TRAUMA, TRUST, AND MEMORY

TRAUMA, TRUST, AND MEMORY

Social Trauma and Reconciliation in Psychoanalysis, Psychotherapy, and Cultural Memory

Edited by
Andreas Hamburger

Routledge
Taylor & Francis Group
LONDON AND NEW YORK

First published 2018
by Routledge
2 Park Square, Milton Park, Abingdon, Oxon OX14 4RN

and by Routledge
711 Third Avenue, New York, NY 10017

Routledge is an imprint of the Taylor & Francis Group, an informa business

British Library Cataloguing-in-Publication Data
A catalogue record for this book is available from the British Library

Library of Congress Cataloging-in-Publication Data
A catalog record has been requested for this book

ISBN: 978-1-78220-447-3 (pbk)

Typeset in Palatino
by V Publishing Solutions Pvt Ltd., Chennai, India

DAAD Deutscher Akademischer Austauschdienst
German Academic Exchange Service

CONTENTS

PREFACE AND ACKNOWLEDGEMENTS

This book is the result of international and interdisciplinary collaboration in social trauma research. Scholars of different disciplines from universities in Bosnia and Herzegovina, Bulgaria, Germany, and Serbia have formed a research network to collaborate in studying the long-term consequences of social traumatisation. This academic research network, Trauma, Trust, and Memory—social trauma and Reconciliation in Psychoanalysis, Psychotherapy, and Cultural Memory, provides a bridge-building model of trauma transformation, reconciliation, and recovery through academic reconstruction and cross-border dialogue. Post-war and post-dictatorial societies are marked by the effects of massive, large-group traumatisation, and if these are not acknowledged, explored, and mourned, long-term rehabilitation and social recovery cannot be expected. Moreover, unprocessed cumulative trauma that has become deeply embedded in the collective memory leads to periodical reactivations. This is true for immediate post-war and post-dictatorial societies, but also for long-term sequelae, for example, in the aftermath of the Holocaust. The research projects connected in the network deal with consequences of social trauma in psychopathology and culture from a trans-regional and trans-disciplinary perspective.

The collaboration started in 2012, funded by the German Academic Exchange Service (DAAD) under the European Stability Pact programme, Academic Reconstruction in Middle and South East Europe, as will be reported in detail in the contribution of the speaker and the coordinator of the project (Hamburger & Scher, Chapter Twenty-Seven).

The main scientific objective of the collaboration was the interdisciplinary approach to social trauma. Social trauma cannot be sufficiently understood from one perspective only. Clinical psychology and psychiatry describe individual and subjective pathology resulting from traumatic experience, and study the pathogenesis, coping mechanisms, and psychotherapeutic approaches. However, especially in the field of social trauma, individual pathology is but one quite limited perspective. Society as a whole has to be studied, where traumatogenic actions like persecution of religious, societal, and ethnical groups emerge and continue, and it is society and culture as a whole that have to deal with the historical scars and traces.

This cultural aspect of social trauma provides a connection to the second objective of our collaboration. Social trauma research in the network is conducted not just "on", but also "in" the situation of social post-traumatic states, that is, in the very region where just two decades ago a war and persecution took place, and is connected to the Western countries that were deeply involved. Young researchers are encouraged to reflect on their personal and emotional experiences while planning, conducting, and sharing their studies in multinational, multi-ethnic, and multidisciplinary groups. The scientific purpose is to deepen our understanding of the roots of collective (social) trauma and the specific traumatic experiences of different groups, and to offer different perspectives and information on how trauma can be dealt with. As an international enterprise, the network connects young scientists in our local research groups across the boundaries of nations and disciplines. They engage in joint research projects, international research supervisions, summer schools, workshops, and seminars, and their enthusiasm constantly inspired our venture whenever it threatened to slow down. Working together on the topic of social trauma establishes a new perspective for each of us, whether we come from experiences of post-war or from post-dictatorial situations—conditions we share in different ways in Bosnia and Herzegovina, Bulgaria, Germany, and Serbia. This new perspective may lay the foundations for a new European identity, commemorating and openly addressing the past while developing in the future.

We wish to thank, first, our PhD, master's, and bachelor students, who engaged in this collaboration so enthusiastically. More than 700 students were with us during the course of the collaboration: some of them have contributed their results to this book, others are still writing their theses and we look forward to their publications. We hope that this project will open the way for young scholars of all our countries to enter the international academic discourse.

Second, our thanks go to colleagues who were with us for part of the way but for various reasons had to leave before this book could be published: Esmina Avdibegović (Tuzla), Jasna Koteska (Skopje), Ferenc Erös and Antal Bokay (Pecs), and Tatjana Stefanović-Stanojević (Niš). We are grateful for the experience of working with them. Our saddest loss was the sudden and premature death of our dear colleague, Academician Dubravko Lovrenović, to whose inspiration and integrative capacity we owe so much. We miss him.

Third, we are most indebted to the outstanding international scholars who have helped us so much in setting perspectives and sharing their inspiration: Anna Buchheim (Innsbruck), Hariz Halilović (Melbourne), Astrid Hirschelmann (Rennes), Suzanne Kaplan (Uppsala), Dori Laub (Yale), Serge Lecours (Montreal), Mark Solms (Cape Town), Mary Target (London), Svenja Taubner (Heidelberg), and Vamık Volkan (Charlottesville). Some of them gave us their keynote lectures or other publication for this book, and we are proud to have them with us. If we have become a family in the network, then it feels good to have relatives all over the world.

It feels good to have relatives nearby, too, and therefore we thank colleagues from our network countries, who have shared their knowledge and enthusiasm with us in our summer schools and conferences: first of all, Amra Delić (Tuzla, Sarajevo, & Leipzig), who gave us incredible support and motivation; as well as the invited lecturers Damir Arsenijević (Tuzla), Faruk Bajraktarević

(Sarajevo), Srdjan Dušanić (Banja Luka), Lilli Gast (Berlin), Jasmina Gavrankapetanović-Redžić (Sarajevo), Nina Hadžiahmetović (Sarajevo), Aleksandra Hadžić (Banja Luka), Dubravko Lovrenović (Sarajevo), Merima Osmankadić (Sarajevo), Adila Pašalić Kreso (Sarajevo), Tatjana Paunović (Niš), Zlatiborka Popov Momćinović (East Sarajevo), Vivian Pramataroff-Hamburger (Munich), Amira Sadiković (Sarajevo), Anna Thüngen (Berlin), Vladimir Turjačanin (Banja Luka), Svetlozar Vassilev (Sofia), and Kalina Yordanova (Sofia).

We are glad to have enjoyed the constant support of the "holding environment" of our rectors and deans, professors Drago Branković (Banja Luka), Miloš Arsenijević and Vojin Nedeljković (Belgrade), Martin Teising (Berlin), Goran Maksimović (Niš), Ksenija Kondali (Sarajevo), and Dimitar Denkov (Sofia).

The most important part of this holding environment is a helpful administration—and if we have learned anything, then it is that such a network is a lot of work. We wouldn't have survived without the help of Bojana Bursać Džalto from the Belgrade Faculty of Philosophy's International Office, Silvia Dröge and Anna Henker from the IPU Berlin International Office, and Kerstin Thesenvitz, our indefatigable IPU Head of Finance and Personal Affairs, as well as our partners from DAAD, in the first years Anne Rörig und Birgit Profittlich-Bauch, now Randolf Oberschmidt und Ljuba Konjuschenko.

For invaluable assistance with this book, the editor wishes to express his sincere gratitude to Amir Djuliman (Sarajevo) for his immense and constant editorial help with the manuscript, particularly with language revision.

We do hope that our efforts have not been in vain, and that the collaboration we have started and fostered through these years will help young researchers to acquire new perspectives and to collaborate within the region and beyond.

Sabina Alispahić

Nikola Atanassov

Aleksandar Dimitrijević

Andreas Hamburger

Camellia Hancheva

Vladimir Hedrih

Horst Kächele

Larisa Kasumagić Kafedžić

Carmen Scher

Biljana Stanković

Annette Streeck-Fischer

Slavica Tutnjević

Lutz Wittmann

ABOUT THE EDITOR AND CONTRIBUTORS

Editor

Andreas Hamburger is a professor of psychology at the IPU Berlin, a psychoanalyst (German Psychoanalytic Society), a training analyst, and a supervisor (DGPT). He is chair of the Trauma, Trust, and Memory network. His main research interests are scenic-narrative microanalysis, social trauma and testimony, psychoanalytic supervision, and literature and film psychoanalysis. He has recently edited books on film psychoanalysis, supervision, and social trauma.

Contributors

Sabina Alispahic is a gestalt psychotherapist under supervision and an assistant professor of clinical psychology. She is President of the Sarajevo branch of the Society of Psychologists in Bosnia and Herzegovina and teaches memory studies on the Trauma, Trust, and Memory social trauma course. Her book *Psihologija boli* [Psychology of Pain] was published in 2016.

Damir Arsenijević PhD, is an associate professor in literary studies and critical theory (Tuzla University, Bosnia and Herzegovina), a psychoanalyst in training, and founder of the Tuzla Psychoanalytic Seminar. His artistic and theoretical interventions enhance discussion of painful topics after war and genocide. He edited *Unbribable Bosnia and Herzegovina: The Fight for the Commons* (2015).

Nikola Atanassov, PhD, is an associate professor of clinical psychology in the cognitive science and psychology department of the New Bulgarian University, and leads its Trauma, Trust, and

Memory division. He is a training and supervising analyst in the Bulgarian Psychoanalytic Society (International Psychoanalytical Association study group), and a former president. His research interest is points of contact between metapsychology and general psychology; his monograph is entitled *Psychoanalytic Theories of Human Development*.

Esmina Avdibegović, MD, is a professor of neuropsychiatry, a group analyst, and head of the department for traumatic and stress-related disorders (Tuzla University, Bosnia and Herzegovina). Her main research interests are mental health and human rights, social psychiatry, suicidology, psychotraumatology, and psychotherapy.

Vedrana Berleković was a doctoral student at the psychology department in the philosophy faculty at the University of Belgrade. Her main research interests include early development, attachment, and mentalization. She is currently working as a school psychologist in Belgrade.

Jasmin Bleimling is a psychoanalyst in training and wrote her PHD on "Countertransference and social trauma" at the University of Munich (Wolfgang Mertens)/International Psychoanalytic University Berlin (Andreas Hamburger) in collaboration with the Sigmund-Freud-Institut Frankfurt (Kurt Grünberg). Her work and research is on social trauma and moments of meeting in video material.

Maša Božović, MSc clinical psychology (Belgrade), is a PhD candidate cooperating with International Psychoanalytic University, Berlin and a psychotherapist in training. She has a background in clinical work and human rights advocacy and is currently involved in an organization that makes psychoanalytic topics available to the general public. Her research interests are mentalization and attachment theory, prevention and treatment of mental disorders, and psychology and art.

Anna Buchheim is a professor of clinical psychology at Innsbruck University, a psychoanalyst (International Psychoanalytical Association), and leads the Adult Attachment Projective Picture System (AAP) trainers' consortium in Austria/Germany. Her research and numerous publications focus on attachment, psychoanalysis, psychotherapy, neuroimaging, and psychoneuroendocrinology. She is co-editor of the *German Journal on Personality Disorders* and vice president of the *German Society of Personality Disorders*.

Amra Delić, MD, MSc, a neuro-psychiatrist and psychotherapist, is a research associate at the University Medicine Greifswald in Germany. Following psychiatric, humanitarian and trauma work in Bosnia and Herzegovina, she joined the Marie Curie Innovative Training Network, Children Born of War, and works as a visiting researcher at the Department for Medical Psychology and Medical Sociology of Leipzig University. Her research interests are in psychotraumatology, sexual violence, human rights, and mental health.

Jonas Diekhans, MA psychology, BA philosophy and literature, studied at the International Psychoanalytic University Berlin, the University of Hamburg, and TU Dresden. His research interests are affects in clinical and social psychology, and constitution of subjectivity and trauma.

Aleksandar Dimitrijević, PhD, teaches clinical psychology and psychoanalysis at the University of Belgrade, the IPU Berlin, and Alpe-Adria University, Klagenfurt. He is a psychoanalyst (International Psychoanalytical Association) and psychoanalytic psychotherapist (EFPP). His research interests include attachment, mentalization, psychoanalysis, and Shakespeare studies. He has edited or co-edited ten books and journal issues.

Ulrike Ehlert, PhD, is a professor of clinical psychology and psychotherapy at the University of Zurich (UZH), Switzerland, and heads the task force for behavioural neurobiology at the Centre for Neurosciences (UZH and ETH). She directs postgraduate training courses in cognitive behavioural therapy and behavioural medicine as well as in clinical supervision. She is head of the outpatient clinic for cognitive behavioural therapy and behavioural medicine at the UZH centre for psychotherapy.

Emin Eminagić is an activist and researcher with an MA in nationalism studies (Central European University, Budapest). His research looks at the intersection between psychoanalysis and politics and he is currently working as a researcher for the Friedrich-Ebert-Stiftung (Sarajevo). He is an initiator of the Tuzla student movement and founder of the leftist political organisation Lijevi, Bosnia and Herzegovina (Tuzla, Sarajevo).

Jusuf Hafizović is a psychology student at the University of Sarajevo working on his MA thesis about experiences of war photographers. He is a gestalt psychotherapist under supervision, and a photographer.

Camellia Hancheva is a senior assistant professor in developmental psychology, a psychotherapist, and a supervisor. Her clinical experience is with terminally ill patients, traumatic loss, and developmental psychopathology. Her research interests are early socio-emotional development, relational psychoanalysis, and intergenerational transmission of trauma. She leads the Trauma, Trust, and Memory network division for Bulgaria and coordinates the master's study course "social trauma" (CST).

Pascal Heberlein, PhD, is head of an institution for child and youth services in Hamburg. He has an MA in the science of education from Kassel University, and his doctoral dissertation was *Microanalysis of videotestimonies of chronically hospitalized Holocaust survivors* (Kassel, 2015).

Vladimir Hedrih is an associate professor, Vice Dean for International Cooperation, Faculty of Philosophy, University of Niš, and a leader of a national scientific research project. His research mainly focuses on vocational interests and psychometrics. He is the current leader of the University of Niš Trauma, Trust, and Memory division.

Martina Heeren, PhD, is a clinical psychologist and psychotherapist in private practice. She specialises in treating children, adolescents, and families as well as in psychotraumatology and migration. She received her PhD from the University of Zurich on the topic of asylum seekers' mental health.

Horst Kächele, MD, PhD, is a specialist in psychosomatic medicine, a psychoanalyst (International Psychoanalytical Association), a former chair of psychosomatic medicine and psychotherapy at the University of Ulm, and since 2009 has been a professor at the International Psychoanalytic University Berlin.

Svetlina Koleva is an assistant professor in child and adolescent psychology (Sofia University) whose main research interests are adolescent conduct problems, aggressive behaviour in particular, and psychopathic traits. Her psychotherapeutic work is influenced by ideas of attachment and psychoanalytical theories.

Siniša Lakić, PhD, is an assistant professor at the Department of Psychology, University of Banja Luka, who teaches quantitative research methods. His main research interests are psychometric validation, personality assessment, self-regulated learning, and evaluation in higher education.

Dubravko Lovrenović (1956–2016) was a professor of history (University of Sarajevo), and a member of the Academy of Science and Art of Bosnia and Herzegovina. His main research was on Bosnian medieval history and deconstruction of historiography myths of the nineteenth and twentieth centuries. His book *Stećci—Bosnian and Herzegovinian Medieval Tombstones* was published in 2010.

Thomas Meier, MD, is medical director for acute psychiatric interventions, addiction-related and psychotherapeutic treatment at Psychiatric Services of St Gallen, Switzerland. Among his main research interests are psychotraumatology, psychotherapy, and transcultural psychiatry.

Marija Pejičić, is a doctoral student and teaching assistant at the Department of Psychology in the Faculty of Philosophy, University of Niš. Her teaching and research focuses mainly on intergroup and interpersonal relations, specifically communication and emotional experience.

Julia Müller, PhD, is a clinical psychologist and psychotherapist in cognitive behavioural therapy. She is a qualified therapist for psychotraumatology and a certified supervisor in cognitive behavioural therapy. She is director of the trauma counselling service at Münsterlingen Clinic in St Gallen, Switzerland.

Jasmina Nedeljković is an assistant professor of psychology (Faculty of Legal and Business Studies, Novi Sad) whose main research interests are methodology, procrastination, and time perspective. In 2013 she coauthored (with A. Kostić) *Studije vremenskih perspektiva u Srbiji* (Time perspectives in Serbia).

Chrysanthi Papadopoulou is a master's student of psychology (International Psychoanalytic University Berlin), with experience of fieldwork with unaccompanied refugee minors in Lesvos, Greece. Current research is looking at secondary trauma of interpreters working with refugees, and transgenerational transmission of trauma.

Margarita Papazova is a psychologist and psychotherapist in training with an MA in child, adolescent, and school psychology (Sofia University). Her research is in attachment, social trauma, and residential care. She is the project coordinator in the field of early childhood development at For Our Children Foundation.

Ivana Pedović is a doctoral student and teaching assistant in the Department of Psychology at the University of Niš. Her teaching and research is on psychometrics, research statistics, and perception. After entering TTM, together with Vladimir Hedrih and Marija Pejičić, she started working on studies and publications in the area of social trauma.

Sonja Protić is a postdoctoral research associate at International Psychoanalytic University and a research assistant at the Institute of Criminological and Sociological Research in Belgrade. Her main research interests are attachment, mentalization, emotional development, and juvenile offending.

Sara Ristić is a master's psychology student with an academic and research focus on social trauma, large-scale conflicts, mental health, and human rights. Her practical work is based on providing psychosocial support to some of the marginalised groups in Serbia, including refugees, the Roma people, the homeless, and psychiatric patients.

Duška Šain has an MSc in psychology and works at a penitentiary institution in Banja Luka. Previously, she was a teaching assistant at the Department of Psychology, University of Banja Luka. Her research focuses on cognition and logical inference.

Svetoslav Savov, PhD, is a clinical psychologist and assistant professor in the Department of Cognitive Science and Psychology, New Bulgarian University. An associate member and candidate of the Bulgarian Psychoanalytic Society, he is currently in private practice with children, adolescents, and adults.

Carmen Scher has an MA in comparative literature, German, and Islamic studies. She is head of the International Office, International Psychoanalytic University Berlin, and coordinator of the Trauma, Trust, and Memory project. From 1999–2002, she was founding director of the Goethe-Institut Sarajevo (Bosnia and Herzegovina). She has worked as a German Academic Exchange Service lecturer for German, European, and intercultural studies and as a manager of international university programmes in Canterbury/UK, Tirana/Albania, and Hanoi/Vietnam.

Ulrich Schnyder, MD, is professor and head of the Department of Psychiatry and Psychotherapy at University Hospital Zurich. His research interests are psychotraumatology (epidemiology, neurobiology, psychotherapy, and pharmacotherapy of PTSD) and resilience. He is past president of the European Society for Traumatic Stress Studies (ESTSS), the International Federation for Psychotherapy, and the International Society for Traumatic Stress Studies (ISTSS). He received the Wolter de Loos Award for Distinguished Contribution to Psychotraumatology in Europe (2013, ESTSS) and the Lifetime Achievement Award of the ISTSS (2016).

Paul Schröder is a PhD student and clinical psychologist at the Institute for Psychosocial Prevention in the medical faculty of the University of Heidelberg. His main interests are in mentalization and statistical modelling.

Mark Solms is a professor and Director of Neuropsychology at the University of Cape Town. He is a member of the South African and American Psychoanalytical Associations and of the British Psychoanalytical Society, and is Research Chair of the International Psychoanalytical Association. He was awarded the Sigourney Prize in 2012.

Biljana Stankovic has a PhD in psychology and is an assistant professor at the University of Belgrade, Serbia. She is working with qualitative and mixed method approaches on the topics at the intersection of health and social psychology, and she is increasingly applying qualitative methods to the area of psychological trauma research. She is the current leader of the University of Belgrade Trauma, Trust, and Memory division.

Tatjana Stefanović Stanojević is a psychologist, a professor of psychology (Universities of Niš, Serbia, and Banja Luka, Bosnia and Herzegovina), and President of the Section of Psychology of Close Relationships in the Serbian Psychological Society. She has written or co-written five books on attachment, and is editor or co-editor of numerous publications on developmental psychology. Her research interests are attachment and the psychology of close relationships.

Aleksandra Stojilković is a doctoral student and teaching assistant in the Department of Psychology at Nis University. Her teaching and research interests are child and adolescent mental health and psychopathology.

Annette Streeck-Fischer is director emerita of the department for clinical psychotherapy of children and adolescents at Asklepios Fachklinikum Tiefenbrunn/Göttingen; professor of clinical psychology and psychoanalysis at the International Psychoanalytic University in Berlin; training and supervising analyst (German Psychoanalytic Society); editor of the journal *Praxis der Kinderpsychologie und Kinderpsychiatrie*; and president of the International Society of Adolescent Psychiatry and Psychotherapy (ISAPP). Her books and main research interests focus on adolescence, violence, trauma, and maltreatment.

Svenja Taubner is professor and director of the Institute for Psychosocial Prevention at the medical faculty of the University of Heidelberg; clinical psychologist and psychoanalyst (German Psychoanalytic Society); editor-in-chief of *Mental Health & Prevention*; editor of *Praxis der Kinderpsychologie und Kinderpsychiatrie*, and of *Psychotherapeut*. Her main interests and publications are about mentalization, psychotherapy research, adolescence, and conduct disorder.

Slavica Tutnjevic, PhD, is an assistant professor at the University of Banja Luka, who focuses on psychology, teacher training, and preschool education. She has researched and published in the field of early categorisation development in infants. She is the current leader of the University of Banja Luka Trauma, Trust, and Memory division.

Tomi Tzolov has an MSc in clinical psychology from the New Bulgarian University. Having worked as a school and child psychologist for four years, he is currently a psychotherapist.

Gloria Velinova has a BA in public administration and is an MA student of clinical psychology at the New Bulgarian University. She works with children and adolescents and has experience as a psychologist in psychiatry and in a rehabilitation centre. She is co-author of a handbook for psychosocial work with people affected by rare diseases and her research interests are adolescence, trauma, addictions, eating disorders, and political psychology.

Vamık Volkan is an emeritus professor of psychiatry (University of Virginia), a training and supervising analyst (Washington Psychoanalytic Institute), a senior Erik Erikson scholar (Austen Riggs Center, Stockbridge, MA), and a former president of the International Dialogue Initiative, the International Society of Political Psychology, the Virginia Psychoanalytic Society, and the American College of Psychoanalysts. He is a leading expert on large group conflict and "enemy" dialogue, and has published widely in many languages on clinical and political psychoanalysis.

Lutz Wittmann, PhD, is a professor of psychodynamic psychotherapy and psychotherapy research, and head of the psychotherapeutic university outpatient service at the International Psychoanalytic University. He serves as international editor for the APA journal *Psychoanalytic Psychology*. He is a recipient of the Young Minds in Psychotraumatology Award (2009) and a former member of the board of directors of the European Society for Traumatic Stress Studies (ESTSS).

INTRODUCTION

Social trauma research in a collaborative network

Andreas Hamburger

Psychological trauma has become one of the central topics not just in healthcare, but also in political and cultural discourse. Some diagnose a fashionable trauma paradigm (see Luckhurst, 2013; Van der Wiel, 2014). Others, concerned by the endless slaughtering in the world's economic and military battlefields, insist that this is less a matter of discourse construction, but of cruel reality. Psychoanalysis and general psychotherapy, as well as the public discourses of memory culture and in the arts, face severe suffering of victims of genocide, war, persecution and dictatorship, systematic abuse, and mistreatment. Scheduled pogroms are different from natural or individual disasters. The general symptoms of post-traumatic disorders resemble each other in both groups of traumatic experiences, but social trauma sequelae display a stronger tendency towards chronification and transgenerational transmission. Moreover, social trauma is not just a clinical phenomenon, it has to be addressed, understood, and coped with as a societal symptom.

When trauma discourse evolved in psychoanalysis and psychiatry, it articulated a need in society to acknowledge how the cataclysms of civilisation resonated in individual suffering (see Chapter Two). Acknowledgement, however, is just the first step to solid and extensive research. Meanwhile, a huge corpus of clinical and epidemiological research has evolved; however, the specificity of societal, group-targeted traumatisation as compared to individual trauma is still a relatively neglected field.

Crossing bridges

The collaboration documented in the present volume addresses the intersection of individual and social aspects of trauma, by connecting the efforts of researchers from countries whose history is characterised by social trauma. These histories, however, are very different: Germany with its history stigmatised by the civilisational catastrophe of the Shoah and two offensive World Wars; the former Yugoslav countries with their tormenting histories of wars, civil wars, and genocides; and Bulgaria with a relatively "ordinary", but nevertheless socially traumatising backstory of dictatorship and group persecutions. But across all differences, these social scars resonate in the political processes as well as the prevailing mentalities in our countries.

Scientific approaches in this dialogue range from social, psychological and culturological research on acknowledgement and memory culture, through attachment and mentalization research, to conceptual outcome and process research in psychotherapy.

Rather than listing and connecting the chapters of the book in order of their appearance (which is provided in the five section introductions), I will highlight the main research approaches presented in this book, and group some of the chapters appertaining to them.

Collective trauma

One central reason for organising this research collaboration (see Hamburger & Scher, Chapter Twenty-Six) was to contribute to acknowledgement of the social trauma at stake. From here came the most inspiring, even stirring contributions to our group work. The starting point was a captivating lecture by Mark Solms who, instead of teaching neuropsychoanalysis, where he is a leading researcher, told us about his ambivalent family heritage as a landowner in South Africa and his analytic way of dealing with it (Chapter Four). Other distinguished researchers have also contributed, like Vamık Volkan (Chapter One) from the viewpoint of social and political psychoanalysis and Dubravko Lovrenović (Chapter Five) from history. Amra Delić and Esmina Avdibegović's study on war rape (Chapter Seven) was another stirring input our group had to work on—remarkably enough, presented at Belgrade University. This, as I had learnt, cannot be taken for granted. In fact, it was the first lecture on this topic ever given at the Faculty of Philosophy. In the field of collective trauma, marked by these key chapters, this book presents many studies on the vicissitudes and difficulties of remembering. Studies on the way people deal with collective trauma were conducted, like acknowledging (or denying) responsibility (Ristić, Chapter Eight), or telling war jokes (Arsenijević & Eminagić, Chapter Nine). Hancheva's ongoing oral history study on the transmission of historical memory (Chapter Six) promises to gain a deeper understanding of how memories of social trauma are formed and handed on in the family in different countries, reflecting different histories.

Attachment and mentalization

Parts of the network were linked from the beginning by a shared research topic. The concepts of attachment and mentalization are two major bridge concepts between clinical and developmental research, both highly relevant for understanding how traumatic experiences affect mental life. Accordingly, they contribute to the clinical as well as to the developmental section of this book. Anna Buchheim (Chapter Eleven) summarises the impact of trauma and attachment, and gives a convincing clinical example. Pertinent chapters for the field of attachment research comprise Stefanović Stanojević and Nedeljković's study on attachment in former Yugoslavia (Chapter Thirteen), which inspired a follow-up study by Hedrih, Pejičić and Pedović (Chapter Fourteen). Interestingly, both studies result in quite different findings, requiring further research. More specific even for trauma research than attachment research is the concept of mentalization (Fonagy, Gergely, Jurist, & Target, 2002; Bouchard & Lecours, 2008), because it helps explain one of the mechanisms by which traumatic childhood experiences result in post-traumatic personality. The volume presents several studies on mentalization in trauma-connected psychopathologies, like drug addiction (Atanassov & Savov, Chapter Sixteen), and PTSD (Berleković & Dimitrijević, Chapter Fifteen). Taubner and Schröder (Chapter Twenty) and Protić (Chapter Twenty-One) study the role of mentalization in the circle of violence in adolescents. Still, there is much work to be done. The research instruments are not always compatible—this is why we work on a multilingual translation and validation of questionnaires—and the link between the social scale of the traumatisation and resulting deficits in mentalizing capacity should be studied in large-scale comparative investigations.

Psychotherapy research

Beyond assessments of psychological consequences of social trauma in large samples, the close experience in the consulting room is a most important way to gain insight in what social trauma does to people. Historically, clinical awareness of social trauma started the trauma discourse, and still, clinical research contributes a major part to it. Clinical research contributes prominently to this volume—not just in the clinical section. Approaches informed by psychotherapeutic experience are to be found in conceptual chapters on social trauma (Hamburger, Chapter Two) and traumatic memory (Alispahić, Chapter Three), and of course in the clinical section, with case vignettes on patients enmeshed in traumatic circumstances from the side of a perpetrator's family (Kächele, Chapter Ten) as well as the victim's side (Streeck-Fischer, Chapter Nineteen). Nearly all contributions to this interdisciplinary book highlight consequences and suggestions for psychotherapeutic practice, such as scrutinising the importance of the unconscious transference-countertransference re-enactment (Heberlein & Hamburger, Chapter Seventeen; Bleimling, Chapter Eighteen).

Developmental approaches

Regrettably, lasting consequences of social trauma are quite frequent—on the one hand, because one of its major social aspects is collective denial. Silence is an unequalled way of preserving mental pain, and thus, denied atrocities cannot be mourned and overcome. But on the other hand, the persistence of social traumatic symptoms is due to the fact that, especially, child survivors of genocide and persecution are often structurally affected in their psychological functioning. A large part of the studies in our group were conducted on developmental aspects. Of course, the whole set of attachment and mentalization research mentioned above contributes to the developmental psychology of social trauma. Moreover, findings on family memory (Hancheva, Chapter Six) add to the question of how traumatic experiences are engraved in the deeper level of post-traumatic memory. Clinical chapters illustrate their reconstruction in psychoanalysis (Kächele, Chapter Ten) or the central diagnostic and therapeutic aspects of developmental trauma (Streeck-Fischer, Chapter Nineteen), as well as the microanalysis of survivors' testimonies (Heberlein & Hamburger, Chapter Seventeen; Bleimling, Chapter Eighteen). The social psychology of school bullying, empirically connected to lack of empathy (Koleva, Chapter Twenty-Three), opens another perspective here on possible developmental symptoms of social trauma.

Academic collaboration

The book concludes with a reflective section on our academic collaboration. We knew from the onset that combining the efforts of researchers not only from different disciplines and methodological habits, but also from different nations and cultures, many previously war enemies, was a challenging enterprise. It was the very challenge we looked for, because we were conscious that research in the field of social trauma, if it remained "academically" aloof, would often fail to achieve the reality it aims at—even more, if it is research in the most painful and unresolved parts of our different histories. The challenge is dealt with in the network organisers' account (Hamburger & Scher, Chapter Twenty-Seven), as well as in a group of students' study on the low frequency of teaching the topic of social trauma in the participating universities (Chapter Twenty-Five). Taking into account these preliminary results, we are proud to report that our network meanwhile successfully organised a sustainable international master's study course on social trauma in order to remedy this situation (Hancheva, Scher, & Hamburger, Chapter Twenty-Six).

Overall, the book presents an adventure. Building bridges between former war enemies, between the East and the West, and between psychoanalysis and empirical research, could have resulted in mayhem in the sense of a revival of arrogance and mutual debasement. But it did not. We often had to struggle with personal and scholarly discord, and the attentive reader will without a doubt detect some of its traces. We did not insist on unanimous consent, and even if we empathised with others' perspectives, we often still maintained our own. In certain areas we have to accept that all we get is that we agree to disagree. But still, we keep in contact and find it worthwhile to talk to each other. This is what democracy is about, as well as academia.

References

Bouchard, M. A., & Lecours, S. (2008). Contemporary approaches to mentalization in the light of Freud's project. In: F. Busch (Ed.), *Mentalization: Theoretical Considerations, Research Findings, and Clinical Implications.* New York: Taylor & Francis.

Fonagy, P., Gergely, G., Jurist, E. L., & Target, M. (2002). *Affect Regulation, Mentalization, and the Development of the Self.* London: Karnac.

Luckhurst, R. (2013). *The Trauma Question.* London: Routledge.

Van der Wiel, R. C. (2014). *Literary Aesthetics of Trauma. Virginia Woolf and Jeanette Winterson.* London: Palgrave Macmillan.

PART I

GENOCIDE AND PERSECUTION ARE NOT EARTHQUAKES: THE CONCEPT OF SOCIAL TRAUMA

Introduction to Part I

The initial section of this book deals with concepts of social trauma and related research. This is much less an academic approach than the section title might sound: in the field of social trauma, the term "concept" is anything but a neutral, technical term. It is at the core of the matter. Because what differs in social as compared to individual trauma—or more precisely, what characterises the social aspects of trauma, present in any traumatising event whatsoever—is its conceptual framing. When we understand that a concept is what people use in discourse to name a phenomenon, then social trauma is in itself something like a "concept". It is conceptualised from the start, when groups turn against other groups, and when enacted, it is enacted as a specimen of a concept (like Auschwitz is a materialisation of the concept of annihilation)—and eventually, when we talk about it afterwards, it is a concept we have to develop and foster in social discourse as well, according to the theory of cultural trauma, which will be extensively dealt with in the next section of the book. However, understanding social trauma as a concept cannot mean separating its manifestations from non-social traumatisations, simply because there are no non-social events in the social world. If a girl is abused "in private" the abuse is still part of a society's tolerance and denial, and thus has a social aspect. If a flood destroys a city, leaving thousands of people homeless and deprived of everything they need for survival, it is an important question whether their huts or houses were built on ground within the reach of a deluge, and whether public security and assistance are available to them. It is the (sometimes silent) decision of a society to leave some of its citizens unprotected. From this viewpoint, earthquakes can be manmade disasters, at least through a lack of prevention. Still, there are differences. Social acceptance of pauperisation of a large group is a social trauma, but it differs in quality from plotted persecution, mass killings, and extinction. We should be aware of these differences, and not prematurely unify the concept of trauma.

In the first chapter, Vamık Volkan, the world's leading scholar in the field of political psychoanalysis, having been a consultant in socially traumatising national and international conflicts for decades, will describe the psycho-social scars and unconscious consequences of large-scale social traumatisations. Then, Andreas Hamburger takes up his previous approaches to distinguish between social and individual trauma and attempts to clarify some crucial bridge concepts between clinical and sociological trauma discourse. The section is concluded by Sabina Alispahić from Sarajevo University, an early member of the Trauma, Trust, and Memory network, who connects theories of trauma memories to clinical approaches.

CHAPTER ONE

From earthquakes to ethnic cleansing: massive trauma and its individualised and societal consequences

Vamık Volkan

In 1977, the then Egyptian President Anwar Sadat went to Jerusalem. During his speech at the Knesset, he stated that there is a psychological wall between Arabs and Israelis that was the cause of seventy per cent of the problems between these two peoples. In response, the American Psychiatric Association's Committee on Psychiatry and Foreign Affairs, of which I was a member, brought influential Arabs and Israelis together for unofficial dialogues for six years to make this wall permeable. In 1988, at the University of Virginia School of Medicine, I opened the Center for the Study of Mind and Human Interaction (CSMHI), with a faculty of psychoanalysts, other mental health professionals, former diplomats, political scientists, historians, an environmentalist, and a linguist. This interdisciplinary team and I visited many areas of the world where international conflicts existed and brought together enemy representatives for years-long unofficial dialogues. After my retirement from the University of Virginia and after the closure of CSMHI in 2005, I established the International Dialogue Initiative (IDI) in 2008. The IDI is a private, multidisciplinary group comprised of psychoanalysts, academics, diplomats, and other professionals who meet biannually to examine large-group differences. The present IDI members come from Germany, Iran, Israel, Russia, Turkey, the United Kingdom, the United States, and the West Bank.

Prior to my involvement in the Israeli-Egyptian dialogues, I studied the Cypriot Turkish society that had been living for eleven years (1963–1974) in enclaves surrounded by their enemies and their responses thereafter to the Turkish army's de facto dividing of the island into north Cypriot Turkish and south Cypriot Greek sections (Volkan, 1979). Working in the international arena I also observed refugee Palestinians who were settled in Tunisia after the 1982 war in Lebanon (Volkan, 2013, 2014a) and visited traumatised Georgian and South Ossetian societies many times for five years after the war between these two societies, following the collapse of the Soviet Union. I observed Croats, Bosnians, and Serbians following the collapse of Yugoslavia and witnessed Kuwaitis' response to the Iraqi invasion after the Iraqi forces withdrew. I also examined societies traumatised by dictators: Romanians and Albanians following the deaths of Nicolae Ceauşescu and Enver Hoxha (Volkan, 1997, 2004, 2013). I also spent four months in Israel in the period 2000–2001, interviewing Israelis and Arabs living there.

My observations of societal consequences of natural disasters, however, are very limited. I visited Mexico City ten days after the impact of an 8.1 magnitude earthquake that occurred on the morning of 19 September 1985, followed by a 7.5 magnitude earthquake thirty-six hours later. This natural disaster resulted in the collapse of more than 400 multi-storey buildings in the city. Official figures for the number of fatalities vary between 9,500 and more than 30,000. A magnitude 7.6 earthquake devastated Izmit, near Istanbul in Turkey, on 17 August 1999. Officials estimated that 17,000 people were killed, although other sources gave much higher figures, and more than 40,000 were injured. Two weeks later I went to Istanbul and consulted with dozens of psychiatrists and psychologists who were still working with survivors and injured individuals. The helpers themselves, stunned by what they had seen, needed psychological support as well.

News about shared massive catastrophes is continually brought to our attention. Some result from natural causes, such as earthquakes, floods, or volcanic eruptions; some are accidental catastrophes like the 1986 Chernobyl disaster. Sometimes, the death of a leader, or of a person who functions as a "transference figure" for many in the society, creates individualised as well as societal responses. We witnessed this after the assassinations of John F. Kennedy in the United States (Wolfenstein & Kliman, 1965) and Yitzhak Rabin in Israel (Erlich, 1998; Moses-Hrushovski, 2000). Other shared experiences of disaster are due to the *deliberate* actions of an ethnic, national, religious, or ideological enemy group. Intentional catastrophes themselves range from wars to terrorist attacks, and from the traumatised group actively fighting its enemy to the traumatised group rendered passive and helpless. In this chapter I will not focus on the impact of massive trauma on individual psychology; I will instead examine psychological responses to a massive trauma shared by thousands or millions of people.

Sharing jokes

Sharing jokes is one of the first societal responses to a massive trauma. A psychoanalyst picked me up at the airport and drove me to Mexico City at the start of my visit ten days after the earthquake. While we were driving she asked me: "What is the similarity between a doughnut (a round pastry with a hole in the middle) and Mexico City?" The answer was that the middles of both were missing. I was surprised that the psychoanalyst was joking about a major tragedy within her own country, but later I would notice similar responses elsewhere. After the 28 January 1986 Space Shuttle Challenger disaster, the United States experienced a shared trauma. Classrooms all over the country had tuned in to the event on television so the children could witness and celebrate teacher Christa McAuliffe going into space. Instead, they witnessed a terrible tragedy and, starting with children, the whole country was traumatised. Soon tasteless jokes were heard countrywide. One described how the shampoo, "Head and Shoulders," could be found on Miami Beach, symbolically referring to body parts of the dead crew members. Tasteless jokes also circulated in the United States following the events of 11 September 2001.

Sigmund Freud (1905c) identified unconscious elements within a person by examining dreams and slips of the tongue (parapraxis), as well as jokes, and illustrated some similar psychodynamic elements in jokes and dreams (see reviews of Freud's ideas on humour by Altman, 2006; Newirth, 2006). Still, circulating jokes within a society after a massive trauma has not been studied in depth within the psychoanalytic literature. On the surface, sharing jokes during and after a massive trauma, even while expecting such a trauma, sounds like an unreasonable thing to do. A closer look, however, illustrates that circulating certain jokes is part of the shared grieving and mourning processes, and also utilises defences against the impact of a shared trauma. By sharing jokes, traumatised members of a large group—such as a national, ethnic, religious, or ideological group—discharge their emotions after defensively reversing their affect and laughing instead of crying. They celebrate staying alive while hiding their "survival guilt" (Niederland, 1968).

Some jokes reflect discharging a shared sense of helplessness and humiliation. During dictator Nicolae Ceauşescu's regime in Romania from 1965 to 1989, there were many jokes about a fictitious character named Bula (in Romanian, "bula" is a vulgar term for penis). A typical buffoon, he was an impotent, humiliated coward. In one story, Bula goes to a meeting, opens his briefcase, pulls out a revolver, and aims it at Ceauşescu. He shoots and shoots, but in their enthusiasm, the encouraging crowd push Bula to and fro, causing him to constantly miss his target in a pathetically comic manner.

Under authoritarian governments, other shared jokes are used with an opposite aim: to minimise the danger or humiliate a "bad" leader. I have no information about jokes shared by the Jewish population during the Nazi period, but today both types of jokes about Nazi Germany can be heard. The following joke, for example, illustrates an attempt to minimise danger: a German child happens to pass through a ghetto and notices another child with the yellow star. The German child asks the second child: "Are you Jewish?" The Jewish child answers: "No, I am the sheriff!"

Dictators, authoritarian political leaders, and people in their close circle do their best to suppress jokes about such traumatizing leaders. During the Third Reich, Joseph Goebbels forbade jokes about Adolf Hitler (Reimann, 1976). After the death of Joseph Stalin, I interviewed his two private interpreters, Valentin Berezhkov (Volkan, 1991a) and Zoya Zarubina. I learned that Stalin was unable to tolerate any jokes about himself. During the last decade, as the leadership in Turkey has become authoritarian, liberal-minded citizens have begun to experience, using Leonard Shengold's (1991) term, "soul murder". Shengold originally used this term to refer to the abuse or neglect of children that deprives them of their identities and ability to experience joy in life. In Turkey, many academicians circulate jokes about the present Turkish political leadership, while experiencing fear of going to jail.

I know of only one occasion in which the psychological meanings of jokes after a major trauma were not only understood, but were used therapeutically. Damir Arsenijević (see Chapter Nine), founder of the Psychoanalytic Seminar Tuzla in Bosnia and Herzegovina, and his colleagues collected jokes after horrible events following the collapse of the former Yugoslavia. They were successful in opening what can be called "public classrooms" where they presented their findings on jokes. During these occasions laughter was lost, but Arsenijević and his colleagues were able to open up difficult topics of war, genocide, loss, and mourning.

Shared jokes that are circulated soon after a massive trauma takes place can indicate to an investigator whether a massive trauma is going to break the tissue of the affected society or not.

Breaking or not breaking the tissue of a society

Williams and Parkes (1975, p. 304) referred to a process after a shared trauma that they named "biosocial regeneration". They informed us that for five years following the deaths of 116 children and 28 adults in an avalanche of coal slurry in the Welsh village of Aberfan in 1966, there was a significant increase in the birth rate among women who had not themselves lost a child. Thirty-three years after this disaster there was a follow-up on survivors of the Aberfan tragedy illustrating that trauma in childhood can lead to PTSD, and PTSD symptoms can persist into adult life for at least as long as thirty-three years (Morgan, Scourfield, Williams, Jasper, & Lewis, 2003). Nevertheless, Williams and Parkes' (1975, p. 304) finding that psychosocial transitions "are not entirely destructive in their effects when viewed from the perspective of the total community in which they occur" remains important.

Six years after the Aberfan tragedy, the Buffalo Creek flood in West Virginia in 1972 killed 125, injured 1,121, and left more than 4,000 homeless out of a population of 5,000. This trauma would be studied in literature from a variety of different angles—legal, cultural, and psychological. Sociologist Kai Erikson (1978) examined the "tissue" of the Buffalo Creek community and opened a door, as Williams and Parkes had done, to look closely at how natural or man-made disasters evoke various societal responses. If the "tissue" of a society is not broken, the society eventually recovers. Expanding Williams and Parkes' observations, we can say that after a massive trauma, a society can exhibit "biosocial regeneration" and "biosocial degeneration".

A type of biosocial regeneration occurred among Cypriot Turks during the six-year period (1963–1968) in which they were forced to live in ethnic enclaves in subhuman conditions surrounded by their enemies. Though they were massively traumatised, their "tissue" was not broken because of the hope that the motherland, Turkey, would come to their aid. Instead of bearing increased numbers of children like the inhabitants of Aberfan, they raised hundreds and hundreds of parakeets (not native to Cyprus) in cages, representing the "imprisoned" Cypriot Turks. As long as the birds sang and reproduced, the Cypriot Turks' anxiety remained under control (Volkan, 1979).

The art and literature stemming from the Hiroshima tragedy (Lifton, 1968) might also be considered a form of symbolic biosocial regeneration. In Hiroshima's case, however, the society also exhibited biosocial degeneration and showed "death imprints" for decades after the catastrophe; the society's "backbone" was in fact broken, and biosocial regeneration could only be limited and sporadic.

The nuclear accident at Chernobyl, with at least 8,000 deaths (including thirty-one killed instantly), provides an example of biosocial degeneration. Shared fear about radiation contamination lasted many years and had an impact on the social fabric of communities in and around Chernobyl. Thousands in neighbouring Belarus considered themselves contaminated with radiation, and they did not wish to have children, fearing birth defects. Thus the existing norms for finding a mate, marrying, and planning a family were significantly disrupted.

If the jokes following a trauma are connected with the society's own lost people and things, in general this indicates that the society's backbone is not broken. Jokes that appeared following the 1986 Challenger tragedy illustrate this. Such jokes directly link the surviving citizens to images of their own lost objects; telling jokes, in a peculiar way, becomes part of the grieving and mourning process. When nature shows its fury and people suffer, victims tend ultimately to accept the event as fate or as the will of God (Lifton & Olson, 1976). After man-made accidental disasters, survivors may blame a small number of individuals or governmental organisations for their carelessness, but even then there are no "Others" who have *intentionally* sought to hurt the victims. When a trauma results from war or other ethnic, national, religious, or ideological conflicts however, there is an identifiable enemy group that has deliberately inflicted pain, suffering, humiliation, and helplessness on its victims. Such trauma affects ethnic, national, religious, or ideological large-group identity issues—such as: we are Germans; we are Syrians; we are Sunnis; we are communists—in ways entirely different from the effects of natural or accidental disasters.

When a massive trauma occurs at the hand of the other, the victimised large group's tissue is broken and shared jokes are more directly related to dealing with shame, humiliation, and threats to one's large-group identity. They are not helpful for grieving and mourning. Under such situations, the reference in the jokes is to the enemy's shared identity, and the usual psychological aim of these jokes refers to a wish to make the enemy less dangerous or to deny humiliation. After the Iraqi invasion of Kuwait in 1990, one popular joke was about Iraqi soldiers who thought that when you knocked on certain walls in Kuwait City, money would pour out. It referred to Iraqi soldiers' unfamiliarity with automated teller machines, implying that Iraqis were not as rich or sophisticated as Kuwaitis.

The shared joke in Kuwait that would bring the most anxious laughter had to do with the city zoo. In the jokes, "stupid" Iraqis do not know the difference between animals, especially which ones are edible and which are not. They open cages at the zoo and eat inedible animals. When I first heard this joke I did not yet know the true story of how the Iraqi soldiers raped a Kuwaiti woman, put her in a cage at the zoo, and kept her there for days. This horrible story later came to public attention (Saathoff, 1995). When I learned of it I came to the conclusion that this woman's dreadful fate and the Iraqis' inability to differentiate between a human being and an animal stimulated the content of this joke. Shame and anxiety about what had happened in the zoo was covered up by the storyline of the joke, reversing horror into laughter.

Perennial mourning, monuments, and artistic expression

In 1972 I coined the terms "linking object" and "linking phenomenon". A mourner utilises certain objects or things in order to create a meeting ground between the mental representation of a lost person or thing and the corresponding self-representation. For example, a young man "chooses" a broken watch owned by his dead father and, psychologically speaking, makes it magical. In this case, the mental representation of the dead father is externalised and meets the son's mental representation "out there". Internal adult-type mourning becomes replaced by a continuous preoccupation and relationship with the broken watch. By controlling the linking object (or phenomenon), the mourner controls the wish to bring back (love) or kill (hate) the lost person or thing, and thus the mourner avoids the psychological consequences of either of the two wishes. The mourner becomes a *perennial mourner*.

Societies build monuments to honour their heroes killed during a war. They also build monuments after suffering a massive trauma at the hand of an other, such as Yad Vashem. These types of monuments become *shared* linking objects postponing the societal mourning, sometimes over many decades (Volkan, 2006). Like an individual perennial mourner's linking object, a monument as a shared linking object is associated with the wish to complete a group's mourning and help its members accept the reality of their losses. On the other hand, it is also associated with the wish to keep mourning active in the hope of recovering what was lost; this latter wish may fuel feelings of revenge. Both wishes can co-exist: one wish can be dominant in relation to one monument, while the other is dominant in relation to another monument.

Sometimes a monument as a linking object absorbs unfinished elements of incomplete mourning and helps the group to adjust to its current situation without re-experiencing the impact of the past trauma and its disturbing emotions. In the United States, the Vietnam Veterans Memorial evolved as a shared linking object and helped Americans to accept that their losses were real and that life would go on without recovering them (Ochsner, 1997; K. Volkan, 1992).

Establishing memorials, writing books, singing songs, producing art, or making films to remember the trauma are aspects of societal response to a massive tragedy and they are related to the shared mourning processes. Depending on the severity of the traumatizing events and how long they lasted, the influence of the trauma on the victimised group may continue for decades.

After a massive trauma at the hands of the other, members of a large group will face difficult tasks taming and rendering harmless psychological features such as victimisation, dehumanisation, and humiliation. Thousands or millions of victimised individuals *deposit* (Volkan, Ast, & Greer, 2002) their traumatised images into their children. They give offspring tasks to reverse humiliation, to take revenge, or to do the work of mourning. The cumulative effects influence the shape and content of the large-group identity and initiate some significant social movements. Similar processes also may appear in the descendants of victimisers. Among the perpetrators' descendants there is more preoccupation with consequences of shared feelings of *guilt* than preoccupation with the shared feeling of helplessness. Both groups share a difficulty or inability to mourn (Mitscherlich & Mitscherlich, 1971).

Transgenerational transmissions, chosen traumas, and entitlement ideologies

It is the transgenerational conveyance of long-lasting "tasks" that perpetuates the cycle of societal trauma. Though each child in the second generation has her own individualised personality, all share similar links to the trauma's mental representation and similar unconscious tasks for coping with that representation. If the next generation cannot effectively fulfil their shared tasks—and this is usually the case—they will pass these tasks on to the third generation, and so on. Such conditions create a powerful unseen network among hundreds, thousands, or millions of people.

Depending on external conditions, shared tasks may *change function* (Waelder, 1930) from generation to generation. In one generation, the shared task is to grieve the ancestors' loss. In the following generation, the shared task may be to express a sense of revenge. But whatever its expression in a given generation, keeping alive the mental representation of the ancestors' trauma, which I named "chosen trauma" (Volkan, 1991b, 2013, 2014b), remains the core task. Societies do not choose to be devastated; they unconsciously "choose" to make historical events significant large-group identity markers.

Following the end of an occupation by the other, the removal of the oppressive regime, or the break-up of a political system, smouldering narcissistic injuries among the former sufferers and among their descendants through transgenerational transmissions can spark new large-group processes of "entitlement ideologies". Entitlement ideologies refer to a shared sense of entitlement to recover what was lost in reality and fantasy during the collective trauma that evolved as a chosen trauma and during other related shared traumas. Chosen traumas are linked to entitlement ideologies.

Leaders, especially those with narcissistic personality organisation, may reactivate a chosen trauma and manipulate an entitlement ideology within the large group (Volkan, 2004; Volkan & Fowler, 2009). This, in turn, increases the shared narcissistic investment in large-group identity and changes its characteristics. The members of the society, under the influence of large-group psychology, can become preoccupied with repairing old wounds and feel entitled to carry out even inhumane massive destruction in the name of "ethnic cleansing" and genocide.

Last words

This chapter does not explore psychoanalytically informed strategies and therapeutic interventions dealing with societal as well as individualised consequences of massive traumas and their transgenerational consequences. It only describes what happens within a large group after a massive trauma, especially one at the hand of the other, and focuses on reasons for circulating jokes, because this is an area not studied in depth by psychoanalysts.

References

Altman, N. (2006). And now for something completely different: humor in psychoanalysis. *Psychoanalytic Dialogues*, *16*: 573–577.

Erikson, K. T. (1978). *Everything in Its Path: Destruction of Community in the Buffalo Creek Flood*. New York: Simon & Schuster.

Erlich, H. S. (1998). Adolescents' reactions to Rabin's assassination: a case of patricide? In: A. Esman (Ed.), *Adolescent Psychiatry: Developmental and Clinical Studies* (pp. 189–205). London: Analytic Press.

Freud, S. (1905c). Jokes and their Relation to the Unconscious. *S. E.*, *8*. London: Hogarth.

Lifton, R. J. (1968). *Death in Life: Survivors of Hiroshima*. New York: Random.

Lifton, R., & Olson, E. (1976). The human meaning of total disaster: the Buffalo Creek experience. *Psychiatry*, *39*: 1–18.

Mitscherlich, A., & Mitscherlich, M. (1971). *The Inability to Mourn: Principles of Collective Behavior*. B. R. Placzek (Trans.). New York: Grove.

Morgan, L., Scourfield, J., Williams, D., Jasper, A., & Lewis, G. (2003). The Aberfan disaster: 33-year follow-up of survivors. *British Journal of Psychiatry, 182*: 532–536.

Moses-Hrushovski, R. (2000). *Grief and Grievance: The Assassination of Yitzhak Rabin*. London: Minerva.

Newirth, J. (2006). Jokes and their relation to the unconscious: humor as a fundamental emotional experience. *Psychoanalytic Dialogues, 16*: 557–571.

Niederland, W. G. (1968). Clinical observations on the "survivor syndrome". *International Journal of Psychoanalysis, 49*: 313–315.

Marcus, P. and Wineman, I. (1985). Psychoanalysis Encountering the Holocaust. *Psychoanal. Inq., 5*: 85–98.

Ochsner, J. K. (1997). A space of loss: the Vietnam Veterans Memorial. *Journal of Architectural Education, 10*: 156–171.

Reimann, V. (1976). *Goebbels: The Man Who Created Hitler*. S. Wendt (Trans.). New York: Doubleday.

Saathoff, G. B. (1995). In the halls of mirrors: one Kuwaiti's captive memories. *Mind and Human Interaction, 6*: 170–178.

Shengold, L. (1991). *Soul Murder: The Effects of Childhood Abuse and Deprivation*. New York: Ballantine.

Volkan, K. (1992). The Vietnam War Memorial. *Mind and Human Interaction, 3*: 73–77.

Volkan, V. D. (1979). *Cyprus—War and Adaptation: A Psychoanalytic History of Two Ethnic Groups in Conflict*. Charlottesville, VA: University of Virginia Press.

Volkan, V. D. (1991a). An interview with Valentin Berezhkov: Stalin's interpreter. *Mind and Human Interaction, 2*: 77–80.

Volkan, V. D. (1991b). On "chosen trauma". *Mind and Human Interaction, 3*: 13.

Volkan, V. D. (1997). *Bloodlines: From Ethnic Pride to Ethnic Terrorism*. New York: Farrar, Straus & Giroux.

Volkan, V. D. (2004). *Blind Trust: Large Groups and Their Leaders in Times of Crisis and Terror*. Charlottesville, VA: Pitchstone.

Volkan, V. D. (2006). What some monuments tell us about mourning and forgiveness. In: E. Barkan & A. Karn (Eds.), *Taking Wrongs Seriously: Apologies and Reconciliation* (pp. 115–131). Stanford, CA: Stanford University.

Volkan, V. D. (2013). *Enemies on the Couch: A Psychopolitical Journey Through War and Peace*. Durham, NC: Pitchstone.

Volkan, V. D. (2014a). Father quest and linking objects: a story of the American World War II Orphans Network (AWON) and Palestinian orphans. In: P. Cohen, M. Sossin, & R. Ruth (Eds.), *Healing in the Wake of Parental Loss: Clinical Applications and Therapeutic Strategies* (pp. 283–300). New York: Jason Aronson.

Volkan, V. D. (2014b). *Psychoanalysis, International Relations, and Diplomacy: A Sourcebook on Large-Group Psychology*. London: Karnac.

Volkan, V. D., & Fowler, J. C. (2009). Large-group narcissism and political leaders with narcissistic personality organization. *Psychiatric Annals, 39*: 214–222.

Volkan, V. D., Ast, G., & Greer, W. (2002). *The Third Reich in the Unconscious: Transgenerational Transmission and its Consequences*. New York: Brunner-Routledge.

Waelder, R. (1930). The principle of multiple function: observations on over-determination. *Psychoanalytic Quarterly, 5*: 45–62.

Williams, R. M., & Parkes, C. M. (1975). Psychosocial effects of disaster: birth rate in Aberfan. *British Medical Journal, 2*: 303–304.

Wolfenstein, M., & Kliman, G. (Eds.) (1965). *Children and the Death of a President: Multi-disciplinary Studies*. Garden City, NY: Doubleday.

CHAPTER TWO

New thoughts on genocidal trauma

Andreas Hamburger

It is a significant semantic operation to metaphorically apply the term "trauma" to a social and mental phenomenon. The medical term "trauma" was used for physical injury, violently piercing through the skin. Only around the middle of the nineteenth century was the term metaphorically extended to address mental suffering due to an overwhelming experience (Schott, 2005; Fischer-Homberger, 1999). The *tertium comparationis* of the metaphor, "lesion caused by an external intrusion", makes us feel the un-mental, un-recognisable quality of the event. Freud's early concept of traumatic hysteria (Freud, 1896c) was about sexual abuse—however, since he had modified it to introduce infantile phantasy, trauma was less vital in the psychoanalytic discourse and was revived only through the experience of World War I. Sexual abuse and hysteria were replaced by the war experience and shellshock (Freud, 1955c; Ferenczi, 1916; Ferenczi, Abraham, Simmel, & Jones, 1921). Between the wars, Ferenczi's trauma theory (1949) shifted attention to early family trauma again, without a link to social phenomena; and when the world had learned about the Holocaust, in the 1940s and 1950s, there was hardly a reaction to it in psychoanalytic trauma theory (Marcus & Wineman, 1985). There was important work on anti-Semitism and authoritarian personality, but few on trauma and survivors, an exception being Friedman's 1948 paper on displaced people. The topic of the Holocaust survivors was only raised when, in the early 1960s, survivors of German concentration camps were denied compensation on the grounds of supposed previous mental vulnerability (Krystal, 2005), and some important papers on genocidal trauma were issued (Niederland, 1968; Eissler, 1967; Wangh, 1964; Tuteur, 1966; Krystal, 1968).

In general psychiatry, World War II intensified interest in trauma related to the military, which lay the ground for the Diagnostic and Statistical Manual of Mental Disorders (DSM I, APA, 1952):

> DSM … was originally conceived out of the American World War II psychiatric experience, when … consistent psychiatric diagnostic formulations were needed both at the point of induction into the armed forces and, subsequently, under conditions of training, and then of combat stress. (Wallerstein, 2011, p. 153 f.)

While in DSM I (APA, 1952), post-traumatic pathology was categorised as "gross stress reaction (transient situational personality disturbance)", in the second edition (APA, 1968), the diagnosis was omitted. In the ongoing Vietnam War, new APA experts were unwilling to recognise combat stress as a source of psychopathology. The manual advised for such cases the diagnosis of "adjustment reaction to adult life" (Scott, 1990, p. 297).

DSM III (APA, 1980) adopted an explicitly theory-abstinent, symptom-based description; stress reactions were re-integrated, also due to the pressure of the anti-Vietnam movement and the veterans (Scott, 1990). As the only aetiology-based diagnosis in the whole manual, PTSD was defined as "a recognisable stressor that would evoke significant symptoms of distress in almost anyone". Further revisions tried to introduce more precise definitions. In the trauma model of DSM IV and DSM-IV TR (APA, 2000), emotional reaction is crucial (A2 criterion), but astonishingly enough, exclusively if related to a physical threat (A1). This definition obviously excluded many traumatic circumstances, among them the most haunting ones, like "collective identity traumas such as genocide and holocaust that go beyond the threat to the individual's physical integrity" (Kira et al., 2008, pp. 62–87). Subsequently, as the first compromise, DSM-5 (APA, 2013) added sexual violence as the first non-physical stress acknowledged as possibly causing PTSD. This single compromise also mirrors the social discourse of the time, where justified rebellion against the trivialisation of sexual violence was eventually effectively voiced. Genocide, this time, had less of a lobby. Recently, there has been a rising interest in social trauma connected to 9/11 and terrorism in general, as well as in psychoanalytic discourse (Kernberg, 2003; Twemlow, 2004).

We may summarise here, that the interest in trauma, especially social trauma, and consequently the amount of research invested, depends much on concerns and denials prevailing in society.

The specificity of social trauma

Social phenomena, like involvement in wars, genocides and terrorist attacks, but also societal movements and discourses, influence the sensibility for trauma. Trauma is a subject where social and individual aspects are inseparably tied together. In war rape (see Chapter Seven) for example, the core of the act is more than sexual greed—it is a purposefully plotted humiliation of the population group the victim belongs to, committed by the perpetrator as a member of his group, which by the very act loses its dignity, too. Civilised armies prosecute war rape, in order to maintain their reputation. Volkan (1997) underlines that individuals belonging to a massively traumatised, large group do not go through normal mourning processes. Those unresolved processes are often unconsciously transferred to later generations. Socially embedded trauma is transmitted not only to survivors' families, but also to the society as a whole, since such events tend to become tabooed or denied. Lacking acknowledgement, as in the case of the concentration camp survivors in Germany, or the "forgotten survivors" in Israel (Laub & Felsen, 2016) leads to further isolation and retraumatisation. Thus, we have to look at the societal mechanisms.

Trauma theory as a political phenomenon

"You needn't be Jewish to be a Holocaust girl. But it helps." This is how S. L. Wisenberg opens her essay in *Holocaust Girls* (2002, p. 1). The statement points to the fact that besides being a personal experience (even if socially embedded), trauma is also a discourse phenomenon. To become voiced, it needs a voice—and since the social aspects of trauma are deeply connected to silence, it is all but self-evident that there will be voices that can be heard and responded to. Usually in the range of several years after the events, massive defences come in, like denial, counter aggression, global projection, and splitting. Therefore, in the field of social trauma, the case of the public voice is deeply connected with the acknowledgement, and thus with the perpetuating, of the unresolved trauma itself.

Psychoanalytic discourse is one of the voices that brought the concept of trauma to public attention. Here, the mentioning of trauma has had an impressive career. From the first decade of psychoanalytic publications, 1881–1890, to the decade 2001–2010, absolute numbers were constantly rising from zero mentions in title (or five mentions in text) to 352 in titles and 5,565 text hits. Percentages range from 0% for titles (3.76% for texts) to 2.59% (29.14% for texts). In recent years (2011–2016), trauma was mentioned in 34.79% of texts. There is a major difference in psychoanalytic trauma discourse compared with general psychiatry and psychology, where in the same time range the mentioning of "trauma" in the text reached only 1.58% (see Figure 1).

The strongly increasing rates of mentioning trauma seem to indicate a growing discourse, especially in psychoanalysis, rather than a growing incidence rate of trauma. Sociologists and literature scholars have demonstrated that indeed social trauma is in large part a cultural construct. There are two main directions of studies: on the one hand, mainly from literature and history, trauma is understood as the non-symbolised, overwhelming experience, as opposed to the relative stability of society's symbolic universe. Cathy Caruth (1996) describes parallels between the psychoanalytic trauma discourse and literature. She addresses (social) trauma as "a wound that cries out, that addresses us in the attempt to tell us of a reality or truth that is not otherwise available" (Caruth, 1996, pp. 3–4). Kansteiner strongly opposes her view, criticising her "easily adopted model of cultural trauma, one which is stripped [...] of any concrete suffering and which turns us all into accomplished survivors" (Kansteiner, 2004, p. 203). On the other hand, Alexander, Eyerman, Giesen, Smelser, and Sztompka understand "cultural trauma" as "a socially mediated attribution" (2004, p. 8), accrued in a long and multifold process of social negotiation, which includes interest groups, media, religious, and political institutions. Culturally established trauma narratives are considered to stabilise social identities (see also Volkan, Ast, & Greer, 2002).

These various points of view, which can be mentioned here only very briefly (see also Hamburger, 2017b), indicate that the localism of the clinical trauma discourse must be challenged. As clinicians, we empathically accept the survivors' reports. This, of course, is necessary to do justice to them. Being a psychotherapist is, after all, a social role too, and our clinical

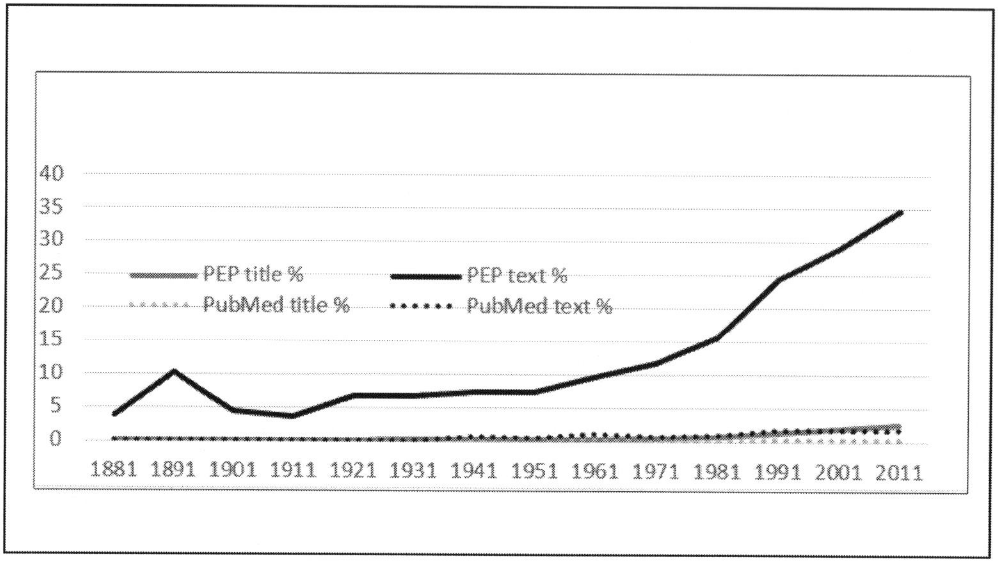

Figure 1. Frequency of mentioning the word "trauma" in psychoanalytic, psychiatric, and psychological publications, in percentages of total publications per decade (from Psychoanalytic Electronic Publishing, pep-web.org and PubMed, www.ncbi.nlm.nih.gov/pubmed).

theories as well as our practice co-author the social construction of trauma, bringing with it the danger of pathologisation (Ornstein, 2013). A psychoanalytic concept of social trauma therefore has to include a theory of its societal conditions, as, in general, the psychoanalytic theory of the subject (Brunner, Burgermeister, Lohl, Schwietring, & Winter, 2013). Freud's belief in the progress of science and civilisation was overshadowed by a pessimistic stance following World War I. This, however, is not a contradiction: Freud's optimism resulted from his trust that civilisation can overcome its own limitations by acknowledging the uncivilised portions of the human mind. What he could hardly foresee was the extent of the irreversible breach of civilisation caused by the Shoah (Arendt, 1976).

Even if the Holocaust hardly resonated in the psychoanalytic discourse of the 1940s and 1950s, the basic position of psychoanalysis requires a concept of trauma beyond a symptom description vaguely linked to "a recognisable stressor that would evoke significant symptoms of distress in almost anyone", as in DSM-III. The psychoanalytic concept of trauma carries with it the cultural notion of an event that would overwhelm theory itself. The paradigm of psychoanalytic trauma theory is the Holocaust. This is why many psychoanalysts object to the inflationary use of the term (Prager, 2011; Young-Bruehl, 2012).

Clinical differences: is there a social trauma syndrome?

Resulting from the acausal DSM definitions, the mainstream of psychotraumatology confines itself to clinical symptomatology, regardless of the type of exposure. Only a minority of clinical or epidemiological studies either draw on stressor-specific psychological symptoms (see Hamburger, 2017a for further discussion), or describe specific symptoms more probable in cases where the social or genocidal aspects of trauma prevail, like the effects of social denial and institutional rejection of coping processes. From their experience with survivors, Laub (1998, 2005), Laub and Auerhahn (2016), Kaplan (2008), and many others describe typical cognitive and emotional symptoms. They frequently influence the specific countertransference reactions of the interviewer (Grünberg & Markert, 2012; Hamburger, 2015, 2017a, 2017b), characterised by Laub (2016) as "traumatic shutdown". The pivot of the symptomatology seems to be a lack of a coherent autobiographic memory narrative and congruent self-emotions, especially frequent in child survivors (Kaplan, 2008). While the specificity of post-traumatic memory in general is doubted by memory research (Greenhoot & Sun, 2014), it might still prevail in cases of survivors of social trauma, where the interactional component of narrative formation is strongly involved, and thus developing a coherent autobiographical memory might be negatively influenced.

One of the most impressing specificities of social trauma is its proneness to transmission to the next generation (Kellermann, 2001), especially if the children grow up deprived of additional resilience resources (Sagi-Schwartz, Van IJzendoorn, & Bakermans-Kranenburg, 2008; Van IJzendoorn, Bakermans-Kranenburg, & Sagi-Schwartz, 2004). Different theories have been presented to explain this phenomenon.

Generational trauma transmission is presumably connected to early parenting conditions, followed by a vicious cycle of passing on dysfunctional parent–child interactions (cf. Brunner et al., 2015). Kaplan (2008) found in survivors of the Rwandan genocide that pregnancy in young women sometimes causes trauma-specific anxiety: "parents who themselves were child survivors and live in areas with ongoing political conflicts are more at risk of transferring trauma from one generation to the next via sudden interruptions in their natural web of emotions towards the infant" (Kaplan & Hamburger, 2017, p. 109). Kaplan distinguishes *generational linking* from *trauma linking* in genocide survivors. The latter is similar to intrusions, flashbacks, and irritability in PTSD, and leads to an immersion in the traumatic memory, while *generational linking* allows subjects to shift their attention towards significant people and objects in the past as well as in the present (Kaplan, 2008). Here, a concept of transgenerational trauma transmission could be connected with children experiencing their parents' inability in terms of generational linking. Correspondingly, Laub's (2005) model of the loss of communication with the internalised other can be understood as a transgenerational mechanism, too.

A mentalization model of generational trauma transmission

The most suitable model for describing the mechanisms of generational trauma transmission is the theory of mentalization (Fonagy, Gergely, Jurist, & Target, 2004; Fonagy, 2010). In emotionally charged relations to caregivers and peers, the infant internalises the image of himself in the caregiver's mind by reading the caregiver's intentions, in situations in which the caregiver shows "marked affects" in exchange with the infant. Repeated experience of the marked affect display helps the child to advance from equivalent mode (where the difference between imagination and reality is not yet established), to pretend mode, where an inner world can be established, uncoupled from outer perception. The establishing of this inner world, tirelessly trained in thousands of pretend play situations, is a major prerequisite for mentalization, where the developing individual can distinguish and shift between perception and imagination of his own feelings to the empathic perception of the feelings and intentions of others. In a more social psychological key, Fonagy and Allison (2014) describe "epistemic trust", as the ability to accept new knowledge from another person as trustworthy, developing in secure attachment relations. Tossin (2007) points out that unavailability of a responding environment leads to a "nonmentalizing state" in children.

Social aspects in mentalization

However, findings on the psychology of trauma and trauma transmission require a more general reading, if we talk about a socially embedded trauma. From a social-psychological point of view, Young-Bruehl (2012) reinterprets Freud's early definition of trauma as a breach of the protective shield by assuming that the protective shield is not a physiological "stimulus barrier", but the social environment.

> A social protective shield could be defined as a relational network of people and institutions that grows up to enwrap basic social units—like families, but also states—in customs, programs, and ideas of *eudaimonia* that prevent the units' failure and remedy their ills medically and psychotherapeutically. Social shields of all sorts develop in societies as different needs and social ills are discovered and addressed (Young-Bruehl, 2012, p. 550).

Sossin (2007) and Fonagy and Target (2005) refer to the small family stem in describing the vicious circles of trauma, which leads to impairments in the development of reflective functioning. However, these vicious circles are much more frequent when the social environment is targeted, rather than the individual survivor.

The systematic influence of childhood genocidal or social trauma on mentalization can be understood, if we keep in mind that by definition the traumatisation is not directed against the child alone, but against his social environment. If "it takes a village to raise a child" (Young-Bruehl, 2012, p. 550), then the attack on the village would affect the child and his basic social experience. If the development of reflective functioning relies on the availability of caregivers, who can playfully help the child overcome the equivalence mode by displaying "as if" affects, then we can expect that a child with deeply wounded, dead, or mentally dead parents and grandparents will have scarce opportunity for a relaxed pretend play. Affects will all too often tend to be serious.

Caregivers under a threat of persecution in reality can hardly provide the secure base the child needs to distinguish between his inner fears, experienced in equivalence mode as outer threats, from reality. And beyond the nuclear family, also the social functions of the wider environment will tendentially be restricted. When a healthy social environment is able to provide a good-enough "eudaimonia" (Young-Bruehl, 2012) through protective social institutions and healing mechanisms like judicial institutions, social security, everyday narratives, urban legends and myths, jokes, and social and cultural events, including the benign subgroup formations celebrated in sports, then all these social processes can be compared to the "pretend play" by which the infant learns to distinguish phantasy and reality and develop pro-social behaviour. If, on the other hand, the social environment itself is under threat of annihilation, many of these pro-social, eudaimonia-producing mechanisms, the digesting capacity of the environment, will fail. Thus, if an infant is overwhelmed by projective fears in equivalence mode, if his family is unable to help him mentalize his fears and understand that they come from inside of the whole village where the family lives, which is humming with catastrophic rumours instead of cosy neighbourhood gossips; if paranoia cannot be distinguished from reality any more, then we have childrearing conditions hardly suitable for developing a stable mentalizing capacity (for further discussion, see Hamburger, 2017b, 2017a).

A perspective on the acknowledgement

If, as discussed in the previous section, the extreme conditions of social and genocidal trauma may likely cause severe pathological consequences, and possibly even be handed down to the next generation, then why does epidemiology show only weak evidence for massive pathology in groups that have suffered from systematic persecution? Why do survivors vigorously claim not to be seen as patients (Ornstein, 2013)? Is it a symptom of our own tendency to conjure a universal trauma, in order to stabilise our postmodern, sensation-seeking identity? Is trauma the other of consumerism? In the previous section on trauma and politics, the question was raised whether a fashionable trauma discourse provides adequate help for survivors, or whether survivors are rather exhibited and exploited. I think that it would be wise to reflect on these challenging questions, and to refrain from abstraction. Not every Auschwitz survivor is sick, and not everyone brought up in the land of milk and honey is sane. The basic scepticism of psychoanalysis is scepticism against the "big concepts". If we meet our patients, the people who decide to start an analytic dialogue with us, there will be many doubts on the way, and we are determined to address any single one of them.

References

Alexander, J. C., Eyerman, R., Giesen, B., Smelser, N. J., & Sztompka, P. (2004). *Cultural Trauma and Collective Identity*. Berkeley, CA: University of California Press.

American Psychiatric Association (1952). *Diagnostic and Statistical Manual of Mental Disorders I*. Washington, DC: American Psychiatric Association.

American Psychiatric Association (1968). *Diagnostic and Statistical Manual of Mental Disorders II*. Washington, DC: American Psychiatric Association.

American Psychiatric Association (1980). *Diagnostic and Statistical Manual of Mental Disorders III*. Washington, DC: American Psychiatric Association.

American Psychiatric Association (2000). *Diagnostic and Statistical Manual of Mental Disorders IV*. Washington, DC: American Psychiatric Association.

American Psychiatric Association (2013). *Diagnostic and Statistical Manual of Mental Disorders* (5th edn). Arlington, VA: American Psychiatric Press.

Arendt, H. (1976). *The Origins of Totalitarianism*. New York: Harcourt.

Brunner, M., Burgermeister, M., Lohl, J., Schwietring, M., & Winter, S. (2013). Critical psychoanalytic social psychology in the German speaking countries. *Annual Review of Critical Psychology, 10*: 419–468.

Brunner, R., Reichl, C., Bermpohl, F., Bertsch, K., Bock, J., Bödeker, K., Firk, C., Fuchs, A., Führer, D., Gröger, N., Heinz, A., Herpertz-Dahlmann, B., Herpertz, S. C., Dahmen, B., Hindi Attar, C., Kluczniok, D., Konrad, K., Lehmkuhl, U., Möhler, E., Neukel, C., Reck, C., Resch, F., Rether, K., Zietlow, A.-L., Ziegenhain, U., Schury, K., Karabatsiakis, A., Braun, K., Gündel, H., Kindler, H., Buchheim, A., Meysen, T., Kolassa, I. T., & Fegert, J. M. (2015). Mechanismen der generationsübergreifenden Transmission belastender Kindheitserfahrungen. *Trauma und Gewalt, 9*: 134–147.

Caruth, C. (1996). *Unclaimed Experience: Trauma, Narrative, and History*. Baltimore, MD: Johns Hopkins University Press.

Eissler, K. R. (1967). Perverted psychiatry? *American Journal of Psychiatry, 123*: 1352–1358.

Ferenczi, S. (1916). Über zwei Typen der Kriegsneurose. *Internationale Zeitschrift für Psychoanalyse, 4*: 131–145.

Ferenczi, S. (1949). Confusion of the Tongues Between the Adults and the Child (The Language of Tenderness and of Passion). *International Journal of Psycho-Analysis, 30*: 225–230.

Ferenczi, S., Abraham, K., Simmel, E., & Jones, E. (1921). *Psycho-Analysis and the War Neuroses. With an Introduction by Prof. Sigm. Freud*. London: International Psycho-Analytical Press.

Fischer-Homberger, E. (1999). Zur Medizingeschichte des Traumas. *Gesnerus, 56*: 260–294.

Fonagy, P. (2010). Attachment, trauma, and psychoanalysis: Where psychoanalysis meets neuroscience. In: M. Leuzinger-Bohleber, J. Canestri, & M. Target (Eds.), *Early Development and Its Disturbances: Clinical, Conceptual and Empirical Research on ADHD and Other Psychopathologies and Its Epistemological Reflections* (pp. 53–75). London: Karnac.

Fonagy, P., & Allison, E. (2014). The role of mentalizing and epistemic trust in the therapeutic relationship. *Psychotherapy (Chicago, Ill.), 53*(3), 372–380.

Fonagy, P., & Target, M. (2005). Bridging the transmission gap: An end to an important mystery of attachment research? *Attachment & Human Development, 7*: 333–343.

Fonagy, P., Gergely, G., Jurist, E. L., & Target, M. (2004). *Affect regulation, mentalization, and the development of the self*. New York: Other.

Freud, S. (1896c). The Aetiology of Hysteria. *S. E., 3*: 189. London: Hogarth.

Freud, S. (1955c). Memorandum on the Electrical Treatment of War Neurotics. *S. E., 17*: 211. London: Hogarth.

Friedman, P. (1948). The Road Back for the DPs. Healing the Psychological Scars of Nazism. *Commentary, 6*: 502–510.

Greenhoot, A. F., & Sun, S. (2014). Trauma and Memory. In: P. J. Bauer & R. Fivush (Eds.), *The Wiley Handbook on the Development of Children's Memory (volume 2)* (pp. 774–803). New York: Wiley.

Grünberg, K., & Markert, F. (2012). A psychoanalytic grave walk: scenic memory of the shoah. On the transgenerational transmission of extreme trauma in Germany. *The American Journal of Psychoanalysis, 72*: 207–222.

Hamburger, A. (2015). Refracted attunement, affective resonance: scenic-narrative microanalysis of entangled presences in a Holocaust survivor's testimony. *Contemporary Psychoanalysis, 51*: 239–257.

Hamburger, A. (2017a). Genocidal trauma. Individual and social consequences of the assault on the mental and physical life of a group. In: D. Laub & A. Hamburger (Eds.), *Psychoanalysis and Holocaust Testimony. Unwanted Memories of Social Trauma* (pp. 66–91). London: Routledge.

Hamburger, A. (2017b). Scenic narrative microanalysis. Controlled psychoanalytic assessment of session videos or transcripts as a transparent qualitative research instrument. In: D. Laub & A. Hamburger (Eds.), *Psychoanalysis and Holocaust Testimony. Unwanted Memories of Social Trauma* (pp. 166–182). London: Routledge.

Kaplan, S. (2008). *Children in Genocide: Extreme Traumatization and Affect Regulation*. London: Karnac.

Kaplan, S., & Hamburger, A. (2017). The developmental psychology of social trauma and violence. The case of the Rwanda genocide. In: D. Laub & A. Hamburger (Eds.), *Psychoanalysis and Holocaust Testimony. Unwanted Memories of Social Trauma* (pp. 104–124). London: Routledge.

Kellermann, N. P. (2001). Transmission of Holocaust trauma—an integrative view. *Psychiatry, 64*: 256–267.

Kernberg, O. F. (2003). Sanctioned social violence. *International Journal of Psychoanalysis, 84*: 683–698.

Kira, I. A., Lewandowski, L., Templin, T., Ramaswamy, V., Ozkan, B., & Mohanesh, J. (2008). Measuring cumulative trauma dose, types, and profiles using a development-based taxonomy of traumas. *Traumatology, 14*: 62–87.

Krystal, H. (Ed.) (1968). *Massive Psychic Trauma*, New York: International University Press.

Krystal, H. (2005). Psychoanalytic approaches to trauma: a forty-year retrospective. In: C. R. Figley (Ed.), *Mapping Trauma and Its Wake: Autobiographic Essays by Pioneer Trauma Scholars* (pp. 111–134). London: Routledge.

Laub, D. (1998). The empty circle: children of survivors and the limits of reconstruction. *Journal of the American Psychoanalytic Association, 46*: 507–529.

Laub, D. (2005). From speechlessness to narrative: the cases of Holocaust historians and of psychiatrically hospitalized survivors. *Literature and Medicine, 24*: 253–265.

Laub, D. (2017). Traumatic shutdown of narrative and symbolization: a failed empathy derivative. Implications for therapeutic interventions. In: D. Laub & A. Hamburger (Eds.), *Psychoanalysis and Holocaust Testimony. Unwanted Memories of Social Trauma* (pp. 43–65). London: Routledge.

Laub, D., & Auerhahn, N. C. (2017). Knowing and not knowing massive psychic trauma: forms of traumatic memory. In: D. Laub & A. Hamburger (Eds.), *Psychoanalysis and Holocaust Testimony. Unwanted Memories of Social Trauma* (pp. 32–42). London: Routledge.

Laub, D., & Felsen, I. (2017). Traumatic psychosis: narrative forms of the muted witness. In: D. Laub & A. Hamburger (Eds.), *Psychoanalysis and Holocaust Testimony. Unwanted Memories of Social Trauma* (pp. 228–241). London: Routledge.

Niederland, W. G. (1968). Clinical observations on the "survivor syndrome". *International Journal of Psychoanalysis, 49*: 313–315.

Ornstein, A. (2013). Trauma, memory, and psychic continuity. *Progress in Self Psychology, 10*: 131–146.

Prager, J. (2011). Danger and deformation: a social theory of trauma, part I: contemporary psychoanalysis, contemporary social theory, and healthy selves. *American Imago, 68*: 425–448.

Sagi-Schwartz, A., Van IJzendoorn, M. H., & Bakermans-Kranenburg, M. J. (2008). Does intergenerational transmission of trauma skip a generation? No meta-analytic evidence for tertiary traumatization with third generation of Holocaust survivors. *Attachment & Human Development, 10*: 105–121.

Schott, H. (2005). Das psychische Trauma in medizinhistorischer Perspektive. In: G. H. Seidler & W. U. Eckart (Eds.), *Verletzte Seelen. Möglichkeiten und Perspektiven einer historischen Traumaforschung* (pp. 41–55). Gießen: Psychosozial.

Scott, W. J. (1990). PTSD in DSM-III: a case in the politics of diagnosis and disease. *Social Problems, 37*: 294–310.

Sossin, K. M. (2007). Nonmentalizing states in early-childhood survivors of the Holocaust: developmental considerations regarding treatment of child survivors of genocidal atrocities. *American Journal of Psychoanalysis, 67*: 68–81.

Tuteur, W. (1966). One hundred concentration camp survivors: twenty years later. *Israel Annals of Psychiatry, 4:* 78–90.

Twemlow, S. W. (2004). Psychoanalytic understanding of terrorism and massive social trauma. *Journal of the American Psychoanalytic Association, 52*: 709–716.

Van IJzendoorn, M. H., Bakermans-Kranenburg, M. J., & Sagi-Schwartz, A. (2004). Are children of Holocasut survivors less well adapted? A meta-analytic investigation of secondary traumatization. *Journal of Traumatic Stress, 16:* 459–469.

Volkan, V. D. (1997). *Bloodlines: from ethnic pride to ethnic terrorism.* New York: Farrar, Straus and Giroux.

Volkan, V. D., Ast, G., & Greer, W. F. (2002). *Third Reich in the Unconscious: Transgenerational Transmission and Its Consequences*. New York: Brunner-Routledge.

Wangh, W. (1964). National socialism and the genocide of the Jews. *International Journal of Psychoanalysis, 45:* 386–395.

Wisenberg, S. L. (2002). *Holocaust Girls. History, Memory, and Other Obsessions.* Lincoln, NE: University of Nebraska Press.

Young-Bruehl, E. (2012). Civilization and its dream of contentment: reflections on the unity of humankind. *Psychoanalytic Inquiry, 32*: 543–558.

CHAPTER THREE

Psychological theory and therapy of traumatic memory

Sabina Alispahić

Traumatic memories have been observed and described in psychiatry and psychology for more than 100 years. Exploration of traumatic memories began with the Jean Martin Charcot's studies of hysterical symptoms in women who suffered violence and sexual abuse (Herman, 1992), continued with Pierre Janet (1889), Breuer and Freud (1895d), and followed during the World Wars (Myers, 1915; Sargant & Slater, 1941) and the Vietnam War (Van der Kolk, 1987). As a consequence of the women's movement in the 1970s, along with combat trauma and the trauma of Holocaust survivors, trauma in the lives of women moved from the private domain of the home to the public arena (Herman, 1992). During the 1990s these clinical reports from the past were not taken so seriously, because traumatic experiences had not been researched in a laboratory setting (Van der Kolk, Hopper & Osterman, 2001). Traumatic memories became an important topic in contemporary life as a result of the mass trauma of 9/11, the ongoing war against terrorism, and ongoing wars in Iraq and Afghanistan, which have led to an increased incidence of post-traumatic stress disorder (PTSD) in returning military personnel (Ringel & Brandell, 2011).

Characteristics of traumatic memory

According to the definition of PTSD in the *Diagnostic and Statistical Manual of Mental Disorders* (DSM-5), *traumatic memory* is:

> a memory of exposure to actual or threatened death, serious injury, or sexual violence in one (or more) of the following ways: 1. Directly experiencing the traumatic event(s); 2. Witnessing, in person, the event(s) as it occurred to others 3. Learning that the traumatic event(s) occurred to a close family member or close friend—In cases of actual or threatened death of family

> member or friend, the event(s) must have been violent or accidental 4. Experiencing repeated or extreme exposure to aversive details of the traumatic event(s) (e.g., first responders collecting human remains; police officers repeatedly exposed to details of child abuse). (American Psychiatric Association, 2013)

It is hard to research traumatic memories in the laboratory, because events encoded into memory cannot be a "controlled" variable in the sense of laboratory science. This is because of ethical reasons, not scientific ones—extreme negative emotions that precede the traumatic symptoms cannot be replicated in a laboratory setting (Van der Kolk, Hopper, & Osterman, 2001). Therefore, to study the nature of traumatic memories, scientists must study the memories of people who have been traumatised. Because of this kind of research we have come to some important notions about the nature of traumatic memories. For example, we now know that traumatic memories are characterised by fragmentary and intense sensations and affects, often with very little or no verbal narrative content. These memories are often vivid and intense (Foa, Molnar, & Cashman, 1995) and most often stay the same over time (Van der Kolk, 2002). They are experienced as if the event and one's sensory, cognitive, emotional, and physiological reactions to it were happening all over again (Van der Kolk, Hopper, & Osterman, 2001).

Small triggers can bring back sensations, emotions, and reactions as if the trauma were happening in the present day (Van der Kolk & McFarlane, 1996). The person is often unable to connect these re-experienced memories to a narrative that will explain them (Rothschild, 2000). Not understanding the connection between present feelings and behaviours to past experiences, people often try to make sense of the experiences in any way they can, which can lead to believing negative messages about one's self including being damaged, unstable, out of control, and unable to deal with everyday life (Swenson, 2012).

Neuropsychology of traumatic memories

Another important question about traumatic memories is how they are stored in our memory system. According to past research, traumatic memories are encoded differently from memories for ordinary events, probably through alterations in attentional focusing, or because extreme emotional arousal interferes with hippocampal memory functions (Van der Kolk, 1997). To fully understand the neuropsychology of traumatic memories, it is important to explain the body's chemical responses and memory functions.

During any type of trauma, neurotransmitters in the brain set off the release of a series of chemicals such as epinephrine and norepinephrine that are responsible for the widely known "fight-flight-freeze" stress response. With everyday stress, these chemicals facilitate a process that allows people to function with greater endurance, strength, immunity, and clarity, but during traumatic events these chemicals may often be released in amounts that are damaging to the brain and could interrupt memory functions (Van der Kolk, 1994).

There are two types of memory: explicit or declarative memory that is stored verbally and logically in the hippocampus; and implicit or non-declarative memory stored as senses and emotions primarily in the region of amygdala. It seems that high level of chemicals such as epinephrine, norepinephrine, glucocorticoids, and cortisol interfere with the storage of explicit (declarative) memory, and that is why traumatic memories are stored in the implicit form, as emotions and senses. This is confirmed with recent studies about the memory in patients with PTSD which show that they perform worse than control participants, especially for working memory, with reduced phonemic and semantic fluency (Alberini & LeDoux, 2013).

Flashbulb memories, "memory wars", and false memory research

In this part of the chapter, it is useful to describe some of the concepts and terms that are important for further understanding of psychological theory of traumatic memory. For example, Brown and Kulik (1977) proposed a case where people are highly confident in their memories—they called these "flashbulb memories" and defined them as "a highly detailed, exceptionally vivid 'snapshot' of the moment and circumstances in which a piece of surprising and consequential (or emotionally arousing) news was heard" (Brown & Kulik, 1977).

Typical examples of flashbulb memories include the assassination of John F. Kennedy or the events of 11 September 2011. People can recall where they heard the news about the event and the people they were with (Bohn & Berntsen, 2007). Although individuals often believe that their flashbulb memories are accurate, research demonstrates that these memories are often not so accurate (Talarico & Rubin, 2007; Schmolck, Buffalo, & Squire, 2000).

Another important topic in the field of traumatic memory is the controversy about repressed memories, known as the "memory wars". This is a debate between individuals who believe that traumatic memories can be repressed and remain inaccessible for years, but can be recovered during therapy, and those who question the existence of repressed memory. Different positions about this topic can have serious consequences for clinical practice and the judicial system. According to Patihis, Ho, Tingen, Lilienfeld, and Loftus (2014) this gap between researches and practitioners in their memory beliefs can be narrowed by encouraging a dialogue between the groups and by focusing the education of students and trainees on the topic of repressed memory.

Finally, the "false memory" phenomenon in which a person recalls a memory that actually did not occur, made an important contribution to our understanding of memory errors, specifically in the field of traumatic memory. Decades of research have demonstrated that human memory can be very malleable, and that there is a risk that techniques used to uncover repressed memories of trauma could actually be creating false memories in patients' minds. Many factors have been tested in attempts to make a difference between true and false memories, but no firm distinguishing characteristic has yet been found (Laney & Loftus, 2013).

Dissociation and traumatic memory

According to Van der Kolk (1997), dissociation refers to a compartmentalisation of experience: elements of the experience are not integrated into a unitary whole, but are stored in memory as isolated fragments consisting of sensory perceptions or affective states. In some situations traumatic memories may have no verbal component at all—the memory can be entirely organised on a perceptual level, without an accompanying narrative about the traumatic event.

Often, people who are used to reacting to trauma by dissociating might do so in response to minor stresses. Also, the severity of the dissociative process is correlated with different psychopathologies that are associated with trauma and neglect, such as somatisation, bulimia, and borderline personality disorder (Van der Kolk, 1997). Only a small number of people will go on to chronically dissociate, or develop a dissociative identity disorder (multiple personality disorder).

Psychoanalysis and the study of dissociation and dissociative disorders have had a long relationship (Kluft, 2000). The concept of dissociation has revolutionised the psychoanalytic treatment and understanding of adults who were abused as children. According to Boulanger (2008), because of the unmanageable stimulation of a traumatic event, a child defensively dissociates and forms split-off self states to encapsulate the traumatic self, leaving other self states free to engage with a less threatening world. Distinction should be made between dissociation as it occurs in childhood and catastrophic dissociation that refers to people who have survived catastrophes as adults. Capacity to dissociate decreases with age. In adulthood, catastrophic dissociation does not create further splits in a developed personality; it does provisionally offer protection from terror, but ultimately it leaves the survivor in a state of confusion and anomie (Howell, 2005).

Recovering from traumatic memories

One of the most important goals in working with survivors of trauma is to assist them to integrate their memory functions so that they can recall the trauma verbally and lessen the immobilising emotional/sensory responses.

Little research has been conducted about treatments for helping clients with traumatic memories. According to Greenwald (2013), there are two lines of such research. In the first line, are traditional talking therapy methods and focused trauma-resolution methods such as prolonged exposure, cognitive processing therapy, and eye movement desensitisation and reprocessing. In the second line, trauma-specific treatments are not more effective then other legitimate psychotherapy approaches. The important thing is to identify and use the best treatment approach that is most suitable for each individual client.

This next section considers some of the psychological treatments for trauma and traumatic memory, beginning with the most widely used trauma therapies and then looking at more contemporary treatments.

Cognitive behavioural therapy

Cognitive behavioural therapy (CBT) is often presented as the therapy of choice for treating trauma. Within the basic CBT framework are variations, some of which are detailed below.

Trauma focused cognitive behavioural therapy (TF-CBT)—first described by Deblinger, Cohen, and Mannarino (2003)—is currently is recommended for PTSD by various treatment guidelines and expert consensus panels (Forbes et al., 2007; Bisson et al., 2010). TF-CBT is a short-term treatment approach that can work in as few as twelve sessions. Key elements of the intervention include psychoeducation, gradual exposure, behaviour modelling, coping strategies, and body safety skills training. Each of these elements may be adjusted according to the treatment needs of the client.

Prolonged exposure therapy (PET) is a trauma-focused intervention that includes psychoeducation, anxiety management, and exposure as its components. The main part of the treatment is asking clients to confront trauma-related reminders and thoughts using both in-vivo (real life) exposures, and prolonged and repeated recall of the story of the traumatic experience (imaginal exposure). The goal of this treatment is to promote processing of the trauma memory and to reduce distress and avoidance elicited by the trauma reminders (Foa, Hembree, & Rothbaum, 2007). PET has been found to be effective in reducing post-traumatic stress disorder symptoms in adults and in adolescents (Gilboa-Schechtman et al., 2010; Nacasch et al., 2011; Powers, Halpern, Ferenschak, Gillihan, & Foa, 2010). Also, Rachamim, Mirochnik, Helpman, Nacasch, and Yadin (2015) provide preliminary clinical evidence for the efficacy of PET in toddlers.

Mindfulness meditation-based therapies include dialectical behavioural therapy (Linehan, 1993), acceptance and commitment therapy (Hayes & Strosahl, 2004), mindfulness-based cognitive therapy (Segal, Williams, & Teasdale, 2002), and mindfulness-based stress reduction (Kabat Zinn, 2005). Unlike CBT, mindfulness-based models advocate staying with states of mind, feelings, and physical sensations rather than using distraction or cognitive restructuring. The newest example of mindfulness-based therapy for traumatic memories is trauma interventions using mindfulness-based extinction/reconsolidation (TIMBER), a translational mindfulness-based psychotherapy for PTSD, which was developed by Pradhan, Gray, Parikh, Akkireddi, & Pumariega (2015). TIMBER involves cognitive-behavioural and standardised yoga and meditation interventions to induce new learning. The approach has been tested in adults, either alone or in combination with medication. Efficacy of TIMBER is currently being evaluated in a double blind randomised controlled trial in adult patients with PTSD (ibid.).

Eye movement desensitisation and reprocessing

Shapiro (1989) first introduced eye movement desensitisation and reprocessing (EMDR) with claims of a near 100% success rate for any trauma-related memory within a single session of EMDR, which is an evidence-based treatment for post-traumatic stress disorder (Van Schie, Engelhard, & Van den Hout, 2015). In EMDR, patients are asked to recall traumatic memories while they simultaneously make eye movements.

The effectiveness of the treatment can be explained by dual taxation of the limited resources of working memory. Dual taxation takes place when a person recalls a distressing memory while also performing a secondary task, such as making eye movements, mental arithmetic, or drawing complex figures. When individuals perform the secondary task and simultaneously recall a memory, both tasks compete for limited working memory resources. During this competition, the distressing memory cannot be retrieved completely and is stored as a blurred memory after this competition. As a consequence, the blurred memory will be retrieved during future recalls. Presently, a body of evidence supports the working memory hypothesis (Van Schie, Engelhard, & Van den Hout, 2015).

EMDR requires that the practitioner is licensed or licence-eligible and must be used carefully as part of a comprehensive treatment plan. A meta-analysis of seven studies suggested that trauma-focused CBT and EMDR tend to be equally efficacious, and superiority of one treatment over the other could not be demonstrated (Acarturk et al., 2015). EMDR is an effective treatment for PTSD and its use is recommended in clinical guidelines (World Health Organization, 2013).

Gestalt therapy

Some of the basic concepts in gestalt therapy are immediacy of the present moment, spontaneity, and authenticity of the contact. The ways in which individuals adjust to trauma are treated in gestalt as creative and the very best a person can do in difficult circumstances. Very often they come from a field of limited choice and become a part of the personality as *fixed gestalt* (Taylor, 2014).

If a person has reacted to trauma with a strong dissociation of sensations and affects, the split of "observing self" and the "experiencing self" could last for a long time. In gestalt this could be reduced by helping the person to enact and recover self-awareness through interventions as life-assuring "I statements" ("I am here and I am alive") and simple exercises for raising body awareness (Vidaković, 2013).

Because of the division between clinical work and empirical research, which most humanistic therapies share, there have been few efforts to empirically prove the efficacy of gestalt therapy on trauma. There are a few existing studies showing that a gestalt approach can be efficacious in the treatment of PTSD (Elliott, Greenberg, & Lietaer, 2004; Greenberg, 2002; Rosner & Henkel, 2010).

Sensorimotor psychotherapy

Sensorimotor therapy comes closest to gestalt therapy, and it is seen as the "step-grandchild" to gestalt because both therapies share a number of concepts, including tracking, contact, and experimentation (Taylor, 2014).

Developed by Pat Ogden, sensorimotor psychotherapy is a method of treatment for trauma that utilises the body as the primary entry point. Sensorimotor processing is the re-experiencing of the sequenced physical sensations and impulses related to trauma as they progress through the body to completion, that is, to a place of stabilisation and rest (Ogden & Minton, 2000). With the assistance of a sensorimotor psychotherapist, the client learns how to track the unassimilated sensorimotor reactions that were activated during a trauma. By working with the body to re-experience and assimilate traumas that are lodged in the sensorimotor level, emotional and cognitive processing is improved (Siegel, 2010).

Although formal research has not been done about this kind of treatment, there is clinical evidence of its usefulness with traumatised clients. In this kind of treatment, the interaction of thought, feeling, bodily sensation, and movement is in focus through mindfulness observations of the "here and now". The client should express experience through action and bodily movements, which can be either protective or aggressive in nature (Ringel & Brandell, 2011). A case study by Flynn (2010) revealed both therapist and client satisfaction with the treatment outcomes of the sensorimotor psychotherapy process for resolution of childhood trauma.

Conclusion

A long history of observing traumatic memories has shown that there are important distinctions between traumatic and ordinary memories. Important progress has been made in researching neuropsychological bases of forming traumatic memories and in their treatment. There are several types of psychological treatments available for recovery of traumatic memories that are shown to be effective for different kinds of traumatic events. Because of its harmful effects on the quality of daily life, traumatic memory will continue to be a very important and intriguing topic for psychological science.

References

Acarturk, C., Konuk, E., Cetinkaya, M., Senay, I., Sijbrandij, M., Cuijpers, P., & Aker, T. (2015). EMDR for Syrian refugees with posttraumatic stress disorder symptoms: results of a pilot randomized controlled trial. *European Journal of Psychotraumatology, 6*: 27414.

Alberini, C. M., & LeDoux, J. E. (2013). Memory reconsolidation. *Current Biology, 23*: R746-R750.

American Psychiatric Association (2013). *Diagnostic and Statistical Manual of Mental Disorders (5th edn)*. Arlington, VA: American Psychiatric Press.

Bisson, J. I., Tavakoly, B., Witteveen, A. B., Ajduković, D., Jehel, L., Johansen V. J., Nordanger, D., Orengo Garcia, F., Punamaki, R. L., Schnyder, U., Sezgin, A. U., Wittmann, L., & Olff, M. (2010). TENTS guidelines: development of post-disaster psychosocial care guidelines through a Delphi process. *British Journal of Psychiatry, 196*: 69–74.

Bohn, A., & Berntsen, D. (2007). Pleasantness bias in flashbulb memories: positive and negative flashbulb memories of the fall of the Berlin Wall among East and West Germans. *Memory & Cognition, 35*: 565–577.

Boulanger, G. (2008). Witnesses to reality: working psychodynamically with survivors of terror, 1. *Psychoanalytic Dialogues, 18*: 638–657.

Breuer, J., & Freud, S. (1895d). *Studies on Hysteria. S. E., 2*. London: Hogarth.

Brown, R., & Kulik, J. (1977). Flashbulb memories. *Cognition, 5*: 73–99.

Deblinger, E., Cohen, J., & Mannarino, A. (2003). *Child and Parent Trauma-Focused Cognitive Behavioral Therapy Treatment Manual*. Pittsburgh: Allegheny General Hospital Center for Traumatic Stress in Children and Adolescents.

Elliott, R. K., Greenberg, L. S., & Lietaer, G. (2004). Research on experiential psychotherapies. In: M. J. Lambert (Ed.), *Bergin and Garfield's Handbook of Psychotherapy and Behavior Change* (pp. 493–539). New York: Wiley.

Flynn, S. (2010). Addressing anger using sensorimotor psychotherapy and cognitive behavioral therapy. *Canadian Journal of Counseling, 44*: 227–230.

Foa, E. B., Hembree, E. A., & Rothbaum, B. O. (2007). *Prolonged Exposure Therapy for PTSD*. New York: Oxford University Press.

Foa, E. B., Molnar, C., & Cashman, L. (1995). Change in rape narratives during exposure therapy for posttraumatic stress disorder. *Journal of Traumatic Stress, 8*: 675–690.

Forbes, D., Creamer, M., Phelps, A., Bryant, R., McFarlane, A., Devilly, G. J., Matthews, L., Raphael, B., Doran, C., Merlin, T., & Newton, S. (2007). Australian guidelines for the treatment of adults with acute stress disorder and post-traumatic stress disorder. *Australia and New Zealand Journal of Psychiatry, 41*: 637–648.

Gilboa-Schechtman, E., Foa, E. B., Shafran, N., Aderka, I. M., Rachamim, L., Rosenbach, L., Yadin, E., & Apter, A. (2010). A pilot randomized controlled trial of prolonged exposure and dynamic therapy for adolescent victims of single event traumas. *Journal of the American Academy of Child and Adolescent Psychiatry, 49*: 1034–1042.

Greenberg, E. (2002). Love, admiration or safety: a system of Gestalt diagnosis of borderline, narcissistic, and schizoid adaptations that focuses on what is figure for the client. *Gestalt, 6*(3): 393–405.

Greenwald, R. (2013). *Progressive Counting within a Phase Model of Trauma-Informed Treatment.* London: Routledge.

Hayes, S., & Strosahl, K. (2004). *A Practical Guide to Acceptance and Commitment Therapy.* New York: Springer.

Herman, J. L. (1992). *Trauma and Recovery.* New York: Basic.

Howell, E. (2005). *The dissociated mind.* Hillsdale, NJ: Analytic.

Janet, P. (1889). *L'Automatisme psychologique.* Paris: Félix Alcan.

Kabat Zinn, J. (2005). *Coming to Our Senses.* New York: Hyperion.

Kluft, R. P. (2000). The psychoanalytic psychotherapy of dissociative identity disorder in the context of trauma therapy. *Psychoanalytic Inquiry, 20*: 259–286.

Laney, C., & Loftus, E. F. (2013). Recent advances in false memory research. *South African Journal of Psychology, 43*: 137–146.

Linehan, M. (1993). *Cognitive Behavioral Treatment of Borderline Personality Disorder.* New York: Guilford.

Myers, C.S. (1915). A contribution to the study of shell-shock. *Lancet,* 316–320.

Nacasch, N., Foa, E. B., Huppert, J. D., Tzur, D., Fostick, L., Dinstein, Y., Polliack, M., & Zohar, J. (2011). Prolonged exposure therapy for combat- and terror-related posttraumatic stress disorder: a randomized control comparison with treatment as usual. *Journal of Clinical Psychiatry, 72*: 1174–1180.

Ogden, P., & Minton, K. (2000). Sensorimotor psychotherapy: one method for processing traumatic memory. *Traumatology, 7*: 149–173.

Patihis, L., Ho, L. Y., Tingen, I. W., Lilienfeld, S. O., & Loftus, E. F. (2014). Are the "memory wars" over? A scientist-practitioner gap in beliefs about repressed memory. *Psychological Science, 25*: 519–530.

Powers, M. B., Halpern, J. M., Ferenschak, M. P., Gillihan, S. J., & Foa, E. B. (2010). A meta-analytic review of prolonged exposure for posttraumatic stress disorder. *Clinical Psychology Review, 30*: 635–641.

Pradhan, B., Gray, R., Parikh, T., Akkireddi, P., & Pumariega, A. (2015). Trauma interventions using mindfulness based extinction and reconsolidation (TIMBER©) as monotherapy for chronic PTSD: a pilot study. *Adolescent Psychiatry, 5*: 125–131.

Rachamim, L., Mirochnik, I., Helpman, L., Nacasch, N., & Yadin, E. (2015). Prolonged exposure therapy for toddlers with traumas following medical procedures. *Cognitive and Behavioral Practice, 22*: 240–252.

Ringel, S., & Brandell, J. R. (2011). *Trauma: Contemporary Directions in Theory, Practice, and Research.* New York: Sage.

Rosner, R., & Henkel, C. (2010). Gestalt therapy in psycho-traumatology–characteristics and efficacy of gestalt interventions for posttraumatic stress disorder. *Trauma & Gewalt, 4*: 294–303.

Rothschild, B. (2000). *The Body Remembers: The Psychophysiology of Trauma and Trauma Treatment.* New York: Norton.

Sargant, W., & Slater, E. (1941). Amnesic syndromes in war. *Proceedings of the Royal Society of Medicine, 34*: 757–764.

Schmolck, H., Buffalo, E. A., & Squire, L. R. (2000). Memory distortions develop over time: Recollections of the OJ Simpson trial verdict after 15 and 32 months. *Psychological Science, 11*: 39–45.

Segal, Z., Williams, J., & Teasdale, J. (2002). *Mindfulness Based Cognitive Therapy for Depression: A New Approach to Preventing Relapse.* New York: Guilford.

Shapiro, F. (1989). Efficacy of the eye movement desensitization procedure in the treatment of traumatic memories. *Journal of Traumatic Stress, 2*: 199–223.

Siegel, D. (2010). *The Mindful Therapist: A Clinician's Guide to Mindsight and Neural Integration.* New York: Norton.

Swenson, C. M. (2012). Addressing the unspoken nature of trauma: utilizing somatic processing to explore implicit memory. Paper submitted during MSc course at Winona State University, MN.

Talarico, J. M., & Rubin, D. C. (2007). Flashbulb memories are special after all; in phenomenology, not accuracy. *Applied Cognitive Psychology, 21*: 557–578.

Taylor, M. (2014). *Trauma Therapy and Clinical Practice: Neuroscience, Gestalt and the body.* New York: McGraw-Hill.

Van der Kolk, B. A., & McFarlane, A. C. (1996). The black hole of trauma. In: B. A. van der Kolk, A. C. McFarlane, & L. Weisaeth (Eds.), *Traumatic Stress* (pp. 3–23). New York: Guilford.

Van der Kolk, B. A. (1987). *Psychological Trauma.* Washington, DC: American Psychiatric Press.

Van der Kolk, B. A. (1994). The body keeps the score: memory and the evolving psychobiology of posttraumatic stress. *Harvard Review of Psychiatry, 1*: 253–265.

Van der Kolk, B. A. (1997). Traumatic memories. In: P. S. Appelbaum, L. A. Uyehara, & M. R. Elin (Eds.), *Trauma and Memory: Clinical and Legal Controversies* (pp. 243–260). Oxford: Oxford University Press.

Van der Kolk, B. A. (2002). Posttraumatic therapy in the age of neuroscience. *Psychoanalytic Dialogues, 12*: 381–392.

Van der Kolk, B. A., Hopper, J. W., & Osterman, J. E. (2001). Exploring the nature of traumatic memory: combining clinical knowledge with laboratory methods. *Journal of Aggression, Maltreatment & Trauma, 4*: 9–31.

Van Schie, K., Engelhard, I. M., & Van den Hout, M. A. (2015). Taxing working memory during retrieval of emotional memories does not reduce memory accessibility when cued with reminders. *Frontiers in Psychiatry, 6*: 45.

Vidaković, I. (2013). The Power of "moving on". A gestalt therapy approach to trauma treatment. In: G. Francesetti, M. Gecele, & J. Roubal (Eds.), *Gestalt Therapy in Clinical Practice. From Psychopathology to the Aesthetics of Contact* (pp. 317–330). Milan: Franco Angeli.

World Health Organization (2013). Guidelines for the management of conditions specifically related to stress. Downloadable at www.who.int/mental_health/emergencies/stress_guidelines/en/ [last accessed 22 February 2017].

PART II

COPING WITH SOCIAL TRAUMA CULTURALLY AND INDIVIDUALLY

Introduction to Part II

The chapters in the following section highlight the reality of trauma in society. Whereas in Part I definitions and concepts were discussed, Part II looks at actual societies and their symptoms. The section begins with an astonishing story: Mark Solms is not just a renowned neuropsychoanalyst, but also a descendant of the Boer family, who have been living on their farm near Cape Town, South Africa, for 350 years. Having grown up in the dusk of a detested apartheid system, he emigrated to England where he trained as a psychoanalyst. In his chapter, Psychoanalysis by surprise, he presents his experience of returning from voluntary exile after the fall of the apartheid system, his failed attempt to start over as a good, integrated, white farmer, and applying psychoanalysis to eventually find a way to heal the wounds. Another story, likewise with its origins in the past, is told by the late Sarajevo academician Dubravko Lovrenović, who sets the agonising history of Bosnia and Herzegovina in a historical perspective, pointing, as Solms does for South Africa, to the deep historical roots of social re-enactments.

From here, we move to a more recent period, where Camellia Hancheva (Sofia) presents a preliminary report about an ongoing oral history project that was developed from the Trauma, Trust, and Memory network: three generations in a family were interviewed about their memories of important personal and political events in their lives. The study aims at understanding the ways families in countries with different trauma histories construct and reconstruct their past differently. The process of joint narrative accrual is central to the creation of a culture or a tradition.

And there are scars and blind spots. It is, understandably enough, not easy for people whose groups were involved in social trauma, to voluntarily remember what they had suffered, and even more difficult to admit responsibility for atrocities committed by their own group. A social psychological experimental investigation by Sara Ristić (Belgrade) demonstrates that the crime of obedience is judged differently if the perpetrators are believed to be part of their own ethnic group. As Nietzsche says in *Beyond Good and Evil* (aphorism 68): "'I did that,' says my memory. 'I could not have done that,' says my pride, and remains inexorable. Eventually—the memory yields."

So, how can social trauma be addressed in society? Damir Arsenijević and Emin Eminagić (Tuzla), describe a project on telling war jokes in Bosnia and Herzegovina. What they report is hard to bear, but the authors observe that this type of conversation is a way for people to find their own language to talk about the trauma that has not been spoken of, escaping the "ossified language" of official trauma rhetoric.

CHAPTER FOUR

Psychoanalysis by surprise

Mark Solms

I'm going to tell a story about the latest period of my own life, the last 15 years, about what I have experienced. Really it is nothing much more than that—just a story—but I think quite an interesting story, about what I found when I returned to South Africa in 2002. I'm not an expert on South Africa; in fact I'm not an expert on many of the topics that I'm going to be touching upon. But I am an expert on my own life. I'm simply telling you something as I experienced it.

I realised only in retrospect, and only very recently, that what I experienced over these last few years in South Africa is of interest to psychoanalysts and to people who think psychoanalytically. I realised, with surprise, that what I've been doing was applied psychoanalysis—not *doing* psychoanalysis but *being* a psychoanalyst in relation to something other than the usual clinical situation. What I did arose from the fact that I am a psychoanalyst, and the surprise in that is why this chapter has the title "Psychoanalysis by surprise". It was by no means intended to be something clinical or scientific or theoretical. It really was just me trying to manage a situation I found myself in.

My family have been in South Africa for a long time. I am the sixth generation there and my children are the seventh. We have been landowners in South Africa for an equally long time and, in fact, we were landowners in Germany, too, before that, for a much longer time. It seems we have always been landowners. Therefore we have a lot to answer for. As they say: "Under every pile of money lies a murder." I have a lot to answer for not only on behalf of my ancestors, but also by dint of being a white South African. South Africa, at this time in history, is a very specific place.

I was born into the apartheid system. In fact I was born at the height of apartheid. It was also thanks to apartheid that I had to leave South Africa. Because I was a white male, I was required by law to enlist in the South African army, to join what was euphemistically called the South African Defence Force. In fact it was an offence force.

Under apartheid, everything was divided. There was a white and a black (or "non-white") version of everything. And the white version of everything was a lot better than the black version. Everything included schools, beaches, parks, post offices, public toilets, pedestrian bridges, shop entrances, buses—everything, including hospitals. My first job was in a black hospital. I worked in the neurosurgery department at Baragwanath Hospital in Soweto. My first job overlapped with my final years of postgraduate study. One way you could stay out of the South African army in those days was by being a student. And so I studied, and studied, and studied, and I became very learned. But, eventually, they wouldn't allow me to study any more, and as a result, toward the end of the 1980s, I had to leave South Africa.

I went to England, thinking I would never go back, because I had broken the law: I did not report for duty at the appointed place and time. I assumed I was going to live in England forever. While in England I underwent training in psychoanalysis, which, as it turns out, was just as well, because it stood me in very good stead later, when I returned to South Africa.

It was a great surprise to learn one day in the 1990s that the South African government had come to its senses, which governments generally don't do—especially fascist governments. They began negotiations with the liberation movements, completely unexpectedly, and one thing led to another, and suddenly apartheid was over. And so the reason why I had left South Africa was gone. My exile had lost its premise.

I felt surprised to see a number of white South Africans pitching up on the shores of England, then, after 1994. I felt superior to them, because I had left for "good" reasons, and I thought: "What on earth are they doing leaving now, coming to England *after* apartheid?" But I gradually started to realise, as time passed, that I wasn't as different from them as I liked to believe. Because the question obviously arose: "Why am I still here? Why don't I go back?" This question asked itself increasingly frequently. Because, obviously, being a white South African and having lived through those decades of apartheid, I had benefited from the system. It doesn't matter whether or not you supported apartheid; it's simply true that you benefited. It was impossible *not* to benefit from apartheid if you were a white person in South Africa, because all of the resources of the state were directed to looking after you. The educational system was for you, the parks, the beaches, and so on, as I mentioned. And the police force was there to protect you against everyone who was unhappy about the fact that everything was given to you. Literally everything was for you, if you were white, and you couldn't not benefit from such a privileged life. All the resources of a very wealthy state were poured into just a few million people.

And so, after 1994, there I was in England with an excellent education, at the expense of roughly thirty-five million black people who had a shocking education, who lived in tiny houses if they were lucky enough to have one, who were for the most part not able to find work, struggling with a miserable existence. The difference between them and me represented that history. And now was my chance to put it right. So I decided to return, partly for that reason, but also because I missed South Africa. One does not choose where one's home is, but one has certain kinds of attachment to it that don't form in any other place. And South Africa is a beautiful and lovely place. But, above all, what motivated me to return, alongside these other reasons, was the fact that when I started saying to my family that I was considering returning to South Africa, they said: "Oh, great, why don't you take over this farm?"

The farm in question is a wine farm called *Solms-Delta*. It was established in 1690. It is very beautiful, with an ancient manor house, rolling vineyards, an established forest, and a majestic mountain. Who wouldn't want to live there? I really would be lying to you if I said I went back as somebody suffering for the sins of his fathers. I went back into the lap of luxury.

I was going to take on the mantle of a white South African landowner, and I was very much aware of the meaning attached to this mantle. The word "Boer" is one of the words for Afrikaners, the ethnic group that held power during the apartheid era. The word Boer means "farmer". The identities of Afrikaner, farmer, and oppressor in South Africa are very closely related. In fact, there's probably only one identity that was more symbolically charged than being a white farmer in South Africa, and that was being a white police officer. I was very much aware that I was now going to take on the mantle of a Boer, and I didn't like that idea. So, my thinking was: I'm going to go back to South Africa, I'm going to take over this property, but I'm going to do it differently from how it was done in the past. This was my simple and naïve idea. I will go back and I will do good. I am just a citizen, not a politician, so I am not going to be responsible for the entire country, but I will be responsible for a small bit of it, and I will try to fix this bit of it. I thought: I will fix the little piece of South Africa that I am responsible for. That was my idea. That was going to be my citizen-sized contribution. There were a few other things I thought I could also do: I could teach at the public university there, I could work at the public hospital, I could train people within my discipline, and I could help patients. But the farm was really the idea that appealed to me most; this was how I would repay my debt. I would take this one bit of the country and its history, and try to transform it in line with the vision that Nelson Mandela and his African National Congress were developing for a new South Africa.

I do not know whether it is common knowledge, that when you inherit a farm in South Africa, or indeed when you purchase a farm in South Africa, particularly in the Western Cape region where the colonisation of the country began, you also inherit *people*. Even in the twenty-first century, land in South Africa comes with the people who live on it. They live on your land; they have nowhere else to go. So, one way or another, they belong to you. And I use that word advisedly. I know it might sound like slavery, but they really do sort of belong to you. They truly are at your mercy. They hope that you will employ them, they have no possessions in the form of property of their own; their house, such as it is, is on your property, and the same applies to their job, if they have one. And if they irritate you, you know, you might just suggest that they leave. And the neighbouring farmers are certainly not going to hire them then, because they know (if you, their "owner", don't want them and didn't hire them) they are trouble. "Why did they leave the Solms farm?" they would wonder. So, these really are extremely vulnerable people. Just think about it: this is effectively a feudal system. I was very much aware of this, and very daunted, upon meeting my people on my farm, by the responsibility that I had taken on. Most of all I was anxious to make sure, as soon as possible, that they saw I'm not a bad person.

There are seven extended families living on my farm, all interconnected with each other and also with the families living on surrounding farms, because these families have been there for a very long time. In fact, I think that it's not an exaggeration to say, in some respects, that these families have been there forever. My plan was to meet with each of them, as soon as possible.

I flew over to South Africa before my own young family arrived. I flew in to sort out a few things in advance, and one of them was to meet in person with each one of the families. Over one Saturday, I arranged seven hours of appointments, with one family after another, plus an hour for lunch. My intention was first of all to tell them: "Even though I look like my predecessors, I'm not like them … I'm good. Even though I'm the new boss, even though I now own this place, and you therefore are very vulnerable in relation to me, please be assured that it's not going to be how it used to be." I literally put it to them like this. I was keen for them to know that I'm good: "I'm not bad like other farmers that you've known, that your ancestors have known, I want to change this place. I want to make it into a different sort of farm, aligned with the new South Africa that we are now all living in. But, I also don't really know much about farming, because I'm in fact trained in a different field. I never thought that I would be taking this route in life. So you're going to have to help me to plan how we're going to farm this place differently from how it has been done in the past, because you know much more about it than I do. We are going to become partners. So, you are going to have to make suggestions to me. What do you think? How can we do it differently? Come on, let's try together to make this a new kind of South African farm. Any ideas?"

Maybe this paraphrased version of what I said is not a verbatim account, but it accurately represents my manic anxiety to shed the ugly mantle that so patently now belonged to me. The response by the farm people was dumbfounding. In fact, they did not respond. They didn't talk to me. They didn't look at me. They looked at each other, they looked at the floor, they clearly were uncomfortable. I very rapidly became equally uncomfortable. They quietly whispered things to each another. It was just awful. I think most of these hour-long meetings lasted just five minutes. It was unbearable. There were, of course, one or two things said, of an awkward, tense, difficult kind. There was one man named Nico Jansen—I will come back to him later—who spoke to me a bit. Since I was returning to London that night, I therefore appointed him as the interim manager. I went back feeling dreadful, thinking: "What on earth am I doing? What am I thinking?" The reality of what I was taking on hit me like a fist, like a punch in the face.

I phoned Nico the next week, because I wanted to be sure that he knew that he really was the manager; and I asked him to tell me how the people had responded to our meetings. I was very anxious to hear. He said—and here I am quoting verbatim, because these words are burned into my brain forever—he said: "The people said a prayer to the Lord last night to thank Him for sending us a new owner who we don't have to be scared of." Please note the word "sending us a new *owner*" and also "who we *don't have to be scared* of". Not who is nice, who we find interesting, who's a breath of fresh air. No, it's somebody who we don't we have to be scared of. That was how they experienced me.

A few months later I finally returned for good, with my family. And there we were. Us and them. In comparison to my house, their houses offered small, cramped accommodation. In fact the old cellar, where the wine used to be produced in the eighteenth century, had been divided into six apartments. It wasn't even built for residential use. Only one family, an elderly couple with mature children, were living in a proper house. A proper house of around eighty square metres. And now I faced the task of actually trying to put into effect my plan, that we are going to make a new kind of South African farm together, and we are going to live a different kind of future together, and they are going to teach me some of the tricks of the trade of farming, and

I'm going to show by my actions that I really do want us to forge a way of being together that won't be like it was in the old days. I said, "Come on, let's do it", and so we began.

Well, it was a disaster. It was a complete and utter disaster. As soon as the farm people realised that I really was different from my predecessors, they came to the conclusion that I was an idiot. They saw not only that they don't have to be scared of me, but also that they can take advantage of me. "We don't have to work for this guy, he's just nice all the time, and he doesn't understand what we are doing. He doesn't know any of the tricks of the trade, so maybe if we come in late on Mondays it will be okay. Maybe if we knock off earlier on Fridays it will be okay. Maybe if we don't go to work at all on Mondays it will be okay. Let's see what happens."

And so things fell apart. Pumps went missing, tractors went missing, a Victorian stove was hacked out of one of the buildings (and sold). Things unravelled completely. This was probably one of the first moments when I had a sort of psychoanalytical thought. I thought: "It seems on this farm, given that it's been here for a very long time (more than 320 years), somebody has always been abusing somebody else; so if I'm not abusing them, then they will abuse me. That's simply how it works. We are not on the same side. Everyone's getting away with whatever they can at the expense of someone else." I had the impression, that what was taking place was some sort of reversal of the only way that people knew how to relate to each other across the owner/owned divide, the employer/employee divide on this farm, and that is getting away with what you can, taking advantage and being as greedy and selfish as you possibly can. Now I started to feel irritated. And I started to think "What's the matter with these people, you know, why can't they see I'm really good, I'm really trying my best, why do they have to do this to me? Why don't they even try, why aren't they grateful?" Those were my thoughts, honestly. And I also started to think "Maybe it's true what my (white) neighbour said: 'These people are lazy', 'These people are not really nice', 'These people are thieves', 'They get away with whatever they can, I mean this is Africa after all'." I admit that I started to have these sorts of feelings, but I doubt that I would be the only person to have them in those circumstances.

An anecdote conveys the atmosphere of that period very well. I already mentioned the stolen pump, and the not turning up for work, and the like. (By the way, the pump on a farm is important, it is where the water comes from. In water-stressed South Africa, pumps are really important.) But this story concerns the forest on my farm. A beautiful forest of established, ancient trees. There are indigenous trees, but also European trees, the most prominently represented being the English oaks. And there are also Eastern trees, the most prominently represented being Javanese camphors. The Cape was on the trade route between Europe and the East, so this is why we have these indigenous and European and Asian influences. The Javanese camphors are exquisite. You see them in those Japanese paintings, beautiful sinuous branches. My camphors were more than two hundred years old.

I noticed one day when walking in my forest that some of them had been chopped down. Well, the pump was gone, the stove was gone, the people weren't reporting for work, and now my trees were being chopped down. By the next day another one had been chopped down, and two days later three more had been felled. And so I went to Nico, the manager, and I asked him what was going on. He said: "You know, professor, the people around here are poor and they need wood, so they go to the forest and they chop down the trees; this is how they survive."

So I thought, well, it makes sense. Among the trees in that forest we also had some horrible ones called black wattle; they come from Australia and they're invasive aliens. And so I decided I would fell all the black wattle, which I wanted to do anyway, and even more, I would chop them into logs and I would put these at the entrance to the section of the farm where my home is situated, and I told the people through Nico that if they wanted wood, they could come and take it—already chopped—from here. (By the way, this was further evidence of how good I am!) But nobody took any of this wood, and what's worse, the camphor trees continued to be chopped down.

Maybe you can imagine; my mood turned. I had brought my family, young children, back from Europe to Africa to reclaim my inheritance. Also to admit to my legacy and try to do something about it. And now, the farm was unravelling; nobody was coming to work, things were being stolen, and now the trees in my forest were being felled, and when I offer a rational and generous solution, they still are chopped down, by some dark forces, in the dead of the night. It really was aggressive. I felt scared and upset and a bit angry, too. I went back to Nico and I said: "What's this with the trees? I don't understand it." He said I should talk to Benny Daniels. I didn't know why I was to talk to Benny but I subsequently discovered it was because Nico had a suspicion that it was the people on the farm next door who were doing this, and they were Bushmen, people of Bushman descent, and so was Benny. His family was interconnected with those people, and Benny would probably be able to sort it out. He didn't explain all of this to me; I subsequently worked it out. All I knew was that I was to talk to Benny.

So, I talked to Benny, who incidentally had never talked to me. And in a sullen sort of way he explained to me: "Yes, I think it's those people," this is what he said to me, "I think it's those people from across the road, they are taking down the trees." So, I said to him: "But why? I don't understand; it makes no sense." He replied: "It's because they are Bushmen." "But why?" I asked. He responded again: "They are Bushmen; they don't think like us." That was the explanation: "These are Bushmen, so they don't think like us."

So now we had some kind of racist explanation. There was a group of irrational people called Bushmen who don't think like us. And Benny is far from being the first person to have said that. In fact, that's where the very word Bushman comes from. The implication is: "These are barely people; they are closer to animals than we are." That was the thinking when European colonists first arrived and found the Bushmen here, living in the bush like other primates. When I said earlier that the people on the farm include some families who have been here forever, I was referring to those of Bushman descent. The Bushmen were here since forever, hunter-gathering people, living in the Cape for as long as human beings have existed. And when the colonists first arrived, their response was: these people are not entirely human. They live like animals, hunting and gathering in the bush; they don't have homes, they don't stay in one place, they don't own anything. They are like animals. So, when a person in modern South Africa, even Benny, says to me, "These are Bushmen; they don't think like us", that's an insult which can't explain anything. The implication was that you can't expect rational behaviour from a Bushman. I understood what he was saying to me. You can imagine how much worse I felt!

I realised that I was in real trouble. Once again, this is where psychoanalytical education came to my aid. One thing we learn in psychoanalysis is to be able to recognise a bad situation for what it is, to not pretend that something nice is going on. There is a famous psychoanalyst who once said to a candidate who he was supervising: "Don't you just do something, stand there!" In English when your child is being naughty, or being lazy, you say: "Don't you just stand there, do something!" This psychoanalytical formulation is the opposite: "Don't you just do something, stand there!" In other words, there's a time to just *be* in a situation, especially if you don't understand what's happening, to just be able to tolerate that something bad is happening. If you don't understand it, then you don't know what to do, so what you should do is do nothing. Rather than do something for the sake of it, as if you know what to do. A non-analytic response would have been to do something stupid, to do *anything* in the hope that it will get rid of the bad feeling. For sure, it is better to do nothing than to do something angry, which also is partly what I felt myself wanting to do. I wanted to say to them "Piss off! I *will* become the Boer! You wanna see a Boer? I'll show you. I'm gonna get you to work! You say somebody is gonna abuse somebody, yeah, okay, well, fuck it, I'm gonna abuse you if you abuse me!" I had those sorts of feelings, tinged with racism, of course, and I'm aware of it. Racist feelings definitely were among those that occurred to me, so it's just as well I did nothing. Thus, after the first psychoanalytic insight I had gained, namely the realisation that somebody has to abuse somebody in this place, that is just how it works, the next realisation was: "This is horrible. I don't know what to do. So I am going to do nothing until I understand what is going on."

Eventually I had a really good idea. It followed the period of just doing nothing. I knew something was horribly wrong. I didn't understand it, but I knew I was becoming my own worst nightmare, I really was becoming a white farmer. I had all these angry feelings, all these indignant feelings. So, in desperation, I had an insight: I must *take a history*. That is what you do when you have a new patient. That is how you begin to lay the foundations for a formulation as to what is wrong. I thought: this is a disaster, we need professional help. I decided: we must stop farming and bring in experts to help us take a history. We must bring in historians and archaeologists. And that's what we did. We stopped farming and we dug up the farm. We all joined in, we started using our skills not for tending the vineyards and fields, but rather to learn what had happened here. We must excavate the place, together, and see what we find. We must learn together how we got to be in the situation we were in now.

It was an extraordinary process—digging up the apartheid history, the colonial history, the pre-colonial history, of my farm. All of us were involved in it, with the archaeologists and historians. And we didn't just take refuge in the distant past; we also excavated the recent past. We included oral historians, taking our own remembered life histories, as we sat in the same room where I had those meetings that I mentioned before. We sat there telling the historians, who recorded us, our lives. This was a very important part of the process of researching what had happened here. It was a most moving experience, to listen to the stories of the farm workers' lives. I mean, to hear the grinding degradation, on an everyday basis, that comes with poverty and with being black in South Africa under apartheid. I knew it in the abstract, but to listen over and again to such stories of, for example, how excited the farm people were when—at the age of eleven or twelve—they got their first pair of shoes, and how before that event they used to put their feet in cow dung to keep them warm.

On hearing these stories I gradually realised how people were living, people like me, like Benny, each individual telling you about his lived life. And part of this process with the oral historians was me telling my life story, while we were all sitting there together. I felt nothing but shame telling about my life, honestly. In the sea of other lives, so utterly unimaginable to me, in excruciating detail, the banal daily reality of poverty and prejudice. Story after story, not told in rage and accusation, but told because the historians wanted to know the facts of their lives. The historians asked sensitively, carefully about each life. I could hardly bring myself to tell the historians about the shameful privilege of my own life, and my own piffling problems, by comparison.

So, we dug up our histories, our memories of living under apartheid, on the two sides of that great divide. In the process we got to know each other, in a way that was quite raw, as I hope I'm describing to you. Then the historians filled in the gaps, the foundations beneath our lives, educating us. As they researched and found documentary evidence about my farm, so they educated us about what had happened there. We also found rock art in the mountains surrounding the farm, painted hundreds (and thousands) of years ago by Bushmen, depicting elephants among other things. The valley where I live used to be called Elephants Quarter. There were thousands of elephants. The Bushmen hunted those elephants. Here was tangible evidence of their having been here. We also found a 6,000-year-old Bushman settlement site on my farm, with literally thousands of their stone artefacts. Not all of these were finished tools, they included flakes from the process of tool-making. But they were proof of the fact that there were people who had lived here for millennia, just a few metres from where my house now stands. There was also evidence of Khoe habitation on my farm. The Khoe were nomadic pastoralists, who moved into the Cape from the north 2,000 years ago, and brought cattle and sheep with them. They made mobile houses from reeds, called "matjieshuise", which they could roll up and move with them as the seasons passed. We found pottery of theirs, too, on my farm.

The historians also told us about the early settlers in my valley. My farm was granted in 1690 by the governor, Simon van der Stel, and he said we (i.e., my predecessors) may have this piece of land, and we may cut down all the trees so long as we planted English oaks to replace them, one for each indigenous tree that we cut down. Now can you imagine what the granting of this land into private settler ownership did to the indigenous hunter-gatherers and nomadic pastoralists? One year they came up the valley and all the fertile land suddenly "belonged" to people like me. They didn't have any conception that one can claim ownership of land. That was an absurdity to them; the land so obviously belongs to everyone, and sustains everyone. So they continued to hunt the farmers' animals and so on. As a result, many of them were put in jail, if they were lucky. I say lucky, because most of them were shot. There was genocide, literally, in my valley. The landowners were permitted to shoot Bushmen, as they were considered vermin. So the Bushmen and Khoe were all driven off our land, and their economies and cultures collapsed, and they were literally slaughtered. The few who remained went into mountains (where you don't farm) or into the desert. People think Bushmen like to live in deserts. They didn't choose to live in deserts! They lived there because that was all that was left to them by the settlers. A few of them stayed on the farms and worked for us, for my lot; but very few, not enough to establish the vineyards and build the homesteads and outbuildings and so on. So, we farmers brought slaves—from India, Sri Lanka, Java, Malaysia, from all of the Indonesian archipelago—and also from Madagascar and the east coast of Africa. By 1665 already, there were more slaves in the Cape than settlers.

In this way, the people living on my farm learnt why they are there. They're there either because their ancestors' land was taken away by my predecessors (some of whom stayed, because they had nowhere else to go) or because their ancestors were dragged over as slaves, against their will, to work on farms like mine. And here's the rub: they are still there now, still working on our farms. That's why they are there. Remember, I said that when you acquire land in South Africa it comes with people. These are the people it comes with: descendants of the indigenous people whose land was taken from them, and descendants of the slaves who were brought here against their will to develop the farmland.

This whole process of digging up the history of my farm was an amazing one to go through, collectively learning about what had happened there, what we had done to each other, how we got to be in the position that we are in today. Of course, if you have been at the receiving end of this history, life just happens to you. Imagine if you are descendent from generations upon generations of slaves. It becomes your culture. The culture is that you just wait for things to happen to you. You keep your head down. You hope nobody notices you. You certainly don't talk with the owner and draw attention to yourself. And when the owner says to you: "What's your idea about the future?" you think "What is he talking about? I don't shape the future." There's also no normal relationship between employer and employee on my farm, because of this history. It perverted the relationship between us. The workers didn't even choose to be there, they didn't come and say: "Hi, I want to sell you my labour; let's agree on a fee." It is delusional for me to think that I'm an employer in any normal way, in a freely chosen way. It's simply not true. The attitude of both parties is actually one of resentment. "I have to work for you and I know that you don't really want to pay me, and you pay me as little as you can, and get away with it. So, as long as I don't get noticed, I'll do the minimum, and if shit happens, I'll just have to accept it." That's how it works.

So much made sense to me now. In America, to be told that you are descended from slaves seems to be something that you're proud of. In South Africa that's not the case at all. It's like being told that you're descendent from paedophiles, or something like that—it's absolutely shameful to be told that your ancestors were slaves. Being called a Bushman, too, is an insult. On the farm, it is the worst thing you can possibly be. And now these historians were clearly telling the farmworkers about their roots, not accusing them of anything, just telling them. They're nice, interesting people, telling them about the Bushmen, about how they used to own this land. They are also telling them how their slave ancestors were brought here and forced to work for people like me. And they are telling them that's why they have the facial features they do. That's why the farmworkers look like Bushmen or like Indians. And that's also why the person who lives in the big house is always white, and so on. It is not God who decreed that the world should be like this; it is like this as the result of *history*. And if historical forces made things turn out like this, then we can change those forces.

Benny Daniels came to me one day during the archaeological dig. He looked me in the eye, properly, for the first time ever, holding a microlithic stone tool he had just excavated, which the archaeologists had told him was a blade that his Bushman ancestors had made, and he said: "You see Professor? My people were here before yours!" Here was the proof. And now it was *his* people, not *the Bushmen* who don't think like us. Most importantly, the implicit question behind what Benny said was this: "So, how come I work for you? How come the farm belongs to you?" Moments like this changed everything. To honestly face up to what happened changed everything. There was no way that we couldn't talk to each other now, no way that we couldn't look each other in the eye. In fact, if there was anyone who was still having difficulty looking people in the eye, it was me.

We then made a museum on my farm, a little museum that tells the true story of what happened there—since the stone ages, through colonisation, disposition of the land, dislocation of slaves—everything that we found is publically displayed there. The centrepiece of the museum is a wall of granite plaques that we made to remember each and every slave, by name, wherever possible. We memorialised each individual who gave their life against their will to the development of my farm. I had to recognise, and still have to recognise, that the house I sleep in was built by these slaves, even my children's bedrooms. And the people who work for me now are descendants of the same slaves. That's why things are like they are between us. The museum was enormously important to everyone on the farm. Their own personal stories were there, for all the world to see. They could go there and see their stories being told, to visitors from around the world. It was extremely moving to see the illiterate farm workers watching this and talking to each other and inviting their friends.

But remember: this was not an academic exercise. We took a history in order to reach a diagnosis. Now we had that diagnosis. The whole problem revolves around the taking of the land. The main thing that was wrong now, the current symptom, when looked at it in light of the history, is this: *I still owned the farm*. And they were still beholden to me. There's no way to deny it. This, again, is where it was helpful to be a psychoanalyst. Because, what I recognised, to be honest, was that I didn't want to give the land back. This is what I thought: "I brought my children here, my family has been here for generations, I want to pass it down to the next generation." That's what I felt. What I felt alongside this was rationalisations. I felt: "It's not Nico that I took the land from. In fact, I didn't take it from anyone. It happened more than 300 years ago. Who do I give it back to? Do I give it to Nico, or to some symbolic bushman? Do I chop it up into seven pieces and give one piece to each family? But productive farms have to be a certain size, you can't just subdivide them". All these thoughts went through my head. But the bottom line was that I didn't *want* to give it back. That was the unvarnished truth. I didn't want to and I couldn't bring myself to.

So, here we have what's called a conflict. And as we psychoanalysts know, when you repress something like this or deny it, defending yourself against the painful overwhelming truth, it prevents you from thinking properly. You don't have access to your mind. There are major parts of the facts you're dealing with that you have to exclude from your reasoning. This is the essence of what psychoanalysis is about. One thing we've learned is that people avoid things they can't cope with by excluding them from their minds; but they do this at a cost. Then they have to find other explanations for the missing facts. Racism is one such explanation. I finally understood the simple truth that racism is a defence against facing the historical facts.

The racist thoughts that I had were of this kind. "Why are they not grateful, these lazy people, what's the matter with them?" rather than thinking "Why would anybody be enthusiastic about my project to transform *my* farm, which was stolen from them?" But the essence of the matter is, when you do face the facts you are defending against, it gives you your mind back. You can think again. And so it was a very straightforward process that we then followed. I had to face the fact I didn't really want to transform my farm. I didn't want to fix it properly. This is because I didn't want to give it back—because of my own self-interest. So now we had to talk about that. I said: "I don't want to give it back. What are we going to do? I can see it's wrong, but I still own it. And, I tell you, I can't give it back, I want to give it to my children, Leon and Ella. I feel badly about this. Can we talk about it? Let's try to find another solution?" And that's what we did. A very simple psychoanalytical process.

The solution we then came to was equally simple. The only reason it hasn't been done before is because people like me are so busy defending themselves against the emotions, the guilt, the fear, the shame, and so on, arising from the facts they can't face. But when you face them, including your own self-interest, and talk about it, you can find solutions very easily.

The solution that we found is this: we went to a bank and we said: "Will you please lend money to the farm workers so they can buy the farm next to me, so that we could *both* have a farm?" And the bank said: "No. They've got no assets." So I said: "Yes, but that's the problem. That's what we are trying to reverse. I will use my farm as security, so that you can lend the farm workers the money."

They have a formula with agricultural loans. They will give you fifty per cent of the value of the land if you put it up as security. A very good friend of mine, a neighbour named Richard Astor, then decided he would join me in this venture. So we both put our farms up as security; so we had fifty per cent plus fifty per cent, which equals one hundred per cent. So the farm workers were able to buy the farm next to both of ours which was every bit as beautiful and big, historic and magical as our own. Now the other white neighbours said: "You're at risk! Think about your children!" (By the way, I don't believe I was taking on a risk; I was acknowledging a risk that was there all along. The risk of an unpaid debt. Acknowledging a risk means that you can do something about it.)

The farm next door now belonged to the farm workers, and if they didn't make a success of it I was going to have to forfeit my farm to the bank. So, this motivated me to help them to make sure their farm succeeds. That self-interest is a realistic basis for what they call "skill sharing". In fact we formed a partnership, the owners of the three farms. Each of us owns one-third of a company, and each of us leases our land to this collective agricultural enterprise. (By the way, each one of the three farms comes with its own people, so now we have got many more people, all in this collective enterprise together, living on the three farms.)

From the money we borrowed from the bank we not only bought land, we also built decent new houses, and we invested in expanding our vineyards and our cellar. Today we have a successful business, and everyone is benefiting from it and everyone is pulling in the same direction. It's nice to live among people who are on the same side, who are honest with each other, and who recognise that their fates are intertwined. Our business is successful, by the way, because wine is made by hand: you can make it with hatred and resentment or you can make it with love and enthusiasm—and the outcome is very different. Our wine is wonderful! People taste it when they visit our farm to see our museum, and then they become customers for life, and tell their friends, and so on. So our business has benefited for precisely the same reasons that I supposedly put it at risk.

But other things happened too. You know what the farm workers did? The first thing was they took their kids out of the farm schools and put them in a good school in town, where you have to pay fees. Since their kids couldn't cope at this school, they also paid to have facilitators in the classrooms to help them catch up, and after school we hired teachers to give homework support, because the parents couldn't help the kids with their homework, they don't know anything about it. And you won't believe how well those kids are doing. The single biggest investment of the farm workers has been in their children, in their future.

But something else happened that I would never have predicted. We have an annual parade down the high street of our town called Franschhoek. Each wine farm is invited to make a float for this parade. Our farm workers had never taken part in it, but now they were farm owners and they said they wanted to participate. It never had occurred to anybody that this parade was for farm workers too. Now we had to make a float. The problem is: we have democracy on our farm, so we had to make democratic discussions about our float. Have you ever heard of a float designed by democracy?! The float was terrible. This is what our float committee decided: each person on the farm will get a box, a wine box, and on that box they will paste a photograph of themselves and write their name, and if they cannot write, they'll make a painted handprint onto the box. So, each box represented one person who lives on the farm. Then we put all the boxes in a pyramid on a trailer, and one of our tractors pulls it down the street. That's our float. In addition, we—all 180 of us—will walk around our tractor, down the high street, and we will sing traditional songs!

It was the most memorable day of my life. At the end of the day, they had a vote for the best float. Ours was surely the worst float … but it won. The next year, we won the competition again. In the third year the village cancelled the float competition. Ever since then, the annual parade simply begins with our farm workers marching down the high street singing traditional songs.

The true history of my farm, as told in the museum, is a tragic one, in which many mistakes were made. Of course, alongside these bad things, there were also good things, and some were even inspiring. For example, alongside the slavery and dispossession and apartheid, there was a particular musical tradition that grew out of that cultural melting pot of the early Cape—just as the blues did in America. We have our own indigenous and slave genres and dance music styles, called *goema* and *vastrap* and *langarm* and *riel*. When we built the museum, we decided to archive this aspect of the farm's history there too. So I brought ethnomusicologists, who asked if anybody on the farm still played the old songs, if anybody had the old instruments, and so on, for our museum. It turned out there was one old man, Hannes Floors, who normally did nothing much, who said: "I know the old songs, but my guitar strings broke in 1973." And under his bed was his guitar. So, the ethnomusicologist restrings it, the man plays the old songs in front of his house, and a camerawoman records it. Next thing, Oom ("uncle") Hannes's wife Tant ("aunt") Hanna comes out of the house, and while Hannes plays and sings, she starts dancing. Now we have an event. Mr. and Mrs. Floors are playing guitar and singing and dancing and there's a white person with a camera, and so on. So all the kids come running. "What is Oom Hannes doing? We didn't know that Oom Hannes plays the guitar! Can he teach me? Can I sing too?" In five minutes, we had formed a little band, with kiddies and old people together. They called themselves the Optel ("pick up") band. They start getting little gigs at local events.

Next thing, the farmworkers say: "But, there's another tradition, the marching minstrel bands, we want to have a marching band also." So, today we have an eighty-piece marching band, called The Delta Valley Entertainers. And there's yet another tradition of so-called Christmas choirs, too. So now we also have women's choir, called the Soetstemme (the "sweet voices"). And there's a stage band, who wanted to show that they are not kids, they're serious; the best musicians among them who started this band called it the Langbroeke (which means "long trousers", as opposed to short trousers, which children wear).

The most amazing thing is that while we just wanted to archive all these old musical styles in the museum, we brought them back to public life. It turned out that the people knew all these old things that they were semi-ashamed of. They didn't dream that white people might be interested in their culture. They didn't even think it was a culture. Now we have a huge musical programme on our farms, with voice teachers, strings teachers, brass teachers, song writing teachers. We farm music as well as wine. I didn't even know these musical traditions existed, and these dance styles, and now they are famous! Our workers are on the radio and television, they get gigs all over the country, and every year we have a harvest festival where we throw a party for all farmworkers in our valley. They come and we dance to this music, and eat traditional food. The farm workers in the valley come for free but visitors pay, to see this incredible music and experience being together at last. We have more than 5,000 people attending this festival every year.

That is my story. The rest is detail.

What happened on my farm was kind of a communal psychoanalysis. I think that because I was trained in psychoanalysis, I didn't do anything too emotionally stupid when I got there and found myself in such a difficult situation. I was able to recognise the bad feelings for what they were, and not react to them. Then I tried to understand them, using professional helpers, who enabled us to take our history. Having done that as truthfully as we could, we were able to arrive at a simple but rational decision about how to change that history—we did something that anybody could have done if they had access to all the emotional facts. The result has been very successful.

So that's it: psychoanalysis by surprise.

CHAPTER FIVE

Bosnia and Herzegovina as the stage for three parallel and conflicted historical memories: is Bosnia and Herzegovina a "failed state"?*

Dubravko Lovrenović

Introductory remarks

I chose the topic connected with an unavoidable issue—the issue of collective identities in Bosnia and Herzegovina, that is, three different and conflicting memories formed through history. The topic is extremely important because in the last decade of the twentieth century, Bosnia and Herzegovina became a stage for struggle and for experiments of world policy; or, more precisely, a battle between different cultural, political, and religious concepts of society and state. In such a web of circumstances, its history and its destiny became much more important than they would have been in other situations.

A small Balkan country, Bosnia and Herzegovina caught the attention of the world especially between 1992 and 1995, having become the stage for a war that was ended by the Dayton Peace Agreement in November/December 1995. Although that Agreement brought peace to Bosnia and Herzegovina, it did not solve, as it could not, any of the deeply rooted historical and psychological problems that had existed before the war broke out. So, despite the ethnonational division sealed by the Dayton Agreement, the historical and political scene of Bosnia and Herzegovina is still almost the same in 2014 as it was in 1991.

Actually, Bosnia and Herzegovina is still in a deep political crisis, exposed to the danger of disintegration. The crisis is very closely related to the different regimes and policies of historical memory being transmitted further by the media and the educational system. The whole society, from top to bottom, is divided along ethno-national lines.

* This chapter appeared in *European Review* (October 2016, 24(4): 481–490) and is published here with kind permission of Cambridge University Press.

Historical experience has taught us that the breakdown of Bosnia and Herzegovina could be reflected on a much broader space than the region of Southeast Europe, that is, the Balkans.

Historical discontinuity and national disunity of Bosnia and Herzegovina

The history of Bosnia and Herzegovina, being part of European development, but breaking ties with it as well, has been crucially determined by foreign and authoritarian political systems—a history without democracy of the western type. That history has developed within seven disparate civilisational, political, and legal paradigms: in the Banovina/Kingdom of Bosnia (ninth century to 1463); the Ottoman Empire (1463–1878); the Austro-Hungarian Monarchy (1878–1918); the First Yugoslavia (1918–1941); the Independent State of Croatia (1941–1945); the Second Yugoslavia (1945–1992); and in the internationally recognised state of Bosnia and Herzegovina since 1992. The history of Bosnia and Herzegovina has not been a straight line, a logical dynamics of transition from one state into another, but rather under the impact of external powers which caused its deep demographic, cultural, and political disintegration. After the period of mediaeval state independence, in the Ottoman period (1463–1878), the ground was destroyed for the common political identity of the three religiously and confessionally divided ethnic communities—today's Serbs, Croats, and Bosniaks—who were and have remained emotionally tied to extra-Bosnian political and religious centres (Belgrade, Zagreb, & Istanbul). Political life in Bosnia and Herzegovina was domineered by pragmatism and dogmatism; thus, none of the political traditions related to all those more or less undemocratic systems was accepted, either emotionally or in memory, in the same way by all inhabitants of today's Bosnia and Herzegovina (Džaja, 1999).

Such a "raw" representation of history, which keeps generating and regenerating trauma, is presented mainly by the intellectual, religious, and political pseudo-elite of Bosnia and Herzegovina to their fellow citizens.

Besides the mediaeval period, marked by the schismatic Bosnian Church and the period between 1941 and 1945 marked by the anti-fascist struggle, Bosnia and Herzegovina has remained an object of European and world history, with its political destiny determined by three treaties: Berlin (1878), Versailles (1919), and Dayton-Paris (1995).

The Turkish Complex—in the case of the Bosniaks, the complex of "lesser value"; in the case of the Serbs and Croats, the complex of "greater value"—has been one of the recurring factors of more than four centuries of the long Ottoman Empire ruling over Bosnia and Herzegovina. That complex left three opposite representations in the psychology of the ethno-national communities of Bosnia and Herzegovina: "We are Turks" (Bosniak); "Antemurale christianitatis" (Croatian); "The Return to Ancestral Faith" (Serbian) (Žanić, 2003; Aleksov, 2003; Elrich, 1964; Lovrenović, 2008).

Political culture as a reflection of the friend–enemy scheme

The fundamental contradictory elements of political culture and political language in these historical time periods are established on stereotypical pictures, that is the friend–enemy scheme. The relations between Christians, namely Orthodox and Catholic Christians (Serbs and Croats), meant deep opposition inherited from the Great Schism in 1054, while the relations between Christians and Muslims included the problem of conversion from Christianity to Islam. At the base of a scheme constructed as such was the opposing system of thought: true believer—false believer. Religious pictures were "translated" into political language and those pictures have outlived all political establishments so far. So, the nationalism of the "Doomsday" is still on. This is discouraging but true: religious communities in Bosnia and Herzegovina as such cannot contribute to reconciliation because they produce conflicted political cultures the same way they are conflicted between themselves on the basis of their own dogmatic standpoints. On the contrary, they contribute to Bosnia and Herzegovina increasingly becoming a religious state and, at the same time, to political representation based on confessional affiliations (Komšić, 2014).

Mutual enmities and resentment generated in the historical period of statelessness, which each of the three communities experiences as a different emotion, continued to exist even after the withdrawal of the Ottoman Empire from Bosnia and Herzegovina, in 1878, first under the guise of the constitutional solution of a "rustic" parliamentary democracy of the First Yugoslavia, and then as part of the mono-party system of the Second Yugoslavia. Traditional, heroised patriarchal order, counting on all differences related to these two state-political systems, outlived them with its heritage based on predominance of the rural over the urban.

Different political identities resting on different perceptions of the Ottoman and Yugoslav epoch of the history of Bosnia and Herzegovina, three divergent traditions that are mutually exclusive, with evident differences in view of the political organisation of the state, have made and still make political consensus impossible to realise. What has always been the unresolvable problem is the taming of political power through the state-controlled institutions and productive confrontation with the deformed political culture inherited from the past without any real possibility of political representation for all ethnic communities.

Under such circumstances the monological and conflicting character of the Bosnian-Herzegovinian society was created, as a closed circle living on revenge, without compromise, except for the compromise gained by extortion. Such state of mind and feelings is good for the climate of interventionism. That process—the process of interventionism—has been ongoing especially since 1992 until today.

Constitutional tradition of Bosnia and Herzegovina (1910–2010): death capital consisting of forgotten paragraphs

The forces that took part in this historical seven-act "drama" had such opposing views of life that a century-long constitutional tradition of Bosnia and Herzegovina (1910–2010) could not generate any common starting position for the negotiations about the reform of the Dayton Constitution in which political, ethno-national elites participate now. The Constitution of 1910, the Vidovdan Constitution of 1919, three constitutions of the Socialist Yugoslavia of 1946, 1963, and 1974, and finally the Dayton Constitution of 1995, as Annex 4 of the Framework Peace Agreement for Bosnia and Herzegovina, speak different languages and always need "interpreters". The political implementation of Bosnia and Herzegovina into these constitutional provisions is of such nature that it could not ensure a stable state and efficient resolution of social and economic problems. However, the Dayton Peace Agreement could have done it even less, with its Annex 4, as the constitution of Bosnia and Herzegovina, which introduced a legal provisional solution without formally annulling the 1974 Bosnia and Herzegovina Constitution, which guaranteed its sovereignty of a republic within the Socialist Federal Republic of Yugoslavia.

The cult of an unfinished past

Viewed in the big picture, the history of Bosnia and Herzegovina appears as a history of *caesuras*. Along this region, the Roman Empire was divided into Eastern and Western, where the Latin and Greek languages separated; it was on this seam of history that the Church schism of 1054 took place. At the end of the West, at the end of the East, here, met and mixed artistic forms, ethnicities, and cultures to a degree of difficult recognition; it was here that the frontier between the Ottoman Empire and the countries of central Europe was established and lasted for centuries. Those divisions led to the mixing of ethnic regions and colonising areas of certain nationalities, which bore the seed of countless problems. In this Balkan "Bermuda Triangle" of history, identities were formed made up of heterogeneous affiliations, composed harmoniously at the same time but sharply polarised as well; split up identities escaping full control, most clearly recognised at moments—and there were too many of them—when they were denied on religious, national, ethnic or other grounds. That is why that history was able to become a struggle for identity and that is why such deviations were possible when people turned into serial killers overnight.

Bosnia and Herzegovina fully shares this historical fate, outlining the fate of the Levantine man and, as Ivo Andrić put it, "human dust which painfully passes between the East and the West, not belonging to either and beaten by both" (1996, p. 262). Under such agonising historical circumstances, there was no other more fertile soil for the appearance of uncanonical forms and dislocated paradigms in which creation of a unique history was impossible as they were in advance—from both inside and outside—cut up, divided, opposed, and at odds with each other. Bosnian man was and has remained a victim of great history, and that is why his identity was not able to form as a sum of independent affiliations, but rather *as a pattern drawn on a tightly stretched parchment* (Maalouf, 2001, p. 26). Thus were created the wounded communities nurturing their cults and myths, their dreams and expectations, immeasurably far away from the rationality with which west Europeans look at the past.

In the Balkans generally—therefore in Bosnia and Herzegovina as well—the cult of an unfinished past was created, which is still waiting for its redeemers and healers, where the clear frontier between the past, the present, and the future was wiped out. Psychoanalysts have established that the feelings of groups affected by traumatic experiences are conveyed from one generation to another and that the "chosen trauma" appears through the collective memory of an event or chain of events: "In short, members of a massively traumatised group cannot successfully complete certain psychological tasks and they, then, transmit such tasks to the children of the next generation(s) along with the conscious and unconscious shared wish that the next generation(s) will resolve them" (Volkan, 2004, p. 1). The cycle of negative generalisations and stereotypes is prolonged and constantly regenerated in that way, especially in patriarchal societies like the Southern Slavic, which has been like that for many centuries (Dvorniković, 1990). That is why all our attempts of modernisation failed to "modernise" archaic patriarchal patterns. Bosnia and Herzegovina finds itself only at the threshold of the development cycle, which in modern societies resulted in a transition from class-hierarchical structures to functional structures; that is, to pluralistic democracy where confession is part of the society, not part of the state.

Different types of memory—different relations to the state: the stage for eternal crisis and doomsday nationalism

That generated a postcolonial political culture, which has never won its own emancipation with the political centre in Bosnia and Herzegovina. Generally, modernisation of the Balkan countries began with the creation of nation states in the nineteenth century, not as a result of long-term continuing processes but rather as a sudden attempt to overcome or even delete the old; so politics as a basic factor acquired a dominant role over society. This made it possible for nationalism to emerge much earlier than the spread of mass literacy began (Stojanović, 2000). Such an order of values left an indelible trace in the field of opposing historical narratives, political culture, and political language.

The memory of the Second World War and the memory of the wars between the Serbs, Croats, and Bosniaks in the 1990s are connected, though structured differently. Following the victory of the anti-fascist coalition in 1945, of which the military National Liberation Movement headed by Josip Broz Tito was a part and which consisted of members of all nationalities, a victorious mentality was formed and, later on, the state, which through the Non-Aligned Movement, was recognised and respected worldwide. Such a model for memory was built into the foundation of the political order of the Second Yugoslavia. Tito's Yugoslavia, especially since 1966, developed an efficient federal model of national representation and equality from republic to the federal institutions, in which Bosnia and Herzegovina reached its historical maximum with developed elements of its own statehood. That period, especially from the present-day aspect, is referred to as its "golden age" (Bilandžić, 2007).

The war (1992–1995) among the Serbs, Croats, and Bosniaks left a different type of memory. However, it would be wrong to comprehend that war as a religious, civic, or ethnic war, or as a result of ancient hatreds or a specific Balkan mentality, or even as an internal conflict in Bosnia and Herzegovina (Velikonja, 2003). That armed conflict continued in other premises and presented a result of varying views by the political elite about the political makeup of Bosnia and Herzegovina as a state. These different concepts, still present in the political life of the country, have resulted in three different memories that are mutually exclusive and obliterate each other. The historical and socio-psychological foundation and alternative narratives of the recent past stay alive because of fictitious enemies who exist for the survival of ethnonationalism, allowing ethno-nationalistic ideology to be established in public as a hate system. The forms of memory building are based first of all on the ideology of "sacrifice", namely "sacrificing" for "our cause"—religion, politics, state, and people. Such memory building from the very start is exclusive, causing the final version to be realised in a fragmentary political life lacking a consensus.

The wars of 1941–1945 and 1992–1995 created different historical memories in Serbs, Bosniaks, and Croats, primarily in their relation to the state. While the idea of a common state—Yugoslavia—was nourished from the Second World War, the idea of Bosnia and Herzegovina, a common state of its citizens, was born as a result of different political wills of Bosnia and Herzegovina peoples but also because of interventionism, that is, interference by the international community headed by the leading world powers. This renders Bosnia and Herzegovina a labile state community without internal and external consensus and divided along its ethnic lines.

Wars and conflicts of the twentieth century—the two World Wars and the recently ended armed conflict—appear as an epic cycle of violence in Bosnia and Herzegovina, primarily targeted against civilians. Genocide, deportations, concentration camps, ethnic cleansing, forced conversion, discriminatory laws, verdicts without trials for those holding different political views, took away thousands of human lives, and tore even more of them from their original ways of life and sent them into emigration. While the number of the most recent victims is still auctioned off, we see again the obscure "auction" with the victims of the Second World War, whose number rises astronomically up to 1,700,000.

The role of religious communities

Equally important is the role of religious communities with a special accent on the distinctive fact that the nations of Bosnia and Herzegovina are in essence religious nations—with religion having a key role in their shaping. The breakup of Yugoslavia was favourable for the return of religious communities to the political scene and the revival of religious-nationalistic mythic structures embodied in the collective memory of nations, especially the myth of the "chosen" nation (Velikonja, 2003). That is why culture, as a criterion of national identity, can hardly be separated from religion, since the perceptions of legitimacy have historically been rooted in religious learning rather than in civil law. Such a state of mind is conducive to turning an administrative state into a sentimental nation based on the feelings of affiliation and attachment of its members. It is favourable for the continual mythologisation of the political space or political mythologisation of the space in which the post-war culturological paradigm—the one that produces a conflicting mindset—holds out. The most difficult consequence of such a state is the creation of a strong feeling associated with the cult of suffering, according to which the culprit for one's own endangered condition is identified in his closest people. The notions *enemy* and *others* thus become synonyms, which is a common trait of the South Slavic nationalisms in their interdependence.

Political religions have been given places on the social scene and, unlike civil religions, which are limited to certain societies and serve to separate them from others, they are limited to some states and have to be in the service of the friend–enemy scheme of those states. All political religions create pictures of animosity and barriers against others by legitimising their own domination and through symbolic integration of their own peoples. In modern, messianic political religions, such enmity is raised to the level of an apocalyptic drama. Modern political messianism teaches fear and hatred of the national enemy or class enemy. By paving the way toward misery, the myth of the enemy turns into a political myth of conspirative and arched community against which an unsparing struggle is the only reasonable way forward. The enemy thus becomes the founder of our political existence. This situation gets its final expression in the culture of remembrance—in conflicting narratives and politically motivated violence and erasing of memories, based on the example of Mostar (Markovina, 2014).

Responsibility of the international community (1992–2014)

This finally brings us to the other side of the coin. If the Ottoman confessional heritage represented an obstacle to forming a common political identity, this dichotomy could have been solved even less by west European nationalism as a role model, together with modernisation defined as catching up (Todorova, 2010). A nation established on the basis of language has remained a great problem of national identities understood in that way, producing fatal disagreements and tragedies. After the experience of the 1991–1995 war and the post-war period, it is clear that we need totally different, atypical solutions. It is not only that the international community cannot do it, but it also does not want to do it. After all, it was said loud and clear that change can come only from the inside.

The state and political subjectivity of Bosnia and Herzegovina, having been accomplished by its international recognition in 1992, has remained questionable and exposed to the pressure of interventionism of the international community, that is, the different viewpoints of its members. This brings up the responsibility of the leading European and world powers for such a state and evokes the thought voiced by Christian Schwarz-Schilling in 1992, during his resignation from the position of Federal Minister of the Federal Republic of Germany. He said then that he was "ashamed" to belong to such a cabinet if it keeps being inactive and that his reason for joining the government was to ensure that the bestialities "would happen never again" (Tibi, 1994). Schilling also said: "The Balkans catastrophe, with its consequences for Europe and the world, will represent the heaviest burden for Europe, for which we are to blame, and it will be a difficult legacy for the twenty-first century" (ibid.).

As a solution for the 1992 political crisis, *political Europe* offered exclusively maps of ethnic divisions, turning the political into a humanitarian problem, a multi-ethnic society and country into a mono-ethnic society and a state in permanent crisis. The combination of neoliberal and ethno-nationalistic conception has proven fatal in Bosnia and Herzegovina.

This is why we still have three parallel and conflicted historical memories.

What is the task of historiography and historians?

Historiography as a scientific discipline, essentially subject to politicisation, has contributed and is still contributing considerably to such a state of affairs. That has become especially evident since 1992 when Serbs, Croats, and Bosniaks, for the first time in their history, found themselves together under the roof of an internationally recognised state of Bosnia and Herzegovina. Mentally displaced from Bosnia and Herzegovina, tied like snails to their shells in the form of extra-Bosnian cultural, political, and religious centres, each one of these peoples, represented by their elites, has remained tied emotionally to a political and cultural paradigm from history: Serbs—to First and Second Yugoslavia; Croats—to the Austro-Hungarian Monarchy and the Independent State of Croatia; Bosniaks—to the Ottoman Empire. Each of these ethno-confessional groups preserved the historical era marked with their own supremacy as the referential point in their collective memories. That mythic concept of historical memories has been kept alive by the media and the education system controlled by politically criminalised elites.

Today, as the political crisis in the country is increasing to a paroxysm, the question poses itself: How to live, with such a mental legacy, in one state (Bosnia and Herzegovina)? And is that state sustainable at all?

The consolidation/reconciliation patterns of a religiously and ethnically complex society such as Bosnia and Herzegovina, formed within different political frames during "statelessness" where each following frame negated the previous, include, above all, establishing a secular state, rule of law, establishing institutions of authority, modernising political life, the truth about the recent war, and full responsibility of the media. On the path of establishing its own historical subjectivity, the following themes have been imposed for historiography and historians in Bosnia and Herzegovina: Slavism, anti-fascism, identity, and secularism. The time "when we were the best, when we made the best for us out of ourselves" serves as a landmark (Bajrektarević, 2014).

Conclusion

After we were promised the end of ideologies and divisions, religiously and nationally coloured societies/states are still our harsh reality. Bosnia and Herzegovina is also among them, looking for its way out of this degrading and non-promising situation after the war (1992–1995). The current ethnic divisions, generated from recent and distant history of this country, are being kept alive by domestic political pseudo-elites as well as by the international community with the different political and economic interests of its members. The state of pseudo-democracy perfectly suits the preservation of three parallel and conflicting historical memories of Serbs, Croats, and Bosniaks. Centuries of statelessness, historical and national discontinuity, disagreement between cultural and state identities of the three constituent peoples in Bosnia and Herzegovina, have led the country to the brink of collapse. A frozen military conflict, as well as a combination of neoliberal capitalism and ethno-nationalism, is proving fatal for Bosnia and Herzegovina. In the situation of un-freedom, with a state that does not have political, economic, educational, and media sovereignty, reconciliation is not possible, and thus instead of the "eternal now" the "eternal past" is present nowadays.

New, atypical solutions are essential for the opening of a true perspective. The "global ethics" interpreted by Hans Küng (1998) is required. Bosnia and Herzegovina is a global problem—Bosnia and Herzegovina needs a global solution. Otherwise, we will witness the "end of history" with all of its unforeseeable consequences.

References

Aleksov, B. (2003). *Poturica gori od Turčina: Srpski istoričari o verskim preobraćenjima* [The Turkicised are worse than the Turks: Serb historians on religious conversions]. In: H. Kamberović (Ed.), *Historijski mitovi na Balkanu* [Historical Myths in the Balkans] (pp. 225–258). Sarajevo: Institut za istoriju.

Andrić, I. (1996). *Bosnian Chronicle or The Days of the Consuls*. London: Harvill.

Bajrektarević, A. (2014). Vrijedi li život bez dostojanstva? [Is life worth without dignity?]. *Dani—Bosanskohercegovački News Magazin*, [Dani, BiH News Magazine], *892*: 79.

Bilandžić, D. (2007). Zlatno doba Bosne i Hercegovine, [The golden age of Bosnia and Herzegovina]. In: M. Filipović (Ed.), *Bosna i Hercegovina prije i nakon ZAVNOBiH-a* [Bosnia and Herzegovina before and after ZAVNOBiH]. Posebna izdanja, knjiga CXXIV, Odjeljenje društvenih nauka, knjiga 37, [Special Publications, Book CXXIV, Department of Social Sciences, Book 37], (pp. 42–46). Sarajevo: Akademija nauka i umjetnosti Bosne i Hercegovine [Academy of Arts and Sciences of Bosnia and Herzegovina].

Elrich, V. S. (1964). *Porodica u transformaciji. Studija u tri stotine jugoslavenskih sela.* [A family in transformation. A study in three hundred Yugoslav villages]. Zagreb: Naprijed.

Komšić, I. (2014). *Vrijeme sjenki (Ethos u politici).* [Shadow Time (Ethos in Politics)]. Sarajevo: Sarajevo Publishing.

Küng, H. (1998). *A Global Ethic for Global Politics and Economics*. New York: Oxford University Press.

Lovrenović, D. (2008). *Povijest est magistra vitae.* [History est Magistra Vitae]. Sarajevo: Rabic.

Maalouf, A. (2001). *In the Name of Identity: Violence and the Need to Belong*. New York: Arcade.

Markovina, D. (2014). *Između crvenog i crnog. Split i Mostar u kulturi sjećanja.* [Between Red and Black. Split and Mostar in Memory Culture]. Zagreb-Sarajevo: Plejada, University Press, Magistrat izdanja.

Stojanović, D. (2000). Nekoliko osobina procesa modernizacije u Srbiji po etkom 20. veka [Several characteristics of modernisation processes in Serbia in the early twentieth century]. In: H. G. Fleck, & I. Garovac (Eds.), *Dijalog povjesničara/istoričara 2* [A Dialogue of Historians 2] (pp. 135–136). Zagreb: Friedrich Naumann Stiftung.

Tibi, B. (1994). Die Zerstörung des Religionsfriedens auf dem Balkan: serbischer Ethno-Fundamentalismus. [Destruction of the religious myth in the Balkans: The Serb ethnic fundamentalism]. *Universitas 49:* 205–215.

Todorova, M. (2010). *Dizanje prošlosti u vazduh. Ogledi o Balkanu i Istočnoj Evropi.* [Blowing up the Past. Essays on the Balkans and Eastern Europe]. Belgrade: Biblioteka XX vek.

Velikonja, M. (2003). *Religious Separation and Political Intolerance in Bosnia-Herzegovina*. College Station, TX: Texas A & M University Press.

Volkan, V. D. (2004). *Chosen Trauma, the Political Ideology of Entitlement and Violence.* Available at: www.vamıkvolkan.com/Chosen-Trauma,-the-Political-Ideology-of-Entitlement-and-Violence.php [last accessed 25 February 2017].

Žanić, I. (2003). Simbolični identitet Hrvatske u trokutu *Raskrižje—Predziđe—Most* [The symbolical identity of Croatia in the *intersection—bulwark—bridge* triangle]. In: H. Kamberović (Ed.), *Historijski mitovi na Balkanu* [Historical Myths in the Balkans] (pp. 163–170). Sarajevo: Institut za istoriju.

CHAPTER SIX

Narratives in the family: history spoken and elided—theoretical considerations and initial observations on a Bulgarian sample

Camellia Hancheva

In storytelling, people are at the same time the actor living the story, the narrator telling it, and the listener (McAdams, 2013). All three positions are connected in a constant process of interpretation and reflection in inner and outer dialogue embedded in a cultural context. Dialogical understanding of human nature is a shared belief of philosophers (Bakhtin, 1986), developmental psychologists (Vygotsky, 1997; Bateson, 1979), psychoanalysts (Fairbairn, 1996), social theorists, and conversational analysts (Cronen & Pearce, 1982).

Human beings define themselves in the context of relationships. After adolescence, the dimension of time is included into the self-definition or general structure of identity. The ingredients of identity are: one, personal histories, sometimes a vague impressionistic picture of an individual past and its inevitable consequences in the present and formed anticipations for the future; and two, historical time ultimately experienced. The challenging and never-ending task of being included in and differentiated from people and groups is supported by the development and mastery of an important capacity of reflection and mentalization.

The present study is an attempt to capture the interwoven fabric of personal memories and historical processes. The material is organised in three sections, addressing relationships of individual stories to official history, to autobiographical memory, and to identity formation.

Oral (hi)story

Discrepancy between history as written in the textbooks and personal accounts of the same events that one has actually taken part in is expected. Different in scale, proportion, and focus, individual and official historical descriptions are nevertheless part of the general process of narrative creation of a certain time. Personal stories as individual attempts to create a meaningful interpretation of experience are embedded and submerged into, but also potentially resistant and subverting, to dominant narratives. Their value is in keeping diversities alive and the potential for another interpretation, giving a different path from past to the present and future. As Hammack (2008) claims, "direct access to the process of social reproduction and change" is provided by the relationship between a "master" narrative and a personal narrative.

The oral as a synonym of the unofficial, apart from the dominant version and written (official) (hi)story, is one aspect of the explored phenomena. More relevant to the main focus is another distinction, made by Pearce (2005). Stories could be untold, told but unheard, and with time could become unknown. Following the processes in Bulgarian society more than a decade after the democratic changes, and susceptible to silence and lack of reflection on certain stories, in 2004 journalists, writers, and scientists created a space for sharing memories and stories from "socialist times" (www.spomeniteni.org). A printed book with 171 personal stories has already had four editions (Gospodinov, 2006). There were a few other publications, reflecting on personal experiences, like *Childhood under Socialism* (Elenkov & Koleva, 2010) or *Love under Socialism* (Koleva, 2015). But silence, masked sometimes as boredom or reluctance, is still the prevailing reaction in society.

Based on the experience of the abovementioned studies and struck by the banality of stories told, a pilot study was designed as a semi-structured interview aiming to reveal the memories of important events. People were invited to "name some important events (some big contemporary events—social, political, economical, cultural, etc.)" that they have personal memories of. Representatives of three generations in 20 families (71 respondents), in three age groups—18–30 (N = 17), 43–57 (N = 37), and 66–83 (N = 17)—were interviewed.

Oral history and autobiographical memory

A phenomenon named "over-general memory" in autobiographical memory describes a tendency to recall certain moments lacking the event-specific details. This tendency was repeated in the present study. Although this phenomenon has been linked to depression (Williams et al., 2007; Heron et al., 2012) and trauma (Nixon, Sterk, & Pearce, 2012), other studies question the validity of inferring the influence of trauma or depression (Harvey, Bryant, & Dang, 1998; Johnson, Foley, Suengas, & Raye, 1988).

However, since our study addresses post-war and post-socialist societies, we have to keep in mind the importance of transgenerational evolution of narrative forms, dynamic themes, and affective organisation connected to the repression of individuality. Taking into account (with all due respect, since the circumstances are not comparable) results of a study of Holocaust survivors and their daughters (Adelman, 1995; Van IJzendoorn, Bakermans-Kranenburg, & Sagi-Schwartz, 2003) the methodology of the present study was revised. The Holocaust study demonstrated that the impact of "tragic historical legacy" (Adelman, 1995) on the next generations is strongly dependent on affect organisation and integration achieved by the narrator. Thus, in the present study, new questions were added, aimed at turning-point events for the whole family and at stimulating extensive reflection of the children on turning-point events resulting in considerable life or personal changes for their parents. Family interviews revealed not only the gaps in recollections of the generation of parents but also the representations of their children and shed some light on the process of replicating or rewriting family scripts. Family scripts (Byng-Hall, 1995) are a set of unnamed guidelines for action usually fixed after a successful resolution of a dangerous situation. Stories told about certain events make the retranslation of the "code of action" possible; they establish a moral and belief system. A powerful script and "master" narrative in Bulgarian culture is the one of "patience". Strongly reminiscent of another period of contradictory naming and interpretation of history (being a part of the Ottoman Empire), the narrative of patience is close to the action guidelines of silent resistance. One can only speculate on the effects of unnamed, unrecognised, and unregulated affects behind those narratives and the individual and social price paid.

Categories of the family script (reconstructed through observation of repetitive patterns of actions) and the family story (explicit, verbal structures) are close to definitions of implicit and explicit memory systems. Implicit memory, repression, dynamic unconscious (Fonagy & Target, 1996; Schacter, 1996), and unthought known (Bollas, 1987) are the concepts used to mark the gaps in the stories told in words. As in therapy, research data gives only indirect hints of the unnamed. It is the choice, content, and manner of told stories that can be analysed.

Research in autobiographical memories examines the interaction between memory processes and the social, emotional, and motivational elements that impact on individuals' experiences of events. Two contradicting hypothesis have been developed and supported by different research. The first claims that autobiographical memory is functionally and structurally related to the use of cultural myths and social narratives (Nelson, 2003; Pearce, 2005); the second, finding proof in fMRI studies, says that autobiographical memories are not inherently social (Wilbers, Deuker, Fell, & Axmacher, 2012). These contrasting views call for a clear distinction between the function of autobiographical memory and self-narrative. Autobiographical memory is a vast range of personal information and experience whereas self-narrative is a set of temporally and thematically organised salient experiences and concerns, and only the second—self-narrative—constitutes one's identity (Robinson & Taylor, 1998). The process of socialisation and sense of belonging to a certain family, community, or society is counting on narrative means to guide an individual in her organisation of autobiographical memories into a life story with a degree of coherency and plasticity. Turning-point memories are most relevant to identity formation. They display greater coherence and greater emphasis on the self than other memories (Grysmann & Hudson, 2011) and they could be considered the paradigmatic self-related, self-defining memories (Pillemer, 2001). The choice of organising interviews around turning-point events is justified by their centrality in the process of temporal organisation of life story.

Oral history and narrative identity

Stories that people tell about their life experiences are among the most entertaining and yet challenging activities. The functional value of sharing beliefs through stories is in keeping connections and group cohesiveness and also establishing a certain moral code of guidance that is passed through generations. The process of identity development in the epigenetic hypothesis of Erikson (1982) is paralleled by similar processes of development of elements of social order. New ideologies attract people in identity formation, especially adolescents, with the promise of clear definitions and predictable ways of status achievement and success, like "primitive ideologies" (Erikson, 1968). Thus, a closer look at the moments of reorganisation, turning points, or crises in individual lives could provide access to the process of turmoil and change in either society or ideology. The argument is consistent with the tripartite model of identity that integrates cognitive, social, and cultural levels and defines identity as an ideological framework of commitment (Hammack, 2008).

Methodology

Participants in the research were invited to recollect and give a detailed account of several turning-point events that had significantly influenced their lives and personality. Any kind of event was appreciated but the "priming effect" of social, political, and cultural events was achieved by encouraging them to remember and share first the important contemporary events (of which they had personal memories). Reflections on the mother's, father's, and family's turning-point events were collected and participants were asked for a concluding remark relating to their explicit formulation of credo or life lesson. Three generations of people from one family were subsequently interviewed (tape recorded and transcribed). At this stage only descriptive analysis was performed, coding the types of events mentioned, content of the narrative, and range of radius of important relations and group identifications. Following McAdams (1993, 2006), stories were coded for agency and/or communion and redemption/contamination themes. Category of agency (Bakan, 1966) means putting the accent on personal growth, success, achievements, responsibility, and empowerment. The communion story is a story developed around psychological and motivational ideas involving relationships of care, love, and friendship. Both themes often come together in the narrative of a happy family creation as a turning point in life. The other thematic couple redemption/contamination is central for development of a personal life script. Redemption narrative is considered a "master" narrative of American identity, with its particular historical foundation. The theme "from rags to riches" often exploited in films is a prototypical "prescription" for a successful and respectable life. Contamination narrative is a pattern of interpretation of sequences of events going from bad to worse. Themes like victimisation, betrayal, loss, failure, illness, disappointment, and disillusionment are developed.

Starting from the premise that identity is a life story (McAdams, 1993), choice of events, their retrospective reconstruction, and assessment of consequences gives an idea about the processes of time perspective, meaning-making, and belief system. Making explicit connections of identity and socio-political processes is one of the aims of the present study.

Initial observations and results

The initial process of remembering events often took the form of free-association thinking. Agitation around recollecting the past (with typical verbal clichés) soon moved on either to reconceptualisation of the emotion as inappropriate, followed by an excuse "these were the times", "we were stupid and blind then"; or to a nostalgic ending like "we can't return to the past". The next shift in interviews was even more abrupt. Asked to connect some of these (or other) events to major personal shifts and changes in life, most respondents remained with normative or non-normative events within the family.

Three types of events were mentioned. First, events specific to Bulgarian socio-political, economic, and cultural history (47%): for example, political system changes to socialist in 1944 and to democratic in 1989; sports competitions; economic crises and shortage of goods; social movements; and strikes. Second, world history events (19%) such as the 9/11 terrorist attack, the fall of the Berlin wall, and the first man in space. Third, normative lifespan events (32%) such as birth, marriage, or death of a relative.

Gender had no effect on recollection of specific type of events.

At the level of words and expressions, a clear dualistic interpretation of social and political events was given, creating from the official historical interpretation two versions for before and after the 1989 changes in Bulgaria. For example, in history textbooks, the event on 9 September 1944 is referred to as: "The 9 September coup d'état", or "The Socialist Revolution of 9 September", or "The Government of the Kingdom of Bulgaria was replaced by a government of the Fatherland Front—the People's Republic of Bulgaria". All of those definitions appear in different personal recollections.

The vague and half-heartedly made connections of personal turning-point events with historical processes were critically analysed in the light of results of some memory researchers, questioning the possibility of a traumatic impact resulting in stereotypical recollections of events. Events chosen as turning points in the vast majority of stories fall into two main categories: political changes in Bulgaria (described as before or after 9 September 1944, and after 1989), and family events (marriage, serious illness, birth, death). Important world events were mentioned, but they were never chosen as turning points. Not a single mention of the events in the Balkan region (the neighbouring countries) was made.

Initial observations on the Bulgarian sample revealed a tendency to narrow the radius of relationships and activities connected to both agency and communion themes. A prototypical story of a young person moving from dependence to autonomy is at the core of many narratives of the people from the younger generation (aged 16–36). Agency was coded more often in narratives of men, whereas the seemingly opposite, but not excluding the category of communion, was equally presented. This might be considered typical for the traditional gender roles. Agency, often presented through the story of successful emancipation from family of origin and achievement of material goods was seldom connected to a story reflecting broader social processes or groups, like achievement of social status, being an influential figure, and so on. Narratives of becoming a prominent and influential part of society are rare in the sample. Respondents who mentioned the social status that they'd had put it in the frame of disillusionment, loss, betrayal, and nostalgic reminiscence that often masked embarrassment and shame: "I was a big boss then, I was respected—and after the changes, no one wanted to say hello to me or offer me a job", or "After changing the name [from Bulgarian Communist Party to Bulgarian Socialist Party] this is not my party any more; I do not belong to anything now".

Being successful in a period still highly contradictory in terms of moral and ethical assessment is a fact that is difficult to integrate in personal narrative. It is representative of agency themes but raises a serious question of cohesiveness in ego identity. Experience of discontinuity is salient in many self-narratives. Even though not compatible with the combat crisis of war veterans, the identity crisis of people who had experienced totalitarian and post-totalitarian society is clearly marked in personal stories. Discontinuity in self-image, belief systems, and perceptions of good and bad is interfering with development of generativity and care. A sharp disconnection of ethical and aesthetical official and unofficial ideologies prevents the process of succession of experience, wisdom, and values from one generation to the other. Lack of intergenerational solidarity is also evident in children's narratives. Reflections on parents' turning-point events reveal surprisingly good insight and knowledge of the facts but enormous difficulties in integrating them as a legacy that has to be received. Children frame their parents' life stories either as devaluation: "It was all ready-made for them; our generation is the one paying the price", or as condescension: "They were fooled and never understood the truth". In both attitudes the capacity for receiving with gratitude is seriously impaired.

In the light of the observed lack of continuity and solidarity it is surprising that the majority of respondents focused on the family and named turning-point events related to personal experiences like finding a partner, or having children and grandchildren. Family creation, assessed as content, is a successful and adaptive development of both agency and communion themes. But in the frame of the whole interviews, starting with naming important events and ending with personal credo, family focus seems to be more of a shelter and escape from the turmoil of identity diffusion. The stories of family creation and development through the life cycle resemble more the process of retranslation of genes than of memes (Dawkins, 1976), lacking specific referral to any symbolic act of continuation of one's deeds, ideas, or even name.

Another coding of narratives is organised around duality of themes of redemption and contamination (McAdams, 2006). The theme "from rags to riches" seems to be irrelevant to Bulgarian narratives. A reflection of it is sometimes noticed in stories told about turning points in family history and they usually include the theme of emigration: "After running away he washed dishes in the west, but now he is respected and rich." However, the broader version of redemption narrative is recognised in stories of some respondents. It is developed in themes like "starting all over again", "fighting for justice", "surviving hard times", and so on. It is a question for further analysis to distinguish between "survival" and "submission". Contamination narrative is a development from bad to worse. Many of the stories told by the middle generation (aged 40–63) were coded in this category. Stories about disillusionment prevailed and often in an ambiguous mixture were perfectly expressed in the Latin saying *nec spe nec metu*. This stance—"Without hope, without fear"—and patience narrative (silent disagreement, passive resistance) need to be further explored in relation to historical, social, and cultural processes in the region.

The listener's position

Breaking the conspiracy of silence is a vital necessity in post-totalitarian societies, but equally important is the prevention of deconstruction of meaning and denial of a need for it. Trapped between the painfulness of silence and hopeless doubt in the significance of words, the listener is struggling together with the storyteller. A postulated need (for purpose, value, efficacy, and self-worth) guiding the narrative construction (Baumeister & Wilson 1996) seems to be deeply buried. Disregarding content, form, and emotional tone of the stories, the very act of giving voice to personal experience is an act of leaving a legacy and a challenge to the assumption of personal insignificance. Appreciation of the courage and humbleness of storytellers who took part in the research is a genuine reaction of the listener. Together with the sadness and temptation to interpret stories via "narrative banalisation" (Bruner, 1991) it presents a challenge to future research interpretations in a search (and crying out) for meaning.

Acknowledgment

The project called Oral History was planned and partly financed by DAAD as a part of the Trauma, Trust, and Memory (TTM) research network.

References

Adelman, A. (1995). Traumatic memory and the intergenerational transmission of Holocaust narratives. *The Psychoanalytic Study of the Child, Vol. 50*: 343–367.

Bakan, D. (1966). *The Duality of Human Existence: Isolation and Communion in Western Man*. Boston: Beacon Press.

Bakhtin, M. M. (1986). *Speech Genres and Other Late Essays*. Austin, TX: University of Texas Press.

Bateson, M. C. (1979). The epigenesis of conversational interaction: a personal account of research development. In: M. Bullowa (Ed.), *Before Speech: The Beginning of Human Communication* (pp. 63–78). Cambridge: Cambridge University Press.

Baumeister, R. F., & Wilson, B. (1996). Life stories and the four needs for meaning. *Psychological Inquiry Vol. 7, No. 4*: 322–325.

Bollas, C. (1987). *The Shadow of the Object: Psychoanalysis of the Unthought Known*. New York: Columbia University Press.

Bruner, J. (1991). The narrative construction of reality. *Critical Inquiry, 18*(1): 1–21.

Byng-Hall, J. (1995). *Rewriting Family Scripts: Improvisation and Systems Change*. New York: Guilford.

Cronen, V., & Pearce, W. B. (1982). The coordinated management of meaning: a theory of communication. In: F. E. X. Dance (Ed.) *Human Communication Theory* (pp. 61–89). New York: Harper & Row.

Dawkins, R. (2006). *The Selfish Gene*. Oxford: Oxford University Press.

Еленков, И., & Колева, Д. (съст.) (2010). *Детството през социализма*. София: Рива. [Elenkov, I., & Koleva, D. (Eds.) (2010). *Childhood under Socialism*. Sofia: Riva].

Erikson, E. H. (1968). *Identity, Youth and Crisis*. New York: Norton.

Erikson, E. H. (1982). *The Life Cycle Completed, a Review*. New York: Norton.

Fairbairn, W. R. D. (1996). *Psychoanalytic studies of the personality*. London: Routledge.

Fonagy, P., & Target, M. (1996). Playing with reality: theory of mind and the normal development of psychic reality. *International Journal of Psychoanalysis, 77*: 217–234.

Gospodinov, G. (Ed.) (2006). *Аз живях социализма. 171 лични истории*. София: Жанет-45. [I Lived Socialism: 171 Personal Stories. Sofia: Žanet-45].

Grysman, A., & Hudson, J. A. (2011). The self in autobiographical memory: effects of self-salience on narrative content and structure. *Memory, 19*: 501–513.

Hammack, P. L. (2008). Narrative and the cultural psychology of identity. *Personality and Social Psychology Review, 12*: 222–247.

Harvey, A. G., Bryant, R. A., & Dang, S. T. (1998). Autobiographical memory in acute stress disorder. *Journal of Consulting and Clinical Psychology, 66*: 500–506.

Heron, J., Crane, C., Gunnell, D., Lewis, G., Evans, J., & Williams, J. M. G. (2012). 40,000 memories in young teenagers: psychometric properties of the autobiographical memory test in a UK cohort study. *Memory, 20* (3): 300–320.

Johnson, M. K., Foley, M. A., Suengas A. G., & Raye, C. L. (1988). Phenomenal characteristics of memories for perceived and imagined autobiographical events. *Journal of Experimental Psychology: General, 117*: 371–376.

Колева, Д. (съст.) (2015). *Любовта при социализма. Образци, образи, табута.* София:Рива [Koleva, D. (Ed.) (2015). Love under Socialism. Prototypes, Images, and Taboos. Sofia: Riva].

McAdams, D. P. (2013). The psychological self as actor, agent, and author. *Perspectives on Psychological Science, 8*: 272–295.

McAdams, D. P. (2006). *The Redemptive Self: Stories Americans Live By*. New York: Oxford University Press.

McAdams, D. P. (1993). The Stories We Live By: Personal Myths and the Making of the Self. New York: William Morrow.

Nelson, K. (2003). Self and social functions: individual autobiographical memory and collective narrative. *Memory, 11*: 125–136.

Nixon, R. D. V., Sterk, J., & Pearce, A. (2012). A randomized trial of cognitive behavior therapy and cognitive therapy for children with posttraumatic stress disorder following single-incident trauma. *Journal of Abnormal Child Psychology, 40*: 327–337.

Pearce, W. B. (2005). The coordinated management of meaning (CMM). In: W. B. Gudykunst (Ed.), *Theorizing About Intercultural Communication, Part II: Theories of Communication Incorporating Culture* (pp. 35–54). London: Sage.

Pillemer, D. B. (2001). Momentous events and life story. *Review of General Psychology, 5*(2): 123–134.

Robinson, J. A., & Taylor, L. R. (1998). Autobiographical memory and self-narratives: A tale of two stories. In C. P. Thompson, D. J. Hermann, D. Bruce, J. D. Read, D. G. Payne, & M. P. Toglia (Eds.), *Autobiographical memory: Theoretical and applied perspectives* (pp. 125–143). Mahwah, NJ: Erlbaum.

Schacter, D. L. (1996). *Searching for Memory: The Brain, the Mind, and the Past*. New York: Basic.

Van IJzendoorn, M. H., Bakermans-Kranenburg, M. J., & Sagi-Schwartz, A. (2003). Are children of Holocaust survivors less well-adapted? A meta-analytic investigation of secondary traumatization. *Journal of Traumatic Stress, 16*: 459–469.

Vygotsky, L. S. (1997). *The Collected works of L. S. Vygotsky, Volume 4: The History of the Development of Higher Mental Functions.* New York: Plenum.

Wilbers, L., Deuker, L., Fell, J., & Axmacher, N. (2012). Are autobiographical memories inherently social? Evidence from an fMRI study. *PLoS ONE 7(9)*, e45089.

Williams, J. M. G., Barnhofer, T., Crane, C., Hermans, D., Raes, F., & Dalgleish, T. (2007). Autobiographical memory specificity and emotional disorder. *Psychological Bulletin, 133*: 122–148.

CHAPTER SEVEN

A user-centred approach to helping women survivors of war rape in Bosnia and Herzegovina

Amra Delić and Esmina Avdibegović

Introduction

Coinciding with the failure of communism all over Central and Eastern Europe and following the death of Marshal Tito, president of the Socialist Federal Republic of Yugoslavia, the process of disintegration of the Yugoslav Federation, which was marked by an intense political and economic crisis, took part during the 1980s and early 1990s. According to Bennett (2016), "the holding of multi-party elections transformed relations among peoples throughout Yugoslavia and especially in those republics where the population was most mixed." Influenced by "the emergence of Serb and Croat nationalism in Serbia and Croatia", and out of anxiety and fear to be ethno-nationally underrepresented, the majority of the population in Bosnia and Herzegovina composed of Bosniaks (mainly Muslims), the Bosnian Serbs (mostly Orthodox) and the Bosnian Croats (mostly Catholic) homogenised within the three newly formed ethnic parties, and a multi-party system had been established (Abazović, Ćurak, Sejzović, Šačić, & Turčalo, 2007; Avdibegović, 2014; Bennett, 2016; Malcolm, 1996). The new Bosnia and Herzegovina presidency was a shared power, with members from each of the three leading parties (the Bosniak Party of Democratic Action; the Serb Democratic Party; and the Croatian Democratic Union), who reached an agreement to form a state-level coalition government that soon proved to be unsuccessful, while the above-mentioned parties developed "their own parallel power structures" (Bennett, 2016). In these complex scenarios in the early 1990s, the collapse of ex-Yugoslavia was followed by Slovenia, Croatia, and Bosnia and Herzegovina declaring independence following referendums largely boycotted by Serbs, which led to their ethnic military consolidation aided by the ex-Yugoslav Army, resulting in bloodshed and violent wars in the region (Abazović, Ćurak, Sejzović, Šačić, & Turčalo, 2007; Malcolm, 1996). However, the most hostile actions and severe fighting ensued in multi-ethnic and multicultural Bosnia and Herzegovina, resulting in war crimes, crimes against humanity, and genocide. After three and a half years, the war in Bosnia and Herzegovina was brought to a halt in late 1995, with the signing of the Dayton Peace Agreement, stipulating the Bosnian constitution. Apart from long-term economic and political damage, mass destruction and atrocities committed in Bosnia and Herzegovina, the war left dramatic consequences, including 103,000 killed (of which 60% were civilians); 30,000 missing people; 170,000 wounded; more than two million refugees and forcibly displaced people; and more than 20,000 girls, women, and men raped (Delić & Avdibegović, 2015). According to the Peace Agreement, Bosnia and Herzegovina comprises two semi-autonomous entities—the Bosniak- and Croat-dominated Federation of Bosnia and Herzegovina (further subdivided into ten cantonal units) and the Serb-dominated Republika Srpska (with its own central institutions)—but also Brčko District as the third region administered by local government, while Bosnia's internationally recognised borders were maintained (Bennett, 2016). The constitution of a highly decentralised Bosnia and Herzegovina with complex and very expensive administrative apparatus proved to be poorly functioning and largely ineffective (Avdibegović, 2014). The political picture of the country is still dominated by former warring nationalist parties, and interethnic divisions continue as a result of previous distrust between the three sides.

* * *

Rape is a horrifying act leaving deep scars on the victim's personality, and when used as a weapon of war it targets not only an individual but the family and the community as well. The use of rape as a weapon of war is a widespread phenomenon, especially in societies where women are exposed to repression and their sexuality is controlled by men.

War rape is defined as "a deliberate and strategic decision on the part of combatants to intimidate and destroy 'the enemy' as a whole by raping and enslaving women who are identified as members of the opposition group" (Hagen & Yohani, 2010; Woodhead & Wessely, 2010). It has been well-documented in literature that, during the war in Bosnia and Herzegovina (1992–1995), an estimated 20,000 bodies of girls and women became a "battlefield" while being exposed to systematic sexual persecution, rape, enslavement, and sexual torture within "ethnic cleansing". Apart from sexual torture, women have been affected in many different ways, having experienced other extremely traumatic events, such as unwanted pregnancies that resulted from rape, forced motherhood, witnessing of atrocities, torture and murder of others, exposure to deprivation, hunger, threats, grenade shelling, forced displacement, loss of their loved ones, entire livelihoods and social network, all of which drastically heightened their traumatisation. Such experiences are associated with higher rates of both short-term and long-lasting mental health disorders, especially in women survivors of conflict-related sexual violence (Kuwert et al., 2014; Lončar, Medvedev, Jovanović, & Hotujac, 2006).

In humanitarian emergencies, a certain number of international aid organisations (UN agencies, charities, and non-governmental women's organisations) offer psychosocial support and health programmes to victims who report rape, and the interventions are mainly based at the individual level (Marsh, Purdin, & Navani, 2006; Inter-Agency Standing Committee, 2005). The societal level of wartime rape aftermath has been neglected (Deiana & Goldie, 2012; Skjelsbæk, 2012). After the war in Bosnia and Herzegovina, international attention and humanitarian assistance gradually shifted to other conflict areas, whereas the cultural effect of rape remains.

Rape is still considered as bringing dishonour and humiliation not only to the victim but to the victim's family and community, which significantly contributes to its underreporting. Negative social attitudes towards rape victims play a critical role in the reluctance of women to come forward to share what happened to them, and this also impedes their ability to seek help. In addition, the national authorities' attitude with regard to the needs and rights of raped women has remained largely unsupportive and tradition-bound, which produces fertile soil for denial and for spreading a "conspiracy of silence". Due to these circumstances, the outer adjustment stage lasts many years after the rapes, as the survivors cope with long-term trauma and neglect (Todorova, 2011).

War rape and access to justice in Bosnia and Herzegovina

In spite of establishing the International Criminal Tribunal for the former Yugoslavia (ICTY) in 1993, which declared that "systematic rape" and "sexual enslavement" in time of war was a "crime against humanity", and the estimates of more than 20,000 war rape victims in war-torn Bosnia and Herzegovina, only thirty-five cases involving wartime sexual violence have been prosecuted, and only in twenty-seven of the cases were perpetrators convicted of sexual violence crimes (Organization for Security and Cooperation in Europe, 2015). Some victims who returned to their pre-war homes reported feeling unsafe and insecure when meeting the perpetrators, and thus unable to bring charges against them. Due to societal blame, stigma, and labelling, some victims lack family support, which is one of the factors influencing underreporting of war rape cases and hindering disclosure for women. In addition, a lack of institutional support, and violation of their rights to justice and a secure environment, also created enormous pressure for women, who often report that both the victims and justice itself have been betrayed. The victim's trust in justice has been compromised, and the process of delivering justice has been challenged by various factors, such as complex and fragmented jurisdictions responsible for prosecuting war crimes cases at all levels (entity, district, and cantonal) in Bosnia and Herzegovina; a number of obstacles to properly understanding, investigating, prosecuting, and sentencing war rape cases; a lack of gender expertise in managing and conducting investigations; the mischarging of conflict-related sexual violence as an ordinary (not a war) crime aimed at denying or trivialising the true nature and gravity of the crime; and insufficient witness protection programmes (Organization for Security and Cooperation in Europe, 2015). All this explains the fear that frequently delays reporting of the war rape crime, and worsens the victim's mental health outlook (Iancu, 2012).

Mental health and human rights of war rape victims during war and in post-war Bosnia and Herzegovina

Due to mass war destruction, the capacities of the existing public and mental health institutions were limited during the war, and there was a shortage of staff specifically trained and experienced to deal with sexual violence (Mann, Drucker, Tarantola, & McCabe, 1994). Support services for victims were mainly available within the non-governmental sector, particularly women's organisations, involving psychologists, social workers, and paraprofessionals as service providers. In the medico-clinical setting, psychiatrists responded in sporadic cases because psychiatric care has been mainly offered within institutions for mentally ill people, which due to the societal stigma attached to mental illness represented the biggest barrier to victims seeking psychiatric help (Mollica et al., 2004). In some places, psychiatric care was very limited due to not recognising the rape trauma, and focusing primarily on symptoms of denial, guilt, and shame, in particular when discussing symptoms with male psychiatrists. Thus, non-governmental organisations (NGOs) continued to operate independently, and coordination with public mental health services was insufficient.

In the post-war period, the status of women survivors of war rape was further complicated by uncertainty, socio-economic hardship, lack of employment opportunities, poverty, and weak implementation of laws and policies related to gender equality (Demény, 2011). On top of that, financial support for local NGOs from foreign donors declined, and most NGOs failed in their fundraising efforts due to a lack of evidence-based data. In spite of guidelines on psychosocial interventions in post-conflict areas, which commonly state that interventions should be based on local needs, no unified database of women victims of rape and other forms of sexual violence or trauma rehabilitation centres have been set up by the government.

Although the Federal Parliament adopted in 2006 a law recognising the status of "women war victims" for women who were wartime rape victims, and granting to all civilian victims of war equal access to social benefits and compensation, the official procedure of obtaining this status and their rights at the Federal level and the Brčko District level still remain difficult, whereas in the Republika Srpska the law has not been adopted. Hence, the majority of war rape victims bury their pain in silence, not receiving any assistance, which is another obstacle to healing and perceiving testifying in court as a beneficial rather than harmful experience. Those who decide to file an official complaint often lack appropriate psychological support and protective service while giving statements, which leads to secondary traumatisation, additionally making many victims reluctant to speak about what they have gone through.

* * *

Despite clear recommendations for government action by leading international institutions, official political bodies in Bosnia and Herzegovina remained indifferent. The International Association of Women's Mental Health and the World Psychiatric Association issued Consensus Statements (Stewart, 2006); and the UN Convention on the Elimination of All forms of Discrimination against Women (CEDAW, 2006) and the UN Special Rapporteur on Violence against Women (2012) recommended action. But more than two decades after war crimes against women were committed in Bosnia and Herzegovina, there is no sign of any action being taken at state level. A full range of supportive and appropriate care services is still lacking or denied, which constitutes a further violation of victims' rights.

Instead of providing protection, support, and equal access to fundamental human rights and justice, there are many complicating factors related to the process of recovery of women rape survivors, including poor access to treatment, health, social, and employment services, lack of free legal aid, stigmatisation, discrimination, and social exclusion. At the end of 2010, this situation resulted in an international re-engagement, and the United Nations Population Fund (UNPFA) and women's groups pressured the Bosnian government that then tasked the

Bosnia and Herzegovina Ministry of Human Rights and Refugees to coordinate the process of drafting and adoption of the "Programme for Improvement of the Status of Survivors of Conflict-Related Sexual Violence". In 2014, the Swiss association Track Impunity Always and thirteen local civil society organisations reported that it took four years to complete and submit the draft programme for feedback opinions to entity-level governments, whereas demonstrating further indifference of the government officials of Republika Srpska is interpreted as paralysing the whole process. Also, the adoption and enforcement of the "Law on Victims of Torture, a Transitional Justice Strategy", and implementation of the "National Strategy on War Crimes Processing in Cases of Rape or other Forms of Sexual Violence" have been repeatedly postponed for years (Track Impunity Always, 2014). The only positive change that has been made since 2006 is broadening the definition of rape and other forms of sexual violence as war crimes and crimes against humanity in accordance with international jurisprudence, which took place in 2015.

* * *

Fischer (2007) stated that justice and healing are also part of the process of conflict transformation and reconciliation, emphasising that this is a task that requires proactive engagement by political decision-makers and the whole Bosnian society. However, facing up to the past fairly and truthfully means acknowledging our own responsibilities and roles. Sadly, it is still avoided at governmental and parliamentary levels, whereas many victims are subject to political exploitation and manipulation.

The user-centred approach in addressing war rape

It is known that rape in the context of armed conflict has "distinct characteristics, consequences, and implications for research and service providers than peacetime rape" (Hagen & Yohani, 2010). Studies indicate that the context of the assault and the socio-cultural factors, including social acknowledgement, influence the victim's reaction to the rape, the symptoms presented, the therapeutic approach, and the recovery process (Kuwert et al., 2014).

In this chapter the term "user-centred" means increased attention to the needs, preferences, and strengths of women survivors of war rape in the delivery of mental health services. Community mental health interventions and supportive programmes (World Health Organization, 2002) aiming at listening to, accepting, and facilitating social reintegration of survivors of sexual violence in war, respecting and reinforcing the concept of human rights, as well as ending the impunity of war rape as a crime against humanity, can make a big difference. This is leading to restoration of faith in human beings, the right to health, the right to protection from human rights violations, and provision of appropriate access to justice that are part of the process of healing and recovery for war rape trauma victims and survivors (Wietse et al., 2013).

In our clinical practice, we have seen that unrecognised multiple trauma of wartime rape victims in Bosnia and Herzegovina, and poor access to appropriate healthcare and social justice, resulted in somatic and psychiatric comorbidities (PTSD, anxiety, depression, suicidal thoughts, dissociative disorder, sexual dysfunctions, social phobia), and lasting changes in their personality. At the same time, socially and culturally imposed notions of dishonour and shame related to rape, as well as fragmentation and destruction of the collective and family structure, led to stigmatisation and social exclusion of the victims, who reported that they have to contend with the "double stigma" of being a victim of rape and having a mental health problem. Women survivors were frequently in crisis, unaware of treatment options, and unsure of the value of treatment interventions offered, often complaining that they get fed up with the position of victim and feeling useless.

In order for our practice to benefit from deeper understanding of the long-term psychological consequences of sexual violence in war, development of evidence-based practices, and sensitive care service delivery, we conducted a cross-sectional study among 105 victims of war rape and eighty-eight controls (non-victims), in the period 2011–2014 throughout Bosnia and Herzegovina. The participants from our sample experienced an average of 16.4 ± 11.24 traumatic events, among which the group of women victims had a significantly higher number of traumatic events (25.55 ± 5.75) than non-victims (6.01 ± 5.40). The most common traumatic events included direct exposure to shelling, lack of food and water, starvation, confiscation or destruction of property, lack of shelter, being forced to leave their home, torture, forced separation from family members, and a huge loss of their loved ones. Women victims were also being exposed to head injury, beatings, knifing, and forced labour; they were forced to betray a family member, and an unrelated party, as well as witnessing the rape or sexual abuse of others. Most victims had multiple war rape experiences, and 54.3% were gang raped. Out of 105 victims, 94.3% had symptoms of post-traumatic stress disorder, and 80% were affected by severe and moderate to severe depression. Significantly higher-intensity symptoms of phobic anxiety were found in women victims than in non-victims, especially those held in concentration camps and detention centres, and those kept locked up (in home prisons) (Delić & Avdibegović, 2015). The results of our study showed that due to devastating multidimensional war trauma effects, and an insecure and non-supportive recovery environment in Bosnia and Herzegovina even twenty years after the end of war, victims of wartime rape are in a prolonged need of appropriate medical, psychological, socio-economic, and free legal aid. We argue that mental health professionals working with vulnerable population groups, including traumatised people, should replace their highly paternalistic approach with modern attitudes to person-centred, gender-sensitive care. Improving the experience of care for war rape survivors using mental health services is required, aimed at ensuring that individuals are making informed decisions about services that directly impact on their health, and are allowed to choose a doctor or caregiver of a particular gender.

* * *

In order to provide respectful treatment, and sensitive and more effective services based on the needs of women victims of war rape situated in the Tuzla Canton, and on the basis of recommendations to improve women's mental health issued by the International Association for Women's Mental Health and World Psychiatric Association in 2012, we employed the user-centred approach to mental health and psychosocial interventions within the community-based Mental Health Centre Tuzla. Apart from individual trauma-focused interventions that have been provided to women rape victims after a delayed disclosure of the victimising event, the user's needs and strengths were assessed, and two cycles of group therapy, skills training, and continuing supportive counselling programme are being offered on a voluntary basis, to protect and achieve women's rights. Addressing the challenges they faced in everyday lives, victims reported that due to the feelings of shame and dishonour, and the fear of stigma and distrust, they even found it difficult to approach medical professionals , and that too often they lacked social support and understanding, while at the same time being ignorant of and/or unaccustomed to the basic rights. Recognising the strength and courage it takes to overcome victimisation, we focused on the needs of a victim/survivor to be informed, well understood, and accepted, providing them with the opportunity to perceive the war rape trauma from another perspective, instead of being trapped in the traditional cultural perception of dishonour and isolation, and to enable them to move from the role of victim to the role of survivor who experienced and witnessed a huge violation of human rights, for which criminal sanctions are prescribed. Thus, the ultimate goal of our approach is to empower survivors as engaged participants in the process of recovery and justice, and to help restore connections between survivors and their communities.

* * *

Addressing both individual and collective aspects in our trauma work, we also advocated the importance of a gender-sensitive societal approach to the subject of sexual violence against women, promoting the process of destigmatisation and reintegration of "women war victims" into society, as well as their basic human rights, social justice, and ending the impunity. Following users' needs, we supported their initiative to establish the Association Helping the Victims and Survivors of Sexual Violence in War "Our Voice" in Tuzla, and to create its promotional material (brochures, leaflets), and a website. Reflexion of such an attitude is strengthening and inducing mental health services users—war rape survivors—to speak openly about their feelings and needs in order to influence the full implementation of the law that regulates victims' rights, protects their integrity, and provides high-quality services and multisectoral resources, along with their social inclusion and improved wellbeing.

Aiming at improving intersectoral collaboration and staff training in recognition and treatment of victims and survivors of sexual violence in war, the Mental Health Centre Tuzla initiated and signed a collaboration protocol with community service providers including the Centre for Social Affairs, the Department for Psychiatry, women's NGOs, and the users' Association Helping the Victims and Survivors of Sexual Violence in War "Our Voice" in Tuzla. During the ceremony marking World Mental Health Day 2013, and Doors Open Days at the Mental Health Centre Tuzla in October 2013, representatives of the users' association Our Voice took part in advocating their equality and reinforcing the concept of human rights by educating the public on a broad array of issues affecting survivors of wartime rape in post-war Bosnia and Herzegovina. Furthermore, in supporting the association Our Voice, we helped survivors in developing positive social networks with local, national, and international NGOs, ICTY, UN agencies, and civil society organisations. A comprehensive effort by partners involved in rebuilding rapport and trust with survivors, and meeting the networking needs of survivors' associations was of significant importance for the perception of social acknowledgement as a predictor of recovery from post-traumatic stress disorder. Confronting years of denial and overcoming deep personal trauma in their efforts to go on with their everyday lives in the aftermath of war, using the slogan "Nothing About Us Without Us!" in the 2012–2015 period, the users' association of women survivors of war rape based in Tuzla engaged in many awareness-raising initiatives, education campaigns, group discussions, public dialogue, roundtables, workshops and international conferences addressing sexual violence in war and accountability, and CEDAW recommendations, assuring justice, reparation, and rehabilitation for victims and survivors of sexual violence in war in Bosnia and Herzegovina. In addition, the association Our Voice participated in marking the UN International Day in Support of Victims of Torture in Tuzla, and in a meeting with the UN Special Rapporteur on Violence Against Women held at the UN headquarters in Sarajevo. The annual reports on Our Voice activities repeatedly state how it feels to be recognised and accepted as a valuable member of society, and that their membership is gradually growing for those who kept silent about their pain due to feeling shame, fear, and stigma more than twenty years after the sexual crimes were committed against them.

Women survivors of sexual violence in war from the Tuzla canton have proved able to rebuild a sense of self-worth and competence in relating to self and world, to make a difference, and to replace isolation and poor social integration with active participation in the process of recovery and rehabilitation.

Future directions

In following the abovementioned international Consensus Statements, service providers dealing with victims and survivors of war rape should focus not only on individuals but also on societal aspects of rape while addressing the needs of women's mental health. Being aware of the impact of "research evidence" for informed policy-making and positive actions, a need for prospective gender-sensitive studies on mental health outcomes in war rape victims should be recognised and addressed.

Law enforcement agencies should engage in continuing capacity building of juridical authorities to respond effectively and fairly to conflict-related sexual violence in line with established international jurisprudence, expanding access to transitional justice for those victimised. Multisectoral collaboration and interorganisational partnerships based on mutual respect should be of high importance in creating a safe place for the victims, strengthening the maximum utilisation of local and domestic resources to sufficiently meet their needs, and in reducing the burden of war rape trauma aftermath.

Conclusion

The nature of war rape and its aftermath, in a specific socio-cultural context in post-war Bosnia and Herzegovina, made women survivors of sexual violence in war one of the most vulnerable population categories, depending on long-term systematic support structures, continuing treatment, social recognition, and prolonged recovery. To achieve the optimal level of improvement of women's mental health and functioning, and to facilitate the process of destigmatisation, empowerment, and social reintegration, a user-centred and rights-centred gender-sensitive multisectoral approach is required. Also, implementing the recommendations of the competent international bodies is of high importance. The government should take greater responsibility in protecting and supporting victims promptly and effectively, and providing safety and security in their lives is essential. Continuing training addressing sexual and gender-based violence issues should be mandatory for all health professionals, in particular for those in situations of armed conflict and in post-conflict countries. Voices and experiences of sexual violence victims must be heard, a comprehensive strategy for rehabilitation needs to be developed together with the service users, and autonomy needs to be provided to move forward through users' initiatives and organisations, self-support groups, occupational therapy, and income-generating projects.

References

Abazović, D., Ćurak, N., Sejzović, Z., Šačić, N., & Turčalo, S. (2007). *Ethno-mobilization and the organized production of violence in Bosnia and Herzegovina—conscious preparations*. MIRICO: Human and minority rights in the life cycle of ethnic conflicts. Available at: http://www.eurac.edu/en/research/autonomies/minrig/Documents/Mirico/Bosnia and Herzegovina Report.pdf [last accessed 23 April 2017].

Avdibegović, E. (2014). Ethnic conflict, mental health, and reconciliation: experiences from Bosnia and Herzegovina. In: U. Mader, B. Schurch, & S. Mugier (Eds.). *Reconciliation: Vergeben ohne zu vergessen?* (pp. 113–139). Basel: Gesowip Basel.

Bennett, C. (2016). *Bosnia's Paralysed Peace*. London: Hurst.

Deiana, M. A., & Goldie, R. (2012). Survivors in peace: government response in meeting the needs of survivors of serious physical injury and sexual assault during conflict, as a legacy for Northern Ireland and Bosnia-Herzegovina. *International Journal of Peace Studies, 17*: 1–23.

Delić, A., & Avdibegović, E. (2015). Shame and silence in the aftermath of war rape in Bosnia and Herzegovina: 22 years later. In: H. Glaesmer & S. Lee (Eds.), *Interdisciplinary Perspectives on Children Born of War—from World War II to Current Conflict Settings*. Conference reader. Available at: http://medpsy.uniklinikum-leipzig.de/medpsych.site,postext,rueckblick,a_id,1412.html [last accessed 26 February 2017].

Demény, G. (2011). *Factors of Socio-Economic Uncertainty in the Bosnian War*. Brighton: MICROCON.

Fischer, M. (2007). *Peacebuilding and Civil Society in Bosnia-Herzegovina: Ten Years After Dayton* (2nd edn). Berlin: Lit Verlag.

Hagen, K. T., & Yohani, S. C. (2010). The nature and psychosocial consequences of war rape for individuals and communities. *International Journal of Psychological Studies, 2*: 14–25.

Iancu, S. (2012). *Support for access to justice for female victims of violence*. Commission on the Status of Women.

Inter-Agency Standing Committee (2005). *Guidelines for Gender-Based Violence Interventions in Humanitarian Settings*. Geneva: Inter-Agency Standing Committee.

Kuwert, P., Glaesmer, H., Eichhorn, S., Grundke, E., Pietrzak, R. H., Freyberger, H. J., & Klauer, T. (2014). Long-term effects of conflict-related sexual violence compared with non-sexual war trauma in female World War II survivors: a matched pairs study. *Archives of Sexual Behavior, 43*: 1059–1064.

Lončar, M., Medvedev, V., Jovanović, N., & Hotujac, L. (2006). Psychological consequences of rape on women in 1991–1995 war in Croatia and Bosnia and Herzegovina. *Croatian Medical Journal, 47*: 67–75.

Malcolm, N. (1996). *Bosnia: A Short History*. London: Macmillan.

Mann, J., Drucker, E., Tarantola, D., & McCabe, M. P. (1994). Bosnia: the war against public health. *Medicine & Global Survival, 1*: 130–146.

Marsh, M., Purdin, S., & Navani, S. (2006). Addressing sexual violence in humanitarian emergencies. *Global Public Health, 1:* 133–146.

Mollica, R. F., Cardozo, B. L., Osofsky, H. J., Raphael, B., Ager, A., & Salama, P. (2004). Mental health in complex emergencies. *Lancet, 364*: 2058–2067.

Organization for Security and Cooperation in Europe. (2015). *Combating Impunity for Conflict-Related Sexual Violence in Bosnia and Herzegovina: Progress and Challenges*. OSCE. Available at http://www.osce.org/bih/171906 [last accessed 26 February 2017].

Skjelsbæk, I. (2012). *The Political Psychology of War Rape: Studies from Bosnia and Herzegovina*. Abingdon: Routledge.

Stewart, D. E. (2006). The international consensus statement on women's mental health and the WPA consensus statement on interpersonal violence against women. *World Psychiatry, 5*: 61–64.

Todorova, T. (2011). Giving memory a future: confronting the legacy of mass rape in post-conflict Bosnia-Herzegovina. *Journal of International Women's Studies, 12*: 3–15.

Track Impunity Always (2014). *Follow-Up Report on the Implementation of the Recommendations Issued by the Special Rapporteur on Violence against Women, its Causes and Consequences after her Mission to Bosnia and Herzegovina*. Sarajevo: TRIAL.

United Nations Committee on the Elimination of Discrimination Against Women (2006). *Concluding remarks: CEDAW/C/THA/CO/5*. Thailand: Committee on the Elimination of Discrimination Against Women.

Wietse, A. T., Stavrou, V., Greene, M. C., Mergenthaler, C., Garcio-Moreno, C., & Van Ommeren, M. (2013). Mental health and psychosocial support interventions for survivors of sexual and gender-based violence during armed conflict: a systematic review. *World Psychiatry, 12*: 93–94.

Woodhead, C., & Wessely, S. (2010). Commentary: what interventions work for victims of conflict-related rape? *British Medical Journal, 341*: 1253.

World Health Organization. (2002). *World Report on Violence and Health: summary*. Geneva: WHO.

CHAPTER EIGHT

Who should be held responsible for war crimes?

Sara Ristić

Human history has been full of conflict, with wars being the most extreme and destructive form of conflict in terms of scope and consequences. My motivation to research certain psychological aspects in the context of war stems from the need to understand situational and other factors that are in different ways related to inhumane behaviour by ordinary people in such situations (Arendt, 1963).

The problem to be examined here refers to a more specific kind of event in war: tolerated massacres and how most people perceive them.

Tolerated massacre is defined as "nonselective, cruel, and often systematic mass violence conducted by members of an army or paramilitary formations during actions against helpless and unprotected civilians, which are officially tolerated" (Kelman & Hamilton, 1989). This implies that events of this kind usually occur in a broader context of explicitly or implicitly genocidal policy. The second important characteristic of a tolerated massacre is that the target of these crimes are people who do not pose any threat to the perpetrators of the violence nor do they take part in any violent actions against them.

An infamous example of this is the case of a USA lieutenant, William Calley, which is today equally captivating for social psychologists as it was for the American public at the time it happened. During the Vietnam War, on 16 May 1968, Calley's unit was given an order to "clean up" the village of Mi Lay where apparently Vietnamese guerrilla fighters were provided with shelter, information, and resources. Upon their arrival at the village, the soldiers found only old people, women, and children, all unarmed. Yet almost all villagers were killed—between 500 and 600 people. When the case was discovered, the trial of lieutenant Calley followed and it caused one of the first major mutinies by the American public. Most Americans thought that the trial was unjustified (79% according to research by Gallup—see Kelman & Hamilton,

1989). Lieutenant Calley was initially sentenced to life imprisonment but the verdict was later commuted to a two-year sentence, which he served in his own home.

Soon after the trial ended, comprehensive research was conducted that looked at views of the American public in terms of first, level of familiarity with the trial of lieutenant Calley; second, attitudes towards the lieutenant's actions; and third, attitudes towards whether the trial had been justified (Kelman, Lawrence, & Hamilton, 1972). Of the three variable groups, the second is of the highest importance here, since it deals with attitudes towards the act, operationalised through the following two questions: first, "In your opinion, what would most people do if they were soldiers?" (with options to shoot or not to shoot); and second, "What would you do if you were a soldier?" (with options to shoot, not to shoot, and don't know).

Apart from confirming the previous finding that the public was highly united in opposing Calley's trial (79% of the respondents to the survey), another finding is also of high importance: most respondents stated that in the given circumstances, most people would obey the order and shoot (67%), and that they themselves would do it too (51%). High correlation of answers to the two questions ($r = 0.82$) fuels the interpretation that this act (obedience) was considered the social norm (ibid.).

In the other two pieces of research into crimes of obedience, conducted in Serbia, participants were given a short story about what lieutenant Calley and his unit did in Mi Lay, with the story being set in the context of the Bosnian war (1992–1995). In addition, the nationalities of the victim and perpetrator were changed, as well as who gave the decision to attack—was it the lieutenant himself or had he just forwarded an order issued by his superior.

Participants in the first piece of research were students in the Faculty of Philosophy at Belgrade University, and this research dealt with the level to which the nationalities of the perpetrator and the victim, and the locus of decision-making, influenced the level of (dis)approval of the tolerated massacre and the decision of who is to be put on trial. The results showed that the level of (dis)approval depended solely on the nationality of the perpetrator, while information on the locus of decision-making only influenced opinions on who should be put on trial (the person who issued the order, those who carried it out, or nobody) (Popadić, 1996). Participants disapproved more in the case when Bosnian perpetrators acted violently towards Serbian victims, compared to the level of disapproval of crimes of Serbian perpetrators towards Bosnian victims. Most participants disapproved equally of shooting civilians, regardless of whether the crime was perpetrated by the person who issued the order or the soldier who carried it out. Nevertheless, there was a tendency to hold the person who issued the order more responsible and guilty than his subordinates. This implies that participants believe the officer who gave the order has more responsibility than those who directly carried it out, regardless of their nationality.

The second research related to this chapter was carried out on graduates of a high school in Pančevo, Serbia, and is in part a replication of and addition to the research described above (Popadić, 1996; Sretenović, 2002). The data proved to be in accordance with the previous research showing that the attitudes towards the act are significantly influenced by the nationality of the perpetrator, but not by the locus of decision-making. This means there is a tendency to view the act of the person who issued the order as a crime rather than the act of the soldier, but the difference has not proven to be statistically significant. On the other hand, even though the massacre is classified as a crime, the participants do not think everyone should be put on trial for carrying it out. Statistically, a significant proportion of participants think that the one who issued the order should be put on trial, but not the one who only carried out the orders. The author saw this finding as a consequence of information about nationality blocking the influence of information on locus of decision-making.

In the present study, this assumption will be tested by including a control group (described below), but also by collecting a sample of participants who, unlike the participants from the previous research, were not born during the conflict in which the story they will be presented with is set, so the assumption is they will be less involved.

The research presented here aims to examine the relation of nationality of the perpetrator and the victim and locus of decision-making to attitudes towards the act of perpetrator, to the trial, and to attributing guilt. More precisely, analysis will be available because a control group as a referential point for the level of (dis)approval of the act is introduced. This research adds to previous work and aims to compare data and seek possible tendencies in attributions of this type.

Method

The research design is experimental with three factors (3 × 2). The first factor refers to the nationalities of the perpetrator and the victim with three options: one, Serbs as perpetrators and Muslims as victims; two, Muslims as perpetrators and Serbs as victims; and three, nationalities of perpetrators and victims is unknown (the control group). In order to examine how participants think of the act itself, regardless of the nationality of people taking part in it, a third (control) group was presented with identical stories with only a change in perpetrators being neutrally marked as "group A" and the victims as "group B", while the context was "a war in a country", with no further specifications. This control was needed in order to make more viable comparisons of levels of (dis)approval in the two aforementioned experimental situations. The second factor is locus of decision-making, with two options: one, the commander of the unit issued the attack order to his soldiers; and two, the commander of the unit forwarded to his subordinates the order he was given by his superior.

There are five groups of dependent variables: one, attitudes towards the act itself; two, attitudes towards the trial (relevance here in terms of shedding light on how participants attribute responsibility for crimes of obedience); three, subjective estimation of the effect of information on the two factors of attitudes; four, opinions about what factors contribute to some war crimes of obedience towards civilians; and five, demographic data such as nationality, gender, and level of identification with the nation.

Each participant was presented with one of the six (factors 3 × 2) versions of the story and was told that a real event was portrayed that occurred during the war in Bosnia (1992–1995). After reading the story, they filled in a questionnaire consisting of items operationalising each of the five groups of dependent variables described previously. At the end, participants were provided with a short debriefing, consisting of information on the subject of the research, the fact that events were not real, and their feedback. An example of a story in which Serbs are the perpetrators, Muslims are the victims, and the commander issued the order himself, presented to one of the six groups of participants, is:

> Near the line between the Serbian and the Muslim army there was a Muslim village. The villagers provided shelter and information to the Muslim army. Several actions had been carried out from the village and in them some of the Serbian soldiers had been killed. An army unit commanded by lieutenant X was given the task of occupying the village. During their approach, they were met with no resistance, and in the village only old men, women, and children were found. The lieutenant decided to kill all the imprisoned villagers. He issued an order to his soldiers who gathered and shot all the villagers—between 500 and 600 of them.

The formulation of the story has been taken and adapted from the previously described research of Popadić (1996).

The sample comprised 474 high-school students in Serbia (coming from four schools in the capital and one in the central-southern part of the country), with an average age of 17.24 (SD = 0.692). Female participants comprised just over half (60%) of the sample and 90.7% of all participants declared themselves to be of Serbian nationality. These are the participants whose answers have been included in the following analyses. All participants were equally distributed in regard to gender and the six versions. One quarter of the participants stated that their nationality is highly important to them (grade 3 on a scale –3 to 3–25.6%), and 38.1% said it was important (grade 2 20.2% and grade 1 17.9%). This means that for more than half of the participants, nationality is important.

Results

As for a general level of (dis)approval of the act of the commander, participants graded it with an average M = 3.77 which makes it around –2 on a scale of –5 to 5, while the highest percentages were where the groups of participants graded the act with a "–5—strong disapproval" (31.9%) and a "0—neither disapprove nor approve" (17.5%). The data implies that for most participants the situation is either morally clear and deserves a strong condemnation or the act is not to be easily judged, so they could not decide.

If this general mark is examined more thoroughly, the level of (dis)approval can be seen in regard to two factors: nationality of the perpetrator and the victim, and locus of decision-making. When nationality is taken more closely into account, the data shows that participants condemn the act of the commander strongest when members of their group are victims (M = 3.18/11; SD = 2.614), which is on average grade of one point lower than when members of their group are the perpetrators and Muslims are the victims (M = 4.26; SD = 2.896), and the difference is statistically significant (Sidak post-hoc test, p = 0.02). The grades given by participants from different groups (who were presented with different stories regarding nationality of the perpetrator and victim) differ significantly (F(2) = 5.915; p = 0.003), yet this difference seems to stem from the difference between the two experimental groups, and each group does not statistically differ from the control group (M = 3.83, SD = 2.612) in a significant manner. As expected and in accordance with the data of the previous research, it is once again shown that the disapproval of the crime does depend on the nationality of the people involved in it and will be highest in the situation when members of one's in-group are attacked.

The data obtained from this research, using students who were not born during the war, is in accordance with the data from the previous research in which participants were alive during the war. Results in both cases show that disapproval of the act is significantly higher ($F(1) = 6.566$; $p = 0.011$) when the commander personally issued the order to attack ($M = 3.38$ on a scale of –5 to 11) than when the order was only forwarded by him ($M = 4.07$ on a scale of –5 to 11). This can also be seen in the following comparison: the group that was told that Serbs were the perpetrators and that the commander issued the order ($M = 3.33$ on a scale of –5 to 11) and the group in which Serbs were also perpetrators but the commander only forwarded the order ($M = 5.00$ on a scale of –5 to 11). Apart from the comparison, statistical significance of the difference between the groups ($F (5) = 4.665$; $p = 0.000$) stems from the following differences: control group in which the commander issued the order himself ($M = 3.52$) and the group in which Serbs as perpetrators had a commander who forwarded the order ($M = 5.00$; $p = 0.003$), where presumably the difference is due to the change in locus of decision-making ($p = 0.028$), which is not the case also in the groups that differ significantly ($p = 0.027$) given that the locus is the same (the order was forwarded). However, in one group Serbs were the perpetrators ($M = 5.00$) and in the other, the victims ($M = 3.58$). All three post-hoc tests are Bonferroni corrections, which reduces the chance of false-positive results.

Conclusion

When it comes to estimating the level of (dis)approval of the crime of obedience, the data has shown no difference between people who experienced the Bosnian war more closely and those who did not. In both cases, disapproval is higher when members of one's own group were the victims and if the commander himself issued the order to attack. Although the results are as expected, the pattern of judging when it comes to locus of decision-making seems to imply that participants defined the situation as an act of obedience and not a crime (for the soldiers who carried out the orders) and therefore do not find the direct perpetrators guilty. On the other hand, feelings caused by a situation in which one's in-group is threatened may prompt participants to take into account the consequences of the act when forming their opinion—and they are more likely to portray the act as a crime. Further research may shed more light on the mere process of creating an individual definition of the situation of a crime of obedience as either a "crime" or an "obedience act" through use of qualitative methodology, which would provide deeper insight.

The type of crime of obedience examined in this chapter is also an example of social trauma, in which a defenceless group of people is attacked by another group (both groups defined by their ethnicity), in a war situation supported by a policy of almost utter annihilation of the enemy group. The victims are usually provided by their culture, society, or group with a narrative that can convey meaning to the atrocities they endured, thus making them communicative and able to assimilate. This chapter has also attempted to take a closer look at ways in which other people, who are not completely neutral given that they are members of an involved group, but with a certain time distance between the event and themselves, define the event, how they make sense of it in regard of who is to be held responsible, and how they form their opinion and attitude towards it. The social trauma in question is more persistently continued because the groups of both the victims and the perpetrators (who have at times, exchanged the roles in different events) belonged to the same society prior to the conflict. Another interesting point is that the students who were subjects in this research had not yet been born when the traumatic event they were asked to form an opinion about took place, so it can be argued that their definition of the crime of obedience is at least in part influenced by what has been transferred to them by the socialising agent of their groups: parents, media, and education. Having in mind that these are the people who form general public opinion, learning about their attributions of responsibility is relevant for understanding reactions to and implications of trial processes that are one of the stepping stones towards reconciliation and creating conditions for peaceful relations between the groups in conflict. Furthermore, what makes the issues of trial and assigning responsibility even more relevant, is the fact that neglect of the acts or events by which the trauma was inflicted on a group, by society as a whole (either society of the perpetrator or the victim), fuels the "conspiracy of silence" (Hamburger, 2017). Addressing the issue through society's relevant institutions (such as the justice system, the government, the media) helps acknowledge and validate the pain and suffering that victims endured and deliver the feeling and notion that they will be provided with what they are entitled to, fostering their belief that they are an equal part of a just and moral system. Conducting a scientific psychological research on the topic is also a way to fight the neglect of the issue, to address it and make public an alternative discourse on the topic. Also, given that every approach to social trauma is inevitably intertwined in a social framework, approaching the topic from a social psychology and sociological-constructionist perspective can shed some light on aspects of the issue that are not thoroughly looked into when social trauma is examined from a clinical, psychoanalytic stance. Keeping in mind the importance of the actual traumatic event and its clinical consequences, social psychological investigation of the topic of social trauma can add to it by examining the society in which the traumatic experience is created and continued.

References

Arendt, H. (1963). *Eichmann in Jerusalem: A report on the Banality of Evil*. London: Penguin [reprinted 2006].

Hamburger, A. (2017). Genocidal trauma. Individual and social consequences of the assault on the mental and physical life of a group. In: D. Laub & A. Hamburger (Eds.), *Psychoanalysis and Holocaust Testimony. Unwanted Memories of Social Trauma* (pp. 66–91). London: Routledge.

Kelman, H. C., & Hamilton, V. L. (1989). *Crimes of Obedience*. Binghamton, NY: Vail-Ballou.

Kelman, H. C., Lawrence, L. H., & Hamilton, V. L. (1972). American response to the trial of Lt. William Calley. *Psychology Today, 6*: 41–45; 78–81.

Popadić, D. (1996, February). Suđenje o ratnom zločinu: Uticaj podatka o nacionalnosti počinioca i o lokusu odlu ivanja [War crimes judgement: Effect of data on perpetrator's nationality and decision making locus]. Paper presented at Empirical Research in Psychology congress, Belgrade.

Sretenović, M. (2002). Stavovi maturanata prema ratnim zlo inima nad civilnim stanovništvom [Secondary school graduation students' attitudes towards war crimes against civilians]. Graduation paper from Department of Psychology, Faculty of Philosophy, University of Belgrade.

CHAPTER NINE

Genocide can be mourned: the wager of psychoanalysis in Bosnia and Herzegovina

Damir Arsenijević and Emin Eminagić

The year 2015 marked the twentieth anniversary of the Dayton Peace Agreement in Bosnia and Herzegovina. To end the war (1992–1995), the Agreement put in place a tripartite constitution, which exclusively defined the people of Bosnia and Herzegovina through their ethnicity, that is, Bosniak, Croat, Serb. This in turn created a political economy where any political agency citizens can have, will exclusively be defined by their ethnicity, while continuing the fear-mongering and politics of terror of everyday life. We thus witness a certain *Denkverbot*, suturing Bosnia's citizens into a position of constant melancholia, which is then proliferated through the dominant modes of commemoration.

Bosnian society is locating, exhuming, identifying, and re-burying its dead. After the war, there are still around 8,000 missing people in Bosnia and Herzegovina buried in hidden mass graves.

Each day in this country, bodily remains are exhumed, counted, re-associated, managed, and consecrated as *ethnic* remains. This is done through the strategic collaboration of forensic science; multiculturalist post-conflict management with its politics of reconciliation; and religious ritual—an uncouth alliance between the scientist, the bureaucrat, and the priest.

In doing so, the scientist, the bureaucrat, and the priest assume the perspective of the perpetrator of the crime. For it is in the fantasy of the perpetrator that the executed person is the ethnic *other*.

In the public domain, those who survived can only mourn their loved ones as ethnic dead victims, themselves being politically reduced solely to members of an ethnic group. So, the surviving ethnic victims mourn the dead ethnic victims, while the elites who fought the wars and got rich in the chase for the capital through genocide, remain in power.

The so-called peacebuilding carried out by international agencies, and adopted by many national civil society groups for the purposes of receiving the much-needed funds, promotes multiculturalist politics as the panacea. Multiculturalist politics reduces social conflict to a friction among many identities, recasting cultural, religious, and ethnic difference as "sites of conflict that need to be attenuated and managed through the practice of tolerance" (Brown, 2006). In the discourse of tolerance, what is taken as a given is that each ethnic victim has her own micro story, each ethnic group its own "destiny", and what is promoted as life is the image of life led on parallel tracks, in one never-intersecting apartheid.

In such internationally driven and locally supported management of loss, the logic of the executioner and genocide is upheld and genocide becomes genocide in perpetuity. This new regime of governing produces the subject—the ethnic victim; whether dead or alive, it matters little.

Death was not the only thing produced during the war in Bosnia and Herzegovina between 1992 and 1995. There was also life—a particular kind of life—that was produced amidst the overwhelming production of death in Bosnia and Herzegovina during wartime. In the centre of this production of death one hears the obscene laughter of the ethno-capitalist, who has profited by death and who continues to laugh as he continues to extract more value from death itself. This ethno-capitalist laughs just like the capitalist who laughs when extracting surplus value from labour, when he converts money into capital.

Opposed to this obscene laughter of the ethno-capitalist is the anxious laughter after the joke about war and genocide has been told. This anxious laughter is an interval in the laugher of the ethno-capitalist, reminding us that this obscene laughter is not all that exists. The joke about war and genocide interrupts the stalemate of the post-war period in Bosnia and Herzegovina:

> Sometime after the war in Bosnia has ended, Mujo and Fata decide to have a child. After nine months the child is born and Fata asks Mujo what the child's name should be. Mujo, all proud of himself, says the child should have a nice Bosniak name, and that he should be named Muhamed. So little Muhamed turns four and goes out to play with the other kids in the street, when a bus runs him over. Naturally Mujo and Fata are grief-stricken. Two years pass, and they decide to try again—the child is born and Mujo, again very proud of himself, says the child should have a nice Bosniak name, and that he should be called Ahmed. The same situation: Ahmed turns four, goes out on the street to play with the other kids, and also gets run over by a bus. Again they are grieving. Five years pass and they decide to try one final time. So after nine months, the child is born and Mujo now asks Fata what they should name the child—and Fata says, "Milan!" Mujo, all confused, says, "But Fata, we're Bosniaks, how can you give the child a Serb name?" To which Fata replies "Well Mujo, if ours die, let theirs die as well."

It is always a matter of risk when deciding whether, when and to whom to tell a joke about war and genocide. Such jokes are very efficient ways of opening a critical discussion around topics that are seldom discussed in public, as well as of creating space to discuss the unease created by these jokes.

The working group *Vic, rat i genocid* (Jokes, War, and Genocide) was founded in 2012 in Tuzla, Bosnia and Herzegovina, to explore alternative ways of commemoration beyond the predominant petrification of ethnic victim. For three years, between 2013 and 2015, the group also convened the international Psychoanalytic Seminar Tuzla, as the first sustained effort in Bosnia and Herzegovina to explore the connection between psychoanalysis and society, bringing together analysts, artists, academics, and activists. The working group was guided by the following question: what different practice could deactivate the reification of bones as ethnic victims, would stop the prolongation of the injurious gaze of the perpetrator and would return the bones to such common use through which we can contemplate hope after genocide? In other words, what is the politics that will enable us to be hopeful subjects in relation to these bones?

What mattered was to pose these questions in a public space saturated by the imperative of ethnic identification. This space is colonised and constantly enclosed through routine normalisation of terror—ranging from the enforced devaluation and privatisation of companies, that leaves workers, who once were actively involved in decision-making in the daily lives of their companies, completely financially and politically destitute, all the way to normalising the logic of the perpetrator of genocide, through the mechanisms of counting and identifying the mortal remains as ethnic.

What does it mean to insist on a hopeful stance in such a context? It means to lay claim, recuperate, and restore that which was stolen and destroyed through the war and genocide—a particular type of public and social relations of the commons. By commons, Jokes, War, and Genocide posits all that is left out, discarded, destroyed, weakened, and exhausted—from our capacity to collectively think and materialise demands for a more inclusive justice and societal transformation, to all the excluded forms of life, as well as new forms of life, or new subjectivities that produce a space for solidarity and commonality in the claims for equality for all.

How can psychoanalysis take the context of Bosnia and Herzegovina into account for its theory and practice? That there is no organised psychoanalytic practice in Bosnia and Herzegovina is a symptom in its own right. The working group Jokes, War, and Genocide posits that analysing the parapraxis—such as jokes related to war and genocide—is a productive way to explore the unconscious of war and genocide and counter the predominant denial and silence around painful topics.

Therefore, Jokes, War, and Genocide starts with a position that jokes about war and genocide are specific forms of witnessing. In doing so, the group has posited that "[t]he jokes we have collected and analysed testify to the *unconscious* of war and genocide, which is located in jokes, and our task is to explore that unconscious part" (Jokes, War, and Genocide, June 2012, unpublished). Between 2012 and 2015, the working group collected, analysed, and publicly presented jokes on war and genocide with the aim of opening up a public space for a collective exploration of the unconscious influences that dominate our speech and language.

The working group produced statements that framed its internal and external work. In devising the statements, the group took into account how to create the setting for a public discussion in which different positions around war and genocide can be articulated and confronted without breaking into conflict. Based on insights of the emergent psychoanalytically informed artistic and theoretical interventions in Bosnia and Herzegovina, in its public presentations and lecture performances, Jokes, War, and Genocide created opportunities for *relationality* when speaking of topics. This is strengthened by explicit articulations of mistrust and anger, all of which enables a discussion about loss caused by war and genocide to be properly social, rather than ethnically dominant or merely private (Arsenijević, Husanović, & Wastell, 2016, p. 267).

The first statement of the working group was produced from close reading of the jokes that the group collected, alongside Sigmund Freud's book *Jokes and Their Relation to the Unconscious* (1905c). In the statement, the group outlined the forms of enjoyment produced by the jokes in relation to society:

> Our work starts with Freud's position that jokes and the enjoyment gained through jokes, are psychical short circuits. Jokes are created in language, as opposed to the comic, which is found in a situation, this being a crucial difference for our work on jokes about war and genocide. On the one hand, these jokes testify to loss and continuing pain, and on the other, they enable enjoyment through the mechanism of the joke. Enjoyment through jokes is greater if the individual images (fields of representations, as Freud calls them) that are short-circuited are more widely apart. We perceive a short circuit as a way to examine predominantly held positions and entrenched ways of thinking, whereby a short circuit sheds light on their silenced and disavowed assumptions and effects. In a short circuit created by a joke on war and genocide not only do we understand something new, but also we gain an insight into something more important and more disturbing— "the rediscovery of what is familiar", of what we have always already known, but about which we had to be silent.
>
> In such short circuits, we locate that which Freud calls the "help" of jokes: to secure enjoyment in something that would otherwise be repressed, to secure enjoyment from objection on the part of criticism, which would put an end to enjoyment. In our analysis, in relation to jokes on war and genocide, we start with some questions. What is the technique of jokes? What kind of enjoyment do such jokes provide? In relation to what kind of objection or criticism do these jokes secure and provide enjoyment?
>
> A joke, as a "double-dealing rascal who serves two masters at once" (Freud, 1905c, p. 155), is simultaneously in the domains of both sense and non-sense. Jokes, as the most social of "all the mental functions that aim at a yield of pleasure" (ibid., p. 179), need three people to secure pleasure: the person who tells the joke, the person or situation about which the joke is told, and the person to whom the joke is told, and through whose pleasure is secured the pleasure of the first person.
>
> Our work is bringing together the first assertion—that a joke is a type of witnessing—not only as speech about war, but also through the need for the presence of a third person—and the psychoanalytic insight about a joke as the most social of all functions that secure pleasure. Through our analysis, we open up space for witnessing as part of the commons—as space for collective action, speech, and thinking. Our thesis is that jokes, though short circuits, enable us to open up such space as lies beyond the prohibitions and oppression for speech about topics that we have identified through our work: witnessing war and genocide, the denial of genocide, the position of life that remains after war, and the role of myth in cementing the positions gained in the war. (Jokes, War and Genocide, June 2012, unpublished)

The unconscious of the war and genocide that the group has encountered in its work has been the predominant denial, in Bosnia and Herzegovina, of the existence of jokes on genocide. Moreover, the main objection that has been raised was the conjunction "and" being put between "joke" and "genocide". Therefore, in July 2015, the group posited the following:

> We have come together in this working group to acknowledge the existence of the joke on genocide. In his 1905 text *Jokes and their Relationship to the Unconscious*, Freud's analysis of the structure and psychical purposes of jokes allows us to posit the joke on genocide as a commemorative practice. Freud proposes a distinction that continues to be crucial for our work; the joke is made, and the comic is found. This pluralisation of commemorative register problematizes the dominant regimes of commemorating genocide in Bosnia and Herzegovina today, and promotes the joke as engaging and exiting the repetition of grievance and affect, which robs the victim of the capacity to grieve. In other words, the joke constructs a new position from which a subject can mourn a loss and lay a melancholic identification to rest. (Jokes, War and Genocide, July 2012, unpublished)

Freud's proposition, that the joke as the most social "mental functions aiming at the yield of pleasure" is created in language, whereas the comic is always found in the situation (Freud, 1905c, p. 179), is crucial for the group's work. Such a structural analysis allows us to posit jokes as a mode of commemoration for war and genocide. It is through this pluralisation of commemorative registers that the joke allows us to problematise the dominant commemorative practices found in Bosnia and Herzegovina today.

The dominant commemorative practices insist on the ethnification of the victim, rendering any other metaphorisation of terms like Srebrenica impossible. The subject is demarcated always exclusively ethnic, thus causing it to disavow its own past. Through such an ethnification victims become included into a reified imagined past that was never their own, while being entwined in the privatisation logic that followed the war (Here we refer to the constitutional changes made in 1994, where socially owned property—*društvena svojina*—becomes state owned in order to facilitate privatisation, while discursively erasing traces of labour, commonality, and solidarity that produced such property). Walter Benjamin in his *Thesis VI on the Philosophy of History* writes:

> Articulating the past historically does not mean recognizing it "the way it really was". It means appropriating a memory as it flashes up in a moment of danger. Historical materialism wishes to hold fast that image of the past which unexpectedly appears to the historical subject in a moment of danger. The danger threatens both the content of the tradition and those who inherit it. For both, it is one and the same thing: the danger of becoming a tool of the ruling classes. Every age must strive anew to wrest tradition away from the conformism that is working to overpower it. The Messiah comes not only as the redeemer; he comes as the victor over the Antichrist. The only historian capable of fanning the spark of hope in the past is the one who is firmly convinced that *even the dead* will not be safe from the enemy if he is victorious. And this enemy has never ceased to be victorious. (Benjamin, 2006, p. 391)

This quote pinpoints the stalemate the dominant commemorative practices in Bosnia and Herzegovina create today. Freud claims that the joke's work liberates pleasure by getting rid of inhibitions. Jokes either strengthen the purpose that they serve, by assisting them with impulses that are kept suppressed, or they put themselves entirely at the service of suppressed purposes. Therein lies the novelty of the syntagm "jokes *and* genocide". The conjunction *and* functions as a joke in itself, as it connects the farthest fields of representation while pointing to the interplay of subjectivity and discourse (The work of Jokes, War, and Genocide was guided in particular by a close reading of Jacques Lacan's Seminar V *The Formation of the Unconscious*. We have used the unpublished translation of this seminar made by the analyst Peter Geoffrey Young who is one of the co-conveners of the Psychoanalytic Seminar Tuzla).

The conjunction "and" draws attention to the two mutually linked dimensions in Freud's work on jokes: the dimension of subjectivity and the dimension of discourse. Central in the interplay between these two dimensions—and tying them together—is the pleasure that the joke produces, in the displacement and condensation of signifiers in our speech. This pleasure rests on the simultaneous authorising of the joke in the dimension of subjectivity and the dimension of discourse.

Placing "and" between "joke" and "genocide" precipitates the crisis in the dominant regimes that manage speech about genocide. The crisis speaks of the possibility of a decision; it is a risk and a choice: "and" is a signifying conjunction. The joke—in its outset as free use of words and thoughts—cracks open the managed set of signifiers around "genocide". It introduces both sense and nonsense around "genocide"; in the horizon of need and demand, characteristic of every speech, the joke communicates to the discourse (other) "some-sense" (which functions as a façade or a preparation of the punchline), it continues the displacement of signifiers, it places a demand of sense. The nonsense in a joke is voided of every kind of need. It is the place for the subject, who introduces non-sense, (and also, as Freud asserts, the confusion of the sources of pleasure). In this nonsense, the subject is the one who communicates the novelty of the joke in the dominant discourse. We could also perceive jokes on war and genocide as profanation in the sense that they enable speech itself to be liberated through its "desacralisation" (Felman, 1992, p. 219)—through giving back to the commons that which has been sacralised. To profane, according to Agamben (2007, p. 85), means "to return to common use that which has been removed to the sphere of the sacred" but which is not a mere restoration of a "natural use" of that which was removed. The activity that results from profanation becomes "a pure means, that is, a praxis that, while firmly maintaining its nature as a means, is emancipated from its relationship to an end; it has joyously forgotten its goal and can now show itself as such, as a means without an end. The creation of new use is possible only by deactivating an old use, rendering it inoperative" (ibid., p. 86).

New social bonds, in the direction of which the joke about war and genocide points us, are possible. The joke reminds us that in the face of the anonymity of the victim stands the proper name of the subject. In the passage to the subject, the joke also reminds us that even the closed circuit of the commemoration must be engaged in order to be traversed. In other words, the joke reminds us that genocide can be mourned.

To illustrate this, here is one of the responses to the jokes that Jokes, War and Genocide has collected and analysed:

This is horrible. It's a very sensitive topic because I am a member of the family of victims. Honestly, these kinds of jokes, although insulting, cannot hurt me because I think such jokes are part of a latent campaign to lie about or lessen the genocide.

How do you feel when you hear such a joke?
Betrayed! But at the same time I realise that the person who tells it is so stupid that there is no point to enter into an argument ... they are hopeless cases ... I am a bit taken aback by the question ... but however, this is shameful and terrible. This way of speaking should *never* be thought of by people living here. Why mock anything? I have never liked the jokes about the Holocaust or the jokes about children with special needs. This is the point of fearing God.

If anything, jokes on genocide cannot be said to be lying about or denying genocide; quite the opposite, these jokes make us confront genocide all too closely albeit through a certain distance that the joke creates.

It seems apposite to conclude with another response, this time by Šejla Šehabović, a Bosnian woman writer. Having herself participated in one of our public classrooms, she took up the invitation to work with us on the material we have collected and analysed. Particularly inspired by this previous response, this is an excerpt of the unpublished working paper she wrote in late 2012 for the working group Jokes, War and Genocide:

> There was a moment at which, having heard the responses of the audience, I felt a complete defeat ... What was so defeating in this response? What frightened me? Other respondents also expressed their desire to ban, ignore or despise the telling of jokes on genocide. The content of this response was therefore not the reason why I felt defeated. *The language* which was used in the response is for me terrifying. Because the respondent did not say: my father, brother, and uncle were killed; I suffered greatly; I am sad; I am alone; I am afraid ... He said he was a member of the family of victims. In our language, to be a member of anything means to be removed from one's personal experience and feelings. This meagre language of news reports disables any possibility of a person relating anything to another. The expressions such as the *latent campaign, point of God fearing* are learned, repeated so many times that they say nothing about the one who uses them. This does not mean that horrible and unsayable feelings of loss disappear. Quite the contrary. The inability to speak your own words about the pain, repeating phrases used in TV reports, petrified expressions, ossified language, precisely talk about the trauma that has not been talked about. Instead of the speech about pain, the man repeats Betrayal! And *never*! That is why the man despises and pronounces people hopeless. And nothing is ever hopeless.
>
> That is why I think it is highly valuable to think about that which is inappropriate. Nothing appropriate, tasteful and correct can enable a human being to use human language. In the end I would like to record what I felt when in our meeting I heard several jokes on the genocide in Srebrenica. I laughed, several times. I felt like weeping, several times. I thought one should be silent about this, several times. Then, I thought several times that these jokes should be told and retold. That some people must not enjoy this. That some people have to enjoy this. That it is a lie that we all do not enjoy the crime at least a little bit. That the truth about the crime can only be told in this way. That I have the right to feel all of this simultaneously and that at any moment I have the right to call on others for any of these feelings.

References

Agamben, G. (2007). *Profanations*. Brooklyn, NY: Zone.

Arsenijević, D., Husanović, J., & Wastell, S. (2016). A public language of grief: art, poetry and transitional justice in post-conflict Bosnia. In: V. Beronja & S. Vervaet (Eds.), *Post-Yugoslav Constellations: Archive, Memory, and Trauma in Contemporary Bosnian, Croatian, And Serbian Literature and Culture* (pp. 259–279). Berlin: De Gruyter.

Benjamin, W. (2006). On the concept of history. In: H. Eiland & M. W. Jennings (Eds.), *Walter Benjamin: Selected Writings Volume 4*. Cambridge, MA: Harvard University Press.

Brown, W. (2006). *Regulating Aversion: Tolerance in the Age of Identity and Empire*. Princeton, NJ: Princeton University Press.

Felman, S. (1992). The Return of the Voice: Claude Lanzmann's Shoah. In: S. Felman & D. Laub (Eds.), *Testimony: Crises of Witnessing in Literature, Psychoanalysis, and History* (pp. 204–283). New York: Routledge.

Freud, S. (1905c). *Jokes and Their Relation to the Unconscious. S. E., 8*. London: Hogarth.

PART III

CLINICAL PERSPECTIVES ON SOCIAL TRAUMA

Introduction to Part III

When the concept of trauma moved from surgery to psychiatry in the nineteenth century, it was about social trauma. Individual suffering from overwhelming social forces was at stake. It took a long time until the psychological nature of such suffering was acknowledged by the medical discourse strictly limited to the physiological paradigm. Two major clinical fields were discussed: railway accidents and combat trauma. Both had social implications. The huge discourse on railway accidents mirrored the new and overwhelming experience of large-scale technology beyond control, and combat trauma became all the more discussed, as technology increasingly dominated warfare, subjecting soldiers and civilians to the machinery of mass destruction. In comparison, individual trauma, especially sexual abuse, was a neglected topic (the early Freud and Ferenczi being exceptions) and came into major discussion only in the third quarter of the twentieth century.

This section of the book reflects the many ways clinicians encounter individuals suffering from hardships they experienced as a part of a social group. It opens with two contributions differing largely in the method and subject.

Horst Kächele (Berlin), a leading psychotherapy researcher and author of the influential textbook *Psychoanalytic Practice*, opens the section with the psychoanalytic case report of a thirty-two-year-old daughter of an SS officer, one of the guards of Hitler's personal refuge on the Obersalzberg. The patient suffered from depression and engaged in sadomasochistic relationships, which in analysis turned out to be the unconscious compensation for her father's Nazi involvement. Analysis helped her understand how deeply her whole life was entangled with her father's role.

From another methodological perspective, Martina Heeren and her colleagues, distinguished trauma researchers, address migration, one of the most disturbing topics recently discussed in traumatology. Research shows that refugees display high psychiatric morbidity, with increased vulnerability in asylum seekers and irregular migrants.

Looking closer at the mechanisms of trauma impact on psychopathology, research on attachment and mentalization provides important key concepts and findings. A series of studies from attachment research are presented here, starting with distinguished attachment researcher, Anna Buchheim (Innsbruck), who explains the impact of trauma on attachment, illustrated with a case report. She provides an introduction to the following large-scale studies investigating the impact of war-related experiences on students in the countries of former Yugoslavia. Subjects were still in their early childhood by the time of the war. The theory predicts that in the extent to which they had experienced or witnessed war events, they would influence the development of a less secure attachment style.

The first study, by Tatjana Stefanović Stanojević and Jasmina Nedeljković from Belgrade, compared student samples from three cities with different war impacts. Their findings, among others, show a higher *fearful* attachment pattern in Niš (where bombings had taken place), as well as a higher *preoccupied* attachment pattern, strongly exceeding the usual proportion, in Banja Luka, which was the scene of intranational war and forced migration.

A follow-up study, by Vladimir Hedrih, Marija Pejičić; and Ivana Pedović, investigated a much larger sample from all ex-Yugoslav countries. However, this study used different instruments to assess attachment styles, and—unlike the previously mentioned study—compared them to scored measures of traumatic impact. They also found differences in attachment patterns, which, however, seemed to be more related to economic and religious differences between the home countries than to exposure to war. The results of both these studies require further investigation due to their inconsistent findings, possibly owing to the fact that only self-report attachment measurements were available, whereas test assessments using the Adult Attachment Projective Picture System (AAP), as in Buchheim's contribution, would probably have been more valid.

Vedrana Berleković and Aleksandar Dimitrijević (Belgrade and Berlin) provide a closer insight into the impact of war experience on psychopathology in their study on attachment and mentalization in war veterans with and without post-traumatic stress disorder (PTSD). Still based on self-report measurements, but completing the attachment approach pursued in the previous papers by a mentalization questionnaire, this study provides a better understanding of how traumatic experience leads to PTSD. Authors found that a group of veterans suffering from PTSD displayed a much higher number of insecurely attached probands with a significantly lower capacity for mentalization than healthy veterans.

Thus, mentalization seems to be a major aspect of post-traumatic pathology, and it is necessary to further investigate the mechanisms. In their study of drug addicts in Bulgaria, Nikola Atanassov and Svetoslav Savov (Sofia) hypothesise a background of psychic trauma in childhood. The study scrutinises the factor of mentalization using Lecours' interview-based assessment instruments GEVA and MICA. Heroin-addicted patients displayed a lower quality of affect mentalization, as well as a lower level of personality organisation, than the control group. The findings demonstrate that early traumatic experiences impair mentalization capacity and therefore lead to disturbances in the development of the self.

Two microanalytic empirical studies narrow the focus even more to look at the mechanisms in which traumatic experiences influence clinical interaction. Pascal Heberlein and Andreas Hamburger (Kassel, Berlin) describe the method of scenic narrative microanalysis in conjunction with grounded theory as a rich description of the testimonial process, while Jasmin Bleimling (Berlin) adds quantitative measures of verbal and nonverbal content to the hermeneutic assessment. Results of both approaches point to necessary research on the deep level processes between the interviewer and the interviewee, as well as between the therapist and the patient, to understand the re-enactment of the social dimension of trauma in clinical practice.

CHAPTER TEN

In the shadow of the Obersalzberg: the daughter of an SS officer

Horst Kächele

A thirty-two-year-old female patient, a psychologist working at a consultation centre, had applied for psychoanalytic training two years ago and been rejected. During the following months she felt humiliated by this experience and it got even worse when a colleague of hers, whom she'd known from when she was a student, was admitted; it struck her all the more as he was a very mediocre character in her opinion. As a consequence, she developed a severe depressive symptomatology, which impaired her professional activity. When she sought psychoanalytic help, two female colleagues of our institute had already conducted a first interview (who without the patient's knowledge were in psychoanalytic training). Consent to include this patient in analysis was not given by the training committee, which felt this constellation was not a good arrangement. So the patient was referred to me. Both interviewers had described the patient as a likeable, elegant, yet distant person.

When the patient came to me the first time, I encountered a highly attractive woman, clad in black, elegant clothes, with blonde hair, silver bracelets, and rings. Her appearance was just perfect.

Her deprecatory self-presentation was well organised and professionally worked out. She was able to recount that the rejection to be accepted for psychoanalytic training was the last straw that broke the camel's back.

Everything started when she left a German city where she had "a wonderful time with her friends". She moved as her husband's professional career led them to a small town not very far from Ulm. In the city, when she was a psychology major, she had many erotic and sexually gratifying relationships with men, later including her husband. The couple had shared a flat for some years before they got married. Out of many admirers she picked him, as he was the only one with whom she could share an intense pleasure in making cynical remarks about everything. She told me that she had grown up in a small Alpine town. She was the elder child of a blonde-haired, beautiful, spoiled, and very young mother, and a blond-haired and beautiful former SS soldier who was one of Hitler's lifeguards on the Obersalzberg, his mountain retreat. Later I learned that her mother was the only child of a rich, Catholic merchant family ("the best address in town"). She started the relationship with the SS soldier against her parents' wishes at the age of sixteen, in 1944. Slowly I realised that in this Bavarian, deeply Catholic, nationalistic family it was one thing to do business with the Nazis from the Obersalzberg, but being sexually involved with them was something completely different. Alas, one might think that the sixteen-year-old blonde-haired, beautiful adolescent daughter was acting out what was best for the family's business.

Immediately it occurred to me that her beauty (which reminded me of Jean Marais in the film Orphée)—this shiny, yet stiff blackness of her outfit—would be connected to this background. However I knew that she was born in 1946—a year after the collapse of Nazi Germany. So overall there would be no simple connection. When it was all over, her father who was once characterised by the patient as a psychopath—a primitive beast who hadn't learnt anything other than killing—disappeared in the woods. He escaped all political purges and never underwent denazification, but he must have remained in contact with her mother. Later on in the analytic work, the patient started to realise that even her kind, Catholic grandfather must have been involved in the survival and political cleansing process. The patient was born eighteen months after the surrender of the Reich, the mother only just eighteen years old staying with the jobless father in Heidelberg financially supported by the grandparents.

Experiences concerning her early life were shaped by the post-war normality of bourgeois life in the small town she came from. On the first floor of a big building at the market place there was a shop, the grandparents were living on the second floor, and on the third floor was the patient's family. Two years later, in 1948, a brother was born and for reasons still unknown to her the patient was moved to the grandparents' floor. She assumes that she was a noisy infant and a naughty toddler, and that her mother was unable to adjust to the radical change of circumstances. Her former lover in fancy shiny black uniform had mutated into an unqualified office clerk and remained a great believer in his former idolised leader. He was not only dependent on financial support from his in-laws but most probably also on their agreed-upon silence concerning his former professional activity.

The patient's transfer to the grandparents became a pattern of her life. She assumes that the mother was glad to have a good reason to get rid of her, to send her away for she was a "plague". An intense jealousy of her brother derives from this experience and has also been a topic in our analytic work (Thomä & Kächele, 1992, patient Käthe X).

The grandparents reinforced the patient's firm belief that only a nice girl is a lovable girl. They continuously pointed out: "If you don't behave yourself, we'll send you back to your mother." This was actually practised from time to time, so the patient spent her early years moving between the two flats and two different atmospheres.

Nevertheless, generally life with the grandparents was much warmer than life with the over-emotionalised quarrelsome parents. Grandpa used to tell her wonderful stories, bought her all those nice clothes, and called her "my wonderful doll". Grandma nurtured the patient's prudish attitude towards her body, which is still typical in a traditional Catholic upbringing. As a child she was not allowed to take a bath without a bathing suit so that she would not have a chance to look at herself with sinful thoughts. However, she remembers the feeling of being observed while having a bath. This was the case for years. Grandpa's stories were full of angels and devils. He provided the spiritual frame for grandma's practicalities. As a child she nevertheless felt that she was taken care of and looked after: the most beautiful thing was going to Holy Mass with grandpa on a Sunday, feeling that grandma was really jealous.

The relationship between her mother and father deteriorated quickly. The man, castrated in all respects, was not able to satisfy the unfulfilled hunger of the immature mother. She criticised him a lot and was supported by her father's grim contempt and so he left his job, worked as a sales representative, and started having affairs.

Until puberty, the patient had been a rather ugly duckling. Only her grandfather's eyes beautified her. This changed rather suddenly and the patient turned into a swan, as beautiful as images of the Botticelli paintings. Her mind was still asleep and her soul was confined in God—one of her favourite daydreams was pondering whether God would find the right man for her—when her father openly involved her in his sexualised world, for instance, by taking the fourteen-year-old to a nightclub in order to try out a new type of dancing, she flatly denied its sexual significance. She managed to organise these experiences in line with her grandfather's "gold angel" type of interactions, thus denying the erotic qualities of this over-infusion of paternal attention.

At the same time, her mother started to rediscover her own uncompleted adolescent life in her blossoming adolescent daughter. Both women started to interact like sisters, both blonde and beautiful, just eighteen years apart. The patient developed a very intense sensual relationship with her mother. She helped her with the issues of dressing, combed her hair, and became a source of intimacy and confidence for the mother who used the patient's naivety to learn about the husband's infidelities.

When she was seventeen, the patient for the first time experienced a very intense, platonic relationship with a sensitive young man of her age and upbringing. For both of them it was clear that they would enter marriage untouched and sacrifice their innocence at the altar of the sacrament of marriage. This relationship was wholly in tune with her Catholic teachings and there was nothing to confess to her spiritual father; she had not even discovered masturbation at the time. Parallel to this "normal" developmental involvement, the described incestuous infringements were happening, and that continuously increased marital tensions.

Finally the father was expelled from home with the patient clearly being on the mother's side. Then the mother formally initiated the divorce. The father tried to avoid this development (as it would have had disastrous financial consequences) by seductively talking his wife into negotiations. These resulted in his wife becoming pregnant again. All this made the patient feel very isolated, as she had sided with the mother for all the past years. She also rejected her father's "uncontrolled carnal desires". Then the drama took another course: the mother found unequivocal proof that the father was cheating on her all along. After having found unequivocal proof that the father had been cheating on her all along, the mother had a spontaneous miscarriage. It was then that the patient's intense hatred for men appeared for the first time. She pronounced her father dead and rediscovered her hatred towards her mother, which had been counterbalanced by the over-involvement mentioned above. Aged eighteen, the patient left for the city to study psychology.

The change from the small town to the big city and the autonomy of being a student financially well off caused a major reorganisation of her adolescent personality. Now she wanted a real sexual relationship. Her first boyfriend was not able to adapt to the new situation. After a few failed attempts she dropped him and soon discovered that the lesson she had learned with her grandpa also worked with other men: "I'm pretty good in getting men where I want them, and I know from one look whether they want me."

Part of the change became the habit of wearing elegant black and only black clothes. "I'm a specialist in black," she said, "there are so many shades of black, so many nuances." So we discovered that the patient presenting the image of being a super attractive, seductive person was the outcome of a betrayal that had many forerunners in her life history. Alas, from that time onwards she reversed the active and passive role: from then on she would never be in a passive situation again. When this connection had been cleared up, we understood her depressive mood changes as a loss of control and identified her typical defensive ways to counteract depression by initiating seductive relationships with men: whenever she felt lonely, deserted by her very successful engineer—who was sent around the world—some of her former friends would show up eager to console her.

After one year, the patient felt balanced again and was about to leave treatment. By pointing out to her that she had used me like all the other men, to fill in a gap, to get back control, but had avoided investigating the reason for her having become such a black angel, she was able to redefine the goals of the treatment and continued with the analysis.

The Jew

While the patient was a student in the city, the still juvenile-looking forty-year-old mother regularly came to spend time with her daughter during carnival. On one of these festivities, the two of them met a Jewish-looking businessman. The patient vividly remembers that she was convinced that he was a Jew—which turned out to be a false assumption later on—and this conviction was connected with a desire to undo an injustice in which her father had been involved in some undetermined yet cruel way. Out of this acquaintance developed a very intensive sadomasochistic relationship (besides all her other one-night stands), which was still alive in a way when the patient came for treatment. To please this "Jew", as she continued to call him, the man who, in fact, was of Middle Eastern origin, she started to buy extravagant, black lingerie, as he seemed to appreciate these on her very pale skin. The relationship was unilateral insofar as she never knew when he would be around in Munich. As soon as he phoned her she would drop everything else to spend a weekend with him. At first, sexual experiences were very ecstatic for her and they satisfied something "deep inside of me" as the patient was able to formulate late in treatment. When she finally realised that there was no Holocaust victim in her "Jewish lover's" family she felt deeply disappointed. However it took a while before this influenced their relationship. Finally his praising of the German philosemitism as something very profitable for his business helped her to slowly disentangle herself. At the time when the analytic treatment began, the patient was not yet able to clearly disentangle herself from this man. When he got in touch with her from time to time he still got her to have sexual intercourse though the ecstatic qualities had been gone for a long time. There was something coercive in this relationship.

When the patient first talked about this strange relationship in the seventh session, she remembered a recurring dream she'd had for first time when her parents got divorced:

> The father returns to the family, I am pushing him out again, I am astonished how little resistance he displays but then he is back again.

A few sessions later, she reported another dream that underscores her desperate battle against intrusion:

> A doctor wants to anesthetise me for surgery. I do not know the reason for the surgery. Whatever the physician tries, I remain awake and keep telling the doctor that I am not yet asleep.

The patient was surprised because she had never had a problem when anaesthesia was necessary. On the contrary, she liked the very thought of a deep and dreamless sleep. However, she does not like her lovers to stay overnight, and so she has to throw them out. The transferential aspect of the dream needs no further comment besides mentioning that many years later the patient was able to tell me that from the very first moment she had entered my room and had seen me, she had decided that she would not fall in love with me.

What is the role of the "Jew" in the patient's unconscious relationship role model? I think the patient herself pointed out the functional value: to undo something very important. Politically, the patient had never done more than read the weekly and moderately liberal magazine Spiegel and certainly had never made any effort to explore her father's past. She pronounced him dead and she had never seen him again until we were able to work on the topic. Instead of the dead father she had engaged with a living victim.

For the first time we encountered the full psychological significance of the repressed past of her father during the third year of the analysis. Up to then, we had done a lot of work mainly referring to the basic problems of her self-esteem, of her not being in control of space and objects, and therefore acting defensively by herself being cool, distant, and over-controlling.

At that time, I told the patient that I would be abroad for ten weeks in the summer. For some countertransferential reason I told her directly that I would go to the University of Chile in order to teach there. I suppose I wanted to excuse myself for being away for so long by pointing out my scientific reputation. After this announcement, the patient plunged into a deep, long silence. After a while she was back, back into her most delicate, sharp voice with which she had come to treatment: "So, you too!" No longer a question just a statement. I didn't understand at all. All I understood was that she felt deeply betrayed. Even though I tried to communicate this affect and connecting it to the fact that this betrayal also entailed the feeling of being deserted for a long time, the patient left ten minutes early commenting: "I'd rather cry on my own."

In the next session she was able to query the reasons why I was going there. She made clear that she was convinced that I was a right-wing radical supporting Pinochet's dictatorship. It turned out that her husband had lost the youthful anti-establishment attitude in the course of the years and mutated into a solid bourgeois conservative; his father had been a Nazi too. "I was hoping I'd never meet this kind of people again." I pointed out that up to now since the analysis had started she had been very successful in avoiding meeting "this kind of people". The great shock that was caused by my information must be because these kinds of people still inhabit her mind without her acknowledging it. The session ended with her discovery that Salvador Allende was a psychiatrist and her assumption that probably there are some, just a few, non-rightwing people, too.

It took another two years before we got the next chance to tackle the shadows of her past—it was embedded in our work on her resistance against a positive-erotic transference towards the analyst—a very conscious, well-developed resistance. At the end of the fourth year we found out that she maintained a representational world where men are either very soft, maternal, reliable like her grandfather with no open erotic qualities allowed, or where men are brutal, sexual, beasts, criminals. For the first time she accepted the idea that her father should have been arrested for his crimes. I asked what kind of crimes.

[P is used for Patient; A for Analyst]

P: The crimes he must have committed to get the job on the Obersalzberg; I mean, there has certainly been gratification for being very effective in the concentration camps.

She then remembered a childhood memory when she had spattered him with holy water having in mind that he would go to hell like a devil as she had learned from her religious teachings that this is the way you identify devils.

A: Who told you that he is likely to be a devil?
P: Grandma was telling it all the time.

It turned out that the patient from an early age had been imbued with the idea that there was something very bad about her father; the grandparents had related it to his poor social behaviour and his womanising habits, but she had always felt that there was more to it.

The patient was splitting the representational world into good and bad guys with her father belonging to the category of the bad. Six months later, she reported a dream:

> I'm entering my father's room. He is half asleep in his bed. There is a shower in the room. I wonder whether I should undress or whether I can keep my nightie on as the Thai women do. I keep the nightie on and I am soaping myself under the shower. I have a clear sensation of sexual pleasure in the dream.

The associative work concerning the dream focused on her activity regulating closeness and distance. She was clearly afraid that if she were to get involved with the analyst something dirty about him would appear or that she would lose the regulatory power in that particular relationship.

The next dream dealt with two lovers chasing her. One is Eli the "Jew"; the other one is her husband who follows her to Israel. Her first association was directed at her husband: he always being the wrong person at the wrong time and place. While working on the transferential implications of the dream, she was reminded of a terrible dream—a nightmare that she had dreamt during her summer holidays in her small home town.

> I am standing on the balcony of our house and, like in a film, I observe a great number of naked, dirty people, ready for deportation. Many people are on their balconies, as it is at Corpus Christi or any ecclesiastic festivity, but no one is doing anything about it. I am also doing nothing, but I feel very bad about it.

In her association, the patient soon identified the people as Jews. She herself also felt like someone who is not looked after in an adequate way. She then proceeded to talk about her total abstinence from politics, which she rationalised as the only way to cope with helplessness.

We were able to parallel her retreat from personal engagement into her syndrome of being the active deserter with her retreat from politically engaged activity. In this context, the patient was able to approach the issue of whether she should inform herself in more detail what had happened in the concentration camps. She remembered from her adolescence in the small town that she once found a weapon with a swastika on it. The father proudly exclaimed that he had used it to kill Russians. During the following sessions, the patient's work on these issues continued. She inquired of her mother how the father had survived the times immediately following the end of the war. Her mother's family provided a false identity card in order to protect and hide her involvement in it. Her mother followed her husband to Heidelberg against the will of the family. There quite a few of the old guards had found ways to survive in the neighbourhood of the American army. My line of interpretation caused confusion in the patient: herself being a victim of the domestic disruptions she identified with the victims and was well advised to hide her true feelings. The patient then cried a lot and reported another dream:

> Yesterday I observed how cattle were transported to the butcher. The guilelessness of the animals—not anticipating what was waiting for them—made me cry even in the dream.

This was the feeling she also connected to the dream with the Jews.

A: It is your own guilelessness, your not knowing what your father and your mother were doing to you that made you so vulnerable. So you had to learn to avoid looking too closely in order not to be confronted with another example of them maltreating you and your feelings.

P: It is true, I knew that he was in Dachau, nothing more, and I have never asked. I have never even been to Dachau.

A: So by not knowing you tried to protect yourself; at the same time you had to protect yourself from thoughts and surmises, which led to your very self-estranged manner.

The patient then reported that she had attended a physician in her little town and stated: "Didn't Dr. Mengele come from Günzburg? So how can I know that this doctor didn't experiment on me?" My interpretation connected the acute paranoid feeling with the acute transference issue, that I would experiment forcing her to face the political circumstances of her biography. Our experiment was about finding out whether it would be possible to convince the patient that her negative experiences with close relationships do not necessarily have to continue.

P: I am reminded of the story of the little prince and the fox. The little prince has tamed the fox but what will happen when they depart? Is the little prince not going to suffer? Wouldn't it be better if the prince hadn't become involved with the fox?

[I joined in and continued the story:]

A: The fox said to the little prince: the colour of the wheat will remind me of you. If you need me again you will remember me and you may return.

Parallel to working through her suppressed anxieties concerning her father's criminal involvement in the Nazi regime, the patient changed in different ways that even her colleagues in the consultation centre noticed. She became more open and relaxed, was less controlled and to her own great surprise she became pregnant. She was surprised, as she had never taken great care of birth control. She had been convinced that she would not conceive. During her pregnancy, she visited her father who had settled down with another woman. He was suffering from cancer and it was certain that he would not live much longer. At least she found out that he was now taking care of his stepdaughter and she also found out that I too was a caring father of three daughters.

After the delivery of her baby—a daughter—the patient insisted on reducing the frequency of sessions and also insisted on sitting face to face. Again she had to be the one in control in order to find out whether I was a reliable person.

It was obvious. The patient was moving into a strong positive transference, which she had to keep under control. She initiated the idea of terminating the treatment, as the idea of separating was calming and disturbing at the same time. A series of dreams followed. In the dreams, she was always second to some other woman to me. After having worked through these topics for a reasonable amount of time, the patient was ready to enter the phase of termination.

Both of us were surprised about the severity of depression that overwhelmed the patient. She was possessed by the idea of losing me again, of losing her favourite position due to her baby, which would get all the attention she had wanted for herself. One more time the patient recapitulated the deep loss she had suffered at the age of two when her brother was born. We finally arranged an agreement: she might continue on a "feeding on demand basis"—a somewhat less analytical technique, which in my experience works with patients traumatised by repeated separations.

The treatment ended after six years (512 sessions). One year later she consulted me again as she was having repetitive dreams. She dreamed she was in the gas chambers hearing the gas pouring into the room. She woke up and found herself crying endlessly. My immediate reaction to these very oppressive dreams was to ask whether her father had died. Indeed he had and the patient had noticed that she didn't want to go to his funeral after she had heard about his death. Instead, these dreams menaced her. It took another six months of again working through the kind of experiences the father might have had. I assumed that these dreams pointed out what she was afraid to find out about him now that he was dead. In this phase of treatment I encouraged her (accompanied by a good friend) to visit the concentration camp memorial at Dachau to actively inquire about her father's career, which she finally did. For the first time in her life her inquiry at the Berlin Document Center provided her with an accurate account of the kind of activities her father was involved in at Dachau. However, he had not been in Auschwitz, but due to his physical properties he was delegated to the Obersalzberg in 1940.

Without belittling his deeds, the nightmare of non-remembering came to an end. She finally became sad about being the daughter of such a father who had never shown any signs of remorse. Her mother was disgusted with her development and so the patient decided to reduce contact with her.

During all this battle of remembering the past, the patient gave up her habit of wearing those black festive garments. To me this way of expressing her enmeshment with a family world full of guilt and disruption was based on a private unconscious identification composed of being in mourning for the loss of her family. Her strong hysterical involvement with both parents made her receptive for the notions of death prevailing in the Nazi world: *Der Tod ist ein Meister aus Deutschland* (Death is a master from Germany).

Reference

Thomä, H., & Kächele, H. (1992). *Psychoanalytic Practice. Vol. 2: Clinical Studies*. Berlin: Springer.

CHAPTER ELEVEN

Psychopathology and resident status—comparing asylum seekers, refugees, irregular migrants, labour migrants, and residents*

Martina Heeren, Lutz Wittmann, Ulrike Ehlert, Ulrich Schnyder, Thomas Maier, and Julia Müller

Introduction

Generally speaking, the term "migrant" applies to all people who have left their home country either due to "push" factors in the country of origin (i.e., asylum seekers and refugees; International Organization of Migration, 2007) or due to "pull" factors of the immigration country (i.e., economic incentives, as in the case of labour migrants). Irregular migrants may be found in both groups. As Carta, Bernal, Hardoy, and Haro-Abad (2005) state, it is not possible to consider migrants as one homogeneous group, as conditions of migration differ widely.

With respect to migrants' mental health, high rates of psychiatric morbidity and mental health problems have been consistently reported. Asylum seekers and refugees in particular were found to suffer from symptoms of post-traumatic stress, depression, and anxiety (e.g., Heckmann & Schnapper, 2003; Laban, Gernaat, Komproe, & De Jong, 2007; Ryan, Dooley, & Benson, 2008). Several studies report associations of psychopathology not only with traumatic experiences prior to migration but also with the living situation in exile (Laban, Gernaat, Komproe, Van der Tweel, & De Jong, 2005; Porter & Haslam, 2005; Silove et al., 1997). Less is known about the mental health of labour migrants and irregular migrants. Labour migrants appear to suffer less depression and anxiety compared to refugees (Lindert, von Ehrenstein, Priebe, Mielck, & Brähler, 2009), but frequently the duration of stay in the immigrant nation, which may contribute to variations in symptoms, was not considered in these studies. Regarding irregular migrants, a lack of knowledge about their mental health has been reported (Sullivan & Rehm, 2005).

*This chapter is a shortened version of an article in *Comprehensive Psychiatry*, 2014, 55(4): 818–825.

Whereas isolated comparisons of different migrant groups have been conducted, these results cannot be merged into an overall picture of migrant mental health. Comparisons between different studies are hindered by methodological differences as well as inequalities in socio-political and economical characteristics of immigrant nations (Lindert, von Ehrenstein, Priebe, Mielck, & Brähler, 2009; Sullivan & Rehm, 2005). There is a lack of studies comparing the mental health of different groups of migrants to that of residents and identifying different migrant conditions specifically associated with mental health problems. Moreover, existing studies are frequently limited by methodological shortcomings such as disregard of length of stay in the immigrant nation or failure to consider differential exposure to violence and other traumatic events in the nation of origin (Lindert, von Ehrenstein, Priebe, Mielck, & Brähler, 2009).

Aims of the study

This study aimed to describe, compare, and predict mental health outcomes in four different migrant groups and one group of residents in Switzerland. For the assessment of mental health, a multifaceted approach considering general as well as trauma-specific markers of psychopathology was chosen. In order to overcome shortcomings of previous studies, variables such as length of stay in the receiving country or level of integration, trauma history, and potentially confounding variables such as social desirability were considered.

Material and methods

Participants and procedure

Five groups of subjects residing in the Swiss canton of Zurich were recruited for assessment: (1) asylum seekers (AS; n = 65) still waiting for their claim to be processed and living in asylum centres at the time of assessment; (2) refugees (RE; n = 34) whose claims for asylum had been accepted and who now held permanent resident visas; (3) irregular migrants (IM; n = 21) having entered Switzerland without visas and living without permission to remain at the time of assessment. Former asylum seekers whose claims had been rejected and who were now living without permission to remain were excluded from this sample, as were irregular migrants working as dancers or sex workers, due to possible trafficking and hence involuntary immigration; (4) labour migrants (LM; n = 26) having come to Switzerland for work with pre-issued visas. In order to enable certain comparability with the other samples, German native speakers were excluded from this sample, as were subjects holding academic positions; and (5) Swiss residents (SR; n = 56) without a migrant history, that is, with at least third-generation residency in Switzerland.

AS were randomly drawn from the national register of adult asylum seekers in Switzerland and approached by asylum centre staff with the request to participate in our study. The participation rate was 67.7%. RE were recruited with the help of various refugee organisations in Switzerland, with a response rate of 68.0%. IM were approached during a two-week occupation of a church in Zurich where irregular migrants and their supporters were claiming better treatment for non-visa holders. The participation rate in IM was 77.8%. LM and SR were recruited by migrant organisations and by direct personal recruitment in public, with a response rate of 70.3% and 74.7%, respectively. Assessments took place between August 2008 and April 2009. The study protocol was approved by the ethics committee of the canton of Zurich. All participants completed a self-rating questionnaire of about forty minutes in length. Using established translation procedures including back-translation (Bontempo, 1993), questionnaires were translated into eleven of the languages most frequently spoken by migrants in Switzerland. Provided languages were Albanian (n = 11), Arabic (n = 29), Bosnian/Serbian/Croatian (n = 9), English (n = 10), Farsi (n = 18), French (n = 8), Kurdish (n = 13), Russian (n = 1), Tamil (n = 4), Turkish (n = 6), Spanish (n = 9), and German (n = 82). Two subjects spoke neither German nor any of the provided languages; that is, Chinese (n = 1) and Tibetan (n = 1). For these subjects, interpreters translated the questionnaire items into their native languages onsite.

AS were visited at asylum homes and IM at the occupied church. Instructions for these subjects were issued by a licensed clinical psychologist. Where necessary, interpreters assisted during the assessment (61.5% for AS and 23.8% for IM). RE, LM, and SR were asked to fill in the questionnaires at home and return them by mail. Subjects did not receive any financial compensation for their participation.

Instruments

The demographic variables assessed included age, gender, marital status, level of education, and region of origin. Potentially traumatic experiences pre-migration (23 items) were assessed using the first sections of the Harvard Trauma Questionnaire (HTQ) (Mollica et al., 1991) and the Post-traumatic Diagnostic Scale (PDS) (Foa, 1995). Both instruments are widely used in research with refugees (e.g., Momartin, Silove, Manicavasagar, & Steel, 2004; Silove et al., 2007). We used both trauma lists in order to assess the widest possible range of traumatic experiences. To avoid repetition, we removed the seven overlapping items from the HTQ. Only traumatic events experienced or witnessed by the respondents themselves were considered for analysis.

Section III of the PDS (Foa, 1995) was used to measure symptom severity of post-traumatic stress disorder (PTSD). The seventeen items in this section assess post-traumatic stress symptoms experienced in the month prior to assessment. Items are rated on a four-point scale (0–3), and sum scores range from zero to fifty-one. A probable diagnosis of PTSD was established using an algorithm (Foa, 1995) that requires at least one symptom of re-experiencing, three of avoidance, and two of hyperarousal. The PDS has demonstrated good psychometric properties (Foa, Cashman, Jaycox, & Perry, 1997).

The Hopkins Symptom Checklist-25 (HSCL-25) (Mollica et al., 1991) was used to measure symptoms of anxiety and depression. This checklist was developed for use in refugee populations. It comprises ten anxiety and fifteen depression items scored on a four-point scale. Mean scores range from zero to four. It is common to use a cut-off score of 1.75 for both scales as an indication of symptoms equivalent to an anxiety or depressive disorder. The instrument has been shown to have good psychometric properties (Mueller, Postert, Beyer, Furniss, & Achtergarde, 2009).

An integration index was calculated specifically for this study. Originally, a list of fifteen items assessing different aspects of the post-migration living situation had been generated.

Items were based on Heckmann and Schnapper's (2003) integration concept, which comprises structural, cultural, interactive, and identificational integration of migrants. In order to select the most significant post-migration factors out of this original list, we included items with the highest item-total correlation, yielding a final list of six items with an internal consistency of $\alpha = 0.72$. These six items cover the areas of work satisfaction, social contacts outside the family, social contacts with Swiss citizens, leisure activities, news consumption, and German proficiency. Individuals with better versus poorer current integration outcome were differentiated by a median split on the resulting scale.

To assess social desirability of responses, we used the Marlowe-Crowne Social Desirability Scale Short Form X1 (Fischer & Fick, 1993). Its seven items yield a sum score ranging from one to seven points. In analogy to the original extensive version of this instrument, we defined a cut-off score of four points.

Data analysis

Data was analysed using IBM SPSS Version 19.0. Kolmogorov-Smirnov tests were used to analyse whether the interval data was normally distributed. Except for the number of traumatic event types, none of the data was normally distributed. Chi-square and Fisher's exact tests were calculated for between-group comparisons for nominal data. Kruskal-Wallis H-Tests with post-hoc Mann-Whitney U-tests were conducted for non-parametric group comparisons, and ANOVAs with post-hoc paired samples t-tests for parametric comparisons (number of traumatic event types). Associations between mental health outcomes and pre- and post-migration factors were tested by Chi-square (dichotomous variables) and Spearman coefficients (rank data).

Three stepwise logistic regression analyses were used to test for associations between predictor variables and mental health outcomes (probable diagnosis of PTSD, clinically relevant symptoms of depression, and anxiety). After testing for bivariate associations of mental health outcomes with all assessed socio-demographic, pre- and post-migration variables, only factors showing significant associations with at least one mental health outcome were included in the regression models. Accordingly, social desirability, number of traumatic event types, integration, and residence status were entered in this order into four different steps of the regression models.

Residential status was entered as an indicator contrast into the regression analyses. Accordingly, the effect of each of the four categories referring to migrants was compared to the effect of the Swiss residency category.

With respect to several measures, missing values were detected. Overall missing rates were 6% for PTSD, 1.9% for depression, and 1.5% for anxiety. For post-migratory indexing and social desirability, missing rates were 2% and 3%, respectively. The twelve missing values for PTSD were distributed evenly across subsamples. Nine of these twelve missing values resulted from participants not completing any of the PDS section III items. Rather than imputing PTSD values based on information from other variables, participants with missing values were excluded per analysis. As the missing data for most variables was low, and missing PTSD values were distributed evenly across subsamples, we do not expect strongly biased results due to missing data.

Results

Demographic characteristics

Demographic variables are summarised in Figure 1. Fifty-two per cent of all participants were female, without between-group differences. About half of the participants were married, with

	Groups						
Characteristic	AS (n = 65)	RE (n = 34)	IM (n = 21)	LM (n = 26)	SR (n = 56)	Overall group comparisons	Significant between group differences
Female gender, n (%)	27 (41.5)	22 (64.7)	10 (47.6)	15 (57.7)	31 (55.4)	ns	
Missing values	0	0	0	0	0		
Age in years, M (SD)	33.7 (9.8)	34.8 (10.3)	37.8 (10.2)	39.0 (13.5)	39.4 (13.8)	ns	
Missing values	1	0	0	0	0		
Married, n (%)	27 (41.5)	25 (73.5)	8 (38.1)	15 (57.7)	26 (46.4)	X^2= 11.12, p = .025	AS vs. RE**
Missing values	1	0	0	0	0		RE vs. IM/SR*
Employed, n (%)	11 (16.9)	18 (52.9)	11 (52.4)	16 (61.5)	53 (94.6)	X^2= 74.91, p < .001	AS vs. RE/IM/LM/SR***
Missing values	0	1	1	0	0		RE/IM/LM vs. SR***
Education (years), M (SD)	9.8 (4.3)	10.5 (5.3)	10.4 (5.5)	12.2 (4.1)	11.9 (2.3)	ns	
Missing values	2	1	0	1	0		
Number of children, M (SD)	1.2 (1.5)	1.4 (1.4)	.95 (1.5)	1.1 (1.5)	1.0 (1.3)	ns	
Missing values	0	0	0	0	0		
Region of origin, n (%)						X^2= 75.67, p < .000	
Missing values	0	0	0	0	0		
Asia	42 (64.6)	24 (70.6)	3 (14.3)	7 (26.9)	0 (0.0)		AS/RE vs. IM/LM/SR**
Europe	9 (13.8)	3 (8.8)	0 (0.0)	11 (42.3)	0 (0.0)		AS/RE vs. LM***
							IM vs. LM*
Africa	14 (21.5)	6 (17.6)	8 (38.1)	3 (11.5)	0 (0.0)		
South America	0 (0.0)	1 (2.9)	10 (47.6)	4 (15.4)	0 (0.0)		AS/RE/SR vs. IM**
							IM vs. LM***
Switzerland	0 (0.0)	0 (0.0)	0 (0.0)	0 (0.0)	56 (100.0)		AS/RE/IM/LM vs. SR***
Time in Switzerland (years), M (SD)	3.7 (3.1)	8.2 (5.3)	5.0 (3.3)	12.3 (8.1)	39.4 (13.8)	H = 38.53, p < .000	AS vs. RE***
Missing values	1	0	0	0	0		RE vs. IM*
							AS/IM vs. LM***
Family members in Switzerland, n (%)	33 (50.8)	21 (61.8)	7 (33.3)	18 (69.2)	56 (100.0)	ns	
Missing values	0	0	0	0	0		
High integration index, n (%)	18 (28.1)	20 (60.6)	7 (33.3)	22 (88.0)	55 (98.2)	x^2 = 76.31, p < .000	AS vs. RE***
Missing values	1	1	0	1	0		AS/IM vs. LM***
							RE vs. IM/LM*
High social desirability, n (%)	34 (52.3)	15 (54.5)	10 (52.4)	12 (46.2)	13 (24.1)	x^2 = 12.81, p < .05	AS/RE/IM/LM vs. SR*
Missing values	5	1	0	0	0		
							AS vs. IM/LM/SR***
Traumatic event types, M (SD)	8.4 (5.5)	6.3 (6.2)	2.6 (4.2)	3.1 (3.0)	2.0 (2.2)	F = 14.77, p < .000	RE vs. LM*
Missing values	0	0	0	0	0		RE vs. SR**

Figure 1. Demographic characteristics and psychosocial variables.
Notes: AS = asylum seekers; RE = refugees; IM = irregular migrants; LM = labour migrants; SR = Swiss residents; *p < 0.05; **p < 0.01, ***p < 0.001.

more RE being married than AS, IM and SR. Fewer AS were employed than all other groups and SR were more likely to be employed. RE, IM and LM did not differ in employment status. The mean length of education was 10.8 years, without significant between-group differences. More AS and RE originated from Asia than did the other groups, more IM from South America, and more LM from Europe. Among migrants, length of stay in Switzerland ranged from less than one year to thirty-six years. AS and IM had shorter residency than RE and LM. More than half (54.1%) of the non-residents had family members living in Switzerland, without significant differences between samples.

Integration and social desirability

Fewer AS and IM were indexed as having good integration outcomes as compared to RE and LM (Table 1). Fewer RE were categorised as having good integration outcomes as compared to the LM subgroup, which, in turn, did not differ significantly from SR.

Rates of high social desirability for the migrant groups ranged from 46.2% to 54.5% without significant differences. With 24.1%, Swiss residents showed significantly less frequent high social desirability as compared to all migrant groups.

Traumatic event types

The numbers of traumatic event types are reported in Figure 1. With a mean of 8.4 ($SD = 5.5$) event types, AS reported the highest number of lifetime potentially traumatic event types. The difference between numbers of traumatic events for RE and AS approached significance ($t = 1.83$, $df = 97$, $p = 0.070$). AS reported more traumatic event types than IM, LM, and SR. RE reported significantly more event types than LM and SR. IM, LM, and SR did not differ in the number of reported traumatic event types.

Mental health

Findings on mental health are presented in Figure 2. AS showed a much higher rate of probable PTSD diagnoses as compared to IM, LM, and SR. RE also had more probable PTSD diagnoses as compared to IM and SR, but not compared to LM. Duration of stay did not correlate with the total symptom score of the PDS for any of the samples.

AS reported a significantly higher frequency of clinically relevant symptoms of depression than all other samples. Rates did not differ between RE and IM. These samples had higher rates than LM and SR. LM and SR did not differ regarding depression. No associations were found with duration of stay for any of the samples.

Rates of clinically relevant anxiety were highest for AS and IM, without significant differences between the two samples. Rates for AS were higher than for RE. AS, RE, and IM reported more clinically relevant anxiety than LM and SR. LM and SR did not differ in this respect. Only for RE was a longer duration of stay associated with higher levels of anxiety ($r = 0.40$, $p = 0.021$).

	Groups						
Symptomatology	AS (n = 65)	RE (n = 34)	IM (n = 21)	LM (n = 26)	SR (n = 56)	Overall group comparisons	Significant between group differences
Probable diagnosis of PTSD, n (%)[a]	34 (54.0)	12 (41.4)	1 (5.6)	4 (17.4)	4 (7.5)	$x^2 = 38.9$, $p < .001$	AS vs. IM/SR***
Missing values	2	2	2	3	3		AS vs. LM**
							RE vs. IM**
							RE vs. SR***
Clinically relevant depression, n (%)[b]	55 (84.6)	14 (42.4)	10 (47.6)	4 (17.4)	6 (10.7)	$x^2 = 75.1$, $p < .001$	AS vs. RE/IM/LM/SR***
Missing values	0	1	0	3	0		RE/IM vs. LM*
							RE/IM vs. SR**
Clinically relevant anxiety, n (%)[b]	41 (63.1)	13 (39.4)	10 (47.6)	3 (12.5)	8 (14.3)	$x^2 = 38.3$, $p < .001$	AS vs. RE*
Missing values	0	1	0	2	0		AS vs. LM/SR***
							RE vs. LM*
							RE vs. SR**
							IM vs. LM/SR**

Figure 2. Mental health outcomes.
Notes: AS = asylum seekers; RE = refugees; IM = irregular migrants; LM = labour migrants; SR = Swiss residents; PTSD = post-traumatic stress disorder; [a]assessed using the Post-traumatic Diagnostic Scale; [b]assessed using the Hopkins Symptom Checklist-25; *$p < 0.05$; **$p < 0.01$, ***$p < 0.001$.

Identification of factors associated with mental health outcomes

Of all socio-demographic, pre- and post-migration factors assessed, only social desirability ($X^2 = 4.51$, df = 1, $p = 0.034$ for depressive symptoms), integration ($X^2 = 14.63$, df = 1, $p = 0.000$ for PTSD; $X^2 = 31.46$, df = 1, $p = 0.000$ for depressive symptoms; and $X^2 = 16.53$, df = 1, $p = 0.000$ for anxiety), potentially traumatic events ($X^2 = 53.86$, df = 16, $p = 0.000$ for PTSD; $X^2 = 55.74$, df = 16, $p = 0.000$ for depressive symptoms; and $X^2 = 45.92$, df = 16, $p = 0.000$ for anxiety) and resident status ($X^2 = 38.92$, df = 4, $p = 0.000$ for PTSD; $X^2 = 75.06$, df = 4, $p = 0.000$ for depressive symptoms; and $X^2 = 38.31$, df = 4, $p = 0.000$ for anxiety) were associated with mental health outcome. These were entered into three stepwise logistic regression analyses to test for associations with probable diagnoses of PTSD and clinically relevant symptoms of depression and anxiety (Figure 3).

Social desirability did not contribute significantly to caseness for any of the three outcome criteria. The number of traumatic event types experienced predicted logistic odds for all three outcomes. Better versus poorer integration outcomes did not contribute additionally to caseness of any outcomes. In comparison to SR as indicator sample, AS and RE membership contributed to probable PTSD. AS, IM, and RE membership contributed to clinically relevant symptoms of depression; and AS, IM, and RE membership to clinically relevant anxiety. Logistic likelihood was explained at 38.9% for probable PTSD, meaning that whether a participant reported PTSD symptoms or not could be explained to 38.9% by the assessed pre- and post-migratory factors. Logistic likelihood was explained at 50.2% for clinically relevant symptoms of depression and

	Probable PTSD[a] (N = 190)				Clinically relevant depression[b] (N = 198)				Clinically relevant anxiety[b] (N = 199)			
Steps and variables	OR	95% CI	Wald	Nagelkerke R^2	OR	95% CI	Wald	Nagelkerke R^2	OR	95% CI	Wald	Nagelkerke R^2
Step 1:				.011				.034				.001
Social desirability (high)	.95	.43–2.08	.02		1.12	.52–2.42	.08		.66	.32–1.35	1.32	
Step 2:				.253				.291				.189
Traumatic event types (number)	1.15*	1.03–1.28	6.46		1.16*	1.03–1.30	6.00		1.14*	1.03–1.26	6.23	
Step 3:				.271				.371				.199
Integration index (high)	.89	.36–2.23	.06		.84	.34–2.10	.14		.87	.38–2.02	.10	
Step 4:				.389				.502				.285
Group membership												
AS	10.88**	2.34–50.57	9.27		25.22***	6.20–102.71	20.30		6.48**	1.88–22.41	8.72	
RE	7.62**	1.74–33.37	7.27		4.47*	1.26–19.85	5.37		3.39*	1.05–10.93	4.17	
IM	.71	.06–8.37	.08		6.92**	1.68–28.57	7.15		5.62**	1.50–21.06	6.57	
LM	3.08	.61–15.18	1.87		1.70	.40–7.17	.52		.90	.21–3.89	.02	

Figure 3. Logistic regression analysis for mental health outcomes.
Notes: AS = asylum seekers; RE = refugees; IM = irregular migrants; LM = labour migrants; PTSD = post-traumatic stress disorder; OR = odds ratio; CI = confidence interval; [a]assessed using the Post-traumatic Diagnostic Scale; [b]assessed using the Hopkins Symptom Checklist-25; $^{*}p<0.05$; $^{**}p<0.01$, $^{***}p<0.001$.

at 31.3% for clinically relevant anxiety. Post-hoc Hosmer-Lemeshow Chi-square test for the final warranty of the three models yielded all models with sufficient predictive value ($X^2 = 6.78$, df = 7, p = 0.453 for PTSD; $X^2 = 10.55$, df = 8, p = 0.228 for depressive symptoms; and $X^2 = 8.16$, df = 7, p = 0.318 for anxiety).

Discussion

The results of this study clearly indicate alarmingly high psychiatric morbidity in asylum seekers, refugees, and irregular migrants, with resident status strongly influencing mental health outcomes.

A crucial question regarding the validity of the presented results refers to the representativeness of the recruited subsamples. Owing to the random sampling method applied for the sample of asylum seekers, this group can be considered as representative of the population of adult asylum seekers in Switzerland during the assessment period. For the other four samples, random sampling was found to be impracticable due to hindered accessibility of migrants under terminable conditions owing to the study's concept as a pilot study for a larger-scaled prospective assessment.

Justified concerns can be raised around selection bias in non-probability sampling (Sulaiman-Hill & Thompson, 2011). In our study, certain questions on representativeness remain unresolved, for example whether, by contacting refugees via refugee organisations, mentally impaired refugees were less accessible to recruitment than healthy ones; or whether irregular migrants participating in the occupation of a church may be more affected by psychopathology than those wishing to remain inconspicuous, thus causing higher prevalence rates of mental disorders.

Regrettably, there is no Swiss prevalence data on the mental health of these groups to which we could have compared our results. As for the group of Swiss residents, our sample is comparable to the Swiss population in the year of assessment regarding statistics on gender distribution, marriage, employment rate, and number of children (Swiss Federal Statistical Office, 2009), and comparable on mental health outcomes of Swiss prevalence studies on PTSD, anxiety, and depression (Buddeberg-Fischer, Stamm, Buddeberg, & Klaghofer, 2009). For the Swiss residents, sample representativeness may therefore be assumed.

Asylum seekers and irregular migrants reported poorer integration outcomes than did refugees and labour migrants. This finding is well in line with our expectations. Social isolation, poor German language proficiency, and lack of leisure activities may well be the result of unemployment, financial strains, and the marginalised position in society (restricted access to supportive institutions) with which asylum seekers and irregular migrants are usually confronted. With respect to social desirability, all migrant groups showed more desirable response tendencies than did the resident group. There is a lack of studies on social desirability in migrants, but clinical observations confirm the finding that migrant patients tend to react to their perceived pressure to adjust to local culture and customs with elevated social desirability.

Further limitations need to be considered for any interpretation of the results. Subsamples differed in size and were rather small. For this reason, we refrained from Bonferroni corrections. Study results are also limited by the cross-sectional design, which does not allow for causal implications of results, as well as by the exclusive use of self-report measures. Lastly, the validity of the created integration index has not previously been assessed.

Notwithstanding these limitations, the present study found strongly increased psychiatric morbidity in asylum seekers, refugees, and irregular migrants as compared to labour migrants and residents. This difference was consistent across trauma-specific as well as trauma-nonspecific symptoms. However, groups with high symptom levels showed specific patterns. Whereas asylum seekers showed high overall psychiatric morbidity, refugees showed increased symptoms of PTSD and depression, but not anxiety. And irregular migrants showed increased symptoms of depression and anxiety, but not PTSD.

Increased psychiatric morbidity in asylum seekers has been confirmed in previous studies (Laban, Gernaat, Komproe, Schreuders, & De Jong, 2004; Silove, Sinnerbrink, Field, Manicavasagar, & Steel, 1997). The finding that refugees did not show elevated incidences of clinically relevant levels of anxiety fits well with the previously noted decline in psychopathological symptoms in asylum seekers after they have been accepted as refugees (Silove et al., 2007). However, symptoms of PTSD were not lower in accepted refugees than in asylum seekers. This finding differs from Gerritsen (2006) who reported fewer PTSD symptoms in refugees than in asylum seekers. As in this study refugees reported significantly fewer traumatic events than asylum seekers, we did not consider these results contradictory to our finding. Both studies indicate a persistence of PTSD symptoms over time if left untreated, independently of improved living conditions after having been granted permanent residency. This contrasts trauma-related symptoms from other psychopathological symptoms such as depression and anxiety, which seem to decrease clearly with a change to a secure visa status.

The low rates of post-traumatic stress in irregular migrants may indicate that these individuals may rather have left their country of origin due to "pull" factors than to "push" factors. However, the strongly increased rates of anxiety indicate high distress, which is likely to be caused by the unprotected legal situation to which irregular migrants are subjected.

None of the assessed socio-demographic variables was associated with mental health outcomes. Other studies have found poorer mental health in asylum seekers with a longer length of stay in the receiving country (e.g., Laban, Gernaat, Komproe, & De Jong, 2007), an association that was not replicated in our sample. One possible explanation for this finding relates to the relatively short duration of stay in our sample of asylum seekers. Compared to the study mentioned above by Laban, Gernaat, Komproe, and De Jong (2007) where asylum seekers had been residing in the Netherlands for more than three years, asylum seekers in the present study had arrived in the country only a maximum of one and a half years prior to the assessment. It is possible that the longer the insecurity of the temporary visa status has to be endured, the greater will be the negative impact on mental health. In this sense, the first one to two years after arrival as assessed in the present study may possibly be considered a buffer zone where mental health is not yet affected by the insecurity of status, and where people's hope, resilience, and coping capacities may override the burden of insecurity.

Social desirability did not contribute to caseness of probable PTSD, clinically relevant depression, or anxiety in multivariate analyses. This implies that even though migrants tended to provide more socially desirable responses than residents, their responses on mental health were not contorted by their response tendencies. Likewise, integration outcomes were found to offer no contribution to mental health outcomes in multivariate analyses. While several large-scale studies found associations between post-migration living difficulties and mental health status (e.g., Momartin et al., 2006), findings on other measures of integration such as social support or language proficiency are inconsistent, one possible explanation being a declining influence of possible integration resources over the course of time after migration (Ryan, Dooley, & Benson, 2008).

As has been established in previous studies (Neuner et al., 2004), the number of traumatic event types experienced predicted probable PTSD, but also clinically significant symptoms of depression and anxiety. Over and above the associations with traumatic events, residence status was strongly associated with all mental health outcomes. Living as an asylum seeker or refugee meant having the highest odds of suffering from probable PTSD; and living as an asylum seeker, irregular migrant, or refugee meant having the highest odds of suffering from clinically relevant symptoms of depression and anxiety. The association between mental health and a permanent versus temporary visa status has been previously confirmed (Momartin et al., 2006). However, the fact that all of the most frequently observed psychiatric syndromes, including trauma-related symptoms of PTSD, are associated with resident status over and above the associations with traumatic events is a surprisingly consistent finding in this study.

These results indicate that the pathological effect of trauma is not comprehensively determined by the traumatic experiences encountered in the country of origin. Rather, successful recovery from traumatic experiences may depend on the social, political, and economic conditions in the receiving country. In this sense, our findings support the concept of sequential traumatisation that was first introduced by Keilson (1979) and later elaborated by Becker (2006). In his follow-up study on Jewish war orphans, Keilson found that the course of the postwar period with its hardships had a stronger impact on future health than previous sequences in the traumatic process. Our findings support the assumption that the social, political, and economic conditions of the receiving country moderate the effect of previous traumatisation in the country of origin on mental health in migrants.

In conclusion, the present study suggests that insecure residence permits as they are issued to asylum seekers increase the risk of psychiatric disorders. At the same time, asylum seekers and refugees can be considered especially vulnerable due to pre-existing burdens such as frequent traumatic experiences. It would be worthwhile for future research to focus on effective ways to offer specific preventions and interventions for vulnerable migrant groups, which would include focusing on resources and resilience in asylum seekers, refugees, and irregular migrants. Future efforts should aim at turning migration into a process that, instead of worsening the pre-existing problems, enables individuals to successfully cope with the challenges of their migration. Until this is accomplished, it is vital that individuals suffering from psychopathological strain should be granted access to health services including psychiatric screening and treatment independently of their resident status.

References

Becker, D. (2006). Das Konzept der sequentiellen Traumatisierung und seine Erweiterung. In: D. Becker (Ed.), *Die Erfindung des Traumas: verflochtene Geschichten* (pp. 188–197). Freiburg: Freitag.

Buddeberg-Fischer, B., Stamm, M., Buddeberg, C., & Klaghofer, R. (2009). Angst und Depression bei jungen Ärztinnen und Ärzten-Ergebnisse einer Schweizer Longitudinalstudie [Anxiety and depression in residents—results of a Swiss longitudinal study]. *Zeitschrift für Psychosomatische Medizin und Psychotherapie, 55*: 37–50.

Carta, M. G., Bernal, M., Hardoy, M. C., & Haro-Abad, J. M. (2005). Migration and mental health in Europe (the state of the mental health in Europe working group: appendix 1). *Clinical Practice and Epidemology in Mental Health 1*: 13.

Fischer, D., & Fick, C. (1993). Measuring social desirability: short forms of the Marlowe-Crowne social desirability scale. *Educational and Psychological Measurement, 53*: 417–424.

Foa, E. (1995). *Posttraumatic Diagnostic Scale (PDS) (manual).* Minneapolis, MN: National Computer Systems.

Foa, E., Cashman, L., Jaycox, L., & Perry, K. (1997). The validation of a self-report measure of posttraumatic stress disorder: the Posttraumatic Diagnostic Scale. *Psychological Assessment, 9*: 445–451.

Gerritsen, A. A. (2006). Physical and mental health of Afghan, Iranian and Somali asylum seekers and refugees living in the Netherlands. *Social Psychiatry and Psychiatric Epidemiology, 41*: 18–26.

Heckmann, F., & Schnapper, D. (2003). *The integration of immigrants in European societies.* Stuttgart: Lucius & Lucius.

Heeren, M., Mueller, J., Ehlert, U., Schnyder, U., Copiery, N., & Maier T. (2012). Mental health of asylum seekers: a cross-sectional study of psychiatric disorders. *BMC Psychiatry, 12*: 114.

International Organization of Migration (2007). *Migration and the right to health: a review of European community law and Council of Europe instruments.* Geneva.

Keilson, H. (1979). *Sequentielle Traumatisierung bei Kindern*. Stuttgart: Enke.

Laban, C. J., Gernaat, H. B., Komproe, I. H., Schreuders, B. A., & De Jong, J. T. (2004). Impact of a long asylum procedure on the prevalence of psychiatric disorders in Iraqi asylum seekers in the Netherlands. *The Journal of Nervous and Mental Disease, 192*: 843–851.

Laban, C. J., Gernaat, H. B., Komproe, I. H., Van der Tweel, I., & De Jong, J. T. (2005). Postmigration living problems and common psychiatric disorders in Iraqi asylum seekers in the Netherlands. *The Journal of Nervous and Mental Disease, 193*: 825–832.

Laban, C. J., Gernaat, H. B., Komproe, I. H., & De Jong, J. T. (2007). Prevalence and predictors of health service use among Iraqi asylum seekers in the Netherlands. *Social Psychiatry and Psychiatric Epidemiology, 42*: 837–844.

Lindert, J., von Ehrenstein, O., Priebe, S., Mielck, A., & Brähler, E. (2009). Depression and anxiety in labor migrants and refugees—a systematic review and meta-analysis. *Social Science and Medicine, 69*: 246–257.

Mollica, R. F., Wyshak, G., Marneffe, D., Tu, B., Yang, T., & Khuon, F. (1991). *Hopkins Symptom Checklist 25. Manual*. Harvard Program in refugee trauma. Harvard, MA: Harvard School of Public Health.

Momartin, S., Silove, D., Manicavasagar, V., & Steel, Z. (2004). Complicated grief in Bosnian refugees: associations with posttraumatic stress disorder and depression. *Comprehensive Psychiatry, 6*: 475–482.

Momartin, S., Steel, Z., Coello, M., Aroche, J., Silove, D., & Brooks, R. (2006). A comparison of the mental health of refugees with temporary versus permanent protection visas. *Medical Journal of Australia, 185*: 357–361.

Mueller, J., Postert, C., Beyer, T., Furniss, T., & Achtergarde, S. (2009). Comparison of eleven short versions of the Symptom Checklist 90-Revised (SCL-90-R) for use in the assessment of general psychopathology. *Journal of Psychopathology and Behavioral Assessment, 32*: 246–254.

Neuner, F., Schauer, M., Karunakara, U., Klaschik, C., Robert, C., & Elbert T. (2004). Psychological trauma and evidence for enhanced vulnerability for posttraumatic stress disorder through previous trauma among West Nile refugees. *BMC Psychiatry, 4*: 1–7.

Porter, M., & Haslam, N. (2005). Predisplacement and postdisplacement factors associated with mental health of refugees and internally displaced persons: a meta-analysis. *JAMA, 294*: 602–612.

Ryan, D., Dooley, B., & Benson C. (2008). Theoretical perspectives on post-migration adaption and psychological well-being among refugees: towards a resource-based model. *Journal of Refugee Studies, 21*: 1–18.

Silove, D., Sinnerbrink, I., Field, A., Manicavasagar, V., & Steel Z. (1997). Anxiety, depression and PTSD in asylum seekers: associations with pre-migration trauma and post-migration stressors. *The British Journal of Psychiatry, 170*: 351–357.

Silove, D., Steel, Z., Susljik, I., Frommer, N., Loneragan, C., Chey, T., Brooks, R., le Touze, D., Ceollo, M., Smith, M., Harris, E., & Bryant, R. (2007). The impact of the refugee decision on the trajectory of PTSD, anxiety, and depressive symptoms among asylum seekers: a longitudinal study. *American Journal of Disaster Medicine, 2*: 321–329.

Sulaiman-Hill, C., & Thompson, S. (2011). Sampling challenges in a study examining refugee resettlement. *BMC International Health and Human Rights, 11*.

Sullivan, M., & Rehm, R. (2005). Mental health of undocumented Mexican immigrants: a review of the literature. *Advances in Nursing Science, 28*: 240–251.

Swiss Federal Statistical Office (2009). *Statistical Yearbook of Switzerland 2009*. Neuchatel.

CHAPTER TWELVE

Trauma and attachment

Anna Buchheim

Introduction

John Bowlby (1969) was the first psychoanalyst of his generation to use ethological concepts to describe the infant's biologically predisposed attachment to a primary caregiver. He viewed relatedness in early childhood as a primary and independent developmental goal that is not subservient to a physiological needs (e.g., hunger) or psychoanalytically defined primary processes. The infant is perceived from an interactional perspective, with a focus on the relationships with primary attachment figures. According to George and Solomon (1999, 2008), Bowlby defined defence as forms of exclusion (deactivation or cognitive disconnection) directed to modulating difficult and anxious experiences with attachment figures, and the child's experiences with incomplete or failed bids for parental protection, care, and comfort. Bowlby posited that so-called segregated systems were the intrapsychic root of symptoms related pathological mourning and severe psychopathology. Attachment theorists have since demonstrated that segregated systems are associated with experiences of failed protection and unresolved trauma (George & West, 2012; Solomon & George, 2000,). Empirical investigations of unresolved attachment are based on Main and Goldwyn's operational definition of lack of resolution (i.e., unresolved) using the Adult Attachment Interview (AAI) (George, Kaplan, & Main, 1984; Main & Goldwyn, 1985). The Adult Attachment Projective Picture System (AAP) (George, West, & Pettem, 1999; George & West, 2012) defines the dimension that is used to identify unresolved attachment following Bowlby's (1980) view of defensive exclusion for pathological mourning.

Results on unresolved attachment and psychopathology

The association between unresolved attachment and psychopathology is consistent with Bowlby's original predictions regarding psychiatric instability as a potential response to the death of attachment figures (Bowlby, 1980).

Any attachment study using interview measures (George & West, 2001; Main & Goldwyn, 1985) and approximately half of the attachment style studies reported a strong association between borderline personality disorder (BPD) and indices of disorganised/unresolved, fearful, preoccupied, or angry/hostile attachment (e.g., Agrawal, Gunderson, Holmes, & Lyons-Ruth, 2004; Levy et al., 2006; Bakermans-Kranenburg & Van IJzendoorn, 2009; Buchheim & George, 2011). For PTSD and abused patients (n = 271), the review of Bakermans-Kranenburg and Van IJzendoorn (2009) reported sixty-eight per cent of unresolved individuals, while only fourteen per cent were classified as secure. Studies investigating the association between attachment and trauma revealed that attachment disorganisation (unresolved trauma) was related to high levels of distress and PTSD symptoms in the aftermath of a traumatic event in adulthood (e.g., rape, stillbirth, war veterans) (Hughes, Turton, Hopper, McGauley, & Fonagy, 2004; Stovall-McClough & Cloitre, 2006).

In sum, and in line with the recent meta-analysis reporting on the distribution of attachment patterns in clinical and non-clinical groups, we can conclude that clinical subjects show highly more insecure and unresolved attachment representations than healthy controls. Bakermans-Kranenburg and Van IJzendoorn (2009) suggest in their meta-analysis that in future studies more differentiated scales or dimensional approaches should be assessed in order to study the range of attachment disorganisation in different clinical disorders.

Before reporting on results on attachment trauma, an established, valid measure of adult attachment, the AAP, will be discussed. We used this in our research to begin to unravel the nuances of unresolved disorganised attachments (Juen, Arnold, Meissner, Nolte, & Buchheim, 2013) and also in the case of a severely traumatised patient (George & Buchheim, 2014).

The adult attachment projective picture system

The AAP is a set of eight drawings: a neutral scene and seven attachment scenes. The AAP stimuli are line drawings indicating a range of theoretically derived attachment events (e.g., illness, separation, solitude, death, and threat). The interviewee is asked to describe the events that comprise a "story" for each picture.

The stories are audio-recorded and analyses are done from verbatim transcripts (George & West, 2012). In sum, the AAP designates four attachment classifications based on the analysis of the coding dimensions across the entire set of seven attachment stories. Individuals with secure attachment (F) show a high level of agency, connectedness, and synchrony in attachment relationships in their narratives. If they use defensive strategies, they serve a more flexible integration at the representational level (high agency, e.g., thinking processes). Individuals with insecure-dismissing or insecure-preoccupied (E) attachment are characterised by functional or absent relationships in the stories. Those with dismissing representation tend to use "deactivation" (represented, e.g., by rejection, power, or achievement), whereas those with a preoccupied representation use a high amount of "cognitive disconnection" as a characteristic defence (represented, e.g., by conflicts, vagueness, or anger). Individuals with unresolved trauma (U) are overwhelmed by topics related to attachment-related trauma (e.g., danger, isolation, fear, or threat) and loss with no indications of the character's capacity to act, like protection from frightening and dangerous situations, and no internalised available attachment figure providing comfort and security.

Studies provide evidence of excellent convergent validity of the AAP with the Adult Attachment Interview (AAI), test-retest reliability, inter-rater reliability, and discriminant validity in healthy controls and clinical patients (George & West, 2001; George & West, 2012; Buchheim & George, 2011).

Study on unresolved attachment in different clinical groups

Juen, Arnold, Meissner, Nolte, and Buchheim (2013) analysed several clinical groups using the AAP and assumed that disorganised/unresolved attachment is predominant compared to healthy individuals. Moreover, the authors included an analysis of the degree of self-other boundary confusion by evaluating personal experience (PE) material in order to potentially deflect and differentiate disorder-specific characteristics of attachment disorganisation. The overall sample consisted of n = 218 adults of which 72.9% suffered from a psychic illness compared to 27.1% healthy individuals. Clinical samples were diagnosed along DSM-IV (2000) criteria with addiction and substance abuse (25.7%), PTSD (8.3%), depression (13.3%), BPD (15.6%), or schizophrenia (10.1%). As expected we found significantly more attachment insecurity in the clinical groups (Chi2 = 65.33, p < 0.001) with a predominance of the disorganised/unresolved classification (Chi2 = 18.72, p < 0.001). More than half of our clinical participants showed attachment disorganisation (51.6%) and almost any (96.2%) of these individuals showed an insecure inner working model of attachment (see Figure 1). The differences within the diverse clinical groups were significant ($Chi^2 = 30.11$, $p < 0.01$).

When analysing the number of AAP stories including personal experience (PE) and segregated systems material (unresolved, U) we found the following characteristics (see Figure 1):

PTSD patients (U = 3.11, p < 0.001) compared to patients with schizophrenia and BPD patients (U = 4.73, p < 0.001) demonstrated the highest amount of unresolved material in their narratives. Regarding personal experience in the stories, BPD patients (M = 0.85, SD = 1.26) and especially addictive patients (M = 2.13, SD = 2.30) had struggles with self-other boundaries by showing the highest amount of personal experience material compared to the other clinical groups.

In our study (n = 218) using the AAP, we found that PTSD and BPD patients showed the highest amount of attachment disorganisation. This result is in line with the data from the meta-analysis by Bakermans-Kranenburg and Van IJzendoorn (2009) demonstrating that individuals exposed to abuse and suffering from PTSD were virtually always classified as unresolved. The authors stated that, indicated by several studies, unresolved attachment is a fruitful marker for dissociative disorders like PTSD, which sheds light on the etiology and underlying mechanisms involved.

N = 218	F	Ds	E	U	Insecure	Chi²
Controls	54.2%	23.7%	6.8%	15.3%	45.8%	*Chi*^{2} = 82.96
Patients	3.8%	21.4%	23.3%	51.6%	96.2%	$p < 0.001$
PTSD	–	–	16.7%	83.3%	100%	*Chi*^{2} = 30.11
BPD	2.9%	5.9%	14.7%	76.5%	97.1%	$p < .01$
Depression	3.4%	34.5%	20.7%	41.4%	96.6%	
Addiction	5.4%	26.8%	25.0%	42.9%	94.6%	
Schizophrenia	4.5%	31.8%	40.9%	22.7%	55.5%	

Figure 1. Distribution of attachment classifications (four-way) in healthy and clinical groups (Juen, Arnold, Meissner, Nolte, & Buchheim, 2013).
Notes: F (secure), Ds (Dismissing), E (preoccupied), U (unresolved).

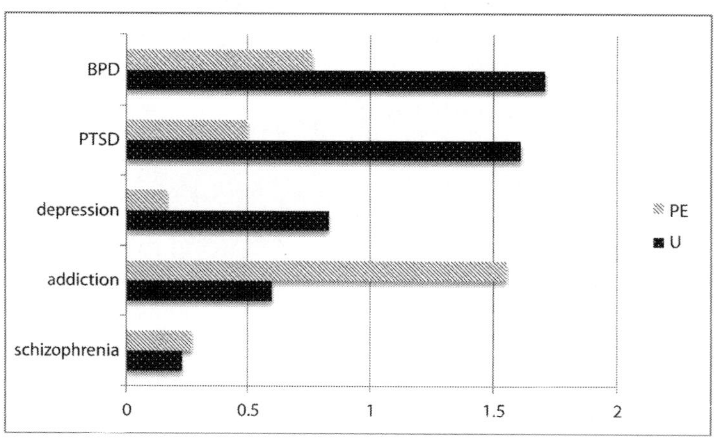

Figure 2. Number of stories including personal experience and unresolved material (Juen, Arnold, Meissner, Nolte, & Buchheim, 2013).

In our study (Juen, Arnold, Meissner, Nolte, & Buchheim, 2013), BPD patients and especially addictive patients had severe struggles in keeping self-other boundaries by showing the highest amount of personal experience material compared to the other clinical groups. Personal experience indicates whether or not the individual's stories include statements regarding her own life experiences. In our sample these two clinical groups included elements from their own abuse or maltreatment stories or addiction history with alcohol in their narratives statements. So these two patient groups seem incapable of staying in the hypothetical story by slipping into their own biography. These preliminary exploratory findings might serve as a fruitful framework for further hypotheses in order to differentiate the disorganised/unresolved categories in different clinical groups. Also, the fact that the intruding personal experience stories are often connected to trauma, might reflect the traumatic aspects included in these two conditions and thus confirm even more the close relationship of trauma and attachment.

In several studies we demonstrated the feasibility of the AAP in the neurobiological context to assess neural correlates of attachment dysregulation and trauma in BPD compared to controls (Buchheim et al., 2006, 2008, 2012). As predicted BPD patients were classified as "unresolved" with respect to attachment trauma and showed significantly more dysregulated attachment trauma language indicators in monadic picture stories compared to controls. In fMRI, BPD patients showed significantly more anterior midcingulate cortex activation in response to monadic pictures than controls. Patients showed more activation of the right superior temporal sulcus and less activation of the right parahippocampal gyrus compared to controls in response to dyadic pictures. These findings provided evidence for potential neural mechanisms of attachment trauma underlying interpersonal symptoms of BPD (Buchheim et al., 2008).

In a recent study we used the AAP to assess neural changes in chronically depressed patients (MD) during psychodynamic treatment. These patients showed a significant higher percentage of unresolved attachment status with respect to loss experiences compared to controls (Buchheim et al., 2012). In this study we again demonstrated the feasibility of the AAP to activate the participants' attachment system by presenting personalised attachment relevant core sentences from the participant's own stories to the AAP pictures (Buchheim et al., 2012). Patients showed a higher activation in the left anterior hippocampus/amygdala, subgenual cingulate, and medial prefrontal cortex before treatment and a reduction in these areas after fifteen months when confronted with the attachment material. This reduction was associated with improvement in depressiveness specifically, and in the medial prefrontal cortex with symptom improvement more generally (Buchheim et al., 2012). Summarising these neurobiological studies on attachment and patients with BPD and MD we conclude that the AAP instrument is capable of activating the attachment system in adults by demonstrating relevant differences between patient groups and healthy controls.

The following section will consider the use of the AAP with a traumatised patient in an inpatient setting, using a case study "Gloria" to illustrate the components of the AAP that are particularly relevant to a psychodynamic conceptualisation and intervention (George & Buchheim, 2014). The following passages present an abridged version of the published single case.

Assessment of the AAP with a severely traumatised patient

Gloria, a middle-aged patient reported that five years ago she had a gruesome experience with a therapist who had suggested trauma therapy for her rape experience immediately at their first meeting. Gloria was terrified and she left therapy.

Gloria's parents divorced when she was seven years old. Her mother remarried five years later. Her stepfather, whom she viewed as her "actual" father, not speaking at all about her biological father, is described as being humorous, beloved, and trusted, but also impulsive and irascible. She tested him by deliberate misbehaviour and her stepfather's beatings were central to their relationship.

After a sadistic rape experience in adolescence, Gloria suffered from sudden headache and fainting attacks up to three times a day, and chronic dissociation experiences. Her symptoms appeared to be associated with feelings of being exposed and with school or performance-related pressure. Although these problems persisted, she did not seek psychological treatment. Her symptoms, especially fainting, diminished when she studied abroad. When her symptoms reoccurred after returning home two years later, she decided to go back abroad.

Gloria's second major traumatic experience was when, aged thirty, her boyfriend of two years died in an accident, shortly after she had separated from him due to her increasing inability to tolerate physical closeness. She developed masochistic guilt feelings and renounced intimate relationships for many years.

Gloria had shortly before seeking treatment experienced a third trauma, a severe car accident. Her fainting episodes increased dramatically and she was unable to work. She was unable to recall what preceded the headaches and described herself as being on autopilot. This was the "defensive mechanism" that had saved her life more than twenty years ago, but now this automatic mechanism was out of her control. Her decision to seek therapy was entirely about regaining control and "to get rid of it".

The AAP was administered after Gloria had been in inpatient treatment for two weeks. Her adult attachment classification was judged to be pathological mourning for unresolved trauma. Pathological mourning is a state of chronic mourning that endures for years because trauma-produced segregated systems block completion of the mourning. Mourning in attachment theory is defined by conscious awareness and reorganisation of memories and feelings related to trauma, which leads to a representation of self that integrates current reality with the past (Bowlby, 1980; George & West, 2012). Gloria's AAP responses demonstrate the prominent role of attachment trauma in her representation of self and attachment relationships. The unresolved designation associated with her classification group signifies that she is not able to maintain regulatory processes to manage pain and fear. In Gloria's case, we see her attempt to keep attachment trauma walled off or segregated as fortified by defensive deactivation. When working well, this form of defensive exclusion neutralises and shifts attention away from distress and pain (George & West, 2012).

Out of the many AAP narratives indicating her traumatogenic unresolved attachment, representation was predominantly in the AAP pictures Bench and Window. Only one AAP stimulus will be demonstrated here (for a more detailed discussion, cf. George & Buchheim, 2014).

The last stimulus in the AAP set is an alone scene that portrays a child in the corner, drawn with solid lines that designate perceptual boundaries that potentially confine the child. The child is turned askew into the corner with one arm reaching outward away from the corner.

Gloria told a story of trauma and self-protection, with trauma (in italics), personal agency (underlined) and her interpretation (in brackets) designated in her response:

> A small child stands in a corner and cannot get away. He defends, *fends off with his hands.* And he looks to the side and down because he tries in this way to *protect* his face or also not see what is coming next … he only thinks, hopefully it will not be so bad. Afterward? He will be *beaten.* (It doesn't help him that he fends against it … he should not have tried to avoid it because then he will be even more severely punished.) Yes, the scene repeats itself again and again. Until the child is someday simply big enough and can run away. *And he will surely never do that because he knows what it feels like to stand in the corner and not be able to return and get away.* So, he will have to get over it.

Gloria's final alone response describes the helplessness of abuse, the defining quality of her relationship with her stepfather. She describes a child who is helplessly trapped in the cycle of abuse. Important in her response, however, is the description of self as having the personal agency of protection. In those moments of abuse, this child was able to protect himself, a capacity to act. This was likely the source of Gloria's capacity to go forward in life. What we see too, though, is that she currently sees the uselessness of trying to protect one's self. This may have been the impetus for seeking therapy. Unable to escape, she has not been able to "get over it". The child's agency in the Corner picture did not change anything and Gloria's overall representation of self in the alone stories demonstrates that she is caught in a cycle of pathological chronic mourning for attachment trauma.

Gloria's overall AAP response patterns (see George & Buchheim, 2014) demonstrated a representation of self as helpless, desperate, and abandoned, managed by deactivating defences that created representational and relationship distance to shift her attention away from her pain. It is notable that none of these stories mirrored the independent or rebellious self she described during her clinical interview. Her AAP responses get beyond her desperate attempts to "get rid of" her feelings and demonstrate how frightened and helpless she really is. Gloria is caught in what seemed to be an endless cycle of trauma. Gloria's response to starting trauma therapy was traumatic in itself. She did not want to look inside and remember the rape that she has tried to repress for more than 20 years. Since the fainting attacks are probably strongly connected to the trauma, an avoidance of treatment of the trauma would probably not improve her disease. A premature treatment of the trauma without an established working alliance would however be contraindicated, because of Gloria's "gruesome" previous experience.

George and Buchheim (2014) suggested the following key tasks in a psychodynamic treatment plan for this patient based on the AAP:

1. Establish a secure base for this patient. This would mean not being intrusive and postpone delving into the rape experience until an alliance was established. Gloria's unresolved-pathological chronic mourning classification on the AAP also supports delaying exploring trauma and parenting failures because they are disorganising and she is not

able to contain feeling desperate, stranded, and helpless. She could not trust others to help her, and this would extend to an inability to trust her therapist. Other features of the secure base position would help Gloria change her representation of object; that is, change the idealisation of the stepfather to become more realistic. She would also need to accept the fact that, in attachment theory terms, her mother rejected her and did not protect her enough, which is why she had to learn to protect herself. Her avoidance, facilitated by deactivating defences, is a reasonable response to her experience but is maladaptive.

2. Diminish deactivating defences. Strengthen Gloria's ability to tolerate negative feelings. This can help her face and accept the physical signs of distress in order to reduce the autopilot autonomic reactions. This can also help mitigate feelings of blame and foster increased ability for affect tolerance.
3. Reorganise attachment dysregulation that is strengthened by deactivation. Help Gloria not reject and be frightened by intimacy and closeness, and accept relationships with an authentic self who has weaknesses.

The therapist should be careful of being silent and appearing anonymous, since for Gloria, who is already neutralised and deactivated, this behaviour would mean rejection. With this patient, it would be expected that the silence of the analyst could activate the previous mode with the mother and described in her childhood as her mother's withdrawal of love: "She did not speak to me for days." One can readily expect also that this relationship pattern will probably appear in the transference.

Conclusion

As Juen, Arnold, Meissner, Nolte, and Buchheim (2013) demonstrated in accordance with existing meta-analytical data, trauma is one major component of unresolved attachment and can be hypothesised as an aggravating factor in other disorders where an unresolved attachment pattern prevails. A case study by George and Buchheim (2014) demonstrates the personal processes linking traumatic memory, interaction, and attachment style. In consequence, suggestions for adequate therapeutic attitudes and interventions could be derived from the thorough analysis of AAP narratives. It was demonstrated how response to trauma is embedded in patients' interpersonal difficulties and representations of self and attachment figures. Attachment representations should receive at least as much attention as their traumatic memories and symptoms (i.e., dissociative experiences, dissociative defences). Knowledge of the mental processes linked to traumatic dysregulation and disorganisation of attachment should guide the therapist's understanding of these difficulties especially with respect to social trauma, where major denial of sexual and physical abuse are present and mostly these issues are excluded from awareness of the individual, the familiar environment, and the society.

References

Agrawal, H. R., Gunderson, J., Holmes, B. M., & Lyons-Ruth, K. (2004). Attachment studies with borderline patients: a review. *Harvard Review of Psychiatry, 12*: 94–104.

American Psychiatric Association (2000). *Diagnostic and Statistical Manual of Mental Disorders IV*. Washington, DC: APA.

Bakermans-Kranenburg, M. J., & Van IJzendoorn, M. (2009). The first 10,000 adult attachment interviews: distributions of adult attachment representations in clinical and non-clinical groups. *Attachment & Human Development, 11*: 223–263.

Bowlby, J. (1969). *Attachment and Loss: Volume 1. Attachment*. London: Hogarth [reprinted London: Pimlico, 1997].

Bowlby, J. (1980). *Attachment and Loss: Volume 3. Loss, Sadness and Depression*. London: Hogarth [reprinted London: Pimlico, 1998].

Buchheim, A., & George, C. (2011). Attachment disorganization in borderline personality disorder and anxiety disorder. In: J. Solomon & C. George (Eds.), *Disorganization of Attachment and Caregiving (Volume 2)* (pp. 343–383). New York: Guilford.

Buchheim, A., Erk, S., George, C., Kächele, H., Ruchsow, M., Spitzer, M., Kircher, T., & Walter, H. (2006). Measuring attachment representation in an fMRI environment: a pilot study. *Psychopathology, 39*: 144–152.

Buchheim, A., Erk, S., George, C., Kächele, H., Kircher, T., Martius, P., Pokorny, D., Ruchsow, M., Spitzer, M., & Walter, H. (2008). Neural correlates of attachment trauma in borderline personality disorder: a functional magnetic resonance imaging study. *Psychiatry Research: Neuroimaging, 163*: 223–235.

Buchheim, A., Viviani, R., Kessler, H., Kächele, H., Cierpka, M., Roth, G., George, C., Kernberg, O., Bruns, G., & Taubner, S. (2012). Changes in prefrontal-limbic function in major depression after 15 months of long-term psychotherapy. *PLOS ONE 7*(3). http://dx.doi.org/10.1371/journal.pone.0033745

George, C., & Buchheim, A. (2014). Use of the adult attachment projective picture system in psychodynamic psychotherapy with a severely traumatized patient. *Frontiers in Psychology, 5*: 865. https://doi.org/10.3389/fpsyg.2014.00865

George, C., & Solomon, J. (1999). The development of caregiving: a comparison of attachment and psychoanalytic approaches to mothering. *Psychoanalytic Inquiry, 19*: 618–646.

George, C., & Solomon, J. (2008). The caregiving system: a behavioral systems approach to parenting. In: J. Cassidy & P. R. Shaver (Eds.), *Handbook of Attachment: Theory, Research, and Clinical Applications* (2nd edn) (pp. 833–856). New York: Guilford.

George, C., & West, M. (2001). The development and preliminary validation of a new measure of adult attachment: the Adult Attachment Projective. *Attachment and Human Development, 3*: 30–61.

George, C., & West, M. (2012). *The Adult Attachment Projective Picture System: Attachment theory and assessment in adults*. New York: Guilford.

George, C., Kaplan, N., & Main, M. (1984). *Adult Attachment Interview protocol*. Unpublished manuscript. Berkeley, CA: University of California; 1996.

George, C., West, M., & Pettem, O. (1999). The adult attachment projective: disorganization of adult attachment at the level of representation. In: J. Solomon & C. George (Eds.), *Attachment Disorganization* (pp. 462–507). New York: Guilford.

Hughes, P., Turton, P., Hopper, E., McGauley, G. A., & Fonagy, P. (2004). Factors associated with the unresolved classification of the adult attachment interview in women who have suffered stillbirth. *Development and Psychopathology, 16:* 215–230.

Juen, F., Arnold, L., Meissner, D., Nolte, T., Buchheim, A. (2013). Attachment disorganization in different clinical groups: What underpins unresolved attachment? *Psihologija 46:* 127–142.

Levy, K. N., Meehan, K. B., Kelly, K. M., Reynoso, S., Weber, M., Clarkin, J. F., & Kernberg, O. F. (2006). Change in attachment patterns and reflective function in a randomized control trial of transference-focused psychotherapy or borderline personality disorder. *Journal of Consulting and Clinical Psychology, 74*: 1027–1040.

Main, M., & Goldwyn, R. (1985). *Adult attachment scoring and classification system*. Unpublished rating and classification manual. Berkeley, CA: University of California; 1994.

Solomon, J., & George, C. (2000). Toward an integrated theory of caregiving. In: J. Osofsky & H. Fitzgerald (Eds.), *WAIMH Handbook of Infant Mental Health* (pp. 323–368). New York: Wiley.

Stovall-McClough, K. C., & Cloitre, M. (2006). Unresolved attachment, PTSD, and dissociation in women with childhood abuse histories. *Journal of Consulting & Clinical Psychology 74*: 219–228.

CHAPTER THIRTEEN

Attachment in students from cities of the former Socialist Federal Republic of Yugoslavia

Tatjana Stefanović Stanojević and Jasmina Nedeljković

Growing up in transition

The 1990s were dramatic for the former Socialist Federal Republic of Yugoslavia (SFRY): wars, bombings, inflation; essentially, suffering and a battle for survival. The children growing up then are today young people aged around twenty. The question we encounter on a daily basis, both as parents and as experts, is to what extent and in what way have the turbulent times marked their development? Or, to be more precise, where are these young people in the development continuum and how do they solve the development tasks characteristic of their age?

According to the majority of psychological periodisations of development (Erikson, 1950), in provisionally normal life circumstances, twenty-year-olds are young people who have mostly worked out the so-called "identity crisis", connected the past with the future, and adjusted their capabilities, interests, and tendencies in accordance with their surroundings. They should have also worked out the "ideals crisis" and accepted sex, status, and ethnic identities. Finally, they should have developed fidelity as a virtue on which to construct marital and family relationships. The theory appropriates all the described processes based on the behaviour of the majority of young people in provisionally normal circumstances.

Wishing to find out what happened to the young people in former Yugoslavia and how the turbulent times affected their development, we decided to test a sample of young people from some bigger cities or capital cities of the former Yugoslav republics. We chose Banja Luka, Skopje, and Niš, aware of the fact that the transitional occurrences during the 1990s were very different in each of these cities and that the differences themselves could be a part of the researched problem. Three different former Yugoslav republics saw a different sequence of events in the 1990s, starting with Bosnia and Herzegovina (Banja Luka), where civil, as well as intranational war lasted for several years; then Serbia (Niš), which was bombarded for months and suffered fierce inflation; and Macedonia (Skopje) in which such dramatic occurrences did not take place, but which endured major consequences in all of the vital functioning aspects after the dissolution of the country.

Of course, not all of the described development aspects could have been tested. The final decision on the research area was influenced by the interests of the researchers, but also by the assumption that the quality of attachment is both an indicator of early life interactions as well as the basis for the formation of actual partner relationships. Before presenting the results, it is necessary to facilitate understanding of the acquired data by a short presentation of the theoretical framework (attachment theory).

Attachment theory

The founder of attachment theory was an English psychiatrist and psychoanalyst, John Bowlby (1907–1990). He defined attachment as a specific, asymmetrical relationship which is formed in the earliest childhood between a mother and a child and which lasts throughout the lifetime. The concept of the "internal working model" enables the theory to overgrow the initial "mission" of the interpretation of early relations between a mother and a child and grow into a lifetime development theory. Based on the ways in which a mother reacts to her child's signals (laughter, crying, cooing, etc.), the child forms an internal working model of himself (an image of himself) and internal working models of others (images of others). These models, relatively unchanged, persist throughout a person's maturing period, influencing the shaping of dominant adult relationships. We will try to present both aspects concisely with the following classifications.

Type "A" or avoidant attachment

Insecure, avoidant babies develop working models of their mothers as consistently resistant throughout their everyday experiences. However, a mother might be present and care about the child in a certain manner, while not connected with the emotions and signals that the child sends. The child, exposed to a repeated experience of the mother not answering his needs, develops an image of the world as an insecure, unkind place and decides not to send signals anymore and not to expect affection from others. The child defends himself by creating a shell, by depending, expecting, and also investing only in himself. If the pattern persists throughout the maturing period, people of this type of attachment avoid closeness with other people but reflect a sense of their own value emphasising the importance of the achieved independence and defensively negating the value of close relationships.

Type "B" or secure attachment

"A secure child has an internal working model of a responsive, reliant parent who can give love and of itself as a being worthy of love and attention and it carries these assumptions as a trademark into all of the other relationships." (Bowlby, 1969) The quality of the early experiences with a mother in babies with secure attachment can be marked as a consistent availability and responsiveness of a mother to the child's signals. Babies with secure attachment, thanks to the repeated experiences of the mother's emotional responsiveness, become secure with their mothers, developing a model of secure motherly availability. Thus, they form an image of themselves as beings who deserve love and attention from their mothers, and an image of the world as a secure and comfortable place, in which there is room for them. Trusting the world and themselves, these babies develop into secure children.

Type "C" or ambivalent attachment

Insecure, ambivalent babies develop a working model of others as inconsistently available. To be more precise, a baby is insecure in the availability of his mother, because the mother reacts selectively to signals. According to the teaching theories, an irregular, unpredictable substantiating regime reflects behaviour, in this case attachment. The internal working model is determined by the struggle to which a child must consent, in order to secure a minimum of attention and affection from his mother. Consequences of such working models are manifold: primarily, a baby develops a more pronounced emotional attachment to his mother (emotionally dependent, so-called clingy children). Fearing that he will lose his mother, a baby monitors and controls her more. To sum it up, a baby of this type forms a positive model of others, but a negative model of himself and everything that he does is connected with the futile attempts at bettering the image of his own self.

During the maturing period, if the internal working model does not change for any reason, individuals of this type try to improve the image of themselves through pronounced closeness in partner relationships. Therefore, we recognise them as symbiotic partners in partner relationships. This pattern is hence most often called "preoccupied" in literature (Feeney & Noller, 2004).

Type "D" or disorganised attachment

This group did not exist in initial classifications but was formed afterwards. Analyses of children whose parents were molested (Crittenden, 1989) or suffered from manic-depressive psychosis (Radke-Yarow, Cummings, Kuczynski, & Chapman, 1985), showed that some of the children could not have been classified into any of the given categories. What separated these children was not a new quality but a different degree of disorganisation and disorientation: running towards a wall and leaning against it, as a form of frightened reaction to a stranger; climbing and falling when a parent enters the room; stiffness in all movements; behaviour stereotypes. Research at Berkeley University by Mary Main and the so-called Charlottesville Studies (Ainsworth & Eichberg, 1991) confirms the existence of irrational, unsystematic thinking as a response to the stress of the parents in type "D" children.

Thus, children of this type grow up with negative models of both themselves and the world. Most often, this pattern is called "fearful" attachment in adults. People who belong to it are highly dependent on others, because they search for affirmation of their own value through relationships with others. At the same time, they have negative expectations from other people, so they tend to avoid closeness in order to avoid the pain of potential loss and rejection.

Within the described theoretical framework, we were interested in the quality of affective relationships, as well as in possible differences in the examinees from the former SFRY territory.

Methodological framework

The problem and hypotheses of research

The research problem could be defined as an attempt at determining the quality of attachment in samples of students from the cities of former SFRY. Alongside the fundamental problem, a line of specific problems was defined: the comparison of the attachment distributions received in the three cities, the comparison of attachment dimensions distributions with the distributions from previous domestic research, and (based on the attempt to reach the attachment patterns through the dimensions) comparison of the attachment patterns, both between the cities, and with the distributions gathered in numerous foreign research.

Defined in accordance with the problem is also the expectation that the distribution of the attachment patterns acquired from the sample of young people who grew up in adverse, that is, transitional conditions, will differ from the distributions acquired in the more suitable circumstances in foreign research. Furthermore, we expect that the distributions of both attachment dimensions and patterns will differ from city to city and in accordance with the specific aspects of growing up in those cities.

Sample

The research sample comprised male and female students of the Faculty of Philosophy in Banja Luka, Skopje, and Niš (N = 247). The sample is not sex balanced. Since there are more female students at the departments of psychology and pedagogy at these faculties, the sample comprised more female (N = 200) than male (N = 47) students. The conspicuous imbalance of the sample is the reason why the results were not treated based on sex. Unfortunately, due to the sample deterioration, the balancing between the cities was also not achieved (Skopje, N = 100; Niš, N = 92; Banja Luka, N = 55).

Scale	N item	Alpha
Unsolved family traumatisation	11	.88
Fear of losing ESB	11	.86
Negative working model of others	11	.84
Use of ESB	11	.83
Negative working model of the self	11	.82

Figure 1. Socio-demographic data and reliability of the UPIPAV-R scale.

Instruments

UPIPAV-R (Hanak, 2004) is the first domestic instrument that presents the examinee's relation to attachment in seven dimensions. The dimensions are unsolved family traumatisation, fear of losing the external security basis (ESB), negative working model of others, mentalizing capacity, negative working model of the self, use of the external security basis, and anger dysregulation. Figure 1 shows the metrical characteristics of UPIPAV-R acquired from the sample N = 523, age 20–41.

Research results

UPIPAV dimensions in the examinees from different cities

From Figure 2 we see that in relation to the normative sample (Hanak, 2004), the tested young people have a significantly higher mentalizing capacity, which is definitely encouraging. However, the finding that the arithmetic means of the dimensions unsolved family traumatisation and negative self are also higher in relation to the normative sample is alarming. Let us mention here that "our" sample differed from the normative in several aspects: the normative sample is sex balanced, the average age of the examinees is higher, and half of the sample examinees have university education.

Also, Figure 2 shows that the examinees from Banja Luka have more pronounced dimensions unsolved trauma and anger dysregulation than the examinees from Niš (mean diff. = 6.997, sig < 0.005) and Skopje (mean diff. = 7.302, sig < 0.005), and negative self than the examinees from Skopje (mean diff. = 7.485, sig < 0.001). In the examinees from Skopje, the dimensions

	Niš	Skopje	Banja Luka	Total		
	Mean SD	Mean SD	Mean SD	Mean SD	F	Sig
Use of ESB	61.79 10.785	59.94 10.618	61.25 14.314	60.92 11.58	0.641	0.528
Unsolved traumatisation	31.80 13.113	31.48 14.599	38.78 10.500	33.23 13.51	6.253	0.0022
Fear of losing ESB	45.55 13.988	49.07 11.572	49.09 12.364	47.77 12.76	2.224	0.110
Anger Dysregulation	32.97 10.749	37.00 10.525	43.42 8.368	36.93 10.86	18.160	0.000
Mentalizing capacity	57.01 9.309	60.03 6.486	52.44 13.445	57.21 9.85	11.479	0.000
Negative model of others	48.80 12.186	54.18 9.726	47.91 14.524	50.78 12.14	7.008	0.001
Negative self	37.97 12.594	32.66 12.650	40.15 10.730	36.30 12.57	8.004	0.000

Figure 2. The seven dimensions of UPIPAV in the examinees from different cities.

mentalizing and negative others are more pronounced than in the examinees from Niš (mean diff. = 3.019, sig < 0.05; mean diff. = 5.376, sig < 0.005) and Banja Luka (mean diff. = 7.594, sig < 0.001; mean diff. = 6.271, sig < 0.005), while they have more pronounced fear of losing ESB and anger dysregulation than the examinees from Niš (mean diff. = 3.516, sig < 0.05; mean diff. = 4.033, sig < 0.05). The examinees from Niš have only two dimensions more pronounced and these are mentalizing in relation to the examinees from Banja Luka (mean diff. = 4.575, sig < 0.005) and negative self in relation to the examinees from Skopje (mean diff. = 5.307, sig < 0.005).

The relation between the UPIPAV dimensions and attachment patterns

By comparing the results with those from foreign research, we tried to reach the attachment patterns using cluster analysis. The non-hierarchical K-means method was applied, within which we defined four clusters due to the existing four attachment patterns.

The objectivity of the acquired grouping and the stability of the solution were checked by discriminant analysis. The results are shown in Figure 4.

The evident overlapping of the cluster analysis results and the predictions of belonging to certain groups guided us towards the next step—naming of clusters. The clusters were named in the following manner:

1. The argument upon which we can take cluster 1 as the secure attachment pattern is the high level of dimensions. Namely, in this cluster, the lowest scores are those in dimensions negative others and negative self, with weak anger regulation and unsolved family traumatisation, which corresponds to the secure attachment pattern.

	1	2	3	4
Use of ESB	35	77	32	47
Unsolved trauma	11	45	74	54
Fear of losing ESB	11	73	27	14
Anger regulation	11	65	65	32
Mentalizing	59	35	65	66
Negative others	17	61	76	42
Negative self	12	45	17	70

Figure 3. Cluster analysis of UPIPAV dimensions.

	Predicted group for analysis				
	1	2	3	4	Total
Cluster 1	41	0	0	0	41
Cluster 2	2	106	0	5	113
Cluster 3	0	0	16	1	17
Cluster 4	0	0	0	76	76
Total	43	106	16	82	247

Figure 4. Discriminant analysis.

2. The pattern of the so-called preoccupied or ambivalent attachment easily corresponds to the second cluster, characterised by the highest scores in the use of the external security basis, but also in the fear of losing it.
3. The third cluster could be classified as the avoidant attachment pattern cluster also based on the dimensions use of the external security and fear of losing the external security. Both of these dimensions are the lowest expressed in this cluster. Furthermore, it is characterised by the most positive image of self and the most negative image of others.
4. The fourth cluster is the hardest to identify. The assumption is that the highest score of the negative self could be one of the indicators of the fearful attachment pattern.

Attachment patterns

Figure 5 shows the distribution of the patterns in the examined sample.

As can be seen from Figure 5, the highest percentage of young people with the secure attachment, with a slightly lower percentage of the preoccupied attachment pattern, is similar to global distribution (Crowell, Fraley, & Shaver, 1999), as well as to some domestic research (Stanojević, 2000). However, the percentage of people with fearful attachment is higher than usual, and the percentage of the avoidant attachment is lower than the expected and already has acquired distributions. Before discussing the acquired results, let us see whether the distributions differ in the tested cities.

Some of the differences seem pretty clear from Figure 6. First of all, most of the people with secure attachment are from Skopje, then from Niš, while there are none in Banja Luka! As far as the preoccupied attachment is concerned, it is most frequent in Banja Luka (maybe because of the danger to which the children were exposed and their parents' efforts to constantly protect them), which is in a way (but not in such a high percentage) similar to the results acquired in, for example, Israeli kibbutzim (Van IJzendoorn, Sagi, & Lambermon, 1992), while it is the least expressed in Skopje. The avoidant attachment is, in fact, most pronounced in Skopje, which might be in accordance with the pro-European trend of children becoming independent early, which

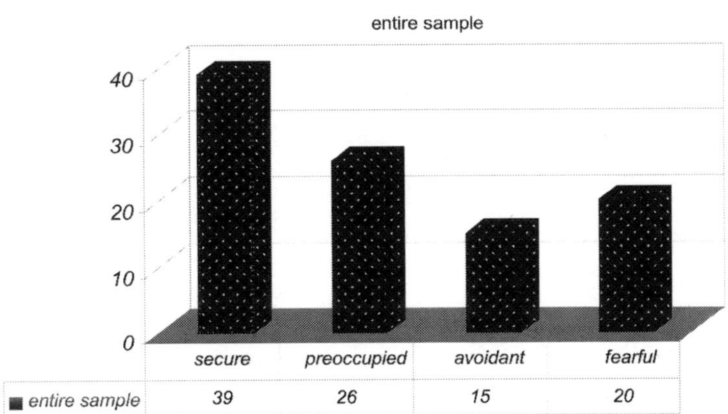

Figure 5. Distribution of the attachment patterns (entire sample).

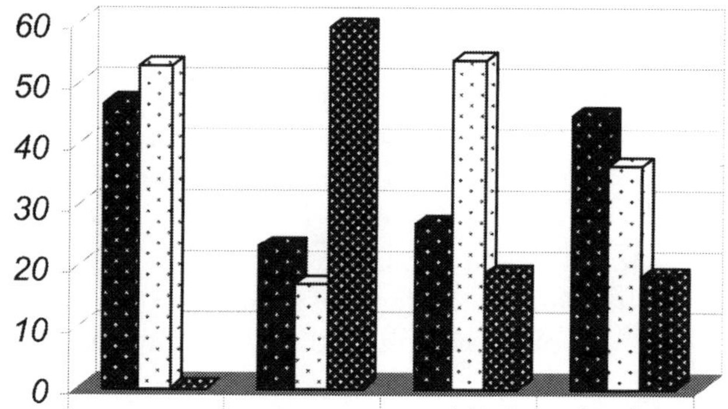

	secure	pre-occupied	avoidant	fearful
NI SR	46.8	23.4	27	44.8
SK MK	53.1	17.1	54	36.7
BL RS	0	59.3	18.9	18.3

Figure 6. The difference in the distribution of patterns in the "tested" cities.
(Legend: NI SR: Niš, Serbia; SK MK: Skopje, Former Yugoslav Republic of Macedonia; BL RS: Banja Luka, Republika Srpska).

could have found new ground only in Skopje since no dramatic war action took place there. And finally, the most unusual fact is that the majority of people with fearful attachment are from Niš! This fact has already been found in some domestic research (Stanojević, 2005, 2007) and has been generally explained by the chaos in which children grew up during the nineties in Serbia.

Discussion

The events in the former SFRY during the 1990s, as well as their consequences, have been the subject of many more significant and representative studies. Aware of the misbalance and the unrepresentativeness of the sample we will not try to answer the general question of how our adolescent subjects have been affected in regard to their development by the childhood war experience. The discussion will be organised around fundamental research hypotheses, and in relation to the cities in which the testing was conducted, but without any pretence at generalising our findings.

The assumption about differences in distribution of attachment in foreign and domestic research has been confirmed only partially, which is encouraging. Namely, in both domestic and the majority of foreign research (Crowell, Fraley, Shaver, 1999), most examinees belong to the secure attachment pattern. Next is the preoccupied attachment pattern, which is also a fact that can be found in distributions acquired in Japan, Israel, and some African countries (Van IJzendoorn, Sagi, & Lambermon, 1992), as well as in some domestic research (Stanojević, 2000). The hypothesis on the existence of differences is in fact confirmed by the two remaining patterns: fearful and avoidant. Namely, we did not find in any of the available foreign research that some of the samples had more fearful than avoidant subjects. This finding can be analysed in light of the fact that the growing up of the tested sample was marked by transition.

Moreover, this basic experience of transition is reflected in the significant differences between the cities included in the study.

Skopje

In Skopje, that is, in the former Yugoslav Republic of Macedonia, unlike in most of the former Yugoslav republics, there were neither wars nor bombings. Even though they felt the economic uncertainty and most of the transitional manifestations, compared to Niš and Banja Luka there were no life-threatening occurrences in Skopje. In accordance with the described situation are the results of the attachment quality assessment. Namely, based on the dimensions of the domestic instrument for attachment assessment, Skopje differed from the other two cities in the more pronounced dimensions: Mentalizing capacity and Negative others. As far as the attachment patterns are concerned, the so-called secure pattern is dominant in Skopje, more dominant than in other cities. Next in abundance is the avoidant attachment pattern. Apart from the fact that this relation of the expressed patterns is characteristic of most of the European countries (Van IJzendoorn & Bakermans-Kranenburg, 1996), it should be emphasised that the number of examinees who belong to the avoidant pattern is greater than in Niš and Banja Luka.

Banja Luka

During the 1990s in Republika Srpska, whose capital is Banja Luka, an intranational civil war raged. It is probable that the dominant emotions of parents toward their children, now students, were worry and fear for their lives, which was reflected in an overprotective, overly worrying attitude towards children.

That may be the reason why in Banja Luka (and compared to Niš and Skopje) the most pronounced dimensions are unsolved family traumatisation, weak anger regulation, and negative self. The situation is even clearer if we look at it from the attachment patterns perspective. In Banja Luka, in the tested sample, there are no examinees belonging to the secure attachment pattern, the globally dominant pattern, but also in the samples from the two other cities! Equally alarming is the fact that in Banja Luka the most dominant pattern is the preoccupied attachment pattern, which is also a fact that cannot be found in literature. The parents of the frightened children probably only reacted to the life-endangering situations, which fits into the selectively responsive manner of reacting, typical for the formation of the occupied attachment pattern.

Niš

Serbia, that is Niš, was certainly not a comfortable place for growing up during the 1990s. Although there was no war, like in Banja Luka, the transition was much more dramatic than in Skopje: utter economic uncertainty, inflation, and strikes. If we add to this the bombing to which the people of Serbia were exposed to, the image is alarming.

* * *

The distribution of the dimensions of the domestic instrument for the attachment assessment in relation to the normative sample, also acquired in Serbia (Hanak, 2004), differs in the increase of the following dimensions: mentalizing capacity, unsolved family traumatisation, and negative self. The distribution of the attachment patterns is highly specific: after the secure pattern, which is the most prominent, comes the fearful pattern! This relation between the representation of the attachment patterns is not typical for any of the tested cities, and does not appear in any of the foreign research results. It is only similar to some of the domestic research (Stanojević, 2005; Stanojević & Kostić, 2007), which did not have the same assessment instrument applied. Certainly, it is not possible to draw further conclusions based on such a small sample.

References

Ainsworth, M. D. S., & Eichberg, C. G. (1991). Effects on infant-mother attachment of mother's unresolved loss of an attachment figure on other traumatic experience. In: C. M. Parkes, J. Stevenson-Hinde, & P. Marris (Eds.), *Attachment Across the Life Cycle* (pp. 160–183). London: Routledge.

Bowlby, J. (1969). *Attachment and Loss: Volume 1. Attachment*. London: Hogarth [reprinted London: Pimlico, 1997].

Crittenden, P. (1989). Internal representational models of attachment relationships. *Infant Mental Health Journal, 11*: 259–277.

Crowell, J. A., Fraley, R. C., & Shaver, P. R. (1999). Measurement of individual differences in adolescent and adult attachment. In: J. Cassidy & P. R. Shaver (Eds.), *Handbook of Attachment, Theory, Research and Clinical Applications.* London: Guilford.

Erikson, E. H. (1950). Childhood and Society. New York, NY: W. W. Norton & Company.

Feeney, J. A., & Noller, P. (2004). Attachment and sexuality in close relationships. In: J. H. Harvey, A. Wenzel, & S. Sprecher (Eds.), *The Handbook of Sexuality in Close Relationships* (pp. 183–201). Mahwah, NJ: Erlbaum.

Hanak, N. (2004). *Afektivna vezanost: provera konstrukta na adolescentnom uzorku* [Attachment: validating a construct on a sample of adolescents]. Master's thesis, Faculty of Philosophy, Belgrade.

Radke-Yarow, M., Cummings, E. M., Kuczynski, L., & Chapman, M. (1985). Patterns of attachment in two-and-three-year-olds in normal families and families with parental depression. *Child Development, 56*: 884–893.

Stanojević, T. S. (2000). Afektivno vezivanje—transgeneracijski prenos [Attachment—transgenerational transmission]. Master's thesis, Faculty of Philosophy, Belgrade.

Stanojević, T. S. (2005). Students: love relationships and the risk of AIDS. In: M. Francesko & M. Zotović (Eds.), *Psychosocial Aspects of Social Transition in Serbia. The Personality of the Multicultural Society, No. 5* (pp. 268–284). Novi Sad: Department of Psychology, Faculty of Philosophy.

Stanojević, T. S., & Kostić, A. (2007). *Afektivna vezanost i odnosprema studiranju u tranzicionim uslovima* [Attachment and studying in transition conditions]. Paper presented at a symposium as part of the convention of psychologists, published in the proceedings from the 55th Scientific Conference of Psychologists in Serbia, Belgrade.

Van IJzendoorn, M. H., & Bakermans-Kranenburg, M. (1996). Attachment representations in mothers, fathers, adolescents and clinical groups: a meta analytic search for normative data. *Journal of Consulting and Clinical Psychology, 64*: 8–21.

Van IJzendoorn, M. H., Sagi, A., & Lambermon, M. W. E. (1992). The multiple caretaker paradox: data from Holland and Israel. In: R. C. Pianta (Ed.), *New Directions from Child Development: No. 57, Beyond the Parent: The Role of Other Adults in Children's Lives* (pp. 5–24). San Francisco, CA: Jossey-Bass.

CHAPTER FOURTEEN

Attachment in postwar societies of the former Yugoslavia

Vladimir Hedrih, Marija Pejičić and Ivana Pedović

Introduction

Social trauma and attachment

Alexander (2004) speaks of cultural trauma as an experience by members of a community who had been exposed to some horrible event which has left indelible traces on their collective consciousness, thus making their memories permanent, and fundamentally and irreversibly changing their identities.

By viewing the social system as an object, psychoanalysts consider this relationship between an individual and the social system to be similar to that between a mother and a child (Hernandez de Tubert, 2006). That similarity reflects in the function of containment, which is analysed by Bion (1962, in Hernandez de Tubert, 2006). In the same manner as the mother is a container for the physiological and emotional needs of the child, the society should also be sensitive to the needs and sufferings of an individual and a group. If the social system does not realise this function, trauma occurs, which can be equally important as the one experienced by a child in his relationship with an unresponsive mother.

According to attachment theory, emotional experiences with a main attachment figure lead to the formation of certain beliefs about oneself and significant others, inner working models, and appropriate patterns of attachment: secure, avoidant, ambivalent, or disorganised. Some research (Stefanović-Stanojević, 2007; see also Chapter Thirteen) indicated an increase in the disorganised attachment style in Niš (Republic of Serbia). It is considered to be not only a consequence of a direct traumatic experience of a child but also an unresolved trauma of a parent, which is transferred onto the next generation (Hesse & Main, 2000). Also, the research by

Stefanović-Stanojević and Nedeljković (see Chapter Thirteen) showed that the most dominant pattern in Banja Luka was the preoccupied style, while in Skopje and Niš it was the secure type, after which came avoidant (in Skopje) and fearful attachment pattern (in Niš).

In the case of war or dissolution of a country, which the population of the Socialist Federal Republic of Yugoslavia experienced, the emotional suffering is very intensive. The feeling that the government, which people trusted, did not manage to find a solution and avoid the war, might have led to increased anxiety in the population, while experience of a sudden change and violation of the collective identity produced cultural trauma, which was manifested through the state of shock and intense fear (Alexander, 2004).

Research by Steinberg (1990, in Stefanović-Stanojević, 2011) has shown early patterns to be irreversible, and that the quality of early affective relationships highly correlates with partner relations in the adolescent period and later patterns in partner relations (Stefanović-Stanojević, 2011).

In partner relations it is also possible to construct four patterns of attachment: secure, anxious-preoccupied, dismissive-avoidant, or fearful-avoidant (Bartholomew & Shaver, 1998). If the phenomenon of attachment is to be viewed through the dimensions of the model of self (anxiety) and the model of other (avoidance), the fearful-avoidant pattern would imply a high prevalence of both dimensions (Bartholomew & Shaver, 1998).

In a partner relationship, anxiety is determined by the image that an individual has of herself, and its expression determines to what extent she will be prone to use the strategies of hyperactivation of the system of attachment (Bartholomew, 1990; Shaver & Mikulincer, 2002). Avoidance, as the second dimension, implies focusing on the maintenance of personal independence and the tendency to deactivate the system of attachment, that is, the alienation and the reliance on oneself. An individual with a high score on the dimension of avoidance has a negative model of others.

In war conditions, the success of the social system in the containment of war victims' emotional needs comes under question. Continuing from the perspective of previous studies (Fraley & Brumbaugh, 2004; Haskuka, Sunar, & Alp, 2008; Okello, Nakimuli-Mpungu, Musisi, Broekaert, & Derluyn, 2014; Ferrajão & Oliveira, 2015), which showed that there were relations between war or combat exposure and attachment style, the goal of this study was to examine how war experience is influencing infant attachment and its aftermath in adult attachment on the territory of the former Yugoslavia. It is questionable how much parents, in their state of intense distress, could have represented the source of safety for their children. More precisely, which pattern of attachment dimensions could be characteristic for these children and would it manifest in their partner relations?

The former Yugoslavia

The Socialist Federal Republic of Yugoslavia (SFRY) was a country situated in the Balkan Peninsula. It was formed after World War I and existed until the dissolution in 1992. At the time of dissolution in 1992 amid the Yugoslav wars, it consisted of six federal republics—Slovenia, Croatia, Bosnia and Herzegovina, Serbia, Montenegro, and Macedonia.

The republic of Slovenia

Slovenia was the wealthiest republic of the former Yugoslavia measured in GDP per capita. The dominant religion is Catholicism and the main ethnic group is the Slovenes. It split from the former Yugoslavia in 1991. Except for a brief clash between the Slovenian Territorial Defence Forces and the Yugoslav People's Army, also known as the Weekend War, it was not actively involved in the Yugoslav wars. It is currently a member state of the European Union. The capital of Slovenia is Ljubljana.

The republic of Croatia

Croatia declared independence from Yugoslavia in June 1991, prompting a four-year war known as the Croatian War of Independence between the forces loyal to the Croatian government on one side and the Yugoslav People's Army and forces of the local Serb minority on the other. The conflict ended with the Croatian victory and the expulsion of the majority of the ethnic Serb population from Croatia. The capital of Croatia is Zagreb. Apart from several air and missile attacks, the city itself was not the site of military engagements during the war. The main ethnic group in Croatia are the Croats and the dominant religion is Catholicism. More than 20,000 people were killed and more than 500,000 were displaced as a result of the war on both sides. Currently, Croatia is a member state of the European Union.

Bosnia and Herzegovina

Bosnia and Herzegovina is home to three main ethnic groups, officially called "constituent peoples", in order of population size—Bosniaks, Serbs, and Croats. The religious composition also follows the ethnic composition with Sunni Islam, Orthodox Christianity, and Catholicism being the three major religions. In 1992, the government of the republic declared independence, after a referendum that was boycotted by the majority of inhabitants of Serb ethnicity. A war ensued, fought mainly between the Bosniak-dominated forces of the Republic of Bosnia and Herzegovina, the Croat forces of the Croatian Defence Council, and the Serb-dominated forces of the Republika Srpska. The war, now known as the Bosnian War, resulted in the internal reorganisation of Bosnia and Herzegovina, through the creation of two parts, called entities—the Bosniak and Croat-dominated Federation of Bosnia and Herzegovina and the Serb-dominated Republika Srpska, with the Brčko District as the third region administered by the local government.

The capital of Bosnia and Herzegovina is Sarajevo, which is also the capital of the Federation of Bosnia and Herzegovina. During the war, Sarajevo was the site of both intense ethnic violence and heavy fighting between the opposing sides. The de facto capital of Republika Srpska is the city of Banja Luka. During the war, the city was the site of some ethnic violence, its inhabitants were involved in the war as soldiers, and it received many refugees, but the city itself was not the site of major military operations.

The Bosnian war was the bloodiest of the Yugoslav wars with more than 100,000 people killed on all sides and more than two million displaced.

Due to the complexities of Bosnia and Herzegovina, samples were collected from both the Federation of Bosnia and Herzegovina and the Republika Srpska.

The republic of Serbia

Although not itself the site of the early Yugoslav wars, Serbia was involved in all of them first through the Yugoslav People's Army whose soldiers during the wars were primarily drafted from Serbia, and after that through support provided to Serb forces fighting in Croatia and Bosnia. Serbia became independent only in 2006, after the dissolution of the successor state it created with Montenegro, following the secession of other republics. Between 1992 and 1995, Serbia was subjected to very broad sanctions imposed by the UN, which devastated the economy. In 1998 and 1999, Serbia, as part of the joint state with Montenegro, fought a war in its Autonomous Province of Kosovo and Metohija (Kosovo for short) against ethnic Albanian rebels seeking independence, known as the Kosovo War. In 1999, NATO forces joined the war on the side of the Albanian rebels and an aerial bombing campaign led to the withdrawal of Serbian forces as well as the displacement of the majority of Serbian and other ethnic minority populations to other parts of Serbia. Kosovo came under the administration of a UN mission. Today, Kosovo remains a disputed territory, with the local Albanian-dominated government of Kosovo claiming independence, which has not been recognised by Serbia.

The majority of the population of Serbia are ethnic Serbs and the dominant religion is Orthodox Christianity. The capital of Serbia is Belgrade. The Serbian subsample was collected in Niš, the third largest city. Apart from the air raids during the three-month NATO involvement in the Kosovo war, no part of the territory currently controlled by the government of Serbia has been a site of military operations in the Yugoslav wars. On the other hand, Serbia became home for large numbers of displaced people fleeing wars in other former Yugoslav republics and many of its citizens participated in the Yugoslav wars as soldiers.

Serbia is currently negotiating its EU accession.

The former Yugoslav republic of Macedonia

Macedonia split from the SFRY in 1991 and remained at peace throughout the Yugoslav wars. It was the site of a minor conflict between the government and ethnic Albanian rebels in 2001, which ended after the arrival of a NATO peace monitoring force. The main ethnic group is the Macedonians, with Albanians being the second largest ethnic group and comprising roughly a quarter of the population. The dominant religion is Orthodox Christianity, with Sunni Islam being the second most widespread. The capital of Macedonia is Skopje.

The smallest of the former Yugoslav republics, Montenegro, has not been included in the study.

The goal of the current study is to explore the level of expression of two attachment dimensions in the five countries and two entities of the former Yugoslavia and examine their relations with a number of country-level variables including exposure to war, war outcome, national wealth, and dominant religion.

Method

Sample

The study included six subsamples from five countries and two entities of the former Yugoslavia—Slovenia, Croatia, Serbia, Macedonia, and the two entities of Bosnia and Herzegovina. As the goal of the study was comparison between countries, one of the issues that had to be resolved was to find a way to maximise the likelihood that results obtained in the study reflected the differences between countries, and not just differences between samples. Following the example of the famous IBM study conducted by Hofstede (1980), it was decided that all the samples from the countries/entities included in the study be as similar as possible. For this reason, all participants were students of social sciences of vocations primarily in the helping field according to the spherical model of vocational interests (Tracey & Rounds, 1996). Participants were students of psychology, education and special education, teacher education, and social work. An overview of samples is shown in Figure 1.

Variables and instruments

Affective attachment dimensions: anxiety and avoidance were measured by using the Serbian, Macedonian, Bosnian, Croatian, and Slovenian versions of the Experiences in Close Relationships—Revised (ECR-R) questionnaire (Fraley, Waller, & Brennan, 2000). The Serbian version of the questionnaire used in the study was created by Hanak and Dimitrijević (2013). Macedonian and Slovenian language versions were created through back-translation. Since differences between Croatian, Bosnian, and Serbian languages can be considered to be minor at most, these two versions were created by asking a colleague from Bosnia and one from Croatia, native speakers of these languages, to correct the spelling and wording of the Serbian version so to make the test conform to the Bosnian and Croatian language norms. The ECR-R itself is a thirty-six-item self-report measure utilising a seven-point Likert-type rating scale for recording participants' responses.

In the study using the Serbian version of the instrument, Hanak and Dimitrijević (2013) reported Cronbach's alpha of the scale to be 0.89 and 0.90 for avoidance and anxiety respectively.

Country indicators: as the goal of the study was to explore if there are differences between the countries/entities that can be related to differences in attachment dimension levels,

Country	City	University	Number of participants
Slovenia	Ljubljana	University of Ljubljana	196
Croatia	Zagreb	University of Zagreb	260
Federation of Bosnia and Herzegovina, BiH	Sarajevo	University of Sarajevo	211
Republika Srpska, BiH	Banja Luka	University of Banja Luka	110
Serbia	Niš	University of Niš	173
Macedonia	Skopje	University of Skopje	237

Figure 1. The sample structure.

especially the experience of war, a number of country indicators have been developed and used in the study:

- Level of war exposure—as Sarajevo was an active ground battlefield during the Bosnian war it was assigned rank one. Banja Luka, Zagreb, and Niš were major cities in countries participating in wars. They suffered economically during the wars, their citizens participated in wars as soldiers, and they each received large numbers of refugees fleeing the wars, but apart from airstrikes and some incidents of missile/artillery attacks, these cities were not sites of battles. They were thus assigned rank two. Ljubljana and Skopje were not sites of battles and their countries did not participate in any major Yugoslav war, so these have been assigned rank three as cities least exposed to war.
- Outcome of the war—Ljubljana and Zagreb are cities in countries that won the wars they have participated in and have thus been assigned category one. Sarajevo, Banja Luka, and Skopje belong to countries/entities that participated in wars resulting in stalemates, and have thus been assigned category two. Niš is located in a country that has lost the wars it participated in and has thus been assigned category three.
- Dominant religion—Zagreb and Ljubljana are cities whose citizens are predominantly Christian Catholic, citizens of Sarajevo are predominantly Sunni Muslim, citizens of Banja Luka, Niš, and Skopje are predominantly Orthodox Christian.
- National wealth—GDP per capita corrected for purchasing power parity for Slovenia is 31,720 USD, and due to this it has been assigned the score thirty-two. Statistics for Croatia, Serbia, and Macedonia are 21,791 USD, 13,944 USD, and 10,718 USD and have been assigned scores twenty-two, fourteen, and eleven respectively. No data was obtained for separate GDPs of the Republika Srpska and the Federation of Bosnia and Herzegovina, so both entities have been assigned scores based on the country level indicator of 9,800 USD, making their score ten.
- EU membership—Croatia and Slovenia are EU member states and have been assigned rank one. Serbia is negotiating its EU membership and has been assigned rank two. Bosnia and Herzegovina and Macedonia are candidates for EU membership and have thus been assigned rank three.

The country indicators were used on two levels: at the individual level each participant was assigned the indicator value for the country he participated in the study in, and at the country/entity level average scores on attachment measures for each country were paired with indicator values for that country. With these two sets of data, individual level and country level correlations were calculated respectively.

Procedure

Students were asked to complete the ECR-R form in their language during classes at the university. This was done in collaboration with the academic staff and authorities of their faculties/universities. Researchers travelled to each of the six cities and asked the faculty authorities and professors of the university to ask their students to participate in the study and to allow a part of their classes to be used for completing the test.

Results

Mean values, standard deviations, and internal consistency measures for all six subsamples as well as for the total sample are presented in Figure 2.

ANOVA comparisons of arithmetic means of subsamples shows statistically significant differences on both avoidance ($F = 5.996$, sig < 0.001) and anxiety ($F = 8.886$, sig < 0.001). Relative to avoidance dimension, post hoc comparisons via Fisher's Least Significant Difference tests show statistically significant differences between Slovenia on one side and all the other subsamples on the other. Relative to anxiety, the same procedure shows statistically significant

Attachment dimension	Country/ entity	Arithmetic mean	Standard deviation	Cronbach's alpha
Avoidance	Slovenia	56.17	14.25	.852
	Croatia	61.30	17.47	.907
	FBiH	63.05	15.94	.857
	RS	62.76	15.91	.891
	Serbia	60.90	16.17	.860
	Macedonia	63.42	13.39	.748
Anxiety	Slovenia	66.18	16.17	.846
	Croatia	65.94	19.28	.903
	FBiH	60.60	18.65	.869
	RS	55.24	19.49	.921
	Serbia	58.12	17.44	.847
	Macedonia	59.43	16.98	.843
Avoidance	Entire sample	61.26	15.53	.854
Anxiety	Entire sample	61.08	18.14	.871

Figure 2. Mean values, standard deviations, and internal consistency measures of attachment measures for the sample included in the study and the six subsamples included in the study. Abbreviations: FBiH—Federation of Bosnia and Herzegovina; RS—Republika Srpska.

	Avoidance		Anxiety	
Country level indicator (correlation coefficient used)	CL/IL mean	CL SD	CL/IL mean	CL SD
Level of war exposure (Rho)	−.185/−.051	−.679	247/.056	−.694
War outcome (Eta)	.794/.337*	.340	.913/.352*	.314
Dominant religion (Eta)	.736/.131*	.274	.950/.192*	.253
National wealth (Rho)	−.754/−.139*	.116	.696/.150*	−.476
EU membership status (Eta)	.794/.361*	.340	.913/.317*	.316

Designations: CL—country level, IL—individual level, *—sig < .05.

Correlations were calculated between subsample mean values and standard deviations on the attachment dimensions and country level indicators as described in the method section. Country level correlations are included in the study on the six countries/entities, while the individual level correlations were obtained by assigning each participant a value of each indicator according to the country/entity in which he participated in the study and calculating correlations between that value and his attachment dimensions' scores. Due to a small number of cases, statistical significance of country level correlations has not been calculated. Spearman's correlation coefficient was calculated for all variables except the dominant religion, where Eta correlation coefficient was used due to the nominal nature of the dominant religion variable.

Figure 3. Correlations between the country/subsample level indicators and mean levels and variability levels (standard deviations) of attachment dimensions on subsamples.

differences between Slovenia and Croatia on one side, and all the other subsamples on the other. It also shows a statistically significant difference between Republika Srpska and the Federation of Bosnia and Herzegovina and Macedonia subsamples.

Relative to the level of war exposure, results show low to medium correlations with the mean levels of both dimensions, but a relatively high one with the country level standard deviation on both dimensions. The direction of the correlations indicates a higher variability of avoidance and anxiety in countries that were more exposed to war. Relative to the outcome of the war, participants from countries that won the wars tend to have lower avoidance and higher anxiety, but this correlation comes mainly from the Slovenian subsample that has both highest scores on anxiety and lowest on avoidance. Dominant religion is in correlation with the attachment dimensions, but it should be noted that the dominant religion differences also follow the wealth differences between territories (Catholic subsamples the wealthiest, Orthodox medium, Sunni Muslim the poorest). National wealth tends to be completely contingent on the EU membership status, with the two wealthiest countries being at the same time EU member states, the third wealthiest (Serbia) being in the process of negotiation, and the poorest countries/entities still waiting for the accession process to begin.

Discussion

Relative to the goal of the study, the results clearly show that attachment measure scores differ across subsamples. Slovenian subsample is the most extreme case, having the lowest average on avoidance and the highest on anxiety compared to all the other samples. Relative to anxiety, the subsamples considered create two prominent groups with one group containing Slovenian and Croatian subsamples, with relatively higher anxiety scores, and the other group containing the other four subsamples. Alternatively, the Republika Srpska subsample could be considered to represent a group of its own, given a prominently lower average level of anxiety scores compared to other subsamples. The study presented here shows that students from Macedonia have a higher mean value on anxiety, compared to the Republika Srpska subsample, while the previous study (see Chapter Thirteen) showed the opposite direction of the difference on the dimension, negative model of self. In contrast to the present study, the previously mentioned study, where UPIPAV-R (see Chapter Thirteen) was used to measure the attachment quality, showed more differences between three subsamples (Serbia, Macedonia, and Republika Srpska), where the Macedonia subsample had a more pronounced negative model of others and less pronounced negative model of self in comparison with students from Republika Srpska and Serbia.

As the main goal of this study was to examine the possible general effects of the recent wars the countries have passed through, the subject of prime interest was to examine if differences in the attachment dimension levels across countries might correlate with some of the war experience indicators of the country. In general, exposure to war can be expected to shift the attachment dimension values towards the insecure part of the spectrum thus increasing both anxiety and avoidance values. It follows that populations of countries that have had more exposure to war should score higher on one or both of the attachment dimensions, thus creating a correlation between the level of exposure to war and one or both of the attachment dimensions. Contrary to this expectation, our results show the mean levels of both attachment dimensions correlate more strongly with other examined country level indicators—like religion and economic wealth—than to exposure to war. Correlations with the war outcome are somewhat higher, but not in the direction expected. The two subsamples from countries that won the wars have the highest mean anxiety scores (Slovenia, Croatia), and the country that lost the wars (Serbia) has its mean score in line with subsamples from the two countries/entities whose wars ended in stalemates (Federation of Bosnia and Herzegovina, Macedonia) and higher than the third (Republika Srpska).

As for the generalisability of the obtained results, it should be noted that, like most studies of postwar societies, this is an ex post facto study, with no data on the pre-war attachment scores to be used for comparison. It should also be noted that the study was not conducted on samples from the general population, but on samples of students intentionally chosen to be similar in many regards except the country/entity they live in. The study detected differences in mean scores on attachment dimensions across the subsamples from the studied countries/entities of the former Yugoslavia, but the patterns of differences correlated more with war outcome, religious composition of the countries/entities the subsamples were collected in, the differences in national wealth, and EU membership status than to the level of exposure to war of each particular country. To try to explain these results the findings of Alexander (2004) might be considered, who states events that are considered the causes of trauma are not by themselves traumatic. Certain events receive the label of trauma based on their representations by certain institutions (for example, mass media, bureaucracy, science, law), and the selection of those pieces of information by the authorities. Also, Hernandez de Tubert (2006) states that when the social system publicly supports but secretly breaks current social values and laws—as in the case of corruption, fraud, or lying—that could also lead to social trauma. The results of the current study were not in concordance with the expectation that war exposure will lead to higher avoidance and higher anxiety. On the other hand, data collected by Transparency International (transparency.org) in 2013 showed that the Global Corruption Barometer among examined former Yugoslav countries reported the highest levels of corruption in Slovenia and Croatia. It is possible that this perception could lead to trauma and therefore to forming adult attachment dimensions, thus resulting in higher scores of anxiety and avoidance in those countries.

This leads to the possible conclusion that exposure to the war itself in former Yugoslav countries had a smaller influence in forming adult attachment than the events and dynamics of societies that occurred after the war. Future studies into socioeconomical factors and narrative constructions around them in societies of former Yugoslav countries might help examine this possibility further.

Acknowledgement

This study was supported by a grant from the Serbian Ministry of Education, Science, and Technological Development through the project 179002, and the German Academic Exchange Office (DAAD) through the Trauma, Trust, and Memory project. A preliminary version was presented at the "Empirijska istrazivanja u psihologiji [Empirical Research in Psychology]" conference in 2017 in the form of an oral presentation.

References

Alexander, J. C. (2004). Toward a theory of cultural trauma. In: J. C. Alexander, R. Eyerman, B. Giesen, N. J. Smelser, & P. Sztompka (Eds.), *Cultural Trauma and Collective Identity* (pp. 1–30). Berkeley, CA: University of California Press.

Bartholomew, K. (1990). Avoidance of intimacy: an attachment perspective. *Journal of Social and Personal Relationships, 7*: 147–178.

Bartholomew, K., & Shaver, P. (1998). Methods of assessing attachment: do they converge. In: J. A. Simpson & W. S. Rholes (Eds.), *Attachment Theory and Close Relationships* (pp. 25–45). New York: Guilford.

Erikson, E. H. (1959). *Identity and the Life Cycle*. New York : International Universities Press.

Ferrajão, P. C., & Oliveira, R. A. (2015). Attachment patterns as mediators of the link between combat exposure and posttraumatic symptoms: a study among Portuguese war veterans. *Military Psychology, 27*: 185–195.

Fraley, R. C., & Brumbaugh, C. C. (2004). A dynamical systems approach to conceptualizing and studying stability and change in attachment security. In: W. S. Rholes & J. A. Simpson (Eds.), *Adult attachment: Theory, research, and clinical Implications* (pp. 86–132). New York: Guilford.

Fraley, R. C., Waller, N. G., & Brennan, K. A. (2000). An item-response theory analysis of self-report measures of adult attachment. *Journal of Personality and Social Psychology, 78*: 350–365.

Hanak, N., & Dimitrijević, A. (2013). A Serbian version of modified and revised Experiences in Close Relationships scale (SM–ECR–R). *Journal of Personality Assessment, 95*: 530–538.

Haskuka, M., Sunar, D., & Alp, I. E. (2008). War exposure, attachment style, and moral reasoning. *Journal of Cross-Cultural Psychology, 39*: 381–401.

Hernandez de Tubert, R. (2006). Social trauma: the pathogenic effects of untoward social conditions. *International Forum of Psychoanalysis, 15*: 151–156.

Hesse, E., & Main, M. (2000). Disorganized infant, child, and adult attachment: collapse in behavioral and attentional strategies. *Journal of the American Psychoanalytic Association, 48*: 1097–1127.

Hofstede, G. (1980). *Culture's Consequences: International Differences in Work-Related Values*. Beverly Hills, CA: Sage.

Okello, J., Nakimuli-Mpungu, E., Musisi, S., Broekaert, E., & Derluyn, I. (2014). The association between attachment and mental health symptoms among school-going adolescents in northern Uganda: the moderating role of war-related trauma. PLoS ONE 9(3): e88494.

Shaver, P. R., & Mikulincer, M. (2002). Attachment-related psychodynamics. *Attachment and Human Development, 4*: 133–161.

Stefanović-Stanojević, T. (2007). Afektivna vezanost kao kroskulturni fenomen [Attachment as a cross-cultural phenomenon]. In: N. Hanak & A. Dimitrijević (Eds.), *Afektivno vezivanje, teorija, istraživanje, psihoterapija* [Affective bonding, theory, research, psychotherapy] (pp. 45–65). Belgrade: Centar za izdavačku delatnost Fakulteta za specijalnu edukaciju i rehabilitaciju [Publishing Center of the Faculty of Special Education and Rehabilitation].

Stefanović-Stanojević, T. (2011). *Afektivna vezanost, razvoj, modaliteti i procena* [Attachment, development, modalities and evaluation]. Niš: Filozofski fakultet.

Tracey, T., & Rounds, J. (1996). The spherical representation of vocational interests. *Journal of Vocational Behavior, 48*: 3–41.

CHAPTER FIFTEEN

Attachment and mentalization in war veterans with and without post-traumatic stress disorder

Vedrana Berleković and Aleksandar Dimitrijević

A psychiatric attempt to objectify and rationalise psychological symptoms and disorders has included the concept of post-traumatic stress disorder (PTSD). The original definition found the main cause of the disorder to be exposure to highly stressful or traumatising event(s). However, at the end of the twentieth century, the view on PTSD was changing and the importance of subjective elements was increasingly emphasised. The fundamental question for understanding PTSD is a dilemma whether the traumatic event possesses objective characteristics of the event or whether it is an individual response to danger, horror, or helplessness.

This standpoint had been confirmed by many research studies showing that the prevalence of the disorder among individuals who suffered highly stressful events is much lower than it would be expected based on the original definitions of PTSD (Nemeroff et al., 2006). In fact, more than fifty-five per cent of the examined subjects did not develop any psychiatric disorders. This led to an increasing number of studies that focused on factors of personality and environment (as factors of vulnerability) and on resilience, instead of on the quality and intensity of trauma. Studies show that among variables such as gender, ethnicity, age, previous psychological problems, life in underdeveloped or developing countries, and the prevalence of exposure to violence, the strongest predictor of PTSD is the person's reaction alone, involving avoiding, psychogenic amnesia, difficulties in close relationships, and seclusion.

The same is the case when we narrow our focus on war trauma. For almost one hundred years, mental health professionals have wondered why, despite being exposed to the same war conditions, some people develop PTSD, while others do not. While all the above-mentioned variables can be at play again, we studied whether attachment and mentalization could be connected to this phenomenon.

According to attachment theory, one of the prime psychological motivators is the search for security (Holmes, 2006). In the period from eight to twelve months of age, infants attempt to establish and maintain optimal proximity to the attachment figure, turning to exploration only after achieving a satisfactory level of security (Bowlby, 1969), and by the end of the first year, individual differences in proximity maintenance and exploration can be observed in both naturalistic and laboratory settings. Mary Ainsworth describes individual differences in attachment through three behavioural patterns: secure, avoidant, and anxious-ambivalent, conceptualised within a two-dimensional space, with dimensions of anxiety and avoidance (Ainsworth, Blehar, & Waters, 1978). Main and Solomon (1990) extend this categorisation by including disorganised attachment in infants. Four analogous patterns were later described in adults, termed "attachment styles" in the research domain of romantic attachment.

According to John Bowlby (1969), the pattern of attachment is a property of the relationship during the first two or three years of life; as a child grows older, however, the pattern becomes increasingly a property of its personality, due to the development of internal working models of self and attachment figures that operate on the unconscious level and affect intimate and social relations throughout life. Secure attachment, characterised by positive internal working models of self and others, is thus considered to be an instrumental system for the development of the most important psychological function—the development of self and its regulatory mechanisms, most of all mentalization (Fonagy, Gergely, Jurist, & Target, 2002; Mikulincer, Shaver, & Pereg, 2003)—since it provides optimal conditions for the maturation of specific neural structures implicated in affective control and interpersonal and intrapsychic aspects of later socio-emotional functions (Schore, 2003).

The concept of mentalization was defined as "the mental process by which an individual implicitly and explicitly interprets the actions of himself and others as meaningful on the basis of intentional mental states such as personal desires, needs, feelings, beliefs, and reasons" (Bateman & Fonagy, 2004, p. 21), or as "a form of mostly preconscious *imaginative* mental activity, namely, interpreting people's actions in terms of 'intentional' mental states" (Fonagy & Target, 2008, p. 17; emphasis in the original).

Research studies uniformly confirm that secure attachment predicts various indicators of, for instance, better social acceptance by peers or a more open relationship with parents (Allen et al., 1998; Sroufe, Egeland, Carlson, & Collins, 2005). Also, attachment is deeply involved in regulating negative emotions provoked by the appraisal of threats and dangers (Mikulincer & Shaver, 2008, p. 507), which makes secure attachment relationship a foundation of effective affect regulation. This assertion has been tested in numerous studies—experimental as well as observational and correlational, developmental as well as clinical and socio-psychological—and "findings are coherent [and] mutually reinforcing" (Mikulincer & Shaver, 2008, p. 526). At the same time, the capacity for mentalization is a key determinant of self-organisation and encompasses the key socio-cognitive capacities that enable us to understand why people think or relate in a certain way.

In sharp contrast to this, extreme forms of insecure attachment, especially the disorganised ones, can compromise the capacity for mentalization throughout life (Holmes, 2006). Studies show that the capacity for mentalization in people who have suffered trauma is significantly underdeveloped (Fonagy & Target, 2008). Periods of crisis and traumatic situations are challenging for those who are characterised by uncertain early development, while the quality of secure attachment increases the chance of the relative adaptive response to trauma. Traumatised individuals are characterised by a lack of imagination, interest, or possibility to access the mental world of others and by the lack of insight into their own internal states (Fonagy, 2006). Traumatised children cannot learn words for feelings, while traumatised adults have significant problems in recognising facial expressions of others (Fonagy & Target, 2008), probably because their cognitive functions that normally prevent confusion between fantasy and memory are compromised. Similar deficits can be observed in people with PTSD (Fonagy, 2006). Therapeutic work with traumatised people, whose condition, among other things, is characterised by intrusive traumatic memories, shows how strongly they are trying to rid their mind of experiences related to the trauma.

Only a few studies have focused on the relationship between attachment and war trauma. It has been found that secure attachment is connected to lower scores on PTSD measures (Dieperink, Leskela, Thuras, & Engdahl, 2001); that attachment anxiety is a significant predictor of how combat exposure affects the development of PTSD (Ferrajão & Oliveira, 2015); and that both anxiety and avoidance play a role (Currier, Holland, & Allen, 2012). On the other hand, a longitudinal study over twenty-four years showed that post-traumatic symptoms led to insecure attachment (Franz et al., 2014). When it comes to mentalization, to the best of our knowledge, there have not been any studies connecting it with war trauma.

Considering that the development of PTSD after encountering a traumatic event may depend primarily on the individual's response to trauma and that the lack of capacity to symbolise and mentalize traumatic events may be shaped by the quality of the attachment system, the aim of this study is to examine the connection between the quality of attachment and the capacity for mentalization with the prevalence of PTSD.

Having this in mind, we hypothesise that there will be a statistically significant difference between groups of war veterans with and without PTSD in terms of distribution of attachment patterns and capacity for mentalization: insecure attachment patterns will be more frequently represented in the group of subjects with PTSD and they will also be characterised by a lower level of capacity for mentalization compared to those who did not develop the disorder.

Method

Participants

The study was conducted on a sample of fifty-eight veterans who participated in armed conflicts in the former Yugoslavia from 1991 to 1999. The sample consisted of two groups with an equal number of subjects; the first group consisted of individuals who had been diagnosed with PTSD, while the second group of individuals participated in the war but did not develop PTSD. Their ages ranged from thirty-one to seventy-one.

Materials

Diagnosis of PTSD was given by attending psychiatrists after the administration of the Clinician-Administered PTSD Scale—CAPS-DX questionnaire (Blake et al., 1990) and IES-R (Marmar, Weiss, & Metzler, 1997) self-assessment of PTSD symptoms.

Attachment patterns were assessed through self-report measures. The first one was the modified Experiences in Close Relationships—Revised (ECR-R) questionnaire (Fraley, Waller, & Brennan, 2000). This 36-item scale assesses attachment avoidance (Av, odd items) and attachment anxiety (Ax, even items) in close relationships in general. Responses are given on a seven-point Likert scale ranging from "disagree strongly" (1) to "agree strongly" (7). The Serbian adaptation (SM-ECR-R) employed in this study was shown to have very good reliability, with 0.89 for Av and 0.90 for Ax (Hanak & Dimitrijević, 2013). The Revised Questionnaire for Attachment Assessment (QAA-R) (Hanak, 2004, 2010) is a self-report measure based on a theoretical analysis of the construct of attachment and of other instruments designed to assess attachment quality, such as the AAI (Main, Goldwyn, & Hesse, 1998) and the Adult Attachment Projective (George & West, 2001). The QAA-R features seven eleven-item subscales, with internal consistencies in the 0.71 to 0.87 range (Hanak, 2010). Using a combination of subscale scores and employing K-means cluster analysis, respondents may be classified into four groups, corresponding to the four attachment patterns: secure, fearful, preoccupied, and dismissing.

Mentalization was assessed through the twenty-eight-item Mentalization Scale (MentS), where responses are given on a five-point Likert scale, ranging from "completely disagree" (1) to "completely agree" (5). It contains three subscales—mentalization of one's own inner states (MentS-S), mentalization of others' mental states (MentS-O), and motivation for mentalization (MentS-M)—all of which are highly reliable and replicated in a clinical sample (Dimitrijević, Hanak, Altaras Dimitrijević, & Jolić Marjanović, 2017).

Procedure

Subjects were tested at the Military Medical Academy in Belgrade. All participants were given necessary explanations about the study and the protection of anonymity and confidentiality of data, and they signed informed consent forms. Psychiatrists trained in assigning the CAPS-DX questionnaire conducted the diagnostic procedure, after which the war veterans were divided into two groups, those with (PTSD) and without PTSD (No-PTSD). Thereafter, all participants filled in the above-mentioned questionnaires. At the end of the procedure, participants were thanked for their participation and informed about the possibility of debriefing if they would need it.

Results

All applied instruments were highly reliable, with the following alphas: for IES-R: 0.95; for SM-ECR-R: 0.89 and for QAA-R: 0.92.

Affiliation to the attachment patterns was determined by the K-cluster analysis method with limitation to four groups, so the theoretical assumption of the four basic patterns is followed. The analysis was conducted separately for the two groups. The results presented in Figure 1 show that 40% of respondents belong to the secure pattern, 14% to the avoidant, 22% to the preoccupied, and 24% to the disorganised.

To verify the hypothesis that veterans who developed PTSD differ significantly in comparison to those without PTSD in terms of attachment quality and capacity for mentalization, K-means cluster analysis and analysis of variance were employed.

As shown in Figure 2, cluster analysis demonstrated that the clinical population is dominated by the insecure form of attachment—86% of respondents belong to this group (disorganised 41%, preoccupied 21%, and avoidant 24%), while only 14% are characterised by secure attachment patterns.

The results presented in Figure 2 show that the group without PTSD includes 66% securely attached participants and 34% insecurely attached ones (avoidant 3%, preoccupied 24%, disorganised 7%).

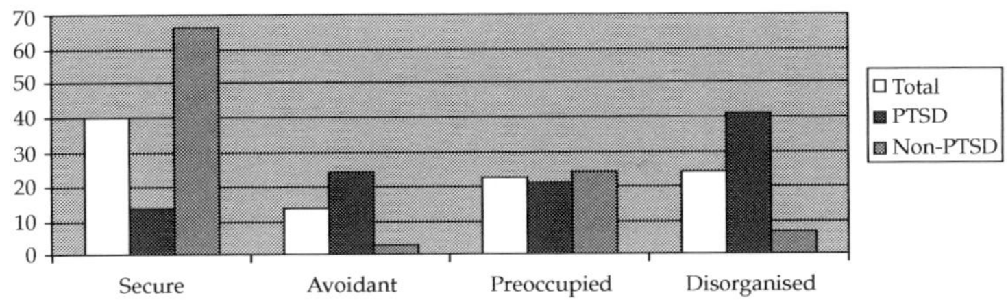

Figure 1. Distribution of attachment patterns in percentages (entire sample, PTSD, No PTSD).

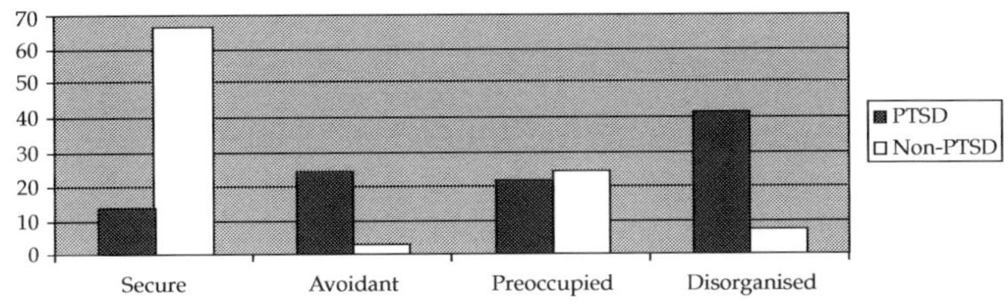

Figure 2. Affiliation of PTSD/No PTSD group to attachment patterns in percentages.

Scale	Group	M	SD	F	Sig.
MentS-S	PTSD	29.6207	7.44222	2.085	.154
	No PTSD	26.7586	7.65159		
MentS-O	PTSD	31.8621	7.61917	14.119	**.000**
	No PTSD	37.9655	4.29687		
MentS-M	PTSD	31.1379	4.77137	9.855	**.003**
	No PTSD	35.2069	5.09467		
MentS-total	PTSD	96.6552	8.78422	8.138	**.006**
	No PTSD	103.8276	10.30280		

Figure 3. Analysis of variance in MentS scores for PTSD and No PTSD groups.

Results of the analysis of variance (Figure 3) indicate that there is a statistically significant difference between people with PTSD and subjects from the control group in terms of the capacity for mentalization ($F = 8.138$, $p < 0.01$). The comparison of descriptive statistics suggests that, in general, the PTSD group ($M = 96.6552$, $SD = 8.78422$) is characterised by a lower capacity for mentalization parameters compared to the No PTSD group. We can see that the latter is characterised by significantly higher parameters on two of the three MentS subscales.

Discussion

The purpose of this study was to examine whether attachment (in)security and/or mentalization are connected to war trauma. In order to achieve that we surveyed equally sized groups of war veterans who developed PTSD and those who did not.

When we looked at the sample as a whole, it turned out that the largest group of respondents was categorised as securely attached—40%, which is consistent with other findings that show the general population in Serbia has a smaller proportion of secure attachment style (Dimitrijević, Hanak, & Milojević, 2011; Hanak, 2010) compared to samples in other parts of Europe or North America (Bakermans-Kranenburg & Van IJzendoorn, 2009). It seems that the group of war veterans is not significantly different from other samples in Serbia and one might even speculate about the whole population being traumatised to a certain extent. The distribution of the three insecure patterns included an unexpectedly high proportion of the disorganised—24%, while the preoccupied with 22% and the avoidant with 14% were in their usual range for Serbia. Here we see that the exposure to war experiences does have specific consequences in terms of attachment disorganisation: veterans are equally rarely as secure as other citizens of Serbia, but are more frequently without any constant strategy in establishing a close relationship.

The situation becomes strikingly different once we look at subgroups. The group of veterans without PTSD is dominated by the secure quality of attachment, its 66% is above the international average and in stark contrast to other studies in Serbia. One could hypothesise that this is a group of men with particularly well-established attachment, but one must not forget the option that these subjects were particularly motivated to present themselves in a very favourable light. The distribution of attachment patterns in the PTSD group shows that 86% of subjects belonging to this group are characterised by insecure and just 14% are securely attached. This is a characteristic of clinical samples defined by a severe mental disorder, like that of heroin addicts where we found 9% were securely attached (Grubac, Dimitrijević, & Hanak, 2011). The results also confirm the hypothesis that insecure attachment patterns are more frequently represented in subjects with PTSD in contrast to the No PTSD group. Unfortunately, our research design does not enable us to offer any causal conclusions.

People with the diagnosis of PTSD are also characterised by a reduced capacity for understanding mental states of others and motivation to deal with the mental world compared to people without this disorder. The finding is consistent with the aforementioned theoretical and empirical assumptions that mentalization is lower in the victims of trauma and patients with PTSD. We add to the body of knowledge the detail that the same is true of war veterans who develop PTSD. Contrary to expectations, however, the results of our study show no statistically significant difference between the respondents from two groups in terms of the capacity for mentalization of inner mental states. The starting point for the interpretation of the findings can be the fact that mentalization does not constitute a unitary concept, and that impairment or "distortion" of this capacity is not necessarily reflected in all its aspects. It should also be kept in mind that MentS is a self-report measure, so its reliability cannot be perfect. The obtained result should certainly be the subject of further research. However, the data obtained confirms the hypothesis that people with PTSD are characterised by a lower level of capacity for mentalization.

More than four-fifths of the respondents in our sample diagnosed with PTSD belong to one of the insecure attachment patterns, while half of them belong to the disorganised pattern. On the other hand, more than two-thirds of the respondents without a post-traumatic diagnosis belong to a secure form of attachment. In addition, the veterans without PTSD are characterised by a higher capacity for mentalization in relation to the ones with PTSD.

The quality of attachment and the capacity for mentalization related to it provide the optimal level of emotional excitation and are in fact a significant protective factor in the face of stressful and traumatic situations. Greater awareness of affective states leads to greater opportunities for their modulation and the regulation of reactions that follow. Periods of crisis and traumatic situations are far more challenging for those who are characterised by insecure attachment and low mentalization, as they can easily be flooded by anxiety and lack the skills required for eliciting social support in times of need.

One of the limitations of our studies is related to the characteristics of the sample. Although it was possible to reach statistically reliable conclusions and the number of subjects is on the level of other studies in the field (e.g., in Ferrajão & Oliveira, 2015, N = 30 + 30), the sample size should be bigger in future studies, especially if the plan is to form four groups of patients in order to study differences among attachment patterns. Likewise, the results obtained should be verified with more sophisticated instruments, like Adult Attachment Interview, Reflective Function Scale, or Adult Attachment Projective, and not only with questionnaires.

Having in mind the results of our study and the theoretical framework, we can conclude that secure attachment and mentalization can be thought of as a kind of intra-psychological filter, a protective factor in facing traumatic experiences in general, and war trauma in particular, which can help against the development of chronic psychiatric syndromes such as PTSD.

References

Ainsworth, M. D. S., Blehar, M. C., & Waters, E. (1978). *Patterns of Attachment: A Psychological Study of the Strange Situation*. Hillsdale, NJ: Erlbaum.

Allen, J. G. (2006). Mentalizing in Practice. In: J. G. Allen & P. Fonagy (Eds.), *Handbook of Mentalization-Based Treatment* (pp. 3–31). Chichester: Wiley.

Allen, J. P., Moore, C., Blake, D., Weathers, F., Nagy, L., Kaloupek, D., Klauminzer, G., Charney, D., Keane, T. G., & Bell, K. (1998). Attachment and adolescent psychosocial functioning. *Child Development*, 69(5): 1406–1419.

Bakermans-Kranenburg, M. J., & Van IJzendoorn, M. H. (2009). The first 10,000 adult attachment interviews: distributions of adult attack representations in clinical and non-clinical groups. *Attachment & Human Development*, *11*: 223–263.

Bateman, A., & Fonagy, P. (2004). *Psychotherapy for Borderline Personality Disorder: Mentalization Based Treatment*. Oxford: Oxford University Press.

Blake, D., Weathers, F., Nagy, L., Kaloupek, D., Klauminzer, G., Charney, D., & Keane, T. (1990). *Clinician-Administered PTSD Scale (CAPS)*. Boston, MA: National Center for Post-Traumatic Stress Disorder, Behavioral Science Division.

Bowlby, J. (1969). *Attachment and Loss: Volume 1. Attachment*. London: Hogarth [reprinted London: Pimlico, 1997].

Bowlby, J. (1973). *Attachment and Loss: Volume 2. Separation: Anxiety and Anger.* London: Hogarth [reprinted London: Pimlico, 1998].

Currier, J. M., Holland, J. M., & Allen, D. (2012). Attachment and mental health symptoms among US Afghanistan and Iraq veterans seeking health care services. *Journal of Traumatic Stress, 25*: 623–630.

Dieperink, M., Leskela, J., Thuras, P., & Engdahl, B. (2001). Attachment style classification and posttraumatic stress disorder in former prisoners of war. *American Journal of Orthopsychiatry, 71:* 374–378.

Dimitrijević, A., Hanak, N., & Milojević, S. (2011). Psychological characteristics of future helping professionals: empathy and attachment of psychology students. *Psihologija, 44*: 97–115.

Dimitrijević, A., Hanak, N., Altaras Dimitrijević, A., & Jolić Marjanović, Z. (2017). The Mentalization Scale (MentS): a self-report measure for the assessment of mentalizing capacity. *Journal of Personality Assessment*.

Ferrajão, P. C., & Oliveira, R. A. (2015). Attachment patterns as mediators of the link between combat exposure and post-traumatic symptoms: a study among Portuguese war veterans. *Military Psychology, 27*: 185.

Fonagy, P. (2006). The mentalization-focused approach to social development. In: J. G. Allen & P. Fonagy. (Eds.), *Handbook of Mentalization-Based Treatment* (pp. 53–101). Chichester: Wiley.

Fonagy, P., & Target, M. (2008). Attachment and mentalization and psychoanalysis. In: E. L. Jurist, A. Slade, & Bergner, S. (Eds.), *Mind in Mind. Infant Research, Neuroscience and Psychoanalysis* (pp. 15–50). New York: Other.

Fraley, R. C., Waller, N. G., & Brennan, K. A. (2000). An item response theory analysis of self-report measures of adult attachment. *Journal of Personality and Social Psychology, 78*: 350–365.

Franz, C. E., Lyons, M. J., Spoon, K. M., Hauger, R. L., Jacobson, K. C., Lohr, J. B., McKenzie, R., Panizzon, M. S., Thompson, W. K., Tsuang, M. T., & Vasilopoulos, T. (2014). Post-traumatic stress symptoms and adult attachment: a 24-year longitudinal study. *The American Journal of Geriatric Psychiatry, 22*: 1603–1612.

George, C., & West, M. (2001). The development and preliminary validation of a new measure of adult attachment: the adult attachment projective. *Attachment & Human Development, 3*: 30–61.

Grubac, K., Dimitrijević, A., & Hanak, N. (2011). Attachment and heroin addiction. Conference paper presented at *Attachment—the Importance of Intimate Relationships from the Cradle to the Grave*, Oslo.

Hanak, N. (2004). Construction of the new instrument for assessment of adult and adolescence attachment. *Psihologija, 37*: 123–142.

Hanak, N. (2010). Razlike između trudnica sigurnog obrasca i nesigurnih obrazaca afektivne vezanosti u pogledu tranzicije ka materinstvu [Differences between securely and insecurely attached pregnant women related to transition to motherhood]. *Psihološka istraživanja* [Psychological Research], *13*: 131–147.

Hanak, N., & Dimitrijević, A. (2013). A Serbian version of modified and revised experiences in close relationships scale (SM–ECR–R). *Journal of Personality Assessment, 95*: 530–538.

Holmes, J. (2006). Mentalizing from a psychoanalytic perspective: what's new? In: J. G. Allen & P. Fonagy (Eds.), *Handbook of Mentalization-Based Treatment* (pp. 31–51). Chichester: Wiley.

Main, M., & Solomon, J. (1990). Procedures for identifying infants as disorganized/disoriented during the Ainsworth strange situation. *Attachment in the Preschool Years: Theory, Research, and Intervention, 1*: 121–160.

Main, M., Goldwyn, R., & Hesse, E. (1988). *Adult attachment scoring and classification system*. Unpublished manuscript. Berkeley, CA: University of California.

Marmar, C. R., Weiss, D. S., & Metzler, T. J. (1997). The peritraumatic dissociative experiences questionnaire. *Assessing Psychological Trauma and PTSD, 2*: 144–168.

Mikulincer, M., & Shaver, P. R. (2008). Adult Attachment and Affect Regulation. In: J. Cassidy & P. R. Shaver (Eds.), *Handbook of Attachment: Theory, Research, and Clinical Applications (2nd edn)* (pp. 503–531). New York: Guilford.

Mikulincer, M., Shaver, P. R., & Pereg, D. (2003). Attachment theory and affect regulation: the dynamics, development, and cognitive consequences of attachment-related strategies. *Motivation and Emotion, 27*: 77–102.

Nemeroff, C. B., Bremner, J. D., Foa, E. B., Mayberg, H. S., North, C. S., & Stein, M. B. (2006). Posttraumatic stress disorder: a state of the science review. *Journal of Psychiatric Research, 40: 1–21.*

Schore, A. N. (2003). *Affect Regulation and the Repair of the Self*. New York: Norton.

Sroufe, L. A., Egeland, B., Carlson, E., & Collins, W. A. (2005). Placing early attachment experiences in developmental context. In: K. E. Grossmann, K. Grossmann, & E. Waters (Eds.), *Attachment from Infancy to Adulthood: The Major Longitudinal Studies* (pp. 48–70). New York: Guilford.

CHAPTER SIXTEEN

Psychic trauma and drug addiction*

Nikola Atanassov and Svetoslav Savov

The onset of drug addiction is determined by a complex combination of constitutional, social, and psychological factors. Although it is the individual who is affected, the role of social factors is of crucial importance for both the genesis and the persistence of the disturbance.

Psychodynamic thinking has from the very beginning associated addiction with experiences of early childhood trauma. Early experiences were regarded as a predisposition for a pathology triggered by later events: these involve interactions with other people, or—as is the case of social trauma in the narrow sense—constitute calamities affecting large social groups (Garland, 1998). More recently, the concept of relational trauma has gained influence. Addiction has been related to concepts of "relational autonomy", identity, and psychosocial integration (Johansen, Darnell, & Franzen, 2013). It has been demonstrated that psychic trauma in childhood leads to a disturbance in the capabilities for mentalization and affect regulation. Mentalization theories, too, see childhood trauma as a consequence of failure of the environment to provide the conditions necessary for the development of self and identity. Clinical data relates psychic trauma to the basic characteristics of the personality organisation in patients with drug addiction, most often described as borderline (identity diffusion, partial object relations, domination of primitive defence mechanisms), but extensive research is still lacking.

In this chapter, after a brief review of some important trends in the development of the psychodynamic conceptualisations of addictions, we present our study on the interconnections between the basic personality characteristics of heroin addicted patients and their mentalization capacities.

*The present study was supported by a grant from the International Psychoanalytical Association. An extended version of the theoretical part can be found in our previous publication (Savov & Atanassov, 2012).

Classical psychodynamic approaches to addictions

Many psychoanalytic pioneers were interested in the problem of substance abuse and addictions. Abraham (1926) tried to conceptualise this form of pathology from the point of view of libidinal theory, that is, as a symptom of regress to oral fixations and striving for "orgasmic" experiences. Radó (1928) pointed out that not the toxic agent itself, but the impulse to use it, defines addictions. In general, these authors understood substance abuse from the point of view of euphoric-pleasurable experiences, and believed that the symptom has a "hidden" meaning (for example, symbolising an orally gratifying object).

Glover (1932), however, made an important breakthrough with his hypothesis that the psychoactive substance could be used "progressively"—not only for regressive satisfaction, but also for protecting the subject from primitive (destructive and self-destructive) impulses or even psychosis. Later on, Fenichel (1945) underlined the deep-seated depression and anxiety in addicts. These ideas served as a basis for Khantzian's (1980) work on the "self-medication hypothesis".

Affect regulation

The next generation of psychodynamic models came largely from the ego-psychological tradition. The main difference between ego-psychological theories and classical drive/conflict models is that ego psychologists shift the focus from the symptom to the personality deficits of addicts and their incapability for coping with traumatising anxiety. Drug use is related to specific ego pathology manifested in quick shifts from depressive states to intensive arousal in conflictual relations with important others (Woody, 1977). Addicts react to situations of crisis with affect regression (totalisation of feelings), which is dealt with by splitting unacceptable parts of internal or external reality and denying their existence. However, only when these series of operations are pharmacologically reinforced, a sense of mastery and raised self-esteem can be restored (Wurmser, 1977).

This generation of psychodynamically oriented clinicians concentrates on the clinical reality that patients with drug addiction complain of being either overwhelmed by intolerably painful affects or cut off from their emotions. Referring to these characteristics of the affective life of addicts, Wieder and Kaplan (1969) define drugs as "prosthesis" helping patients to regulate their impaired affective life.

The primitive defence mechanisms drug addicts employ do not efficiently protect them from excessive anxious and depressive states. Consequently, addicts present not only interpersonal difficulties, affect storms, and impulsive behaviour, that are typical for patients with borderline personality disorder (Kernberg, 2003), but their whole emotional life is in a way much more easily "somatised". Thus, impaired affect regulation comes into focus as a central diagnostic feature of the disorder.

We can generalise that the contemporary psychodynamic approach to affective disorders in drug addicted patients abandoned altogether early conceptualisation of pleasure seeking and symbolic importance of the drug. Instead, leading authors like Khantzian (1980, 2003) see the motivation behind substance use as an attempt for "self-medication". Patients addicted to opiates rely on the anti-aggressive effects of the substance which block disorganising and threatening affective states of anger, pain, shame, and loneliness. Drug addicts do not just search for an "escape" or "euphoria". They actually *need* a shield that protects them from excess in anxiety.

Clinicians became naturally interested in the developmental origins of these affective disorders. Krystal (1974) points out that only when the small child is protected from exposure to continuous trauma in early relations, can she develop affect tolerance during latency and adolescence. He makes it clear that primary self-regulation deficits in drug addicts encompass a tendency for affective regress, deficient capability for using anxiety as a signal, as well as impaired tolerance for painful emotions, especially the primitive affect of undifferentiated anxiety-depression.

These deficiencies showing failure in the desomatisation, verbalisation, and symbolisation of affective experiences are quite often observable in psychosomatic conditions characterised by the state of "alexithymia" (Sifneos, 1973). Addicted patients often share some of the basic components of alexithymic functioning (Taylor, Bagby, & Parker, 1997). Clinical experience shows that addicts also have severe difficulties in putting their mental states and affectivity into words. Without having an apt understanding of them, these patients cannot modulate emotions and show tendencies for direct discharge of anxiety in behaviour or somatisations. Interpersonal disappointments easily trigger rapid changes in mood, which an individual with certain predispositions would try to regulate by pharmacological means. Interestingly, alexithymia—a concept highly applicable to addictions—is also one of the roots of contemporary mentalization-based theories.

Mentalization

The concept of mentalization was introduced by Pierre Marty in the 1960s as an extension of the research into psychosomatic phenomena (De Mijolla, 2005). Classically, it refers to the quality and quantity of psychic representations, their verbalisation, and connections with affectivity. From another perspective—that of modern developmental psychopathology—Fonagy (2008, p. 4) defines mentalization as "a form of mostly preconscious imaginative mental activity, namely, interpreting human behaviour in terms of intentional mental states (i.e., needs, desires, feelings, beliefs, goals, purposes, and reasons)". This conceptualisation integrates the notion of "theory of mind" in cognitive developmental models with attachment theory. It is based on three main assumptions (Weinberg, 2006): (1) the feeling of the self as agent is rooted in the experience of being attributed psychic states by a significant other; (2) this capability is a function of the interaction between the caring figures through a process of mirroring; (3) its development can be impaired by traumatic experiences.

Attachment is seen as the main factor in the development of mentalization and the formation of internal representations of affective states. According to Bateman and Fonagy (2004), patients with borderline personality disorder have difficulty in mentalizing mainly in interpersonal and intimate situations, when they are most vulnerable to excesses in anxiety. Deficits in mentalization prevent them from having a good enough "buffer" from affects and trigger "fight or flight" mechanisms. These observations seem highly relevant for the conceptualisation of addictions, having in mind the high percentage of co-morbidity with borderline personality disorder (Trull, Sher, Minks-Brown, Durbin, & Burr, 2000).

Allen, Fonagy, and Bateman (2008) describe a two-way interaction between substance abuse and mentalizing. Intoxication impairs mentalization of own emotional states as well as those of the attachment figures. Deficits in mentalization on the other hand contribute to an inclination for substance abuse under emotional stress caused by interpersonal conflicts with attachment figures.

Contrasting, but also complementing Fonagy's model, Bouchard and Lecours (2008) present a theory of mentalization focused on the development of thinking through binding of instinctual pressure in representative networks. These processes of psychic working through prevent direct discharge into actions or somatisations. Influenced by psychosomatic research done by P. Marty, Krystal's theory of emotions (1974, 1975) and Piaget's conceptualisation of the child's intellectual development from sensor-motor activity towards formal verbal thought, Bouchard and Lecours understand affects as positively or negatively valanced psychological phenomena with a somato-motor tendency for action. This tendency is "desomatised" by a complex process of psychic working through. They assume that representative deficits lead to an excess of the quantitative element (excitation), which has not been transformed into a psychic conflict. Forms of impulsivity, addicted behaviour, and somatisation are interpreted from this point of view as an expression of accumulated drive impulses with no attributed psychological meaning.

Bouchard and Lecours describe mentalization as the "immune system" of the psyche, because it modifies external and internal pressures. Normally, mentalizing contributes to the coherent and meaningful experience of one's own psychic states. Instead of acquiring this tolerable distance from direct affective pressure, drug addicts often suffer from severe anxiety and depression. These conditions are triggered by the deep conviction that the individual is helpless in regulating not only external reality but also her emotional states. Substance abuse is the copying mechanism that replaces mental processing of helplessness, apathy, and emptiness, and thus brings back temporary control.

There is empirical evidence that a significant number of patients with drug addiction, especially heroin addicts, fall into the category of the borderline personality disorder (BPD), that BPD is predisposing to an earlier onset and a greater severity of drug abuse (Bateman & Fonagy, 2004), and that patients diagnosed as having a personality or behaviour disorder are two times more likely to develop drug dependency (Aleman, 2007). Most patients with BPD have had strongly conflicting relationships with their parents, have been subjected to sexual or physical abuse, and have suffered attachment trauma (Fonagy, Luyten, & Strathearn, 2011). So there is reason to believe that traumatic experiences in childhood are one of the factors contributing to the development of BPD. On the other hand, research on mentalization has shown that traumatised patients have an impaired capacity to mentalize, and that—as suggested above—BPD goes with impairments in mentalization and self-regulation capacities.

Since empirical research on personality organisation and mentalization capacities in heroin-addicted patients is scarce, even absent, in the present study we search for correlations between levels and domains of personality organisation according to Kernberg (1975), the processes and contents of affect mentalization, the addiction severity, and the patient's functioning in a treatment programme. We expected a positive correlation between pathological personality organisation and difficulties in mentalization, especially the mentalization of negative affect (anxiety and depression).

Design and procedure

We formed a clinical group of thirty heroin addicts treated in a methadone maintenance programme. We interviewed them individually with the Structured Interview of Personality Organisation 1.07 (STIPO) (Clarkin, Caligor, Stern, & Kernberg, 2006) and we evaluated the transcribed narratives with the Verbal Elaboration of Affect scale (VEA) (Lecours, 2013) and the Measure of Affect Contents (MAC) (Lecours, 2002). The STIPO administration takes between 90 and 120 minutes, and the length of the narratives is between 14–20 pages (mean: 16 pages). The interviews have been audio recorded and fully transcribed. The data was compared with the results of a control group of thirty healthy individuals, parallel in age, sex, and education.

Participants

The mean age in the clinical group is 29.9 years (SD = ± 4,19, range 22–38 years). The majority (70%) are between 26 and 34 years old. Fifteen participants (50%) are female. Three patients (10%) have completed primary school; twenty-three (76.67%) have graduated from high school; and four (13.33%) hold a university degree. Eighteen (60%) are employed. The mean period of heroin abuse is 11.3 years (SD = ± 4,01, range 5–20 years). The average dose of methadone is 139,83 ml (SD = ± 77,75, range 30–300 ml). The mean age in the control group is 29.3 years (SD = ± 5,08, range 20–44 years). The majority (60%) are between 26 and 34 years old. Fifteen participants are female. Three participants (10%) have completed primary school; seventeen (56.67%) have graduated from high school; and nine (30%) hold a university degree. Eighteen (60%) are employed.

Instruments

STIPO

The Structured Interview of Personality Organisation 1.07 is a manual for operationalised assessment of personality organisation according to Kernberg's structural theory. It measures the following dimensions: identity, quality of object relations, primitive defences, coping and rigidity, aggression, and moral values. The instrument has been translated by two clinical psychologists and their translations have been compared in order to reach an optimal final version. The available data shows that STIPO offers a reliable and valid assessment of the organisation of personality (Hörz, Clarkin, Stern, & Caligor, 2011; Stern et al., 2010).

VEA

Verbal Elaboration of Affect scale (VEA) is an instrument that brings the content analysis tradition into psychodynamic theory. The scale is based on Bouchard and Lecours' (2008) theory of mentalization, and measures verbal elaboration of affect by segmentation and coding of narratives. It consists of two orthogonal dimensions: 1) four channels of affect expression: somatisation, motor activity, imagery, and verbalisation, and 2) five levels of affect tolerance and abstraction: explosive impulsiveness, modulated impulsiveness, externalisation, appropriation (subjectivation), and meaning connection. These are twenty possible forms (4 channels × 5 levels) in which a given affect expression could fit. They are used for calculating a weighted score for the quality of affect mentalization. The scale can be used on verbal material with a free enough expression of affect. The scale has been shown to provide reliable and valid assessment of affect mentalization in individual patients or whole clinical groups (Lecours, Bouchard, St-Amand, & Perry, 2000; Lecours, Sanlian, & Bouchard, 2007; Bouchard et al., 2008). The two experts in the present study have participated in a five-day training with the author of the instrument.

MAC

The Measure of Affect Contents (MAC) is a companion instrument to VEA, allowing categorisation of two affect groups: 1) basic, universal, and inborn emotions (for example, joy), and 2) secondary emotions, which can be regarded as a combination of two or more basic emotions (for example, admiration for others, which can be viewed as a combination of joy, interest, love, and wish). In the present study we have focused on the following affect categories relevant for personality pathology: sadness, anger towards others, love towards others, fear, and contempt, as well as positive and negative affects in general.

Results

Reliability

The internal reliability in the present study is very good. We have calculated Cronbach's α for the six big scales of STIPO, and it ranges between 0.74 (coping and rigidity) to 0.93 (identity), while the total internal reliability for the 87 items is 0.97. These results are comparable with the data from the German adaption of the instrument (Doering et al., 2013).

The inter-rater reliability is assessed by calculation of inter-class correlations of the ratings for the scales. The correlations vary from 0.87 (coping and rigidity) to 0.94 (identity), and 100% for the assessment of the level of personality organisation, which shows a very good inter-rater reliability.

The inter-rater reliability of the narrative analysis has been calculated based on three segmented and coded interviews before the actual start of the coding. These results are in the lower, yet acceptable, spectrum. The percentage of agreement on the identification of affect units between the two experts and the author of the instrument is 0.74 for expert one and 0.70 for expert two. For the categories of MAC we calculated coefficients ranging from 0.83 to 0.60, for the channels—0.55 and 0.54; for the levels—0.62 and 0.54; for the valence—0.76 and 0.62. The differences in the coding procedures were discussed so that a unified approach would be applied in the actual assessment process.

STIPO

The data obtained from STIPO supports previous research showing that patients with BPD receive significantly lower results on all STIPO domains in comparison to a control group (Doering et al., 2013). Our study reached similar results for heroin-addicted patients, who score lower on all dimensions in comparison to the clinical group—the highest difference has been observed in the identity rating (mean: 1.10 in the clinical group and 0.37 in the control group, $p < 0.01$). The lowest difference is observed in the scale coping and rigidity (mean: 38.53 in the control group in comparison to 22.47 in the clinical group, $p < 0.01$).

VEA

The results obtained from VEA show that the clinical group is characterised by a significantly higher use of lower mentalization levels: explosive impulsiveness (mean: 34.47 in clinical group in comparison to 26.53 in the control group; $p < 0.01$) and modulated impulsiveness (0.26 for the clinical group and 0.16 for the control group; $p < 0.01$), as well as lower use of externalisation (0.44 for the control group in comparison to 0.32 for the clinical group, $p < 0.01$). Another significant difference is the higher use of the motor channel in the clinical group (0.27 against 0.22, $p < 0.01$) and a lower use of the somatic channel (24,33 against 36,67, $p < 0.01$). Heroin addicted patients show significantly lower levels of mentalization of negative affects (2,61 against 2,37, $p < 0.01$), and contempt (23,38 against 37,62, $p < 0.01$). An unexpected result is that the control group shows significantly higher use of the somatic channel (24,33 for the clinical group and 36,67 for the control group, $p < 0.01$).

Relationship between STIPO and VEA

A significant negative correlation is found between the identity scale and the affect category contempt ($r = -0.52$, $p < 0.01$), and a moderate one between identity ($r = -0.49$, $p < 0.01$) and the overall assessment of verbal elaboration of affect ($r = -0.38$; $p < 0.01$). There is a significant negative correlation between the aggression scale and the categories contempt and negative affects ($r = -0.52$ and $r = -0.54$; $p < 0.01$). There is a moderate correlation between the object relations scale and contempt and negative affects categories ($r = -0.49$ and $r = -0.47$, $p < 0.01$). Primitive defences is moderately correlated with contempt, negative affects, and overall assessment of verbal elaboration of affect ($r = -0.45$, $r = -0.49$ and $r = -0.32$; $p < 0.01$). Probably the most important result is the moderate negative correlation between the personality organisation scale and the overall assessment of VEA ($r = -0.34$, $p < 0.01$), which shows that personality pathology is indeed related to deficits in affect mentalization.

Discussion

These results indicate several important trends. First, the clinical group shows disturbance in all personality dimensions which is an empirical validation of Kernberg's theory according to which BPD patients suffer from identity diffusion, impaired capacity for establishing and maintaining stable and fulfilling object relations, and predominant use of primitive defence mechanisms (i.e., splitting and projective identification).

Second, heroin-addicted patients mentalize their affectivity to a higher extent on lower mentalization levels of abstraction and tolerance of the affect in comparison to healthy individuals, and they use to a higher degree behaviour-oriented representations. They show lower capacity for mentalization of negative affects, which corresponds to the findings of Walter et al. (2009) and Lecours and Bouchard (2011) who state that the mentalization of the negatively valenced affects is related to the presence of personality pathology. Significantly lower results in the mentalization of contempt category shows once again difficulties in the verbalisation of emotions in intimate interpersonal relationships. Perhaps in the lower levels of verbal elaboration of affect heroin patients face a dilemma—verbalising affects through the somatic or through the motor channel—our results show that they choose predominantly the motor channel, which can be understood in the context of the sample. These are patients in a methadone-assisted maintenance programme who no longer suffer from the typical abstinence syndrome, as they experience a constant anti-anxiety and anti-depressive affect from the substance. This means that they most probably get oriented towards the external reality, hence the use of behavioural representations.

Finally, our results show that the personality dimensions defining the differential assessment of the personality organisation (identity, object relations, and primitive defences) are indeed related to the quality of affect mentalization. The overall level of personality organisation is significantly related to the quality of verbal elaboration of affect and also the mentalization of depressive affects, which is expected since BPD patients typically experience difficulties in working through losses and separations. These results support the findings of Fischer-Kern et al. (2010) who state that personality organisation is related to the quality of reflective functioning.

Conclusion

The present study is an attempt to deepen our understanding of the specifics of the psychic structure and mentalization capacities of heroin-addicted patients. The results show significant impairments in all personality domains, which leads to a fragmented, unbalanced view of self and others, lower capacity for maintaining deep and fulfilling interpersonal relationship, and strong tendencies towards aggressive and self-aggressive behaviour. These impairments in personality organisation are connected to a disturbed capacity of verbalisation and symbolisation of affectivity leading to impulsive behavioural mechanisms.

The results can be interpreted as confirming that psychopathology is a predisposition towards drug dependency (Darke, 2013) and that—more specifically—there is a positive correlation between BPD and heroin dependence. Furthermore, they seem to be supporting the hypothesis that the impulsivity and the difficulties in affect regulation of BPD patients are related to problems in mentalization.

The results can be interpreted as confirming that the early traumatic experiences impair the mentalization capacities and therefore lead to disturbances in the development of the self.

References

Abraham, K. (1926). The psychological relations between sexuality and alcoholism. *International Journal of Psychoanalysis*, *7*: 2–10.

Aleman, K. (2007). Object relation quality, alexithymia, and defense mechanisms of drug abusers with antisocial personality disorder. *Social Behavior and Personality: an international journal*, *35*(10), 1335–1352.

Allen, J. G., Fonagy, P., & Bateman, A. W. (2008). *Mentalizing in Clinical Practice*. Washington DC: American Psychiatric Publishing.

Bateman, A. W., & Fonagy, P. (2004). *Psychotherapy for borderline personality disorder. Mentalization Based Treatment*. New York: Oxford University Press.

Bouchard, M.-A., & Lecours, S. (2008). Contemporary approaches to mentalization in the light of Freud's project. In: F. Busch (Ed.), *Mentalization: Theoretical Considerations, Research Findings, and Clinical Implications* (pp. 103–132). New York: Taylor & Francis.

Bouchard, M.-A., Target, M., Lecours, S., Fonagy, P., Tremblay, L.-M., & Schachter, A. (2008). Mentalization in adult attachment narratives: reflective functioning, mental states, and affect elaboration compared. *Psychoanalytic Psychology*, *25*: 47–66.

Clarkin, J., Caligor, E., Stern, B., & Kernberg, O. (2006). *Structured Interview of Personality Organization*. Ithaca, NY: Cornell University.

Darke, S. (2013). Pathways to heroin dependence: time to re-appraise self-medication. *Addiction*, *108:* 659–667.

De Mijolla, A. (Ed.) (2005). *International Dictionary of Psychoanalysis*. New York: Macmillan.

Doering, S., Burgmer, M., Heuft, G., Menke, D., Bäumer, B., Lübking, M., Feldman, M., Hörz, S., & Schneider, G. (2013). Reliability and validity of the German version of the Structured Interview of Personality Organization (STIPO). *BMC Psychiatry*, *13*: 210.

Fenichel, O. (1945). The marihuana addict in the army. *Psychoanalytic Quarterly*, *14*: 578.

Fischer-Kern, M., Buchheim, A., Hörz, S., Schuster, P., Doering, S., Kapusta, N., Taubner, S., Tmej, A., Rentrop, M., Buchheim, P., & Fonagy, P. (2010). The relationship between personality organization, reflective functioning, and psychiatric classification in borderline personality disorder. *Psychoanalytic Psychology*, *4*: 395–409.

Fonagy, P. (2008). The mentalization-focused approach to social development. In: F. Busch (Ed.), *Mentalization: Theoretical Considerations, Research Findings, and Clinical Implications* (pp. 3–56). New York: Taylor & Francis.

Fonagy, P., Luyten, P., & Strathearn, L. (2011). Borderline personality disorder, mentalization, and the neurobiology of attachment. *Infant Mental Health Journal*, *32*(1), 47–69.

Garland, C. (Ed.) (1998). *Understanding Trauma: A Psychoanalytical Approach*. London: Duckworth.

Glover, E. (1932). On the aetiology of drug-addiction. *International Journal of Psychoanalysis*, *13*: 298–328.

Hörz, S., Clarkin, J. F., Stern, B. L., & Caligor, E. (2011). The Structured Interview of Personality Organization (STIPO): an instrument to assess severity and change of personality pathology. In: R. A. Levy, J. S. Ablon, & H. Kächele (Eds.) *Psychodynamic Psychotherapy Research. Evidence-Based Practice and Practice-Based Evidence* (pp. 571–592). New York: Springer.

Johansen, A. B., Darnell F. J., & Franzen E. (2013). Constructing a theory and evidence-based approach to promote and evaluate autonomy in addiction. *Inquiry: An Interdisciplinary Journal of philosophy*, *56*(5): 539–557.

Kernberg, O. (1975). *Borderline Conditions and Pathological Narcissism*. New York: Aronson.

Kernberg, O. (2003). The management of affect storms in the psychoanalytic psychotherapy of borderline patients. *Journal of the American Psychoanalytic Association, 51*: 517–545.

Khantzian, E. (1980). An ego/self theory of substance dependence: a contemporary psychoanalytic perspective. In: D. Lettieri, M. Sayers, & H. W. Pearson (Eds.), *Theories on Drug Abuse: Selected Contemporary Perspectives* (pp. 29–33). Rockville, MD: National Institute on Drug Abuse.

Khantzian, E. J. (2003). Understanding addictive vulnerability: an evolving psychodynamic perspective. *Neuro-Psychoanalysis, 5*: 5–21.

Krystal, H. (1974). The genetic development of affects and affect regression. *Annual of Psychoanalysis, 2*: 98–126.

Krystal, H. (1975). Affect tolerance. *Annual of Psychoanalysis, 3*: 179–219.

Lecours, S. (2002). *Manuel d'Identification des Contenus Affectifs (MAC)*. Unpublished manuscript.

Lecours, S. (2013). *Verbal Elaboration of Affect Scale Scoring Manual (version 7)*. Unpublished manuscript.

Lecours, S., & Bouchard, M. (2011). Verbal elaboration of distinct affect categories and BPD symptoms. *Psychology and Psychotherapy: Theory, Research and Practice, 84*: 26–41.

Lecours, S., Bouchard, M. A., St-Amand, P., & Perry, J. C. (2000). Assessing verbal elaboration of affect in psychotherapy: a preliminary report and single case study. *Psychotherapy Research, 10*: 47–56.

Lecours, S., Sanlian, N., & Bouchard, M.-A. (2007). Assessing verbal elaboration of affect in clinical interviews: exploring sex differences. *Bulletin of the Menninger Clinic, 71*: 227–247.

Radó, S. (1928). The psychical effects of intoxication: attempt at a psycho-analytical theory of drug addiction. *International Journal of Psychoanalysis, 9*: 301–317.

Savov, S., & Atanassov, N. (2013). Deficits of affect mentalisation in patients with drug addiction: theoretical and clinical aspects. *ISRN Addiction, 10*.

Sifneos, P. E. (1973). The prevalence of alexithymic characteristics in psychosomatic patients. *Psychotherapy and Psychosomatics, 22*: 270–285.

Stern, B., Caligor, E., Clarkin, J., Critchfield, K. L., Hörz, S., MacCornack, V., Lenzenweger, M., & Kernberg, O. (2010). Structured Interview of Personality Organization (STIPO): preliminary psychometrics in a clinical sample. *Journal of Personality Assessment, 92*: 35–44.

Taylor, G., Bagby, R., & Parker, J. (1997). The development and regulation of affects. In: G. Taylor, R. Bagby, & J. Parker (Eds.), *Disorders of Affect Regulation: Alexithymia in Medical and Psychiatric Illness* (pp. 7–25). Cambridge: Cambridge University Press.

Trull, T. J., Sher, K. J., Minks-Brown, C., Durbin, J., & Burr, R. (2000). Borderline personality disorder and substance use disorders: a review and integration. *Clinical Psychology Review, 20*: 235–253.

Walter, M., Berth, H., Selinger, J., Gerhard, U., Küchenhoff, J., Frommer, J., & Dammann, G. (2009). The lack of negative affects as an indicator for identity disturbance in borderline personality disorder: a preliminary report. *Psychopathology, 42*: 399–404.

Weinberg, E. (2006). Mentalization, affect regulation, and development of the self. *Journal of the American Psychoanalytic Association, 54*: 251–269.

Wieder, H., & Kaplan, E. H. (1969). Drug use in adolescents—psychodynamic meaning and pharmacogenic effect. *Psychoanalytic Study of the Child, 24*: 399–431.

Woody, G. E. (1977). Psychiatric aspects of opiate dependence: diagnostic and therapeutic research issues. In: J. Blaine & D. Julius (Eds.), *Psychodynamics of Drug Dependence* (pp. 157–178). Rockville, MD: National Institute on Drug Abuse.

Wurmser, L. (1977). Mr. Pecksniff's horse? (Psychodynamics in compulsive drug use). In: J. Blaine & D. Julius (Eds.) *Psychodynamics of Drug Dependence* (pp. 36–72). Rockville, MD: National Institute on Drug Abuse.

CHAPTER SEVENTEEN

Scenic re-enactment in Holocaust testimonies: scenic-narrative microanalysis and grounded theory

Pascal Heberlein and Andreas Hamburger

The Law of Return, adopted in 1950 by the newly founded state of Israel, assured citizenship for every settling Jew. This led to a great immigration movement and thus also brought many traumatised survivors of the Shoah to Israel. For various reasons, these people were not attended to sufficiently but shifted off to clinics and asylums (Davidovitch & Zalashik, 2007, p. 146). Within the institutions there was no documentation of who was a survivor of the Shoah. The neglect of the traumatic background led to questionable diagnoses and medical treatments in many cases. Many of the Shoah survivors did not talk about their traumatic experiences at all for decades, not only because no one asked them, but also due to an inner speechlessness. They believed they had no story to tell. The traumatic experience of the war only continued to exist in them as a dissociation, an "erasure" (Laub, 2005, p. 256 f.; cf. Bohleber, 2007). This loss of history (Laub, 2005, p. 257 f.) was one of the research objectives in Laub's *Videotestimony Study of Chronically Hospitalized Holocaust Survivors in Psychiatric Institutions in Israel* (VCHSI), aimed at conducting video testimonies with these forgotten survivors (Laub & Hamburger, 2017). Twenty-six patients were ready to give their video testimonies. Before, and five months after, the testimony, psychological and psychiatric tests were administered, showing that symptomatology of PTSD were significantly improved (Laub, 2005, p. 262; Strous et al., 2005, p. 2291).

In a follow-up study, the video testimonies were re-analysed, concentrating on subtexts, the representation of the inner-psychical processing, and the re-enactment in the testimonial situation. Four interviews were analysed by a mixed-method approach consisting of scenic-narrative microanalysis (based on a psychoanalytic expert evaluation; Hamburger, 2015, 2017) and grounded theory (Glaser & Strauss, 1967).

Grounded theory

Grounded theory is a widely approved social-scientific research method, developed in 1967 by Barney G. Glaser and Anselm L. Strauss and later enhanced by Strauss and Juliet Corbin (1990). The method aims to discover theories based on data. Unlike the nomological-deductive model, which verifies or falsifies the existing hypotheses, grounded theory tries to generate and validate new hypotheses, using an iterative-cyclical approach (Strauss, 1987, pp. 18–19). Accordingly, at the beginning of the project, the leading question has to be as open as possible, since the research process is supposed to be led only by the data and not by presuppositions.

Initially, the data is coded openly, that is, it is split into separate meaningful units and given codes. These can refer to the content as well as to the form. The gained codes are condensed more and more by permanent comparison and are thereby abstracted. In the second step, axial encoding, codes that appear to be particularly relevant are interrelated. Thus the examined phenomenon is supposed to be worked out. Furthermore, conditions, context, action strategies, and interactional strategies, as well as consequences, are assigned to the phenomenon in the form of further codes. In the third step, selective encoding, the construct that has originated so far systematically becomes a "reflection of reality" (Strauss & Corbin, 1990, p. 95), a theory rooted in data. This view, however, has been challenged in epistemological discussion; in the result, Strauss' naïve assumption can be received as an early concept of a constructivist epistemology (Bryant, 2009) and is compatible with the concept of abduction (Reichertz, 2010)—and, therefore, also with psychoanalytic (de)construction.

However, in the described project, grounded theory faced the difficulty that the phenomenon under examination was expected to get hold of the subtexts, that is, the non-spoken conversational content. Grounded theory, however, refers exclusively to manifest, explicitly spoken content. Therefore, the result cannot reach the depth of psychoanalytical interpretations. Moreover, the project did not aim at a universal theory, but to generate individual facts regarding every single interview. The aimed reconstruction of biographies could be contextualised by elements of content (cognitive and affective-sensory reconstruction). Formal features (changes of subject, sorts of utterance, specifications of framework, formal replying behaviour) made it possible to understand how reconstruction was accomplished strategically within the interviews. The result of the grounded theory analysis was a list of subjects within the life histories that were either positive, stabilising, and relevant or burdening and negative. Thereby some subjects had to be classified as, for example, negative which would have had to be understood positively regarding only the utterance of the interviewee.

Scenic-narrative microanalysis

The second method used to analyse the four video testimonies was scenic-narrative microanalysis (SNMA) (Hamburger, 2015, 2017).

The method builds on "scenic understanding", as the core and gold standard of clinical experience in modern relational psychoanalysis, which has widely replaced a one-body psychological, top-down interpretation in psychoanalytic practice (Scharff & Scharff, 2015). The second element of the method, the narrative, builds on two elementary properties of human mental life. First, it is situated in interaction from the beginning; and second, as the results of infant research have demonstrated, it is situated in time. Affect dramaturgy in interaction is the stuff mental life is made of. The narrative aspect of the method is especially important in cases like the Holocaust survivors' video testimonies, where the narrative function and the capacity to address and respond to the other has broken down in the survivor's mental life. The third property of SNMA, the micro-analytic aspect, is connected to a trend in qualitative research towards a more subtle in-depth analysis of individual texts. As this method is applied here to video material, this *dispositif* requires additional consideration (Hamburger, 2017).

Scenic understanding as a new paradigm in psychoanalysis

Sigmund Freud understood the psychoanalytic situation as a site of detailed observation, allowing for the interpolation of "connecting links" (Freud, 1916–1917, p. 387) that had to be confirmed by the elicitation of further associations and memories; and eventually, like in his former profession of neuropathology, he expected that aggregations of such single case studies, in the long run, would lead to an overall theory of the mind.

Decades later, Devereux's (1967) approach marks a significant difference to Freud's, in concentrating on the countertransference of the researcher as a leading and reliable data source. It parallels the conception of "scenic understanding", as developed in the later Frankfurt School in Germany in the 1970s (Lorenzer, 1970; Kirshner, 2004, 2011).

Scenic-narrative microanalysis assumes as a principle that meaning itself, not only in the field of human psychology, is a relational phenomenon. Experience and behaviour are embedded in a social context and environment from the beginning of mental development. Thus, the former picture of the analyst as an expert for the reconstruction of drive vicissitudes has given way to the analyst as a present, meaningful other (This position has been described in detail elsewhere: cf., Hamburger, 1998a, 2010, 2013a, 2013b, 2017).

Likewise, the psychoanalytic researcher is never disentangled from his subject; he is part of the same society, living the same defensive construction of the world as the social phenomenon he is trying to investigate. Psychoanalytic research in this sense is based on the reflection on countertransference processes, very much like the clinical practice itself. Scenic microanalysis includes an important trait of psychoanalytic hermeneutic depth analysis: a detailed analysis of readers' reactions to the texts (i.e., "reader transference"; see also Marks & Mönnich-Marks, 2003). Interpretive processes take place in three levels: first, the expert research team's reactions to the transcribed text and/or video; second, the interviewer's reactions within the psychoanalytic situation, his interactions with the interviewee; and third, the account of the interviewee herself, representing her interpretation of the narrated experiences.

The method builds upon a hermeneutic procedure guided by Lorenzer's (1986) repeated oscillation between the positions of participant and reflecting psychoanalyst. In the participant position, the analyst introspectively observes his own transference as a recipient of the text; in the reflecting position, he connects this observed participation to the microstructure of the text. This psychoanalytic method draws specifically on the temporal dimension of the listening process (Hamburger, 2013b).

Narrative analysis

The narrative approach has been heatedly discussed in psychoanalysis (e.g., Spence, 1982; Mitchell, 1988; Ahumada, 1994; Govrin, 2006). It conceptualises mental life as a permanent narration. "The 'Ego' is the narrator, the 'Self' the protagonist of a narrative, permanently retold in conscious and unconscious stream of phantasy" (Hamburger, 1998a, p. 229). In a social constructivist key, the narrated meaning is produced in a constitutive "relational scenario" (Gergen, 1994). Thus, to understand the narrative process means to reflect one's own listening position. The definition of the researcher as a listener reflecting his listening is closely related to the analytic process.

If we adopt the viewpoint of mental life as narrative, that is, basically dialogic and meaningfully ordered in shared time, SNMA aims at reconstructing the dynamic process of the dialogue. In this respect, SNMA contradicts most methods of qualitative analysis in the field of clinical research, which are based on additions of coded prominent traits of the material, and thus of the patient. The accent on temporality is essential for the reconstruction of the microstructure of the single session.

Psychological research methodologies exclusively following the paradigm of natural science seem to be outdated (Hamburger & Mertens, 2004). Qualitative social research is flourishing, much of it based on psychoanalytic inspiration (Hamburger, 1998a, 1998b). Unlike physical data, psychological data is of an interpretive nature, connected to subjectivity and communicative relatedness, and is embedded in an experienced autobiographical context. Thus, if we study our subjects' narratives (and not constrict them to questionnaires and tests), we have to take into account the detailed way such narratives unfold in the communicative context: we look at features of the narrative performance, like turn-taking phenomena, breaks, and signs of relatedness (or interrupts in relatedness) to the recipient and vice versa. And as researchers, confronted with the rich data of an audio or videotaped interview, we have to be aware that these features are not just properties of the material—our own relatedness to the document we analyse, including the introspective description of the interpreter's own countertransference reactions, has to be described as well, and subjected to reflection and subsequent analysis.

Influence of documentation and data types

The process of analysing video interviews is comparable, but not identical, to the analysis of a narrative text or an audiotaped interview.

First, a narrative text, for example in the form of a book, refers to the reader in quite a different way than an audio or video document. Reading texts is an activity, where the speed and even the order of receiving the information are literally in the hand of the reader. Written narratives, if they are not transcripts, are produced differently—writing is a much more deliberate process than speaking, and it includes frequent omissions and corrections, which (with the rare exception of French *écriture automatique*, where erasing was forbidden) become invisible in the resulting text, while verbal talk is inevitably unfolding and proceeding forwards in time. Corrections in verbal utterances by the speaker are mostly audible and can be received as such by the listener (in fact there are hidden and even unconscious changes during the preparatory stages when processing an utterance; but still we hear their traces in syntactical, semantic, or phonological irregularities). It might be concluded that verbal communication, with its irreversible temporal order in the process of speech production as well as reception, provides richer data for psychological analysis than a written account.

Therefore, psychoanalytic process research has concentrated on the analysis of audiotaped session protocols. Of course, tape recording intervenes with the psychoanalytic frame, since the price for accurate documentation is the leak in confidentiality and uniqueness of the situation. The microphone is a witness, transcending the sheltering walls of the consulting room, transgressing the uniqueness and unrepeatability of the dyadic analytic situation. The presence of an anonymous "third", as well as the fact that every moment of the session can be traced back in time, changes the potential space and therefore the transferential frame of the session.

This becomes even more important when it comes to video recording, as it is frequent in testimonial interviews. Here, the interviewee is directly confronted with the presence of an external witness; the situation implies that the interviewer is something like an agent of the camera, which represents the public audience as the real addressee of the testimony (Hamburger, 2017). Furthermore, in video, more than in audio transmission, the mimic and gestural display is part of the testimony, drawing the attention away from the message to the medium, from intended content to unintentional affective communication. This additional source of information might enrich the testimony, but on the other hand might also thin it out. The illusion of presence, like the "cinematographic illusion" of the audience to be part of the displayed scene, generally inherent in medial communication, might impede being aware of the only real presence existing in the testimony, which is the mutuality in the ongoing interview. The more the interviewer takes over the moderator role, serving the illusion of unmediated contact through the camera, the less personal is his contact to the survivor. Scenic-narrative microanalysis as a reanalysis of such a real registered situation therefore has to remain conscious of the mediality of its access.

SNMA: steps and procedures

The present chapter describes the design of the first applications of SNMA, as it was adopted in the Yale Video Testimony Study (Hamburger, 2010, 2015) in combination with parallel grounded theory (Heberlein, 2015). Further developing the method, however, is a continuing task. The manual is under permanent revision (Hamburger, 2017). The systematic steps in applying SNMA are (ibid.):

1. Referring to meaningful data, usually in the form of interviews or sessions, where a kind of listening prevails that facilitates the emergence of Moments of Meeting (Stern, 2004). To allow for a micro-analytic approach, this material must be video or audio documented and then transcribed.
2. Identifying of and commenting on such Now Moments and/or Moments of Meeting by at least three independent raters trained for this task either by clinical psychoanalytic training or other specialised preparation. The moments identified are to be assigned to one or two consecutive phrases.

3. Discussing the sentences that have been unanimously marked by all raters in one moderated consensus conference for each analysed interview. The discussion compares and evaluates the individual reasons for qualifying them as a Now or Meeting Moment, and reflects the differences in interpretation, as well as the group dynamics of the consensus conference as indicators of the underlying unconscious relational structure. The conference agrees on a final statement, mentioning also dissenting opinions, on the underlying interpersonal re-enactment scene apparent in the material through discussion of the selected passages.
4. Conclusive discussion of the whole material by the main researcher considering the statements of the raters, the raters' discussion agreement, the dynamics of the consensus discussion, and re-contextualising the chosen passages to broader context of the material.

Results of the study

By means of the elaborate analysis of the four interviews applying SNMA and the appertaining group discussion, it was possible to rudimentarily understand traumas of the survivors and to carefully trace their life stories. The results of the grounded theory also contributed to understanding the biography better to some extent.

This may be exemplified using the case of Rafi R. The interview with the survivor is characterised by strong resistance, manifested through indifference, brief answers, black-and-white thinking, and fragmentation of emotional descriptions, as it could be demonstrated by grounded theory. This phenomenon corresponds to the results from SNMA, but was transformed into another key. The psychoanalytic rating group understood Rafi's resistance as a creative shelter. Unless the inner life of the patient was prone to processes of fragmentations, the analysis of the vivid discussion atmosphere within the rater group indicated that beneath these emotional splitting, Rafi possessed what the raters called a "living core", surviving the traumatic childhood experience. However, a tendency within the group not to contemplate the subjects told by Rafi in their ambivalence, but to connote them as either "only positive" or "only negative", was understood as corresponding with his black-and-white thinking. The complex structure of defence and transference in the rater group could be analysed as mirroring the interview scene as well as the mental conditions of the survivor.

Nevertheless, the analysis of the interviews revealed that many aspects of the biography had to remain opaque and lost. However, this was not so much ascribed to the method but to the particular hardship of the life experiences of the interviewees and the long phase of their hospitalisation. Psychoanalytical methods of examination attain results depending on the psychical constitution of the investigated person. This fact puts them into a special position in relation to other qualitative studies. Still, they are just one paradigm among others. This paradigm, though quite respected by qualitative researchers as one of the most fruitful paradigms of research of the last century (and sometimes even idealised because of the psychoanalytic researchers' unique possibility to access their subjects), now tends to fade out in the academic community, where more "objective" empirical approaches are often preferred. It therefore has to be re-introduced into this discourse, while keeping close contact to psychoanalytic clinical experience and theoretical development.

Psychoanalytic qualitative research is an inductive process. It is not concerned with testing the previously formulated hypotheses, as would be necessary to meet Popper's falsificationist model, but it is rather aimed at generating hypotheses that emanate from the controlled research process itself (Sandler, Dreher, & Drews, 1991; Hinshelwood, 2013). Only as the second step can these hypotheses be submitted to a quantitative analysis and more objective testing procedures. If research is aimed at generating meaningful and non-arbitrary results, the two strategies mentioned above have to work hand in hand. SNMA of video testimony data is one contribution to emerging qualitative psychoanalytic research.

References

Ahumada, J. L. (1994). Interpretation and Creationism. *International Journal of Psychoanalysis, 75*: 695–707.

Bohleber, W. (2007). Remembrance, Trauma and Collective Memory. *International Journal of Psychoanalysis, 88*: 329–352.

Bryant, A. (2009). Grounded theory and pragmatism: the curious case of Anselm Strauss. *Forum: Qualitative Social Research, 10*(3). www.qualitative-research.net/index.php/fqs/article/view/1358/2850 [last accessed 24 April 2017].

Davidovitch, N., & Zalashik, R. (2007). Recalling the survivors: between memory and forgetfulness of hospitalized holocaust survivors in Israel. *Israel Studies, 12*: 145–163.

Devereux, G. (1967). *From Anxiety to Method in the Behavioral Sciences*. Berlin: de Gruyter Mouton.

Freud, S. (1916–1917). *Introductory Lectures on Psycho-Analysis. S. E., 15–16*. London: Hogarth.

Gergen, K. J. (1994). Mind, text, and society: self-memory in social context. In: N. Ulric & R. Fivush (Eds.), *The Remembering Self* (Emory Symposia in Cognition 6) (pp. 78–104). Cambridge: Cambridge University Press.

Glaser, B. G., & Strauss, A. L. (1967). *Grounded Theory. Strategien qualitativer Forschung*. Bern: Huber, 2005.

Govrin, A. (2006). The dilemma of contemporary psychoanalysis: toward a "knowing" post-postmodernism. *Journal of the American Psychoanalytic Association, 54*: 507–535.

Hamburger, A. (1998a). Traumnarrativ und Gedächtnis. In: M. Koukkou, M. Leuzinger-Bohleber, & W. Mertens (Eds.), *Erinnerung von Wirklichkeiten. Psychoanalyse und Neurowissenschaften im Dialog. Bd. 1:* Bestandsaufnahme (pp. 223–286). Stuttgart: Verlag Internationale Psychoanalyse.

Hamburger, A. (1998b). Solo mit Dame. Traumgeschichten einer Psychoanalyse. In: M. Leuzinger-Bohleber, M. Koukkou, & W. Mertens (Eds.), *Erinnerung von Wirklichkeiten. Psychoanalyse und Neurowissenschaften im Dialog. Bd. 2: Folgerungen für die psychoanalytische Praxis* (pp. 96–127). Stuttgart: Verlag Internationale Psychoanalyse.

Hamburger, A. (2010). Traumspiegel. Gegenübertragungsträume in der Beziehungsanalyse. In: H. Hierdeis (Ed.), *Der Gegenübertragungstraum in der psychoanalytischen Theorie und Praxis* (pp. 23–50). Göttingen: Vandenhoeck & Ruprecht.

Hamburger, A. (2013a). Arbeit in der Tiefe. Vorüberlegungen zu einer skeptischen Kulturanalyse. In: H. Hierdeis (Ed.), *Psychoanalytische Skepsis* (pp. 123–183). Göttingen: Vandenhoeck & Ruprecht.

Hamburger, A. (2013b). Via Regia und zurück. Traumerzählungen und ihre Resonanz. In: B. Janta, B. Unruh, & S. Walz-Pawlita (Eds.), *Der Traum* (pp. 123–143). Gießen: Psychosozial-Verlag.

Hamburger, A. (2015). Refracted attunement, affective resonance. Scenic-narrative micro-analysis of entangled presence in a Holocaust survivor's testimony. *Contemporary Psychoanalysis 51*: 239–257.

Hamburger, A. (2017). Scenic narrative microanalysis. Controlled psychoanalytic assessment of session videos or transcripts as a transparent qualitative research instrument. In: D. Laub & A. Hamburger (Eds.), *Psychoanalysis and Holocaust Testimony. Unwanted Memories of Social Trauma* (pp. 166–182). London: Routledge.

Hamburger, A., & Mertens, W. (2004). Book review of "Forschen und Heilen" in der Psychoanalyse. Ergebnisse und Berichte aus Forschung und Praxis ["Research and healing" in psychoanalysis. Results and reports from research and practice] by M. Leuzinger-Bohleber, B. Rüger, U. Stuhr, & M. Beutel. Stuttgart: Kohlhammer, 2002. *International Journal of Psychoanalysis, 85*: 535–565.

Heberlein, P. (2015). *Zerstörte Lebensgeschichten: Mikroanalyse von Interviews chronisch hospitalisierter Holocaustüberlebender*. Hamburg: Verlag Dr. Kovacs.

Hinshelwood, R. D. (2013). *Research on the Couch: Single-Case Studies, Subjectivity and Psychoanalytic Knowledge*. London: Routledge.

Kirshner, L. A. (2004). *Having a Life: Self-Pathology After Lacan*. London: Taylor & Francis.

Kirshner, L. A. (Ed.) (2011). *Between Winnicott and Lacan: a Clinical engagement*. London: Taylor & Francis.

Laub, D. (2005). From speechlessness to narrative: the cases of Holocaust historians and of psychiatrically hospitalized survivors. *Literature and Medicine, 24*: 253–265.

Laub, D., & Hamburger, A. (Eds.) (2017). *Psychoanalysis and Holocaust Testimony. Unwanted Memories of Social Trauma*. London: Routledge.

Lorenzer, A. (1970). *Sprachzerstörung und Rekonstruktion*. Frankfurt: Suhrkamp.

Lorenzer, A. (1986). Tiefenhermeneutische Kulturanalyse. In: H. D. König, A. Lorenzer, H. Lüdde, S. Nagbol, U. Prokop, G. Schmid Noerr, & A. Eggert (1988), *Kultur-Analysen* (pp. 11–98). Frankfurt: Fischer.

Marks, S., & Mönnich-Marks, H. (2003). The analysis of counter-transference reactions is a means to discern latent interview-contents. *Forum Qualitative Social Research, 4*(2). www.qualitative-research.net/fqs-texte/2–03/2–03 marks-d.htm [last accessed 8 March 2017].

Mitchell, S. A. (1988). *Relational Concepts in Psychoanalysis: An Integration*. Cambridge, MA: Harvard University Press.

Reichertz, J. (2010). Abduction: the logic of discovery of grounded theory. *Forum Qualitative Social Research, 11*(1). www.qualitative-research.net/index.php/fqs/article/view/1412/2902 [last accessed 8 March 2017].

Sandler, J., Dreher, A. U., & Drews, S. (1991). An approach to conceptual research in psychoanalysis illustrated by a consideration of psychic trauma. *International Review of Psychoanalysis, 18*: 133–141.

Scharff, J. S., & Scharff, D. E. (2015). *Towards the Interpersonal Unconscious*. IPI eBooks. http://freepsychotherapybooks.org/product/572-towards-the-interpersonal-unconscious [last accessed 8 March 2017].

Spence, D. P. (1982). *Narrative Truth and Historical Truth*. New York: Norton.

Stern, D. (2004). *The Present Moment in Psychotherapy and Everyday Life*. New York: Norton.

Strauss, A. (1987). *Qualitative analysis for social scientists*. Cambridge University Press.

Strauss, A., & Corbin, L. (1990). *Basics of qualitative research: grounded theory procedures and techniques*. Newbury Park, CA: Sage.

Strous, R. D., Weiss, M., Felsen, I., Finkel, B., Melamed, Y., Bleich, I., Kotler, M., & Laub, D. (2005). Videotestimony of long-term hospitalized psychiatrically ill Holocaust survivors. *American Journal of Psychiatry, 162*: 2287–2294.

CHAPTER EIGHTEEN

Assessing traumatic re-enactment—now moments in survivor interviews*

Jasmin Bleimling

Theory

The importance of the concept of countertransference for research and practice is constantly growing. It is mainly understood as the "whole of the analyst's unconscious reactions to the individual analysand—especially to the analysand's own transference " (Laplanche & Pontalis, 1973, p. 92). In contrast to a totalistic definition stands the scientific demand for precision. In discussion between representatives of a practical, though blurred, countertransference term and representatives of a narrowly defined term, Gysling (1995) pleads for a definition that is imprecise though clinically handy and applicable. The following presentation of a single case sheds further light on specific countertransference reactions in the context of trauma.

Loss in dialogue with introjected good objects, and loss of faith in them, are typical consequences of extreme traumatisation as experienced in the Shoah (Laub, 2005). Among other things, post-traumatic difficulties in libidinous cathexis of new objects can arise (Laub & Auerhahn, 1995). Leuzinger-Bohleber, Emde, and Pfeifer (2013) mark this as crucial for the destruction of a protective shield that serves as a representation of good inner objects in clinically non-pathological states. Also, Rosenbaum and Varvin (2007) describe the post-traumatic lack of trust and damage of the inner, empathic other as a post-traumatic symptom. The work with traumatised patients confronts their treating therapists with intensive emotional

*This chapter is based on results from the doctoral dissertation "Assessing Traumatic Re-enactment in Survivor Interviews" (Bleimling, 2016) conducted at LMU Munich and IPU Berlin, Germany (Supervisors: Andreas Hamburger, IPU, and Wolfgang Mertens, LMU), in collaboration with the research project "The Scenic Memory of the Shoah" at the Sigmund-Freud-Institute in Frankfurt, Germany (Kurt Grünberg, Friedrich Markert). The doctoral study was financed by the Ernst Ludwig Ehrlich Foundation.

arousal, mainly heavy negative countertransference reactions. Trauma patients impede their therapists' empathic capacities. As Wilson and Lindy (1994) put it, they are likely to experience an "empathic strain". The authors sketch a differentiated model of countertransference reactions that oscillates between two poles of avoidance (Type I) and over-identification (Type II). Countertransference can be classified as concordant versus complementary, or as disjunctive. Usually two introjects can be found in traumatised patients: an idealised pursued victim introject as well as a haunting offender introject (Gregurek, 1999, p. 496). Knowledge about those variable inner object relational formations is an important factor concerning treatment technique (Wardi, 1999, p. 480). Aggression in particular can determine the whole transference setting (Ehlert-Balzer, 2008).

Grünberg (2007) speaks of an overestimation of verbal aspects in contact with survivors—trauma transmission occurs especially via nonverbal aspects like formation of relations, fear, silence, and gestural behaviours between survivors and their children. Non-verbalised, so called "encapsulated" memories, which contain the inflicted traumatic pain and suffering, express themselves in unconscious and spontaneous emotional utterances.

Current interactional approaches capture actual human experience beyond traditional psychodynamic understanding as a conglomerate of body, affect, and cognition. Intersubjective consciousness and the focus on a two-person-psychology serve as theoretical background for Stern's research on the "now moment". The idea of the presence and the primary, phenomenal subjective reality (Stern, 2004) are of great importance for him: he conceptualises change as a lived experience, a moment in the present. Although it is short (three to five seconds), every now moment has a psychodynamic relevance especially in interaction with another person, leading to a shared experience ("the moment of meeting"). The coherency between soma and psyche, as already pointed out by Stern, is further developed by Leuzinger-Bohleber, Emde, and Pfeifer (2013). Cognition, affect, and problem solving are thus far understood as "embodied" as they are determined by their sensomotoric coordination in an ongoing interactive situation. This insight is far from "deciphering" body language and means; rather, the body is involved in all mental processes (ibid.). Gallese (2014) refers to the concept of intercorporeality. His concept of mirror neurons, rhythm, synchrony, and asynchrony marks the intentional tuning and provides evidence for the very somatic roots of intersubjectivity. In applying interactions between infants and their mothers, Beebe and Lachmann (2002) emphasise the relevance of early synchronicity and attachment. They stress moments of "increased affective moments" in line with significant "interruptions and repairings" in the dialogue (Mertens, 2011, p. 149).

Traumatic memories, as remembered by the survivors of the Holocaust in the video interviews, can be described formally by splitting and fragmentised memory storage (Gurevich, 2008). It is assumed that those peritraumatic defence mechanisms are re-enacted in the course of the conversations. Such moments are hypothesised to be identifiable formally by breaks and splitting in comparison to other, "neutral" classified moments in the videos. Now moments are therefore understood as "irritation moments". Consequences are expected in countertransference reactions on behalf of the listener: helplessness, loss of contact, entanglements, reinforced acting outs, over-identification, and empathic strain—nonverbally accompanied by a loss of synchronicity as well as increased "shielding" behaviour; verbally by greater use of emotional negatively toned words.

Methods

The central methodological question is the operationalisation of psychoanalytically relevant scenes that are marked by an unconsciously re-enacted trauma. A mixed method approach was chosen in order to compare the narratives of the interview partners, the objective methods Cycle Model (CM) (Mergenthaler, 2008) and Motion Energy Analysis (MEA) (Ramseyer, 2010), the clinical hermeneutical assessments, as well as the results of a countertransference questionnaire (CTQ) (Westen, 2005), used for validation purposes. By applying a micro-analytical and interactional approach, knowledge about implicit object relationship formations can be obtained.

In the following, results of the pilot study entitled "Mr. G" are presented. This conversation is part of a sample of five videographed conversations. A psychoanalytical exploration of the traumatic scene and individual life story stood in the foreground. The non-standardised, open, narrative interview was led by psychoanalyst Kurt Grünberg (total length = 131 minutes). Interviewee and interviewer were known to each other beforehand and recordings took place in the domestic environment of the survivor with his consent.

Hermeneutical assessment

The interviewer's goal is to access the survivors in a clinical as well as a non-clinical way by using a "multi-sited ethnography" approach to fathom the unconscious transmission processes and dynamics of their persecution experience as Jewish survivors in the "country of the perpetrators" (Grünberg, 2013). The videotapes are retrospectively investigated by means of an in-depth hermeneutic analysis (Lorenzer, 1983). Psychoanalytically relevant scenes are generated in an intervision by the occurrence of special countertransference phenomena while watching the video. In order to enrich those hermeneutical assessments, additional psychoanalytically trained working groups were established.

Text analysis

Mergenthaler (1997, 2008) tries to identify "key moments" in psychotherapies via computerised methods. He uses a "text analysis system" that includes an automated dictionary of emotion (words of affective experience and processing) and abstraction (contemplating words). The theoretical framework is the resonating minds theory (RMT), which describes the psychotherapeutic process and changes in it. A connection between brain, psychotherapeutic activity, and the mind is assumed (Mergenthaler, 2008, p. 123). Following cognitive processing respectively, speech patterns can be analysed: "relaxing" (low emotion, low abstraction), "reflecting" (low emotion, high abstraction), "experiencing" (high emotion, low abstraction), and "connecting" (high emotion, high abstraction). Furthermore, the emotional valence (positive/negative) as well as the narrative style can be described. The latter relies on concepts of referential activity by Bucci (2001) (and by Bucci & Maskit, 2007) and describes actions combined in words (high versus low in concreteness and vividness).

Movement analysis

The nonverbal scene is an extremely suitable pathway to the traumatic scene, which cannot be detected by text-analytical methods alone. Ramseyer (2010) (and Ramseyer & Tschacher, 2011) developed an automated, objective, reliable, computerised video analysis in order to measure the quantity of body movements and synchronicity in interacting dyads. Nonverbal synchronicity is defined as an alignment process that includes static, dynamic, emotional, and physiological as well as acoustical elements and facilitates empathic sensitivity as an important trace for the quality of the (therapeutic) relationship (Ramseyer, 2010, pp. 5–7). Asynchronicity can accordingly be seen as an indicator for the (momentary) demolition of the relationship, as a rupture in an otherwise empathic synchronic relationship—and movement scenery.

To illustrate the methods used, a neutral scene (i.e., no high emotional relevance) is contrasted with an emotionally relevant scene. Text excerpts are based on the video transcript.

Results

Mr. G, born in Poland in 1926, speaks about his biography. He starts the interview by showing his new apartment, followed by a narration of his life circumstances in the times of the Shoah: from the initial ghettoisation, to transportation to working camps, up to the concentration camp (Buchenwald).

Micro-analytical results: neutral scene

Excerpt from the transcript (the original interview was conducted in German; this translation is by the author):

INTERVIEWEE: You can eat lunch there.
INTERVIEWER: Uh-huh
INTERVIEWEE: You can choose whatever you want; you just need to heat it up in the microwave.
INTERVIEWER: Uh-huh
INTERVIEWEE: And at a very good price. Really unique! I don't choose because I can't see. The whole meal. Super cheap. Half a chicken for two euros twenty-five.
INTERVIEWER: Uh-huh
INTERVIEWEE: A portion of chips costs one thirty or one fifty? I can't even eat it all, that's too much.
INTERVIEWER: So you are a good customer there, right?
INTERVIEWEE: Really much cheaper there.
INTERVIEWER: Uh-huh

Hermeneutical assessment

A neutral scene serves as a baseline for the emotionally relevant scenes. It is hypothesised that there are no moments of specific countertransference or moments of meeting. A hermeneutical assessment is not required.

Text analysis

As in the rest of the interview, the amount of used words is higher for the interviewee than for the interviewer, which is not a surprising result due to the psychoanalytical interview style. Mr. G uses a concrete narrative style; the words are rarely based on his biography and show a positive emotional tone. This positive atmosphere doesn't include a significant use of emotional or abstract words though.

Movement analysis

The interviewer is nodding, eating a cake, touching his glasses, while Mr. G talks about shopping in the department store. According to the results of the MEA movement analysis (Ramseyer, 2010), movements (x mov = 0.36) are below average movement (x mov = 0.58) in the whole video. In-between, nonverbal synchronicity is low (x syn = 0.08), as interpreted by cross correlations per minute.

Micro-analytical results: emotionally relevant scene

Excerpt from the transcript:

INTERVIEWER: It's also possible that there are things you'd rather forget … than well, to remember them?

INTERVIEWEE: I'd rather forget so much. Because. I have those dreams again. I can hardly sleep.

INTERVIEWER: What kind of dreams did you just say?

INTERVIEWEE: From the war. I run, I run. I was screaming at night. Because I was running, I was running, to hide myself. In Buchenwald, I hid myself in dirt, in shit!

INTERVIEWER: How did this come about?

INTERVIEWEE: Because they started with the selection. You already knew that they sent people to Auschwitz.

INTERVIEWER: That was in Buchenwald what you told me right now.

INTERVIEWEE: Now with the shit? That was in Buchenwald.

INTERVIEWER: And there you hid yourself to hide …

INTERVIEWEE: I am churned up inside. The last two years. I need to go to the toilet. I have to leave now.

INTERVIEWER: Yes, yes, sure.

INTERVIEWEE: Please excuse me, I need to … [*Stands up*]

INTERVIEWER: Of course. Is it all right? [*Clears his throat*]

INTERVIEWEE: [*walks out, voice from afar*] You can shut the camera down! So the film doesn't continue.

[*The interviewer holds an old photograph in front of the camera. Meanwhile a ticking clock and the flush of the toilet are the only sounds; the interviewer sits still. The interviewee comes back after six and a half minutes.*]

INTERVIEWEE: You have to excuse me, but it churns everything up.

INTERVIEWER: Of course, Mr. G, you don't feel good right now.

INTERVIEWEE: What?

INTERVIEWER: You don't feel good right now.

INTERVIEWEE: Well it's okay. You get churned up inside automatically. Do you understand? [*A long pause*] The worst picture is the one in the ghetto with a child. With a baby. [*A long pause*] If he'd just shot the mother before! And not after. [*Pause*] Because the mother died in agony. They shot her. Yes. But that was the last picture that she saw. Three months old.

INTERVIEWER: Uh-huh. How did this happen?

INTERVIEWEE: Don't know; I was in the house, screaming. Then SS. He takes the baby out of the bed. The mother lay in bed. He told her to turn to the wall. He takes the baby. Thump. Drops it. And then shoots the mother. Instead of shooting the mother earlier? Or the baby later. No, you cannot imagine. [*weeps*]

INTERVIEWER: Uh-huh. No, no... you cannot.

INTERVIEWEE: If you had seen this picture! Then. I don't need to apologise. I don't need to … I understand why I smashed the bottle against his forehead.

INTERVIEWER: Uh-huh?

INTERVIEWEE: It happened in the morning. There was some drunken guy. He spoke derisively about Jews. I took his bottle. Filled with liquor, broke it. And hit him! He screamed and then there were police.

Hermeneutical assessment (rater Sigmund-Freud-Institute Frankfurt)

My blood runs cold. This in one of the central scenes of the interview: "I need to go to the toilet." The "shit" emerges into the relationship. He remembers the shit of persecution and he needs to go to the toilet. But the shit also saved his life. After he comes back he is moved, holds his hand near his belly; and also I feel very touched and have the need to show him that I am there for him, that I feel with him. He starts to cry when it comes to what hurts him most, the murder of a three-month-old infant. This picture, the image, the sounds, I guess are unbearable. Presumably those memories were later the reason why he reacted in such an aggressive way towards the insulting man.

Text analysis

Like in the neutral scene, Mr. G starts with an abstract narrative style; his words are rarely based on his biography. As the scene progresses, his words become increasingly concrete. The words show a significant negative tone in comparison to the neutral scene.

A significantly higher use of emotional words can be noted; abstract words are barely used by the interviewer or the interviewee. An interesting time leap appears, when at the end of this sequence the interviewee suddenly jumps into the post-war event with the bottle.

Movement analysis

Movements in this scene differ from those of the neutral one, with a higher use of shielding, meaning self-stimulating and regulating behaviour can be observed. Mr. G standing up and going to the toilet is accompanied by the constantly nodding interviewer. As he is left alone, he "freezes" nonverbally. The trauma-associated introjects of victim and perpetrator can be translated into his nonverbal behaviour. In memorising the murdered infant, Mr. G stays nonverbally passive, with little body tension, equivalent to his inner feeling of being a helpless observer. As he describes his aggressive post-war attack, his body tension changes, his movements become active, strong, and assertive. According to the MEA results, movements (x mov = 0.43) are below average (x mov = 0.58), but higher than in the neutral scene. Synchronicity does not differ and stays low (x syn = 0.09).

Macro-analytical results

Text analysis

The first part of the interview is low in emotions and high in abstraction. This cognitive pattern is accompanied by an abstract narrative style and can be assigned to Mergenthaler's (2008) "reflecting" cluster. The second part of the interview, when Mr. G talks about his traumatic experiences, is narrated in a significant negative emotional tone. Results are in line with the hypothesis, that scenic relevant moments contain a higher use of negative emotional words than those in neutral scenes.

Movement analysis

Contrary to the hypothesis, MEA analysis showed no significant difference in either movement quantity or movement synchronicity between the neutral and the emotionally relevant scene, with a slight tendency of less movement in the neutral scene.

Countertransference questionnaire

A one-factor ANOVA was conducted in order to check differences in countertransference feelings towards the five survivors. A German version of the CTQ was used (Kernhof, Kaufhold, & Grabhorn, 2008). Overall, no significant differences between the five conversations were found. Descriptive analysis of comparison of means reveals that Mr. G scores highest on the factor "entangled", high on the factors "protective/parental" and "positive/inclined" and lowest on the factor "aggressive-resigned".

Interdisciplinary supplements

Linguistic analysis

Erras (2014) investigated the parameters "turn-taking, pauses, speed of speech, volume, intonation" via the phonetic computer programme PRAAT. Speaking intensity in the neutral scene was faster and steadier, that is, quieter with smooth turn-takings and more instances of "uh-huh". In the emotionally relevant scene, the speed of speech was slower, with more fluctuation in the speaking intensity as well as in a higher pitch/frequency. In summary, it can be stated that the interviewee speaks louder, with more fluctuation, at a higher pitch, and with impaired turn-takings in now moments, while the interviewer speaks more quietly and more slowly, at an unsteady speed, with impaired turn-takings, and fewer instances of "uh-huh".

Dance movement analysis

Heller (2015) identified a clear orientation of the interviewer towards the interviewee via LABAN analysis. The latter is less focused on the interviewer and turns away from time to time. The strong alignment of the interviewer towards his conversation partner is discussed in terms of "pacing" and "mirroring" phenomena (ibid., p. 3). In the emotionally relevant scene, changes occur in this movement pattern: while Mr. G is talking about the infant's death, the interviewer "answers" nonverbally with high physical involvement (shaking head for fourteen seconds), followed by frequent changes between eye contact and turning away, including longer phases without orientation and gradual detachment of glance. The strongest effects were observed when Mr. G talks about how he hit the man with the bottle (ibid., pp. 5–6).

Discussion

Results of the presented pilot single case study of Mr. G are in line with the hypotheses that relevant now moments in survivor interviews can be understood mainly as irritating moments, including breaks, splitting, and loss of contact. Both speak with more emotional words and with higher emotionally negative tone as well as with a less abstract narrative style in moments of relevance compared to the neutral scene.

Though this result is in line with the hypotheses, a general objection against the use of verbal text analysis needs to be taken into account. Verbal analysis is strongly oriented to the consciousness, which is considered to be of less importance in the traumatic re-enacted relevant scenes. Erras enriched the verbal analysis by linguistic findings. The interacting partners show an unsteady voice pitch and impaired turn-takings in now moments. The hermeneutical assessment of the emotionally relevant scene fits the nonverbal behaviour in the same irritating way including disruptive elements, reported feelings of helplessness, and exclusion.

MEA analysis revealed no significant differences in synchronicity. This finding is not in line with the expected hypotheses. It is important to note the limitations associated in using a solely quantifying objective method that cannot detect qualitative subtle changes in behaviour like facial expression, gesture, eye movements, and the direction of movements necessary for meaningful interpretations. Those indicators can only be assessed in a qualitative analysis.

Significant differences between neutral and emotionally relevant scenes were indeed discovered in the LABAN notation. The interviewer tended to disengage himself from the contact and to regulate pauses by steady headshakes. This finding resembles linguistic results that the interviewee speaks louder at the same time as the interviewer speaks slower in relevant scenes.

Results of the countertransference questionnaire showed that Mr. G scored highest in the entangled factors and lowest in the aggressive factor, both with no significant differences to the other four interviewed survivors. As already mentioned, aggression in contact with extremely traumatised patients are hard to bear, which can be seen as an explanation for the collective defence against aggressive elements and its reversal in high scores on protective-parental and entangled, the latter a typical concordant countertransference feeling, well known from psychoanalytical literature about trauma.

Clinical implications

As it emerges from the discussion of the results, traumatic re-enactment can be assessed in survivor interviews in specific irritating moments, as derived from now moments and Stern's (2004) moments of meeting. Beyond scientific insights this finding has its own clinical value and implications when considering treatment techniques for PTSD patients.

Siri Erika Gullestad advocates inverting the primal conception of psychoanalysis in order to "discover the soul in the body" (2013, p. 389). The nonverbal behaviour of a patient is just as important as the concrete content of free associations as a *via regia* to the unconscious.

References

Auerhahn, N. C., Laub, D., & Peskin, H. (1995). Der zweite Holocaust: Das Leben ist bedrohlich. *Psyche—Zeitschrift für Psychoanalyse, 49*: 18–40.

Beebe, B., & Lachmann, F. (2002). Organizing principles of interaction from infant research. *Journal of Infant, Child, & Adolescent Psychotherapy, 2*: 61–89.

Bucci, W. (2001). Pathways of emotional communication. *Psychoanalytic Inquiry, 21*: 40–70.

Bucci, W., & Maskit, B. (2007). Beneath the surface of the therapeutic interaction: the psychoanalytic method in modern dress. *Journal of the American Psychoanalytic Association, 55*: 1355–1397.

Ehlert-Balzer, M. (2008). Trauma. In: W. Mertens & B. Waldvogel (Eds.), *Handbuch psychoanalytischer Grundbegriffe* (pp. 767–772). Stuttgart: Kohlhammer.

Gallese, V. (2014). Finding the body in the brain: from simulation theory to embodied simulation. In: H. Kornblith & B. McLaughlin (Eds.), *Alvin Goldman and his Critics* (ch. 14). New York: Wiley-Blackwell, 2016.

Gregurek, R. (1999). Countertransference problems in the treatment of a mixed group of war veterans and female partners of war veterans. *Croatian Medical Journal, 40*: 493–497.

Grünberg, K. (2007). Contaminated generativity: Holocaust survivors and their children in Germany. *The American Journal of Psychoanalysis, 67*: 82–96.

Grünberg. K. (2013). Scenic memory of the Shoah—"The Adventuresome Life of Alfred Silbermann". *The American Journal of Psychoanalysis, 73*: 30–42.

Gullestad, S. E. (2013). Die Seele im Körper entdecken. Eine Fallstudie. In: M. Leuzinger-Bohleber, R. N. Emde, & R. Pfeifer (Eds.), *Embodiment. Ein innovatives Konzept für Entwicklungsforschung und Psychoanalyse* (pp. 385–407). Göttingen: Vandenhoeck & Ruprecht.

Gurevich, H. (2008). The Language of Absence. *International Journal of Psychoanalysis, 89*(3): 561–578.

Gysling, A. (1995). *Die analytische Antwort. Eine Geschichte der Gegenübertragung in Form von Autorenportraits*. Tübingen: diskord.

Heller, V. (2015). *Bewegungsanalyse, Szene 8 (Herr G.).* 2. Fassung, unveröffentlichtes Arbeitspapier. Berlin.

Kernhof, K., Kaufhold, J., & Grabhorn, R. (2008). *Fragebogen zur Gegenübertragung. Deutsche Version des CTQ (CTQ-D)* [Countertransference Questionnaire. German version of the CTQ]. Frankfurt.

Laplanche, J., & Pontalis, J. B. (1973). The Language of Psycho-Analysis. *International Psycho-Analytical Library, 94*: 1–497.

Laub, D. (2005). Traumatic shutdown of narrative and symbolization: a death instinct derivative? *Contemporary Psychoanalysis, 41*: 307–326.

Leuzinger-Bohleber, M., Emde, R. N., & Pfeifer, R. (2013). *Vorbemerkungen*. In: M. Leuzinger-Bohleber, R. N. Emde, & R. Pfeifer, (Eds.), *Embodiment. Ein innovatives Konzept für Entwicklungsforschung und Psychoanalyse* (pp. 9–14). Göttingen: Vandenhoeck & Ruprecht.

Lorenzer, A. (1983). Sprache, Lebenspraxis und Szenisches Verstehen in der psychoanalytischen Therapie. *Psyche—Zeitschrift für Psychoanalyse, 37*: 97–115.

Mergenthaler, E. (1997). *Emotions/Abstraktions-Muster in Verbatimprotokollen: ein Beitrag zur computergestützten lexikalischen Beschreibung des psychotherapeutischen Prozesses.* Frankfurt-Bockenheim: VAS, Psycholinguistic Research.

Mergenthaler, E., (2008). Resonating minds: a school-independent theoretical conception and its empirical application to psychotherapeutic processes. *Psychotherapy Research, 18*: 109–126.

Mertens, W. (2011). *Psychoanalytische Schulen im Gespräch. Band 3. Psychoanalytische Bindungstheorie und moderne Kleinkindforschung*. Bern: Hans Huber.

Ramseyer, F. (2010). Nonverbale Synchronisation in der Psychotherapie. *Systeme, 24*: 5–30.

Ramseyer, F., & Tschacher, W. (2011). Nonverbal synchrony in psychotherapy: coordinated body-movement reflects relationship quality and outcome. *Journal of Consulting and Clinical Psychology, 79*: 284–295.

Rosenbaum, B., & Varvin, S. (2007). The influence of extreme traumatisation on body, mind and social relations. *International Journal of Psychoanalysis, 88*: 1527–1542.

Stern, D. (2004). *The Present Moment in Psychotherapy and Everyday Life.* New York: Norton.

Wardi, D. (1999). Therapists' responses in Holocaust survivors and second generation psychotherapy. *Croatian Medical Journal, 40*: 479–485.

Wilson, J. P., & Lindy, J. D. (1994). *Countertransference in the Treatment of PTSD*. New York: Guilford.

PART IV

DEVELOPMENTAL PERSPECTIVES

Introduction to Part IV

Social trauma is most pernicious for children, since it hits them in a developmental phase where they still depend on the expectation of a reliable social environment. If this environment is injured, then we observe that child survivors grow up with basic damages to attachment and mentalization—some of them have been addressed in the previous clinical section.

Like the clinical section, we open here with a case report. Annette Streeck-Fischer (Berlin), an internationally renowned and highly experienced adolescent psychiatrist, who has published seminal books on trauma and adolescence, describes complex traumatisation in the example of a severely traumatised nine-year-old girl. In the long term, complex traumatisation can lead to increased self-mutilation in girls and increased violence towards others in boys. In juvenile offenders we often find a traumatic background, and in consequence a reduced mentalizing capacity.

Since mentalization is a prerequisite for learning prosocial behaviour, it is a most important psychosocial protective variable. Svenja Taubner and Paul Schröder (Heidelberg) describe this relation and advocate a mentalization-based intervention for high-risk adolescents.

An empirical study by Sonja Protić (Belgrade) confirms the hypothesis that the capacity to mentalize trauma is more compromised in juvenile offenders than in their also traumatised non-delinquent peers. It can be assumed that mentalization is a potential protective factor for violent behaviour.

The concluding chapter of this section is an empirical study on school bullying by Svetlina Koleva (Sofia), where we find further evidence for the link between empathy and violent behaviour from the research perspective of educational psychology.

CHAPTER NINETEEN

Marked for life—psychotherapy in the case of a severely traumatised child

Annette Streeck-Fischer

For the past twenty years, we have been able to recognise the problems of these children and adolescents as consequences of mistreatment or abuse. And we understand increasingly adequately the matter of the transmission of traumas and their repetitive re-enactments (Streeck-Fischer, 2014).

What kinds of children and adolescents does this concern?

The children and adolescents in question usually exhibit disturbances in social behaviour, are aggressive and destructive towards others as well as towards themselves; they lie, steal, suffer from anxiety attacks and nightmares, are prone to alcohol and drug abuse, and are subject to severe learning, attention, and contact disorders, to mention only a few types of conspicuous behaviour. Underlying these behavioural disturbances are multiple ego-structural impairments.

These children have been physically mistreated or sexually abused, oppressed within the family and/or neglected. They manifest disorders in self, affect, and impulse regulation as a result of chronic psychobiological dysregulation with states of numbing and hyperarousal, destructiveness towards others or towards themselves, and impulsive and risky behaviour. Moreover, they exhibit typical changes in consciousness, amnesia, hypermnesia, dissociations, depersonalisation and derealisation, flashbacks, and nightmares. They are disturbed in their self-perception and in their perception of others. Their relationships are accompanied by boundary issues, such as the deficient ability to set and maintain boundaries between themselves and others or between self and an object. And they have corrupt value systems and fragile norms; they largely lack stable orientations for want of a basic trust in people, in their surroundings, and in the existing order of things.

Diagnosis and treatment of complex traumatically caused disorders

In the following, we report on the diagnosis and treatment of a now nine-year-old girl (ICD 10: severe post-traumatic stress disorder F 43.1, reactive attachment disorder F 94.1), to illustrate the complexity of the disorder pattern and the necessary approaches to treatment.

Owing to the severe persistent traumatisation during the child's early development, the physical, cognitive, and affective impacts are especially variegated. Our discussion leaves out possible genetic factors.

At the age of five and a half, B was removed from her family by court order following severe sexual abuse, including vaginal intercourse, and other forms of mistreatment by the father, as well as gross neglect by the mother, and moved to a foster family. Hospitalisation in inpatient psychotherapy in Tiefenbrunn began two years later, after B exhibited very conspicuous behaviour such as bulimia followed by vomiting, food hoarding, states of agitation, sudden aggressive acts against the foster mother, sleep disturbances with nightmares and waking up at night screaming with panic anxiety attacks ("No Daddy! Don't do that!"), suspected flashbacks and states of trance, and a significant general lag in development. Despite having the physical appearance of a six-year-old, B gave the overall impression of a four-year-old.

B frequently reacted in everyday life by freezing up. She would show a mask-like frozen face, move about in a tense way, sometimes shyly giggling, without being able to take in anything from her environment. Often she would fall back into toddler-like states, sometimes appearing dreamy and spaced-out, and would suddenly begin to cry in connection with certain actions. It was then unclear whether reactions to being overwhelmed or flashbacks were occurring. At times she became beside herself with delight, fell to the ground and kicked about, or she became restless and hectic. On the ward her sexualised language was noticeable, along with her sexualised self-presentation, her emotional labiality and her avoidance of any fantasy activity. B's play behaviour was monotonous, documental, and low in fantasy. She would often change play scenarios and ran about disoriented in the therapy room. The individual scenarios were juxtaposed in an unrelated form. She had almost no sense of time. She experienced the ending of the session as directed against her personally, as "bad" and as being "pushed away".

Three years ago, prior to hospitalisation, B had already been examined for the first time as to her capabilities in connection with an expert opinion. The results of this examination can be interpreted only to a limited extent. At best tendencies can be pointed out, so that we must do without statistical individual case analyses (The following methods, among others, were employed: Raven's Coloured Progressive Matrices (CPM), Draw-a-Man test (DAM), and the Breuer-Weuffen test. The diagnosis was conducted by Ms Schrader-Mosbach).

At that time, her work behaviour and performance had not at all reached an age-appropriate level, and very much affected her capabilities, which approximately corresponded to the level of a four-year-old child. Her resilience was very limited. In all tasks, she appeared unpractised and reacted with great shame.

In the CPM the missing piece of a geometrical figure or pattern must be found, that is, gestalt principles must be discerned through simple comparisons and the visually supported continuation of a pattern. In performing the task, B repeatedly suffered a considerable loss of attention (dissociative cut-offs from perception), when she would point to selected items multiple times as if automatically. In addition, disorders (later more precisely identified in the physical diagnosis) seemed to prevent her from scanning the provided patterns. There are indications of a bilateral integration disorder and difficulties in spatial orientation, which make crossing the centre line of her body difficult for her. Tactile problems in identifying shapes traced on the skin also prevent B from recognising visually presented shapes as uniform or identical. Her performance levels correspond to a percentage rank of two.

The differentiation test according to Breuer and Walsh, which tests perceptual differentiation, revealed in B's case pronounced partial performance weaknesses in visual spatial perception as well as in acoustic perceptual differentiation due to attention deficiency and seriation problems.

B's DAM test was impressive, performed at the age of six (see Figure 1). The standard instructions had to be changed, as B persisted in drawing faces stereotypically. She was prompted to name the limbs based on those of the examiner. Without prompting she then drew the limbs protruding from the head. The result was a sort of cephalopod, corresponding rather to the developmental level of a barely four-year-old child. The limbs protruding from the head indicated a disordered perception of the individual elements of the child's own body. We may assume a pronounced disorder in bodily awareness to be the case. Even apart from her considerable difficulties in dealing with paper and pencil tasks and the significant lag in development, the drawing indicates a severely mentally disturbed child.

B showed complex impairment in the area of sensory modalities (The following examination methods were applied for the sensory-integrative diagnosis: test sheets for sensory-integrative motor diagnosis according to Kesper and Hottinger (1993); parent questionnaire; motor-diagnostic test according to Professor Eggert (1996); and observation of movement.

Figure 1. Man drawing test, patient B.

Ms Kepper carried out both the diagnosis and the body psychotherapy). Testing of tactile perceptual processing revealed that B could hardly sense pain. She experienced tactile stimulation as unpleasant and fended it off. She was unable to localise and differentiate between touch stimuli. She could not sense or recognise shapes traced on her hand with the back of a pencil.

B became unsettled in matters of vestibular perception. She avoided scaling heights and refused to balance herself on walls. Her entire movement behaviour appeared as though she constantly had to struggle for balance. There existed a hypersensitivity to gravity receptor stimulation (Ayres, 1989). Her tonicity was low and could be adjusted to the necessary circumstances only with difficulty. To stabilise her stance, she required a significantly greater muscle tension when moving to the right than when moving to the left.

B also showed impairment in kinaesthetic stimulation processing and in her coordination skills. She had great difficulty in adjusting to different sorts of objects, such as a bouncing exercise ball. For a long time she was not able to perform more complex coordinated movements, such as learning to ride a bicycle. In performing movements she lacked speed and the ability to respond.

At the beginning of treatment B was hardly motivated to move about the room. She appeared frozen in place. If she agreed on exercises, she held up only briefly. She could not muster the strength to move forwards on the skateboard, for example.

The development of B's body scheme was also conspicuous. She was unable to classify or name the individual parts of her body with any confidence. She avoided crossing the centre line of her body with her limbs and did not feel confident in the two halves of her body working together. Nor did she fully succeed in coordinating her legs with her torso and upper limbs.

Regarding apraxia, it became clear that B could orient herself in the room with her body only with difficulty. She was unable to change direction or recognise pathways in the room when asked to. In the game of hide-and-seek she often did not realise that she was still visible. Conscious and purposeful planning was not possible for B. For a long time she did not develop any ideas of her own in handling materials. She was unable to recognise or carry out temporal and spatial sequences.

How do such impairments arise?

The understanding, provided by neurosis psychology, of primitive defence mechanisms and ego-structural deficits as well as deficient self-object differentiation does not suffice for comprehensively discerning and treating these young patients' problems. Discerning the traumatic disorder complex requires the ability to perceive messages, with their puzzling behavioural patterns, which are the outcomes of previous reactions to existential threats and are not comprehensible in words. This in turn requires different perceptual settings than we would otherwise have (Streeck-Fischer, 2014). The perception of childhood forms of behaviour not determined by neurotic conflicts but developing more or less independently of the ego and communicability altogether, is necessary. In play and in imaginative activity, too, the communicative space remains empty.

Faced with the inevitably recurring experience of a threatening opponent, B repeatedly entered into states of freezing up and shame. She would then endeavour to satisfy any given expectations, while all the time behaving as if she were three to four years old. It then remained unclear whether she was stuck at the temporal developmental level of the traumatic experience or whether she had regressed to the time preceding the traumatic experience. The resulting halt to development also manifested itself in her drawings, at first mere scribblings.

Chronic and complex traumas cause serious relationship disorders in terms of the self, the environment, and being together with others. In a study of maltreated infants, Fraiberg (1982) describes primary reactions with which these children try to survive unbearable conditions: they avoid eye contact and ignore their mothers in order to completely obscure the source of pain from view. Fraiberg also describes reactions of freezing up and, in later development, fighting connected with unrest and destructive activity. Such primary reactions have nothing to do with denial. These children respond to painful traumatic experiences with a sensory shutdown, resulting in a cognitive standstill (Dopart, 1983; Mandler, 1984) and dissociation of unbearable feelings and perceptions. The traumatic break in the early as well as later dialogue between mother and child has the consequence of destroying sensorimotor and affective coordination processes and—in conjunction with them—automatically and constantly self-adjusting re-categorisation processes (Edelman, 1978). That is to say, the classification of current experience through the stimulation of different sensory channels is destroyed as the result of freezing up and shutting-out of view (Streeck-Fischer & Van der Kolk, 2000). Neurobiological studies (Teicher, Anderson, & Polcari, 2012) point out that disturbances in the development and organisation of the child's brain, especially the hippocampus, play a role here. Instead of open responsiveness, the child persists more or less with dream-induced ways of coping, activated either generally or by micro-triggers. As a consequence of early and overwhelming traumatisation, the child lacks the capacity for verbal expression; rather, non-verbal messages in the form of actions come to the fore, such as somatic memories, embodied enactments, and enactments through action (Santostephano, 1995).

The traumatic situation is inscribed in early sensorimotor, physical, and affective defence mechanisms and is therefore not actively recalled. The situation is present in an activated way only state-dependently by virtue of certain triggers. As is characteristic of traumatic forms of memory, detailed fragments of images or sensory sensations emerge that cannot be brought into a holistic history but persist as embodied and sensorimotor-affective in the form of actions or disintegrated in the form of flashbacks. Lacking are contingency experiences for discerning meaningful relationships between interactions that are sensory and affective in nature. Such contingency experiences are destroyed by the traumatic experience.

The treatment of such disorders should aim at breaking vicious circles—control loops or repetition compulsions becoming functionally autonomous on their own—and setting deadlocked developments back in motion. The descriptions from the different therapeutic areas of B's treatment make clear the close intertwining of the cognitive, sensory, and affective reactions.

The course of treatment

During the individual therapy, Ms. Lehmann, an analytical child and adolescent therapist who carried out the individual psychotherapy, got to know the patient who had already been living in Tiefenbrunn for three months and after her previous male therapist had left the clinic. Initially, B ignored her (defence against relationships) and reported to the new therapist on B's apparently more familiar relationship with Mr W, without wanting to build on play experiences. B said that the new therapist's room was different, and that the new therapist did not have what the old one had. The departure of the male therapist rendered unstable her already precarious readiness for attachment.

B at first devalued the new therapist by berating her, for example, if she (B) arrived too early and had to wait. B threatened not to come again and acted out her negative feelings by projecting them on the therapist and making her an "evil object". At the same time, B's behaviour expressed the desire for physical closeness and the readiness to cross boundaries when she would firmly press herself against the therapist's body. B then acted like a small child, with exaggeratedly coy laughter or a masklike frozenness. She could not verbalise grief or anger. Cautious attempts by the therapist to articulate the disappointment over the departure of her colleague were repelled at first. According to B, he did not simply go away, but was rather pushed away by the arrival of the new therapist: "Why did she come to Tiefenbrunn in the first place? That made Mr. W leave!"

After these initial sessions, marked by B's acting out her anger, a more trusting atmosphere was established through shared arts and crafts. B would take away something from each session back to her room—something from the therapist. A more positive therapeutic relationship developed, which B would nevertheless denigrate at the slightest disappointment from the therapist. B felt she was being constantly tested, while all the time clearly desiring greater closeness and security. She did not want to leave at the end of sessions, almost always came too early, and in both situations accused the therapist of providing inadequate and deficient care. In this way she ultimately re-enacted her experiences of neglect. Through endurance of the negative transference and caution in naming things, the therapist gradually managed to stabilise her relationship with B. The therapist would endure B as she is, while at the same time maintaining the reliable framework. There developed a calm phase in which B would write and draw, and thus try out her abilities. B wanted the therapist to write down her name for her, and B wrote down her own name for the therapist.

This "delicate" relationship was put to the test in early September, two years after the discovery of the abuse, when B had to make a statement before the court and in early October had to undergo a gynaecological examination in Hanover, which was indispensable for prosecuting the father. B was re-traumatised most severely by these events, succumbed to flashbacks, and was almost constantly overwhelmed by the traumatising experiences. She told the therapist that one childcare worker reminded her of her father and that she was afraid of him. She feared that her father might come and do her harm. She had severe nightmares, cried often, and was anxious and aggressive.

During this time, B would construct a cave during the therapy sessions—a safe place where she could hide. The therapist had to keep her eyes closed until B was hidden from sight.

The therapist then had to guess what B was doing in her cave. Her desire that the therapist understand what she (B) wanted to say then became clear, while at the same time she was full of shame. The therapist was not allowed to see what she (B) was doing—the therapist had to simply know it. It seemed too difficult for B to call things by their names. During this time the therapist had the sense that it was all or nothing. Reality and fantasy intermingled. Past and present merged. From her hiding place B made signals with her fingers. She would stick her index finger in a hole, "give the finger", and show her little finger. The therapist repeatedly had to guess the different finger signs. B tried to teach the therapist her language as if the latter were illiterate. B would become angry if the therapist did not guess right away what she was doing and saying, and would say that the therapist did not understand anything and was stupid.

B thus re-enacted in a compulsive way her experiences of sexual abuse and projected onto the therapist her unbearable feelings of impotence and worthlessness and of being unloved and stupid. A desperate struggle to escape the violent feelings of anxiety and to communicate them without showing herself took place. The therapist cautiously began to verbalise these feelings and ask herself questions aloud, which B increasingly answered with "Right!" or "You don't understand anything!" B next switched the roles of victim and perpetrator in the game and ascribed both to the therapist.

By the time this intensive phase ended, the relationship had been significantly strengthened. It was now possible to distinguish between past and present. When B was in her hiding place, she was the girl from the past; when she came out of her cave, she was the girl of today. A differentiation between overwhelming traumatic experiences and real, everyday experiences with transference reactions to others outside therapy began. B stated: "Mr. R [childcare worker] reminds me of my father, but now I know he's not."

After feeling more secure and better understood, B began to arrange the room less as a hiding place, but more as a zone, using her own space for self-determination and therefore for safely setting boundaries. She repeatedly stressed that she did not have to do anything, that she wanted to be asked questions, that the therapist had to say "Please" first before asking questions. She would end her friendship if the therapist did not do something the way she (B) wanted her to. There developed a game in which B entirely assumed the role of director. B would hide in her own space, and the therapist had to leave the room, knock on the door, and ask whether she may speak with the girl who lives here. Over many hours B repeatedly ejected the therapist from the room—with increasing pleasure. In the next sequence, the therapist had to enter the room without knocking—thus not respecting her space—and she ejected the therapist from the room with great delight and with increasing aggression. She left her hiding place for this purpose and berated the therapist—"beating me to a pulp". She had changed from victim to perpetrator. During this time, she told the therapist for the first time: "This is a game, you understand, I trust you."

Separation and distinction between reality and fantasy were now possible. Understanding and making understandable her inner traumatising images and working through them have led to a more self-reliant utilisation of her space and to the separation between self and object with an increasing capacity for object constancy. B's current developmental level was examined again by the female psychologist half a year later. By now she had further developed considerably as to work behaviour and performance. While she still showed fluctuations in motivation, she put this motivation to work in building relationships. Her expectations of and sensitivity to failure lessened considerably. For example, while she was unwilling to do tasks she perceived as difficult, she could be easily motivated to continue cooperation. She visibly took pleasure in successes and experienced them as motivational aids. At no point in the second series of examinations did she indicate that she remembered parts of the material. In accordance with her school age (first year in a special needs school), she could now do the work in a persevering and resilient manner.

The qualitative analysis in CPM also continued to indicate difficulties in spatial orientation and in the translation of position. She was still unable to recognise simple addition and subtraction of sample elements. Dissociative cut-offs from perception no longer occurred. B achieved a percentile rank of nine.

The Breuer-Weuffen findings still indicated a significantly pronounced discriminatory weakness for acoustically provided material.

In the man-drawing test B spontaneously drew two people, each a cephalopod, and wrote her name on the smaller and first-drawn figure. For the second figure, she asked me to write down the name of her key carer. The quantitative analysis revealed a developmental age of about six years—still a considerable lag in development. The qualitative analysis indicated developmental progress in bodily awareness, especially compared with her drawing from three years ago. The person now had hands and feet. On the other hand, even now B was still unable to depict a complete person—the torso was still missing.

B has made significant developmental progress in sensory integration.

The first goal of treatment (stage one) was to introduce B to the available materials in order to stimulate her willingness to explore. This was necessary, as she seemed frozen at the beginning of the treatment. She was unable to turn specifically to given materials, but concentrated exclusively on the motion therapist (I. Kepper is the motion therapist in the department). B needed her help in dealing with the skateboard or exercise ball, for example. When she made an attempt on being prompted, she showed little willingness to move and hardly any stamina. She then seemed powerless and would immediately give up again.

During the third session, B finally found the balloon to be the element that would stir her motivation to move with her body. The task of not letting the balloon fall to the ground required so much concentration on her part that she unconsciously increased her movements. She became increasingly brisker in her movements and seemed more relaxed.

After B learned to endure bodily tension better and after her movement motivation was sparked, the motion therapist offered exercises (stage two) to alleviate B's disorders in a topic-focused way. This included arranging pathways through the room, climbing small heights, balance-training tasks, tactile stimulation through offers of relaxation, exercises in pressing and pulling for improving depth sensitivity, and so on.

She increasingly gained confidence in herself and in her own actions. To support the development of her body scheme (stage three), B and the motion therapist together drew the outline of B's body on large puzzle pieces, which they then took apart and put back together. The individual parts of the body were named, moved about, and arranged to form the picture of a body; relationships between the body parts were illustrated in playful exercises. At this point B was still avoiding crossing the centre line of her body with her limbs and refused to enter into the offered exercises in this regard.

With the aim of transferring her body scheme to the spatial scheme, B and the motion therapist constructed different spaces with different entrances (stage four), in which she enthusiastically played hide and seek and catch.

B now practises rhythmic jumping on the trampoline by accompanying small movement sequences by counting, for example. She engages in rhythmic clapping games that she verbally accompanies and which require her to cross the centre line of her body with her limbs.

Altogether B has made significant progress in her everyday social life. She has become more capable of learning and concentrating. She is able to articulate desires, designate negative emotions, and interact with her peers on the ward, and also within the ward group. She expresses anger when her foster mother does not write, whom she also confronts about this. She is able to attend the external school.

Outlook

Our detailed account of the diagnosis and therapy of this nine-year-old, severely abused and neglected girl illustrates the complex manner in which traumas affect childhood development. Multidimensional therapeutic offerings can reduce and/or help the patient overcome sensory, affective, and cognitive impairments. Re-enactments of traumatic experiences and primary reactions as self-protective forms of behaviour, which lead to continued re-traumatisation and accompanied by speechlessness, determine the treatment to pursue for such children and adolescents. The forms of interaction shaped by the abuse inevitably occurring in the patient's everyday life and in the therapeutic setting can be overcome only if these interactions are recognised as such and treated on the macro and micro levels. In addition to the psychotherapy, which gradually approaches and treats this central complex of problems in connection with the development of a space for thinking, playing and symbolic communication (Ogden, 1985), the body therapy covers disorders in bodily awareness and body image as well as disorders in the various sensory modes of perception and their processing, which have hitherto been sustaining the re-enactments (attribution bias: Dodge & Somberg, 1987). Both types of therapy make clear how previous excessive mental stress that had led to a persistence of primitive reactions can be tempered by introspective distancing, development of ego capacities, and the affective state of being held. New experiences involving reliability, stability, and relationships providing security become available on a complex level that creates a condition of "secure readiness" (Cicchetti, 1995) which in turn enables learning from experience (Bion, 1962) and learning from knowledge.

References

Ayres, J. (1989). *Sensory Integration and Praxis Tests.* Los Angeles, CA: Western Psychological Services.

Bion, W. R. (1962). *Learning from Experience.* London: Heinemann [reprinted London: Karnac, 1984].

Dodge, K. A., & Somberg, D. R. (1987). Hostile attributional biases among aggressive boys are exacerbated under conditions of threats of the self. *Child Development, 58*: 213–224.

Dopart, T. (1983). The cognitive arrest hypothesis of denial. *International Journal of Psychoanalysis, 64*: 47–58.

Edelman, G. M. (1978). *The Mindful Brain: Cortical Organization and the Group-selective Theory of Higher Brain Function.* Cambridge, MA: MIT.

Eggert, D. (1996). The Measurement of Motor Abilities: Developments, Problems, and Alternatives. In G. Doll-Tepper, C. Dohms, B. Doll & H. Selzam (Eds.), Adapted physical activity. *International Council of Sport Science and Physical Education* (pp. 389–394). Berlin, Heidelberg: Springer.

Fraiberg, S. (1982). Psychological defences in infancy. *Psychoanalytic Quarterly, 51*: 612–635.

Kesper, G. & Hottinger, C. (1993). *Mototherapie bei sensorischen Integrationsstörungen,* München: Reinhardt.

Mandler, G. (1984). *Mind and Body—Psychology of Emotion and Stress.* New York: Norton.

Ogden, T. H. (1985). On potential space. *International Journal of Psychoanalysis, 66*: 129–141.

Santostephano, S. (1995). Embodied meanings, cognition and emotion: probing how three are one. In: D. Cicchetti & S. L. Toth (Eds.), *Developmental Perspectives on Trauma: Theory, Research and Intervention. Rochester Symposium on Developmental Psychopathology (Volume 6)* (pp. 59–132). Rochester, NY: University of Rochester Press.

Streeck-Fischer, A. (2014*). Trauma und Entwicklung. Adoleszenz—frühe Traumatisierung und die Folgen.* Stuttgart: Schattauer.

Streeck-Fischer, A., & Van der Kolk, B. A. (2000). "Down will come baby, cradle and all": diagnostic and therapeutic implications of chronic trauma on child development. *Australian and New Zealand Journal of Psychiatry, 34*: 903–918.

Teicher, M. H., Anderson, C. M., & Polcari, A. (2012). Childhood maltreatment is associated with reduced volume in hippocampal subfields CA3, dentate gyrus and subiculum. *Proceedings of the National Academy of Sciences, 109*: E 563–572.

CHAPTER TWENTY

Can mentalization disrupt the circle of violence in adolescents with early maltreatment?

Svenja Taubner and Paul Schröder

Introduction

Young offenders pose a major risk for modern societies concerning long-term societal costs, for themselves in terms of criminal careers as well as for their victims. Thus, the development and implementation of effective rehabilitation and prevention programmes is highly desirable, and especially in adolescence, when the so-called "window of opportunity" that goes along with massive neurobiological, psychological, and social changes (Drury & Giedd, 2009), enables profound changes in individual development that can interrupt vicious circles leading into chronic offending. At the same time, adolescents are vulnerable to negative developments and prone to risk-taking behaviour (Steinberg, 2005).

Juvenile justice systems in the USA and other countries have followed different epistemic frameworks in the past century, starting from an unrealistic rehabilitation expectation that was followed by the "get tough" era with stronger punitive intervention strategies (Manchak & Cullen, 2015). Starting in the 1990s, high quality meta-analysis studies led to a new insight about efficacy in offender programmes overcoming the "nothing works" pessimism. Main factors of effectiveness seem to be treatment intervention philosophy, addressing high risk offenders and high quality of implementation (Lipsey, 2009), while the punishment-oriented programmes are ineffective (Manchak & Cullen, 2015) or can even increase recidivism—as is the case of being placed within the juvenile justice system in comparison to being placed in non-system conditions (Petrosino, Turpin-Petrosino, & Guckenburg, 2014). A group of Canadian psychologists (Andrews & Bonta, 2010) developed a highly influential treatment theory for adult and juvenile offenders called the Risk-Need-Responsivity model (RNR). They argued that intensive interventions should only be delivered to high-risk individuals because low-risk individuals may experience negative effects when taken out of risk-reducing communities and being confronted with high-risk peers. Second, interventions should target criminogenic risk factors (e.g., antisocial cognition, family problems, substance use and abuse); and third, programmes should be delivered in accordance with offenders' learning styles.

Developmental psychopathology and psychoanalytic theories deal with the question of how early experiences can have an impact on altering functioning in adolescence and adulthood. From this point of view, any psychopathology is regarded as an adaptation to inner and attachment-related problems associated with impaired functioning or dynamic defences against unbearable mental states. Later in life, these "solutions" may become rigid, may not fit well with the demands of current situations, and may cause suffering both for the individual and for others around her. In that sense, individual antisocial and violent behaviour can be regarded as an expression or symptom of failure of expectable developmental support, in other words, a developmental disorder (Fonagy, 2008). About seventy per cent of children show forms of aggressive behaviour with a peak in aggressiveness at the age of two years (Tremblay, 2003). This is followed by a steady decline in aggressiveness in the majority of children, which leads to the hypothesis that children do not learn to be aggressive, but instead, most children learn *not to be aggressive* in the service of an evolutionary helpful optimal adaptation to the cultural context (Fonagy, 2008; Binks et al., 2006, 2012). Epidemiological and longitudinal studies have convincingly demonstrated the relationship between childhood maltreatment and disruptive disorders, including acts of violence (Jaffee, 2005; Loeber, Burke, & Lahey, 2002; Moffitt, Caspi, Harrington, & Milne, 2002). However, the mechanisms underlying the relationship—that is, how the experience of early maltreatment is transformed into a potential for violence against others is still poorly understood. An understanding of mechanisms linking early abuse with later violent behaviour is needed to be able to interrupt the circle of violence as conceptual framework for resilience research (Ensink, Berthelot, Bernazzani, Normandin, & Fonagy, 2014; Fonagy, Steele, Steele, Higgitt, & Target, 1994; Adshead, Fonagy, & Sarkar, 2007). Research has identified variables with a strong protective effect on the relationship between early maltreatment and later aggressive behaviour, however those are mostly genetic (e.g., Caspi et al., 2002; Weder et al., 2009) or socioeconomic (Beauchaine, Webster-Stratton, & Reid, 2005; Reyno & McGrath, 2006) in nature. As these cannot be addressed by therapeutic interventions, there is a need to elaborate on psychosocial protective variables. Social cognition, in particular mentalization, has been proposed to be inhibiting towards violent and aggressive behaviour (Blair, 1995). Therefore, in this overview, we will focus on the role of mentalization as a protective factor in adolescence.

Effects of early maltreatment

Childhood maltreatment is a worldwide problem with severe negative consequences and long-term effects for victims and high societal costs (Butchart, Harvey, Mian, & Fürniss, 2006). The World Health Organization's definition of childhood maltreatment encompasses physical and emotional mistreatment and sexual abuse. There has been strong variance in the range of prevalence of childhood maltreatment reported by studies worldwide. A study using a retrospective assessment of childhood maltreatment in a representative German population sample reported 14.9% psychological maltreatment, 12% physical maltreatment, 12.5% sexual abuse, 13.8% moderate to severe emotional neglect, and 18.8% moderate to severe physical neglect (Häuser, Schmutzer, Brähler, & Glaesmer, 2011). The values described coincide with studies with American prevalence rates (Afifi et al., 2011). Childhood maltreatment is, among other consequences, closely linked to the development of a heightened potential for violence (Anda et al., 2006; Caspi et al., 2002; Keenan, Wroblewski, Hipwell, Loeber, & Stouthamer-Loeber, 2010). Specifically, experiences of childhood maltreatment are associated with the development of an increased level of aggressive behaviour in the maltreated child or adolescent (Chen, Coccaro, Lee, & Jacobson, 2012; Weder et al., 2009; Afifi, Brownridge, Cox, & Sareen, 2006; Gershoff, 2002, 2013; Lansford et al., 2014; Taylor, Manganello, Lee, & Rice, 2010) and an increased risk of developing conduct disorder (CD) in childhood and adolescence (Caspi et al., 2002; Afifi et al., 2011; Jaffee et al., 2005).

Links between early maltreatment and violence

James Gilligan formed a thesis on extreme violence built upon numerous cases he encountered during his work in the American prison system (described in his monograph; Gilligan, 2000) in which seemingly small insults or even the fantasy of being humiliated appear to get out of hand, leading to extreme violence. Central to explaining this phenomenon is the feeling of shame. The inability to tolerate the feeling of being shamed, to symbolise shame in a non-behavioural manner, and to contain shame, are common in these perpetrators and might originate from past experience of childhood maltreatment. According to Gilligan, violence of physical and/or psychological nature in early attachment relationships is conveying an absolute absence of love. The child, constantly shamed, humiliated, and hurt instead of loved becomes numb in an effort to protect herself. Interpersonal relationships and especially loving others always carries the risk of re-experiencing the rejection of early attachment interactions and thus are extremely dangerous for this person. The incapability of loving coupled with a hypersensitivity to insult leads to a joyless life. Experiencing another person as potentially shaming, which in combination with a hypersensitivity to insult occurs frequently, the individual "drowns in an ocean of hatred" (Gilligan, 2000). In order to prevent this from happening, the person might then commit to the fantasy of never being shamed again by means of being dreadful, strong, or untouchable. In the face of extreme violence, such as with murderers, Gilligan also observed another phenomenon, linked to extreme forms of childhood maltreatment and early close-to-death experiences. These extremely violent men report to have no feelings at all and experience themselves as "living dead". Gilligan hypothesises that the constant and overwhelming experience of shame, rejection, and humiliation most of these people were exposed to in childhood, gradually destroys their self-esteem. Without a minimal amount of self-esteem, the self collapses, leading to a "soul murder" (Shengold, 1979) in a body that is still biologically functioning. As a consequence, Gilligan states that these individuals will ferociously attack and kill others, if they think that it will prevent their own souls from being murdered by further anticipated shame or rejection. They kill for what appears to them as a form of self-defence. However, hurting others does not restore a "living soul" and is a strategy that is self-defeating, and thus extreme forms of self-mutilation occur to create physical sensations, for it is better to feel pain than the feeling of deadness, the absolute absence of feelings. This might also explain the unsurprising fact that many murderers decide to end their own lives as well (Binks et al., 2006).

Inhibition of mentalizing as one key mechanism in the circle of violence

Mentalizing is the ability to understand one's own behaviour and the behaviour of others in terms of mental states (Fonagy, Gergely, Jurist, & Target, 2002). It entails deducing and understanding the cognitive and affective mental states of the self and others on the basis of a psychological theory. Mentalizing can be seen as an essential evolutionary human capacity that enables long-term social collaboration and, probably to assure this function, is capable of inhibiting violent aggressive social action (Fonagy & Target, 2004). The development of mentalizing starts in early childhood in the context of early attachment interactions (Fonagy et al., 2002) and from there goes through various states: from teleological to intentional and finally to mentalizing understanding of self and others, meaning robust awareness of the representational, subjective nature of mental states (Frith & Frith, 2012). A teleological understanding of behaviour is solely based on observable outcomes, while an intentional understanding implies the presumption of motives in terms of feelings and beliefs. Violent individuals frequently experience a merely teleological mode of understanding that is strictly limited to detecting what happens in the physical world—e.g., what is the outcome of an action, regardless of its impact on subjective experience (of either the self or the other). Fonagy and colleagues consider mentalizing, in a similar fashion to language, to be a biologically programmed developmental achievement, which is crucially dependent on the family context. Secure attachment relationships promote rapid acquisition of mentalizing (Arnott & Meins, 2007; Fonagy, Target, Steele, & Steele, 1997). By contrast, mentalizing can be severely impaired when early relationships become brutalised (Cicchetti, Rogosch, Maughan, Toth, & Bruce, 2003; Ensink et al., 2014; Ensink, Berthelot, Bernazzani, Normandin, & Fonagy, 2014; Pears & Fisher, 2005).

The impact of the quality of parenting on behavioural outcomes may be mediated through the mechanisms of affect regulation and selective attention. For example, Derryberry and Rothbart (1997) assume that children who have not experienced support and calming from their early caregivers in anxiety-provoking situations are likely to develop avoiding strategies to hide or deny such situations instead of experiencing inner and social coping possibilities. They suggest two possible long-term consequences from anxiety-avoiding strategies: first, such children will be less attentive to anxiety-provoking information and will not be able to handle difficult social situations effectively and appropriately. Instead, they develop maladaptive coping strategies based on compulsion; and second, the child will not benefit from the positive consequences of felt anxiety in the sense of promoting affect regulation, impulse control, empathy, and anxiety consciousness.

Fonagy, Gergely, Jurist, and Target (2002) have proposed a similar model in conceptualising inhibited mentalization as an adaptation to the brutalisation of an attachment relationship

(Adshead, Fonagy, & Sarkar, 2007; Fonagy, 1999, 2003). Inhibition of mentalizing serves as a protection because children no longer need to think about a perpetrator's frankly malevolent motives when they are simultaneously vulnerable to, or existentially depending on, the same individual. If others' actions are not interpreted in terms of their motives, wishes, emotions, and beliefs, the understanding becomes "concrete"; that is, it is restricted to an understanding in terms of physical or observable reality. If mentalizing is inhibited, the social environment is no longer interpreted from the "intentional stance", but from a "physical stance" (Dennett, 1987). In this case, an angry voice can be perceived as being only loud, and a threatening gesticulation is seen only as a raised arm (Hill, Fonagy, Lancaster, & Broyden, 2007). This specific non-intentional approach to anxiety-provoking situations was demonstrated for children with externalising disorders (Hill, Fonagy, Lancaster, & Broyden, 2007; Hill, Murray, Leidecker, & Sharp, 2008). There is accumulating evidence of substantial mentalizing problems in young people and adults with a combination of histories of maltreatment and of severe interpersonal aggression (Chiesa & Fonagy, 2014; Elsegood & Duff, 2010; Romero-Martinez, Lila, Catala-Minana, Williams, & Moya-Albiol, 2013). Antisocial behaviour has been consistently shown to be associated with observed deficits in mentalizing across a number of measures (Newbury-Helps, Feigenbaum, & Fonagy, 2017), especially in violent subgroups (Levinson & Fonagy, 2004; McGauley, Ferris, Marin-Avellan, & Fonagy, 2013).

In line with these findings, Bateman and Fonagy (2012) propose a probable mediation between childhood maltreatment and externalising problems through inadequate interpersonal understanding as well as limited behavioural flexibility in response to demands from the environment. It is argued that a child who is maltreated by her own caregivers cannot experience being treated as a feeling and thinking being. Being recognised as a feeling and thinking human being is a necessary prerequisite to experiencing oneself and others as thinking and feeling beings, and to be able fully to mentalize others. Thus, individuals who were treated like physical objects are prone to treat themselves and others without reliably attributing intentionality to self or others, especially when intense emotions arise that cannot be contained in a mentalizing way but only by using one's own body or violent action.

Mentalizing interrupts the circle of violence in adolescents with early maltreatment

We conducted a study on 161 adolescents from the community (n = 98) and adolescents with externalising and internalising problems (n = 63) who were recruited from several youth psychiatrists in Germany. The data from our participants was examined using a structural equation modelling to test first, whether childhood maltreatment predicts the development of a heightened potential for violence in adolescence and second, whether mentalization and/or attachment mediate this influence. Mentalizing was measured with the Reflective-Functioning-Scale (RFS) (Fonagy, Target, Steele, & Steele, 1998); attachment was assessed using the Adult Attachment Projective Picture System (George & West, 2001). Since mentalization is thought to develop in early attachment interactions, the reciprocal influence between attachment and mentalization was also considered. Potential for violence was composed from proactive and reactive aggression and the manifestation of CD, in terms of a diagnosis, or lack thereof. The operationalisation of childhood maltreatment in the present study included physical neglect and antipathy, defined as hostility, coldness, or rejection shown to the child by parents or surrogate parents, and physical maltreatment. With regard to potential for violence, the observed values in the present sample are comparatively high: 26.1% of the sample was diagnosed with CD, a rate much higher than in studies with representative samples (Afifi et al., 2011; Ravens-Sieberer, Wille, Bettge, & Erhart, 2007). The mean values of the Reactive-Proactive-Aggression-Questionnaire also range above the mean value from the validation sample of the RPQ (Vloet, Von Polier, Herpertz-Dahlmann, & Raine, 2013). The proportion of disorganised attachment in the present sample (23%) coincides with results from a meta-analysis with 6,000 mother-child dyads from various ethnic, socioeconomic, and cultural backgrounds of 20.4% (Van IJzendoorn, Schuengel, & Bakermans-Kranenburg, 1999). The mean score for Reflective Functioning (RF) in the present sample (M = 3.43) replicates values from Borelli, Compare, Snavely, and Decio (2014), who reported a mean RF score of M = 3.2 in their sample of 84 adolescents which is a lower RF value than in adult samples. Values of childhood maltreatment coincide with German and American prevalence rates (Häuser et al., 2011; Afifi et al., 2011).

Results of the structural equation model replicated former studies in terms of demonstrating that the severity of childhood maltreatment indeed had a strong direct effect on potential for violence with regard to aggressive behaviour and the presence of CD. This effect was mediated partially through mentalizing, but not through attachment. This means that, in the face of childhood maltreatment, higher mentalizing was associated with reduced potential for aggression.

Consequences for treatment and prevention

Addressing the vulnerabilities in mentalization has been successfully achieved in treatments for other psychopathologies such as borderline personality disorders or antisocial personality disorders (Bateman & Fonagy, 2016). In the light of the current state of the art and the present study, it seems promising to integrate mentalization-enhancing therapeutic techniques for treatment of young offenders as well. Although replication of the present study's findings is needed, they still might carry implications for clinical practice. Adolescent violent offending, a core symptom of CD, poses high risks on modern societies through a variety of factors. On the one hand, violent behaviour causes victimisation, on the other hand offending signifies a high risk of criminogenic and psychopathological development. The mediating effect of mentalization, operationalised as RF, on the effect of childhood maltreatment on potential for violence implies that promoting mentalization through prevention and treatment might reduce the potential for violence in adolescence. Thus, the present study's results imply that treatment programmes with a focus on promoting mentalization might be effective in treating children and adolescents with a heightened potential for violence. Above all, early childhood maltreatment seems to be one of the major harmful events that need to be addressed more effectively by early prevention programmes.

References

Adshead, G., Fonagy, P., & Sarkar, S. P. (2007). Violence and gun crime. *British Medical Journal, 335*(7625): 837.

Afifi, T. O., Brownridge, D. A., Cox, B. J., & Sareen, J. (2006). Physical punishment, childhood abuse and psychiatric disorders. *Child Abuse & Neglect, 30*: 1093–1103.

Afifi, T. O., McMillan, K. A., Asmundson, G. J., Gordon, J. G., Pietrzak, R. H., & Sareen, J. (2011). An examination of the relation between conduct disorder, childhood and adulthood traumatic events, and posttraumatic stress disorder in a nationally representative sample. *Journal of Psychiatric Research, 45*: 1564–1572.

Anda, R. F., Felitti, V. J., Bremner, J. D., Walker, J. D., Whitfield, C., Perry, B. D., & Giles, W. H. (2006). The enduring effects of abuse and related adverse experiences in childhood. A convergence of evidence from neurobiology and epidemiology. *European Archives of Psychiatry and Clinical Neuroscience, 256*: 174–186.

Andrews, D. A., & Bonta, J. (2010). *The Psychology of Criminal Conduct* (5th edn). New Providence, NJ: Anderson.

Arnott, B., & Meins, E. (2007). Links among antenatal attachment representations, post-natal mind-mindedness, and infant attachment security. A preliminary study of mothers and fathers. *Bulletin of the Menninger Clinic, 71*: 132–149.

Bateman, A. W., & Fonagy, P. (Eds.) (2012). *Handbook of Mentalizing in Mental Health Practice.* Washington, DC: American Psychiatric Publishing.

Bateman, A., & Fonagy, P. (2016). Mentalization Based Treatment for Personality Disorders: A Practical Guide. Oxford: Oxford University Press.

Beauchaine, T. P., Webster-Stratton, C., & Reid, M. J. (2005). Mediators, moderators, and predictors of 1-year outcomes among children treated for early-onset conduct problems: a latent growth curve analysis. *Journal of Consulting and Clinical Psychology, 73*: 371–388.

Binks, C. A., Fenton, M., McCarthy, L., Lee, T., Adams, C. E., & Duggan, C. (2006). Psychological therapies for people with borderline personality disorder. *The Cochrane Database of Systematic Reviews.*

Blair, R. (1995). A cognitive developmental approach to morality: investigating the psychopath. *Cognition, 57*: 1–29.

Borelli, J. L., Compare, A., Snavely, J. E., & Decio, V. (2014). Reflective functioning moderates the association between perceptions of parental neglect and attachment in adolescence. *Psychoanalytic Psychology, 32*: 23–35.

Butchart, A., Harvey, A. P., Mian, M., & Fürniss, T. (2006). *Preventing Child Maltreatment: A Guide to Taking Action and Generating Evidence.* Geneva: World Health Organization.

Caspi, A., McClay, J., Moffitt, T. E., Mill, J., Martin, J., Craig, I. W., & Poulton, R. (2002). Role of genotype in the cycle of violence in maltreated children. *Science, 297*: 851–854.

Chen, P., Coccaro, E. F., Lee, R., & Jacobson, K. C. (2012). Moderating effects of childhood maltreatment on associations between social information processing and adult aggression. *Psychological medicine, 42*: 1293–1304.

Chiesa, M., & Fonagy, P. (2014). Reflective function as a mediator between childhood adversity, personality disorder and symptom distress. *Personality and Mental Health, 8*: 52–66.

Cicchetti, D., Rogosch, F. A., Maughan, A., Toth, S. L., & Bruce, J. (2003). False belief understanding in maltreated children. *Development and Psychopathology, 15*: 1067–1091.

Derryberry, D., & Rothbart, M. K. (1997). Reactive and effortful processes in the organization of temperament. *Development and Psychopathology, 9*: 633–652.

Drury, S. S., & Giedd, J. (2009). Inside the adolescent brain. *Journal of the American Academy of Child and Adolescent Psychiatry, 48*: 677–678.

Elsegood, K. J., & Duff, S. C. (2010). Theory of mind in men who have sexually offended against children: a U.K. comparison study between child sex offenders and nonoffender controls. *Sexual Abuse: A Journal of Research and Treatment, 22*: 112–131.

Ensink, K., Berthelot, N., Bernazzani, O., Normandin, L., & Fonagy, P. (2014). Another step closer to measuring the ghosts in the nursery: preliminary validation of the trauma reflective functioning scale. *Frontiers in Psychology, 5*: 1471.

Ensink, K., Normandin, L., Target, M., Fonagy, P., Sabourin, S., & Berthelot, N. (2014). Mentalization in children and mothers in the context of trauma: an initial study of the validity of the child reflective functioning scale. *The British Journal of Developmental Psychology, 33*(2): 203–217.

Fonagy, P. (1999). Male perpetrators of violence against women: an attachment theory perspective. *Journal of Applied Psychoanalytic Studies, 1*: 7–27.

Fonagy, P. (2003). Das Verständnis für geistige Prozesse, die Mutter-Kind-Interaktion und die Entwicklung des Selbst. In: P. Fonagy & M. Target (Eds.), *Frühe Bindung und psychische Entwicklung. Beiträge aus Psychoanalyse und Bindungsforschung* (pp. 31–48). Gießen: Psychosozial.

Fonagy, P. (2008). Persönlichkeitsstörung und Gewalt. Ein psychoanalytisch-bindungstheoretischer Ansatz. In: F. Lackinger & W. Berner (Eds.), *Psychodynamische Psychotherapie bei Delinquenz. Praxis der übertragungsfokussierten Psychotherapie* (pp. 326–365). Stuttgart: Schattauer.

Fonagy, P., & Target, M. (2004). Frühe Interaktion und die Entwicklung der Selbstregulation. In: A. Streeck-Fischer (Ed.), *Adoleszenz—Bindung—Destruktivität* (pp. 105–135). Stuttgart: Klett-Cotta.

Fonagy, P., Gergely, G., Jurist, E. L., & Target, M. (2002). *Affect Regulation, Mentalization, and the Development of the Self.* London: Karnac.

Fonagy, P., Steele, M., Steele, H., Higgitt, A., & Target, M. (1994). The theory and practice of resilience. *Journal of Child Psychology and Psychiatry, 35*: 231–257.

Fonagy, P., Target, M., Steele, H., & Steele, M. (1998). *Reflective Functioning Scale Manual.*

Fonagy, P., Target, M., Steele, M., & Steele, H. (1997). The development of violence and crime as it relates to security of attachment. In: J. D. Osofsky (Ed.), *Children in a violent society* (pp. 150–177). New York: Guilford.

Frith, C. D., & Frith, U. (2012). Mechanisms of social cognition. *Annual Review of Psychology, 63*: 287–313.

George, C., & West, M. (2001). The development and preliminary validation of a new measure of adult attachment: the adult attachment projective. *Attachment & Human Development, 3*: 30–61.

Gershoff, E. T. (2002). Corporal punishment by parents and associated child behaviors and experiences: a meta-analytic and theoretical review. *Psychological Bulletin, 128*: 539–579.

Gershoff, E. T. (2013). Spanking and child development: we know enough now to stop hitting our children. *Child development perspectives, 7*: 133–137.

Gilligan, J. (2000). *Violence: Reflections on our deadliest epidemic. Forensic focus: Volume 18.* London: Jessica Kingsley.

Häuser, W., Schmutzer, G., Brähler, E., & Glaesmer, H. (2011). Maltreatment in childhood and adolescence: results from a survey of a representative sample of the German population. *Deutsches Ärzteblatt International, 108:* 287–294.

Hill, J., Fonagy, P., Lancaster, G., & Broyden, N. (2007). Aggression and intentionality in narrative responses to conflict and distress story stems. An investigation of boys with disruptive behaviour problems. *Attachment & Human Development, 9*: 223–237.

Hill, J., Murray, L., Leidecker, V., & Sharp, H. (2008). The dynamics of threat, fear and intentionality in the conduct disorders. Longitudinal findings in the children of women with post-natal depression. *Philosophical Transactions of the Royal Society of London. Series B. Biological Sciences, 363*: 2529–2541.

Jaffee, S. R. (2005). Family violence and parent psychopathology: implications for children's socioemotional development and resilience. In: S. Goldstein & R. B. Brooks (Eds.), *Handbook of Resilience in Children* (pp. 127–142). Boston, MA: Springer.

Jaffee, S. R., Caspi, A., Moffitt, T. E., Dodge, K. A., Rutter, M., Taylor, A., & Tully, L. A. (2005). Nature × nurture: genetic vulnerabilities interact with physical maltreatment to promote conduct problems. *Development and Psychopathology, 17*(1).

Keenan, K., Wroblewski, K., Hipwell, A., Loeber, R., & Stouthamer-Loeber, M. (2010). Age of onset, symptom threshold, and expansion of the nosology of conduct disorder for girls. *Journal of abnormal psychology, 119*: 689–698.

Lansford, J. E., Sharma, C., Malone, P. S., Woodlief, D., Dodge, K. A., Oburu, P., & Di Giunta, L. (2014). Corporal punishment, maternal warmth, and child adjustment: a longitudinal study in eight countries. *Journal of Clinical Child and Adolescent Psychology, 43*: 670–685.

Levinson, A., & Fonagy, P. (2004). Offending and attachment: the relationship between interpersonal awareness and offending in a prison population with psychiatric disorder. *Canadian Journal of Psychoanalysis, 12*(2): 225–251.

Lipsey, M. W. (2009). The primary factors that characterize effective interventions with juvenile offenders: a meta-analytic overview. *Victims & Offenders, 4*: 124–147.

Loeber, R., Burke, J. D., & Lahey, B. B. (2002). What are adolescent antecedents to antisocial personality disorder? *Criminal Behaviour and Mental Health, 12*: 24–36.

Manchak, S. M., & Cullen, F. T. (2015). Intervening effectively with juvenile offenders: answers from meta-analysis. In: J. Morizot & L. Kazemian (Eds.), *The Development of Criminal and Antisocial Behavior* (pp. 477–490). Cham, Switzerland: Springer.

McGauley, G., Ferris, S., Marin-Avellan, L., & Fonagy, P. (2013). The index offence representation scales; a predictive clinical tool in the management of dangerous, violent patients with personality disorder? *Criminal Behaviour and Mental Health, 23*: 274–289.

Moffitt, T. E., Caspi, A., Harrington, H., & Milne, B. J. (2002). Males on the life-course-persistent and adolescence-limited antisocial pathways. Follow-up at age 26 years. *Development and Psychopathology, 14*: 179–207.

Newbury-Helps, J., Feigenbaum, J., & Fonagy, P. (2017). Offenders with antisocial personality disorder display more impairments in mentalizing. *Journal of Personality Disorders, 31*(2): 232–255.

Pears, K., & Fisher, P. A. (2005). Emotion understanding and theory of mind among maltreated children in foster care: evidence of deficits. *Development and Psychopathology, 17*: 47–65.

Petrosino, A., Turpin-Petrosino, C., & Guckenburg, S. (2014). The impact of juvenile system processing on delinquency. In: D. P. Farrington & J. Murray (Eds.), *Labeling Theory: Empirical Tests—Advances in Criminological Theory* (pp. 113–147). New Brunswick, NJ: Transaction.

Ravens-Sieberer, U., Wille, N., Bettge, S., & Erhart, M. (2007). Psychische Gesundheit von Kindern und Jugendlichen in Deutschland. Ergebnisse aus der BELLA-Studie im Kinder- und Jugendgesundheitssurvey (KiGGS) [Mental health of children and adolescents in Germany. Results from the BELLA study within the German Health Interview and Examination Survey for Children and Adolescents (KiGGS)]. *Bundesgesundheitsblatt, Gesundheitsforschung, Gesundheitsschutz, 50*(5–6): 871–878.

Reyno, S. M., & McGrath, P. J. (2006). Predictors of parent training efficacy for child externalizing behavior problems—a meta-analytic review. *Journal of Child Psychology and Psychiatry, and Allied Disciplines, 47*: 99–111.

Romero-Martinez, A., Lila, M., Catala-Minana, A., Williams, R. K., & Moya-Albiol, L. (2013). The contribution of childhood parental rejection and early androgen exposure to impairments in socio-cognitive skills in intimate partner violence perpetrators with high alcohol consumption. *International Journal of Environmental Research and Public Health, 10*: 3753–3770.

Shengold, L. L. (1979). Child abuse and deprivation: soul murder. *Journal of the American Psychoanalytic Association, 27*: 533–559.

Steinberg, L. (2005). Cognitive and affective development in adolescence. *Trends in Cognitive Sciences, 9*: 69–74.

Taylor, C. A., Manganello, J. A., Lee, S. J., & Rice, J. C. (2010). Mothers' spanking of 3-year-old children and subsequent risk of children's aggressive behavior. *Pediatrics, 125*(5): e1057–e1065.

Tremblay, R. E. (2003). Why socialization fails: the case of chronic physical aggression. In: B. B. Lahey, T. E. Moffitt, & A. Caspi (Eds.), *Causes of Conduct Disorder and Juvenile Delinquency* (pp. 182–226). New York: Guilford.

Van IJzendoorn, M. H., Schuengel, C., & Bakermans–Kranenburg, M. J. (1999). Disorganized attachment in early childhood: meta-analysis of precursors, concomitants, and sequelae. *Development and Psychopathology, 11*: 225–250.

Vloet, T. D., von Polier, G. G., Herpertz-Dahlmann, B., & Raine, A. (2013). *The Reactive-Proactive Aggression Questionnaire.*

Weder, N., Yang, B. Z., Douglas-Palumberi, H., Massey, J., Krystal, J. H., Gelernter, J., & Kaufman, J. (2009). MAOA genotype, maltreatment, and aggressive behavior: the changing impact of genotype at varying levels of trauma. *Biological Psychiatry, 65*(5): 417–424.

CHAPTER TWENTY-ONE

Mentalization of trauma in juvenile offenders

Sonja Protić

Introduction

Trauma has been recognised as one of the most important risk factors for many different mental health problems, including, for example, depression (Nanni, Uher, & Danese, 2014), substance abuse (Wilsnack, Vogeltanz, Klassen, & Harris, 1997), and schizophrenia (Matheson, Shepherd, Pinchbeck, Laurens, & Carr, 2013). In relation to that, juvenile offenders seem to be a particularly vulnerable group in terms of early traumatic experiences in the family—records show that about eighty per cent of juvenile offenders experienced certain forms of physical, psychological, and emotional abuse, serious accidents, and losses in their childhood (Fonagy et al., 1997). Furthermore, approximately half of them could have been diagnosed with post-traumatic stress disorder at a certain point (Steiner, Garcia, & Matthews, 1997). However, these two phenomena cannot be associated based on direct causality only, especially in the light of data that has so far shown that only one quarter of children with traumatic experiences become delinquents, while three-quarters turn out not to be involved in any kind of antisocial behaviour (Fonagy et al., 1997). Therefore, the aim of this chapter is to discuss a potential mediator between trauma and delinquency, as well as the preliminary results of a study on the same topic.

The experience of being abused by a parent/caregiver is considered to be particularly hazardous and overwhelming. According to attachment theory (Bowlby, 1973), a parent or a caregiver is the person that provides the child with safety, comfort, and care so as to ensure her survival. A child being raised by an unpredictable parent, who represents both a haven of safety and a source of danger and mystery, can lead to some serious development impairments of that child's self-regulation mechanisms, such as mentalization (Fonagy, Gergely, Jurist, & Target, 2002). Mentalization is the capacity to interpret behaviour based on mental states, such as desires, beliefs, and feelings (Bateman & Fonagy, 2004). However, in a violent relationship, the child is too threatened to think about her own and the maltreating parent's mind since only unbearable fear, hatred, and pain come from there. As a result, the child chooses not to think about her own and her parent's mind in order not to lose the relationship with her parent. The hypothesis that will be discussed here is that some specific characteristics of this developmental impairment can be linked to antisocial behaviour in adolescents.

The collapse of mentalization might be better understood through analysis of deficits in some other developmental processes strongly connected to it, and found within the attachment relationship. One of them is affect regulation (Allen, Fonagy, & Bateman, 2008), which develops in situations when the child feels threatened and the attachment behavioural system is automatically activated in order for the child to establish and maintain closeness with her caregiver and get comfort and security. However, if the parent himself represents the source of anxiety and pain, the child does not succeed in containing these feelings; on the contrary, she feels even more frightened. The feeling of increased intensive fear then reactivates the attachment system, and the child enters into a vicious circle of anxiety, unable to build any kind of strategy to regulate her own emotions (Allen, Fonagy, & Bateman, 2008).

Mirroring, and especially parents' marked mimics, which represent processes and aspects of interaction essential for the development of the child's sense of self and of her inner world representations (Allen, Fonagy, & Bateman, 2008), also become compromised within a violent relationship (Fonagy, 2004). Instead of empathic expressions to the child's facial appearances, aimed at soothing and enhancing development of affect regulation, the child sees only the parent's anger and thus becomes even more agitated and frightened. As a result she might identify the parent's anger as her own feeling, which can lead to certain misinterpretations in the future; for example, the child may equate her own anxiety with someone else's rage and misinterpret it as a threat. Also, the child might learn to perceive certain feelings as unacceptable, incomprehensible, and unbearable, or may adopt some inappropriate strategies to attract her parents' attention (e.g., provoking anger or fear in the parent).

How does the child psychologically survive a trauma in the relationship with an attachment figure? Bowlby (1980) has introduced the concept of defensive exclusion that involves three different processes—deactivation, cognitive disconnection, and segregated systems. Their aim is to prevent the child from facing a threatening or an unbearable content within the attachment relationship or, as we would say today, to stop the mentalization. The concept of cognitive disconnection refers to distracted and unorganised thoughts, aimless ruminations, withdrawal, and abstention from affect, while at the same time the child feels overwhelmed by emotional arousal, anxiety, and anger that are not being contained by her caregiver. Deactivation prevents the child from becoming aware of her negative feelings. It involves different strategies of idealisation of the attachment figure as well as neutralisation, devaluation, minimisation, and isolation of affect. The third group, called segregated systems, is an extreme form of defensive exclusion that is usually activated in attachment-related trauma and leads to segregation of extremely painful emotions, memories, unfulfilled desires, and needs from consciousness. By avoiding thoughts about the caregiver as being the abuser and taking over the guilt, the child manages to survive within the traumatic relationship.

On the other hand, the use of segregated systems has its price. This defensive process hinders the adaptation of internal working models of self and others to the external reality, and leads to their splitting (Bowlby, 1973, 1980). The repressed representations of the violent relationship remain stored and so does the possibility that they are activated in another situation resembling the traumatic experience in some way. In relation to that, the child's actions and behaviours then become dysfunctional, disorganised, and uncontrollable. The consequence of splitting on the level of internal working models is that one or more behavioural systems become partially or completely shut down, while the others take control over the child's functioning (Bowlby, 1980). The child or adolescent is not aware of the factors that influenced the selection of these actions; she can misinterpret her own behaviour and attribute emotions and direct actions towards the wrong person.

Authors have identified three types of mentalization deficits in the face of trauma (Allen, Fonagy, & Bateman, 2008). One of them is psychic equivalence mode in which the experience of the inner world becomes equated with that of the outer world. That type of reduced mentalization includes, among other things, the absence of differentiation between psychological and physical pain, and the lack of abstract thinking and symbolisation. Another deficit is described as teleological mode in which the mental states are not expressed through explicit representations, but through concrete goal-oriented actions. Finally, the pretend mode involves a kind of dissociative thinking that renders the child incapable of finding any emotional implication or separating the fantasy from the real world. When functioning on those pre-mentalizing levels, a child or adolescent tends to be more impulsive and more easily overwhelmed by emotions. The adolescent may interpret her own anger as that of others, or act out unprocessed inner contents, since her only adopted guideline behaviour is the already experienced aggressive one. Compromised judgement, inability to reflect upon an outer event, and absence of consciousness about mutual responsibilities, joined with excessive use of the pretend mode have been known to cause antisocial behaviour in traumatised adolescents.

There is little empirical data on the mentalization capacities in traumatised people and more specifically in delinquents, since it is still a relatively new topic in the research field. Ensink with colleagues reported that sexually abused children demonstrated lower mentalization than their non-traumatised peers (Ensink et al., 2014), and that pregnant women with a history of trauma manifested a deficit in trauma-specific mentalization (Ensink, Berthelot, Bernazzani, Normandin, & Fonagy, 2014). The studies involving delinquents are even more rare. Möller with colleagues reported that juvenile offenders showed lower mentalization than their peers in a non-clinical population (Möller, Falkenström, Holmqvist Larsson, & Holmqvist, 2014). In a sample of adult offenders, Levinson and Fonagy (2004) showed that prisoners obtained lower mentalization scores than people with no criminal record, while the presence or absence of a personality disorder diagnosis did not emerge as a relevant factor.

An important fact is that we also lack data on female delinquents' mentalization even though there are some indications that it might differ from males'. First, gender differences in attachment (Del Giudice & Belsky, 2010) and mentalization (Taubner, White, Zimmermann, Fonagy, & Nolte, 2013) were found in community samples. Additionally, statistics show a high gender disproportion in frequency and context of criminal acts—women commit fewer crimes in general, especially those involving violence, and they usually do it by themselves and against someone close to them (Steffensmeier & Allan, 1996). Some authors suppose these differences come from girls being less exposed to risk and more to protective factors (Agnew, 2005), but others emphasise the existence of different motives and meanings of a crime in men and women, in that women might perceive crime as the only way to escape physical and sexual violence (Chesney-Lind, 2002). Those hypotheses still need to be examined.

A hypothesis about mentalization being the mediator between trauma experiences and aggressive behaviour was confirmed in a community sample of adolescents (Taubner & Curth, 2013; Taubner et al., 2013). To my knowledge, none of the previous studies examining the importance of mentalization as a protective factor has compared incarcerated juvenile offenders with their institutionalised and traumatised peers with no criminal conviction.

Rationale

I was intrigued to examine how attachment and mentalization could help in understanding the differences between traumatised delinquents and their non-delinquent peers with a history of abuse. This study was conducted on ninety adolescents of both genders with a history of severe physical and/or sexual trauma in relationship with their parents. Half of them were convicted minors and the rest, the controls, were adolescents who were taken to an institution for children without parental care because they were victims of family violence. The assumption was that being separated from a maltreating parent and involved in a relationship with another caregiver gave the adolescents a chance to learn a behavioural model different from the aggressive one, and develop a less hazardous relationship together with the chance to (re) build some of their mentalizing capacities (Van IJzendoorn, 1997). In addition, it was supposed that mentalization in the delinquents would be more compromised and that they would show a more insecure attachment style. The preliminary results, related to the adolescents' capacity to mentalize trauma, are presented below and they were obtained from one part of the research within a larger study.

Methodology

Participants and procedure

Approximately one half of the data collected for the larger project described above was successfully coded and analysed for the purpose of this study. Thus, the selected sample consisted of twenty traumatised incarcerated juvenile offenders from the Juvenile Correctional Institution in Kruševac (Serbia) and twenty of their traumatised peers from four institutions for young people without parental care in Belgrade. The age range in both groups was fifteen to eighteen years, with an equal number of female and male participants. All participants in the study had average intellectual capacities and official reports claimed they experienced severe forms of physical and/or sexual family violence during their childhood. In the group of juvenile offenders, only the ones convicted of violent crimes were tested.

Permission to conduct the research in the Juvenile Correctional Institution was obtained from the Serbian Ministry of Internal Affairs. In addition to that, every adolescent's legal guardian gave consent for their participation in the study in each of the institutions involved. The participation was voluntary, the adolescents were informed about the standards of anonymity and confidentiality, and they signed the informed consent forms. All of the subjects were tested individually and an audio recording was made of every interview. Upon completion of the testing, interviewees were financially compensated.

Instrument

In this study, the Reflective Functioning Scale (RFS) (Fonagy, Target, Steele, & Steele, 1998) was used for measuring the participants' mentalization capacity in attachment relationships. The RFS was developed as a specific coding method in order to provide information about the participants' capacity to think and reflect about their own mind and about the mind of their significant other in attachment-provoking situations. The coding procedure of each interview question depends on whether or not it explicitly demands an appreciation of mental states, and whether the qualitative markers of RF or the qualitative markers of absent RF have been detected in the answer. The overall score is obtained by the score function of each interview question, as outlined in the manual. An eleven-point scale is used, with values ranging from minus one to nine, where every score represents one level of mental state explanation, from anti-mentalizing capacities (–1) and absent mentalization (1), through borderline mentalization (3), to basic (5), high (7), and exceptional mentalizing capacities (9). Aside from the value of the total score, the interviewee's performance can be shown through different qualitative indicators (for example, number and type of mentalizing sentences); and specific RF scores regarding some aspects of attachment relationship can also be rated. For this report we measured the participants' capacity to mentalize trauma they experienced (RF-trauma) through all passages in which abuse was directly probed (such as "Do you feel that the experience of having been physically abused by your father affects you now?") or explicitly discussed.

Previous studies have shown the importance of RFS and its good psychometric properties (Fonagy, Target, H. Steele, & M. Steele, 1998; Taubner et al., 2013). Unfortunately, it was impossible to carry out a common research strategy to measure inter-rater reliability for a certain amount of interviews, since there is only one certified RF coder available in Serbia. For future reports, interviews should undergo the process of translation into another language so as to ensure the possibility of collaboration with another qualified RF rater.

Results

In order to establish whether the group and gender differences in mentalization of trauma exist, a two-factor analysis of variance was performed. Results suggested that delinquents have lower scores of RF-trauma compared to their traumatised peers that haven't been convicted of a crime (see Figure 1). Therefore, the score range was different for delinquents and non-delinquents and it presented the following values, respectively: –1 to 3 and –1 to 6 (30% of delinquents have scores of 0 and –1 compared to 10% in controls, while in controls 20% had scores higher than 3). In addition, a large effect size of gender factor was detected—girls' score range was 0 to 6 which was on average one standard deviation unit higher than the values obtained with boys whose scores were –1 to 5.

	Group		ANOVA	Gender		ANOVA
	Delinquents Mean(Sd)	Non-delinquents Mean(Sd)	F(d)	Boys Mean(Sd)	Girls Mean(Sd)	F(d)
RF-trauma	0.90(1.25)	1.95(1.82)	5.33*(.77)	0.75(1.52)	2.10(1.48)	8.81**(1.00)

Figure 1. Group and gender differences on RF-trauma score.

Delinquents		**Non-delinquents**		**Group*Gender**
Boys	Girls	Boys	Girls	**ANOVA**
Mean(Sd)	Mean(Sd)	Mean(Sd)	Mean(Sd)	F(d)
.20(1.13)	1.60(.97)	1.30(1.70)	2.60(1.77)	.01(<.01)

Figure 2. Interaction of group and gender on RF-trauma score.

Interaction of group and gender on the other hand did not emerge as significant. In both groups boys were inferior on the RF-trauma scale compared to their female peers (see Figure 2). Moreover, an additional analysis demonstrated no difference between female delinquents and their female ($F(1) = 2.44$, $p = 0.13$) and male peers from the non-delinquent group ($F(1) = 0.23$, $p = 0.63$).

Discussion

The hypothesis that the capacity to mentalize trauma is more compromised in juvenile offenders than in their also traumatised non-delinquent peers has been confirmed in this study. A medium to large effect size supports the assumption of mentalization as a potential protective factor for violent behaviour (Taubner & Curth, 2013; Taubner et al., 2013). The average scores in both groups were lower than the ones in the general population (Fonagy, Target, H. Steele, & M. Steele, 1998), which is in line with previous studies involving traumatised groups (Ensink et al., 2014; Möller, Falkenström, Holmqvist Larsson, & Holmqvist, 2014), and the theory about the impact of trauma on mentalization (Fonagy, 2004).

On average, delinquents are at the level of absent mentalization. Usually their explanations are descriptive, concrete, and sociological (Fonagy, Target, H. Steele, & M. Steele, 1998), with clear examples of passive evasion of answers and excessive use of deactivation mechanisms (Bowlby, 1980). They also give more bizarre or inappropriate answers with signs of segregated system activation (Bowlby, 1980). On the other hand, controls on average demonstrate naïve and somehow superficial RF with reduction of mental state attribution to social clichés (Fonagy,

Target, H. Steele, & M. Steele, 1998) and frequent use of cognitive disconnection (Bowlby, 1980). Moreover, one fifth of non-delinquents demonstrated "the awareness of the nature of mental states" and/or "explicit effort to tease out mental states underlying behaviour" (Fonagy, Target, H. Steele, & M. Steele, 1998). Finally, the variety of scores is higher in controls, which might suggest this group is more heterogeneous in terms of mentalization capacities than delinquents, but data from the whole sample is needed for drawing more reliable conclusions.

According to these results, it seems that separation from the maltreating parent and experience of qualitatively different relationships in the institution for children without parental care might be connected with higher levels of mentalization. One possible explanation could be that these children, after being provided with physical security and basic requirements for surviving, consequently also reducing their level of anxiety, managed to transfer a bit of this structure and safety into their mind. Even though their inner models are rarely psychological and often one-dimensional and simplistic, they provide them with some level of predictability and understanding of themselves and of others. Also, building a new relationship could have helped them in adopting a repertory of non-violent behaviours and learning to consider violence as wrong in general. An opportunity for exploring their own and the minds of others, together with getting out of traumatic experiences, could have helped controls in developing empathy and more trust in people, and processing the trauma they experienced, even if it just meant being able to feel and bear their own emotions (Van IJzendoorn, 1997).

A pilot study on gender differences in mentalization in juvenile offenders was also presented. The results corresponded to the data obtained in the non-clinical population (Taubner et al., 2013) and support the assumption of female delinquents having higher mentalization than males. It was also found that female delinquents do not differ in mentalization from the controls of both genders. These results render the initial data on differences between groups less clear, as they could indicate that mentalization may not be as relevant a factor in understanding the link between trauma and juvenile offences in females as it is believed to be in males. Thus, it might be assumed that mentalization impairment in female delinquents is more of an acute nature, due to trauma exposure, than a permanent state representing a deficit in general. However, more reliable interpretations of these results could be given only after analysing the data from a larger study, which also includes attachment style, and exploring whether attachment style would be a more important mediator for a trauma-delinquency link in females.

The results of this study are relevant for understanding the connection between trauma and antisocial behaviour and the role of trauma mentalization in both genders. Moreover, after finishing the original larger study more reliable information on mentalization in general and attachment in both groups will be provided, which may offer additional assumptions about the correlation of differences reported above. The implications drawn from this study could prove useful in planning prevention, treatment, and resocialisation of juvenile offenders. Thus the results indicate a possibility that the best preventive intervention could be to stop the violence towards adolescents and to provide a more secure and predictable environment for them. Also, it is possible that (re)building the mentalizing capacity through, for example, mentalization-based treatment (Bateman & Fonagy, 2004), in addition to enabling the processing of trauma, might prevent crime (repetition), especially in male adolescents.

The importance of this study lies in the fact that it represents the first time RFS has been used in Serbia. However, for the same reason, one should be particularly cautious in interpreting the data, as well as because the reported results have been obtained only from one half of the original sample, thus limiting the possibility of their generalisation. This is even more important when it comes to results related to gender differences. Finally, it should be emphasised that a potential discussion on causality between the explored phenomena would require a longitudinal design research study to be performed.

Acknowledgements

The study was conducted as part of a Trauma, Trust, and Memory project. The results presented in this chapter were obtained through an additional analysis of the data collected for my doctoral dissertation (Protić, in 2016; mentor: Aleksandar Dimitrijević, PhD, assistant professor). The original research was financially supported by the German Academic Exchange Service through the Trauma, Trust, and Memory project. Additionally, the study took part in projects number 47011 at the Institute of Criminological and Sociological Research in Belgrade and number 179018 at the Institute of Psychology, University of Belgrade. I am grateful to the management and staff of all the institutions involved in the study, and our special appreciation is reserved for the adolescents who were engaged in the interview process. My particular gratitude goes to professors Andreas Hamburger and Aleksandar Dimitrijević, who encouraged and supported my work on this text.

References

Agnew, R. (2005). *Juvenile Delinquency: Causes and Control.* Los Angeles, CA: Roxbury.

Allen, J. G., Fonagy, P., & Bateman, A. (2008). *Mentalizing in Clinical Practice.* Arlington, VA: American Psychiatric Publishing.

Bateman, A. W., & Fonagy, P. (2004). Mentalization-based treatment of BPD. *Journal of Personality Disorders, 18*: 36–51.

Bowlby, J. (1973). *Attachment and Loss: Volume 2. Separation: Anxiety and Anger.* London: Hogarth [reprinted London: Pimlico, 1998].

Bowlby, J. (1980). *Attachment and Loss: Volume 3. Loss, Sadness and Depression.* London: Hogarth [reprinted London: Pimlico, 1998].

Chesney-Lind, M. (2002). Criminalizing victimization: the unintended consequences of pro-arrest policies for girls and women. *Criminology & Public Policy, 2*: 81–90.

Del Giudice, M., & Belsky, J. (2010). Sex differences in attachment emerge in middle childhood: an evolutionary hypothesis. *Child Development Perspectives, 4*: 97–105.

Ensink, K., Berthelot, N., Bernazzani, O., Normandin, L., & Fonagy, P. (2014). Another step closer to measuring the ghosts in the nursery: preliminary validation of the trauma reflective functioning scale. *Frontiers in Psychology, 5*: 1–12.

Ensink, K., Normandin, L., Target, M., Fonagy, P., Sabourin, S., & Berthelot, N. (2014). Mentalization in children and mothers in the context of trauma: an initial study of the validity of the Child Reflective Functioning Scale. *British Journal of Developmental Psychology, 33*: 20–217.

Fonagy, P. (2004). The developmental roots. In: F. Pfafflin & G. Adshead (Eds.), *A Matter of Security: The Application of Attachment Theory to Forensic Psychiatry and Psychotherapy, Forensic Focus 25* (pp. 13–56). London: Jessica Kingsley.

Fonagy, P., Gergely, G., Jurist, E., & Target, M. (2002). *Affect Regulation, Mentalization, and the Development of the Self.* New York: Other.

Fonagy, P., Target, M., Steele, H., & Steele, M. (1998). *Reflective-Functioning Manual, Version 5.0, for Application to Adult Attachment Interviews*. London: University College London.

Fonagy, P., Target, M., Steele, M., Steele, H., Leigh, T., Levinson, A., & Kennedy, R. (1997). Morality, disruptive behavior, borderline personality disorder, crime, and their relationship to security of attachment. In: L. Atkinson & K. J. Zucker (Eds.), *Attachment and Psychopathology* (pp. 223–276). New York: Guilford.

Levinson, A., & Fonagy, P. (2004). Offending and attachment: the relationship between interpersonal awareness and offending in a prison population with psychiatric disorder. *Canadian Journal of Psychoanalysis, 12*: 225–251.

Matheson, S. L., Shepherd, A. M., Pinchbeck, R. M., Laurens, K. R., & Carr, V. J. (2013). Childhood adversity in schizophrenia: a systematic meta-analysis. *Psychological Medicine, 43*: 225–238.

Möller, C., Falkenström, F., Holmqvist Larsson, M., & Holmqvist, R. (2014). Mentalizing in young offenders. *Psychoanalytic Psychology, 31*: 84–99.

Nanni, V., Uher, R., & Danese, A. (2012). Childhood maltreatment predicts unfavorable course of illness and treatment outcome in depression: a meta-analysis. *American Journal of Psychiatry, 169*: 1–11.

Protić, S. (2016). *Doprinos vezanosti i mentalizacije razumevanju veze između traume i delinkvencije* [The contribution of attachment and mentalisation to understanding the connection between trauma and delinquency]. Doktorska teza [PhD thesis], Filozofski fakultet, Belgrade.

Steffensmeier, D. J., & E. Allan. (1996). Gender and crime: toward a gendered theory of female offending. *Annual Review of Sociology, 22*: 459–487.

Steiner, H., Garcia, I. G., & Matthews, Z. (1997). Posttraumatic stress disorder in incarcerated juvenile delinquents. *Journal of the American Academy of Child & Adolescent Psychiatry, 36*: 357–365.

Taubner, S., & Curth, C. (2013). Mentalization mediates the relation between early traumatic experiences and aggressive behavior in adolescence. *Psihologija*: 177–192.

Taubner, S., Hörz, S., Fischer-Kern, M., Doering, S., Buchheim, A., & Zimmermann, J. (2013). Internal structure of the reflective functioning scale. *Psychological Assessment, 25*: 1–9.

Taubner, S., White, L. O., Zimmermann, J., Fonagy, P., & Nolte, T. (2013). Attachment-related mentalization moderates the relationship between psychopathic traits and proactive aggression in adolescence. *Journal of Abnormal Child Psychology*: 929–938.

Van IJzendoorn, M. H. (1997). Attachment, emergent morality, and aggression: toward a developmental socio-emotional model of antisocial behaviour. *International Journal of Behavioral Development, 21*: 703–727.

Wilsnack, S. C., Vogeltanz, N. D., Klassen, A. D., & Harris, T. R. (1997). Childhood sexual abuse and women's substance abuse: national survey findings. *Journal of Studies on Alcohol, 58*: 264–271.

CHAPTER TWENTY-TWO

Hostility and empathy in adolescence as predictors of aggressive, prosocial, and avoidant behaviour

Svetlina Koleva

Aggression and bullying at school are serious contemporary problems that have provoked a wide range of research. Any form of violence from one group towards another has long-term effects in society. The history of Bulgarian society is a history of a totalitarian regime and social suppression of one group of people due to ideological differences. The phenomenon of school aggression could be viewed also from that perspective, namely as an after-effect of prior violence, which is reproduced at any level of interpersonal relations.

The present study focuses on reactions in conflict situations in the school environment. Being a victim of bullying is a chronic stressor that often results in traumatic responses (Newman, Holden, & Delville, 2005). When this social trauma has a repetitive character, the sense of trust in oneself, others, and the world is disturbed (Janson & Hazler, 2004), and can lead to a severe condition with intrusive trauma reactions (Davidson, Inslicht, & Baum, 2000). Links between personality dispositions (hostility, empathy) and behavioural manifestations in a conflict situation are revealed.

The Bulgarian versions of three self-assessment scales are used: the Social Problems Questionnaire (Lindeman et al., 1992; Kalchev, 2010), the Interpersonal Reactivity Index (Davis, 1983; Kalchev, 2010), and a new self-assessment scale, the Questionnaire of Hostility Aspects (Kalchev, 2008). Results point towards aggression as the least preferred reaction, but with significantly higher mean levels for boys. The withdrawal reaction reduces with age and readiness for prosocial actions shows an irregular pattern. Regression analysis is performed, revealing prediction of aggressive behaviour by personality traits of hostility and impulsivity, and prevention of aggression by two components of empathy. Results are discussed in the light of psychoanalytical, cognitive behavioural, and socio-cultural perspectives.

The complex of constructs is viewed on a larger field of the dynamic period of adolescence. The dominant engagement and focusing of adolescents on peers can be found on several levels, not only as an interpersonal contact, but also as a tool to form a self-image of a high social status individual recognised as an important person by significant others (Erikson, 1968). In this context, aggression defines one side of the social connectedness. Thus, for an adolescent, fighting for a status in a group of peers, aggression could be seen as a factor for shaping social relations and participating in identity formation. From this perspective, Björkqvist, Österman, and Kaukiainen (1992), and Björkqvist, Österman, and Lagerspetz (1994), insist that aggressive styles are subject to developmental change during life. The three types of aggression—direct physical, direct verbal, and indirect aggression—are not just different aggression strategies, but also three partially overlapping phases in the development of aggression. Boys, being more active and often physically stronger, are more likely to react through physical aggression in a conflict situation than girls who typically withdraw or seek help (Björkqvist, Österman, & Kaukiainen, 1992; Björkqvist, Österman, & Lagerspetz, 1994).

Aggression is considered to be any behaviour that aims to harm or hurt another person (Baron & Richardson, 1994). Hostility is regarded as a multidimensional construct with cognitive (negative beliefs about and attitudes toward others, including cynicism and mistrust), affective (unpleasant emotion ranging from irritation to rage), and behavioural components. This is thought to result from the attitudinal and affective component and is an action intending to harm others, either verbally or physically (Anderson, 2004). Evenden (1999) states that impulsivity is a multifactorial construct that involves a tendency to act on an impulse, displaying behaviour characterised by little or no forethought, reflection, or consideration of the consequences.

In the present study, the concept of empathy is based on the model developed by Davis (1983), where empathy is understood as a multidimensional construct representing stable personal dispositions on reaction towards others, consisting of four constructs: perspective-taking—the tendency to spontaneously adopt the psychological point of view of others; fantasy—the tendency to transpose oneself imaginatively into feelings and actions of fictitious characters in books, films and plays; empathic concern—"other-oriented" feelings of sympathy and concern for unfortunate others; and personal distress—"self-oriented" feelings of personal anxiety and discomfort as a reaction in tense interpersonal situations. Empathy is thought to be a core precursor to and motivator for prosociality (de Waal, 2008), playing an important role in moral development (Eisenberg, 2000). Richardson, Hammock, Smith, Gardner, and Signo (1994) found that perspective-taking correlates negatively with self-reported aggression and with conflict responses that reflect little concern for the needs of others. Empathy has been associated with higher levels of conflict resolution skills in adolescents, which is an important factor in maintaining meaningful relationships (de Wied, Branje, & Meeus, 2007).

Therefore, it is expected that the personal traits of hostility, impulsivity, and annoyance will correlate positively with aggressive reactions in a conflict situation. Readiness to act in a destructive way in a conflict situation at school is expected to expand with increase of each of those factors, and aggression—either verbal or physical—accumulates unpleasant emotions. The individual, who tends to focus on his own feelings of anxiety and discomfort in a conflict situation with peers, will withdraw. The adolescent, scoring high on empathy, is expected to react prosocially. An underlying negative connection between aggression and empathy is expected.

Method

Sample and procedure

The sample size is 302 students aged twelve to sixteen; 142 boys, 160 girls. Data collected with the Interpersonal Reactivity Index (IRI) is from a sample of 153 pupils (seventy-eight boys and seventy-five girls), also aged twelve to sixteen. The data was anonymously collected in school classes and in groups, in Sofia, Bulgaria.

Measures

Three self-report questionnaires were used. The first one, the Social Problems Questionnaire (SPQ) (Lindeman et al., 1997), was developed on a large sample of 2,594 of adolescents. Kalchev (2010) adapted the instrument for Bulgaria. The questionnaire is constructed to assess three different types of reaction: aggression, withdrawal, and prosociality in a peer conflict situation. In comparison with traditional self-descriptive aggression scales, SPQ offers a different point of evaluating—not a description of actions undertaken or attitude towards them, but the preferred type of reaction in an imaginary conflict situation. The two situations described in SPQ are developed during interviews with pupils, so they represent recurring problems among peers and therefore personal experiences are presumably brought up (Kalchev, 2010). The situations are: 1) Some pupils at school are teasing one of your classmates, who is neither your friend nor your enemy. What would you do in this situation? and 2) Some of your classmates are talking behind the back of one of the classmates, gossiping and saying offensive things. This child is neither your friend nor your enemy. What would you do in this situation?

Twenty-seven items describing possible reactions are given, seventeen for the first and ten for the second situation. Each item is endorsed on a five-point scale, with reversed items to control for response sets. The instrument has been translated by Kalchev and Hancheva. The three-factor solution, reported by Lindeman, Haraka, and Keltinkangas-Järvinen (1997), is confirmed in the Bulgarian sample. Items loading high on the respective factor are, for example: 1. Aggression: "I would also take part in teasing, then one can make more friends"; 2. Withdrawal: "I would just go away because the conversation is of no importance to me"; 3. Prosocial strategy: "I would say clearly to those who are talking behind the back of the other child how offensive that is, and I would ask them to stop."

Kalchev (2010) states that the situations described in SPQ aim to provoke an initiative towards the "neutral" peer, and actions in such conditions are closest to altruistic prosocial behaviour, described by Persson (2005) as behaviour evoked and motivated by pure concern for the other.

The second instrument used in the present study was the Questionnaire of Hostility Aspects (QHA), constructed to assess hostility aspects in adolescence. It is composed by Kalchev (2008) using the following scales: the Child Version of Cook-Medley Hostility Scale (Liehr et al., 2000); Paranoid Ideation subscale from The Symptom Checklist-90-Revised, developed by Derogatis (1977), modified by Raikkonen, Katainen, Keskivaara, and Keltikangas-Järvinen (2000); Cynicism Factor from the Minnesota Multiphasic Personality Inventory (MMPI) (Hathaway &

McKinley, 1943); the subscale Impulsive/Impatient from the Aggression Inventory (Gladue, 1991).

The QHA consists of thirty-six items, endorsed on a five-point Likert scale. Exploratory factor analysis and Scree test (Cattell, 1966) were performed and both conducted to a five-factor solution. The five factors received were labelled based on the items' content. Examples of typical items for the factors are: 1) Alienation—"Others do not understand me"; 2) Cynical attitude—"Most people would lie to get what they want"; 3) Annoyance—"If something annoys me, I easily lose my temper"; 4) Hostility—"I am glad when people I dislike have troubles"; 5) Impulsivity—"I tend to do things hastily, without considering them enough".

The third measurement included in the study was the Interpersonal Reactivity Index (IRI) (Davis, 1983) in the Bulgarian adaptation by Kalchev (2010). Because IRI is a well-known and widely used instrument, no further presentation of the scale is regarded as necessary.

Results

Statistical analysis conducted on SPQ (see Figure 1) revealed higher means on withdrawal and prosociality as a reaction in a conflict situation at school for both sexes. Results point towards aggression as the least preferred reaction, with a significant effect for gender ($t_{(300)} = 2.61$, $p = 0.009$) and prosociality ($t_{(300)} = 2.14$, $p = 0.016$). Girls report preferring the passive behaviour of withdrawal; however, no significant differences were found.

For exploring the hypothesis that aggression will be the less preferred coping strategy in a conflict situation, a two-way ANOVA was performed. In Bulgaria, adolescents in the sixth grade are at the age of twelve to thirteen, in seventh grade: thirteen to fourteen, in eighth grade: fourteen to fifteen, and in ninth grade: fifteen to sixteen. Results showed a significant main effect for sex ($F(1, 294) = 10.63$, $p = 0.001$), insignificant main effect of the grade ($F(3, 294) = 1.64$, $p = 0.18$), but a significant interaction between the grade and sex ($F(3, 294) = 3.28$, $p = 0.02$) regarding aggression (see Figure 2). No significant effects were found on withdrawal. For prosociality, a significant main effect for sex ($F(1, 294) = 7.95$, $p = 0.005$), and for grade ($F(3, 294) = 4.53$, $p = 0.004$) was found, however interaction between grade and sex is $F(3, 294) = 2.60$, $p = 0.05$ (see Figure 3). The climax of aggressive behaviour is at eighth grade for boys, and seventh grade for girls. Prosociality shows an irregular pattern of unexpected decrease between sixth and seventh grade for both sexes, followed by an increase in girls and decrease in boys in seventh

	Boys (n = 142)		*Girls (n = 160)*				
	M	SD	M	SD	*t*	*df*	P
Aggression	**19.92**	8.31	**17.67**	6.38	2.61	300	0.009
Withdrawal	**20.67**	5.21	**21.33**	5.36	1.07	300	0.284
Prosociality	**29.16**	7.24	**31.06**	6.38	2.14	300	0.016

Figure 1. Scale descriptives—SPQ in Bulgarian sample n = 302.

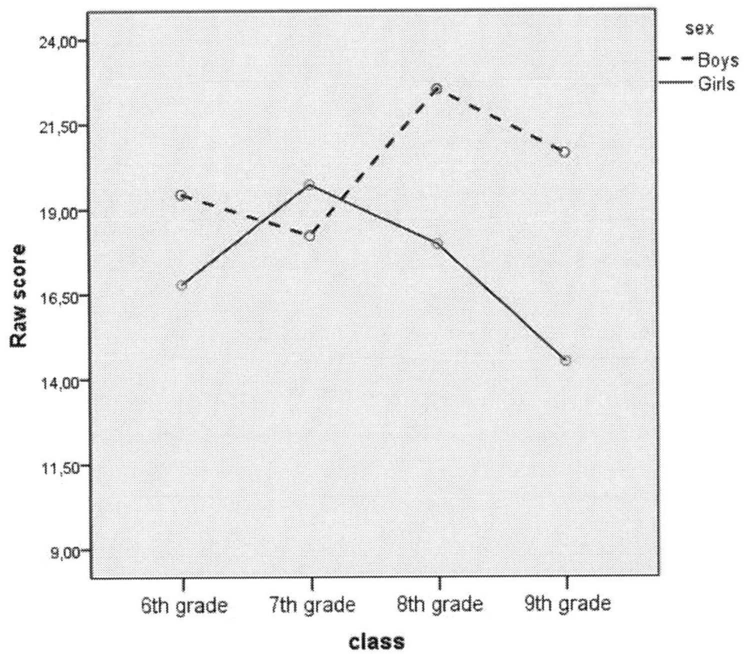

Figure 2. Aggression in boys and girls (n = 302).

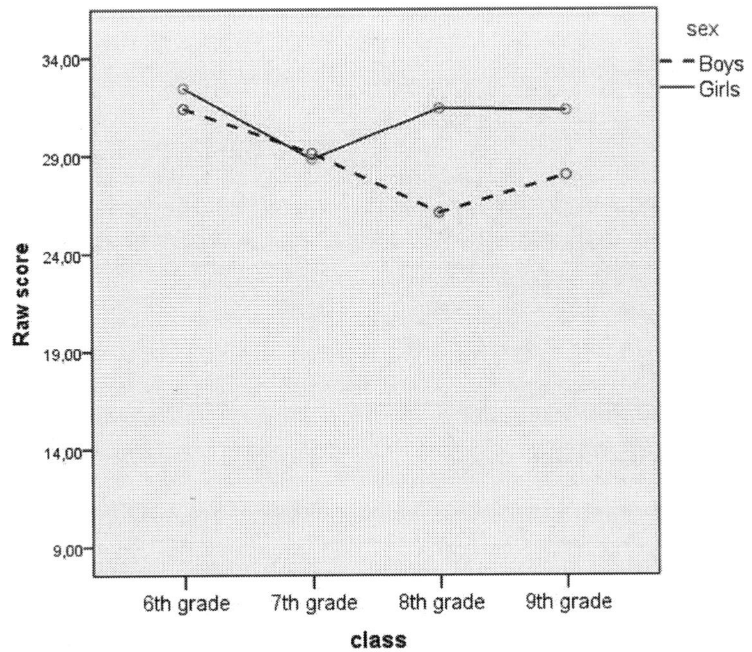

Figure 3. Prosociality in boys and girls (n = 302).

grade. A tendency to increase in boys after eighth grade is found, never reaching the levels of adolescents, aged twelve for both sexes.

Analysis of QHA data showed a significant difference in sex only in hostility, with $t_{(300)} = 3.28$, $p = 0.001$, boys (M = 17.22, SD = 5.03); girls (M = 15.42, SD = 4.71). On all other constructs no significant differences between boys and girls were found.

In the Bulgarian sample, girls showed higher means on all four components of empathy measured with IRI. Significant differences between sexes are found for perspective-taking ($t_{(151)} = 3.13, p = 0.000$), fantasy ($t_{(151)} = 2.85, p = 0.002$), and empathic concern ($t_{(151)} = 2.86, p = 0.005$), suggesting that in the adolescent sample, the capacity to empathise differs significantly by gender, with no significant differentiation on personal distress: boys (M = 14.15, SD = 5.03); girls (M = 14.96, SD = 5.07); $t_{(151)} = 0.98$, $p = 0.326$.

Correlation of aggression and hostility (r = 0.47***), impulsivity (r = 0.36***), and annoyance (r = 0.34***) as personal traits were medium to high (see Figure 4). Negative correlations between prosociality and annoyance (r = –0.19**) and prosociality and hostility (r = –0.37***) were weak to medium (*p < 0.05; **p < 01; ***p < 0.001).

The relations between constructs are assessed via a path model (Figure 5) with observed variables using LISREL 8.72. (Jöreskog et al., 2001), on maximum likelihood, with mediation effects of empathic concern and perspective-taking.

Goodness-of-fit indices are: $\chi^2_{(2)} = 2,40$; $p = 0.30$; SRMR = 0.030; RMSEA = 0.036; GFI = 0.99; AGFI = 0.95; CFI = 1; NNFI = 0.99. Hostility increases the probability of aggressiveness both directly and indirectly, reducing the capacity of perspective-taking and empathic concern. The effect of impulsivity on aggression is significant and direct (p < 0.05). Perspective-taking and empathic concern showed direct effects on preventing aggression.

	Aggression	Withdrawal	Prosociality
Alienation	0.03	0.03	0.14
Cynical attitude	0.12	0.02	–0.06
Annoyance	0.34***	0.18**	–0.19**
Hostility	0.47***	0.04	–0.37***
Impulsivity	0.36***	0.08	–0.14
Perspective-taking	–0.46***	–0.10	0.62***
Fantasy	–0.25***	0.04	0.29***
Empathic concern	–0.46***	–0.07	0.51***
Personal distress	0.03	0.28***	0.00

Figure 4. Correlations among scales in the study (n = 302).
Note: *p < 0.05; **p < 0.01; ***p < 0.001.

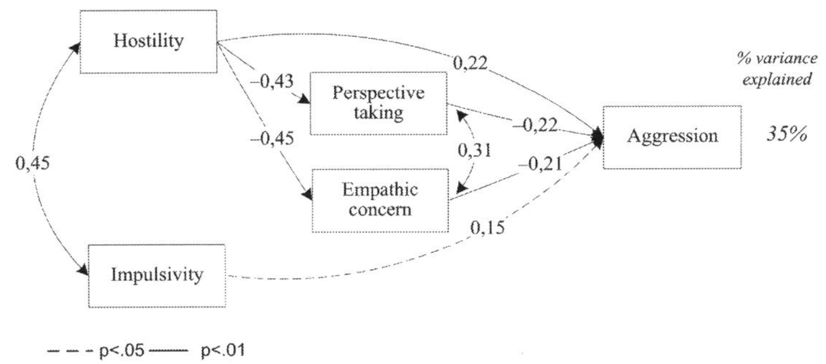

Figure 5. Structural model with dependent variable "aggression" in a conflict situation (n = 153).

Discussion

The results obtained could be viewed in a model of a hostile and self-focused person, whose primary care is his personal wellbeing and survival. It could be speculated, that in a situation of dictatorship, where all forms of solidarity and togetherness are avoided and punished, a coping strategy that is formed and taught to the next generation is suppressing the urge to act prosocially, discouraging mutual care and solidarity, and the effects of this could be found in reactions in a typical conflict situation, such as those occurring at school. In the present study, as hypothesised, significant positive correlation between aggression and hostility, impulsivity, and annoyance was found. However, some, but not all, personal traits mentioned have a predictive power when discussing the aggressive outcome. For a better understanding of the phenomenon, the role of peer pressure and group hierarchy should be considered (Crick & Grotpeter, 1996; Kalchev, 2003) and further researched.

Findings on withdrawal as a coping strategy in a conflict situation could be explained with casual attribution, typically seen in adolescents, together with a personal sense of the lack of control in complex social problems (Weiner, 2000). The prevalence of this reaction in girls, although no significant differences in sex were found, could be regarded in light of the theoretical and empirical data, insisting that females rarely act directly aggressively, due to the gender role stereotypes and to the importance attributed to social relationships (Björkqvist, 1994). Some speculations on withdrawal could be made, viewing it as a sign of a lack of a democratic society or immaturity of a democratic society. Results obtained in the current study on IRI confirm that empathy is more salient in females than in males. Putting social desirability aside, the results could be interpreted as increasing the ability to empathise, enlargement of the capacity and readiness to react prosocially to the distress observed. There is also evidence to suggest that empathy in females may be part of a prosocial affective orientation that includes a tendency to experience guilt over harming others, and females may have a greater tendency than males to imagine themselves in someone else's place (Hoffman, 1977).

Regarding the results found in tendency to increase aggressive behaviour in the eighth grade, it should be stated that this is a period usually connected with a lot of social tension, new school environment, and new group position, and this could provoke the peak of aggressive reactions. Furthermore, in that period, withdrawing could no longer be seen as such an effective strategy by the adolescents, because being passive could bring oneself to the position of lesser importance in the group process. Significant differences found on hostility and aggression between boys and girls support the expectation of boys tending to react aggressively in a situation of conflict and the link between the aggressive behaviour and hostility as a personal trait (Kalchev, 2003).

An interesting finding concerning the factor "cynical attitude" should be mentioned: it showed no predictive power of aggressive behaviour in adolescence. That is coherent with a suggestion by Thornberg, Halldin, Bolmsjö, and Petersson (2013) that cynical attitude could be regarded as a core result of victimisation.

Furthermore, besides the medium positive correlation between aggression and annoyance, annoyance as a personal trait showed no predictive power in aggression. Thus, choice of behaviour in a conflict situation is not influenced solely by personality characteristics, like anger and a low threshold of tolerance, but also by situation factors, like the subjective estimation of the likely consequences of an aggressive act, named effect/danger or cost/benefit ratio of aggression, suggested by Björkqvist, Osterman, and Lagerspetz (1994).

Negative correlations ($p < 0.001$) between the tendency to react aggressively in a conflict situation and the components of empathy (an exception is the personal distress factor) were found, which support the classical findings that the personal tendency to spontaneously adopt the psychological point of view of others, and the ability to perceive feelings of sympathy and concern for others, are likely to lead to non-aggressive behaviour in a situation of social tension (Eisenberg & Miller, 1987). Findings on the medium correlation in personal distress with the reaction of withdrawal ($r = 0.28^{***}$, $p < 0.001$) supports the hypothesis that an individual who tends to focus on his own feelings of anxiety and discomfort in a conflict situation with peers, could be possibly overwhelmed by them, and is likely to react in avoidance, but this needs to be further researched in the Bulgarian sample. Thus, the results suggest that adolescents who share a hostile attitude towards others and get easily irritated, are less likely to engage into prosocial actions (Kalchev, 2008).

Results obtained suggest that aggressive behaviour in adolescence could be predicted by hostility. This, together with impulsivity, showed direct effect on predicting aggression. These findings could be linked with the important social effect of school bullying as a risk factor with a strong contribution to violence later in life. The effect is significant even after controlling for other major childhood risk factors, as found in a meta-analysis of prospective longitudinal studies (Ttofi, Farrington, & Lösel, 2012). They state that school bullying and other externalising problems (violence, delinquency, and offending) later in life are "different age- and context-related manifestations of the same underlying antisocial dispositions" (Ttofi, Farrington, & Lösel, 2012).

Another construct, contributing to social trauma due to bullying is dehumanisation, with its significant role in both bullying and victimisation. Children dehumanise outgroup members more than friends (Van Noorden, Haselager, Cillessen, & Bukowski, 2014).

Bastian and Haslam (2010) found that social exclusion leads people to feel less human, to believe that they are viewed as less human by those who ostracise them, and perceive them as less human too. The results of the current study, regarding the role of empathy in preventing aggression, support previous findings (Nordgren, Banas, & MacDonald, 2011). The influence of empathic concern and perspective-taking as factors blocking destructive and harming behaviour suggests that adolescents who have developed the capacity to sympathise with the pain of others are less likely to act aggressively in a conflict situation. Therefore, empathy could be viewed as playing the leading part in impeding and preventing aggression and bullying at school.

Thornberg, Halldin, Bolmsjö, and Petersson (2013) underline the negative effects of being bullied, such as incorporation of the victim-image, which results in a self-image of being different and a sense of not fitting in with the other classmates, developing distrust in others, as well as perceiving many social situations as unsafe, threatening, and leading to a social withdrawal.

Carlisle and Rofes (2007) report survivors of school bullying describing long-term effects similar to those of survivors of childhood abuse. Carney (2008) states that frequency of exposure to bullying events is the greatest factor in predicting trauma level, as well as traumatic impact of bullying on all participants involved (Baldry, 2004). Therefore, considering the impact of this type of social trauma, our efforts should be concentrated on supporting adolescents to develop and enlarge the capacity to empathise, in promoting positive behaviours towards others, and facilitating social interactions and relationships, so that they too become socially competent people with meaningful social relationships.

References

Anderson, N. B. (2004). *Encyclopedia of Health and Behavior*. Thousand Oaks, CA: Sage.

Baldry, A. C. (2004). The impact of direct and indirect bullying on the mental and physical health of Italian youngsters. *Aggressive Behavior*, *30*: 343–355.

Baron, R., & Richardson, D. (1994). *Human Aggression* (2nd edn). New York: Plenum.

Bastian, B., & Haslam, N. (2010). Excluded from humanity: the dehumanizing effects of social ostracism. *Journal of Experimental Social Psychology*, *46*: 107–113.

Björkqvist, K. (1994). Sex differences in physical, verbal, and indirect aggression: a review of recent research. *Sex Roles*, *30*: 177–188.

Björkqvist, K., Osterman, K., & Kaukiainen, A. (1992). The development of direct and indirect aggressive strategies in males in females. In: K. Björkqvist & P. Niemela (Eds.), *Of Mice and Women: Aspects of Female Aggression* (pp. 51–64). San Diego, CA: Academic Press.

Björkqvist, K., Osterman, K., & Lagerspetz, K. M. J. (1994). Sex differences in covert aggression among adults. *Aggressive Behavior*, *20*: 27–33.

Carlisle, N., & Rofes, E. (2007). School bullying: do adult survivors perceive long-term effects? *Traumatology*, *13*: 16.

Carney, J. (2008). Perceptions of bullying and associated trauma during adolescence. *Professional School Counseling*, *11*: 179–187.

Cattell, R. B. (1966). The scree test for the number of factors. *Multivariate Behavioral Research*, 1: 245–276.

Crick, N. R., & Grotpeter, J. (1996). Children's treatment by peers: victims of relational and overt aggression. *Development and Psychopathology*, *8*: 367–380.

Davidson, L. M., Inslicht, S. S., & Baum, A. (2000). Traumatic stress and posttraumatic stress disorder among children and adolescents. In: M. Lewis (Ed.), *Handbook of Developmental Psychopathology* (pp. 723–737). New York: Kluwer Academic.

Davis, M. H. (1983). Measuring individual differences in empathy: evidence for a multidimensional approach. *Journal of Personality and Social Psychology, 44*: 113–126.

de Waal, F. B. M. (2008). Putting the altruism back into altruism: the evolution of empathy. *Annual Review of Psychology, 59*: 279–300.

de Wied, M., Branje, S. J. T., & Meeus, W. H. J. (2007). Empathy and conflict resolution in friendship relations among adolescents. *Aggressive Behavior, 33*: 48–55.

Derogatis, L. R. (1977). SCL-90-R, administration, scoring & procedures manual-I for the R(evised) version. Baltimore, MD: Johns Hopkins University School of Medicine.

Eisenberg, N. (2000). Emotion, regulation, and moral development. *Annual Review of Psychology, 51*: 665–697.

Eisenberg, N., &. Miller, P. A. (1987). The relation of empathy to prosocial and related behaviors. *Psychological Bulletin, 101*: 91–119.

Erikson, E. (1968). *Identity, Youth and Crisis*. New York: Norton.

Evenden, J. L. (1999). Varieties of impulsivity. *Psychopharmacology, 146*: 348–361.

Gladue, B. A. (1991). Qualitative and quantative sex differences in self-reported aggressive behavioral characteristics. *Psychological Reports, 68*: 675–684.

Hathaway, S. R., & McKinley, J. C. (1943). *The Minnesota Multiphasic Personality Inventory*. Minneapolis, MN: University of Minnesota Press.

Hoffman, M. (1977). Sex differences in empathy and related behaviors. *Psychological Bulletin, 84*: 712–722.

Janson, G. R., & Hazler, R. J. (2004). Trauma reactions of bystanders and victims to repetitive abuse experiences. *Violence and Victims, 19*: 239–255.

Калчев, П. [Kalchev, P.] (2003). Тормоз и виктимизация от връстниците [Bullying and victimisation by peers]. София: Парадигма [Sofia: Paradigma].

Калчев, П. [Kalchev, P.] (2008). Въпросник за аспекти на враждебността [Questionnaire of Hostility Aspects] (unpublished manuscript).

Калчев, П. [Kalchev, P.] (2010). *Скали за агресия в юношеска възраст. 2 част* [*Youth aggression scales. Volume 2*]. София: Изток-Запад [Sofia: Istok-Zapad].

Liehr, P., Meininger, J. C., Mueller, W. H., Chan, W., Frazier, L., & Reyes, L. R. (2000). Psychometric testing of the adolescent version of the Cook-Medley hostility scale. *Issues in Comprehensive Pediatric Nursing, 23*: 103–116.

Lindeman, M., Haraka, T., & Keltinkangas-Järvinen, L. (1997). Age and sex differences in adolescent reactions to conflict situations: aggression, prosociality and withdrawal. *Journal of Youth and Adolescence, 26*: 339–351.

Newman, M. L., Holden, G. W., & Delville, Y. (2005). Isolation and the stress of being bullied. *Journal of Adolescence, 28*: 343–357.

Nordgren, L., Banas, K., & MacDonald, G. (2011). Empathy gaps for social pain: why people underestimate the pain of social suffering. *Journal of Personality and Social Psychology, 100*: 120–128.

Persson, G. (2005). Developmental perspectives on prosocial and aggressive motives in preschoolers' peer interactions. *International Journal of Behavioral Development, 29*: 80–91.

Räikkönen, K., Katainen, S., Keskivaara, P., & Keltikangas-Järvinen, L. (2000). Temperament, mothering, and hostile attitudes: a 12-year longitudinal study. *Personality and Social Psychology Bulletin, 26*: 3–12.

Richardson, D. R., Hammock, G. S., Smith, S. M., Gardner, W., & Signo, M. (1994). Empathy as a cognitive inhibitor of interpersonal aggression. *Aggressive Behavior, 20*: 275–289.

Thornberg, R., Halldin, K, Bolmsjö, N., & Petersson, A. (2013). Victimising of school bullying: a grounded theory. *Research Papers in Education*, *28*(3): 309–329.

Ttofi, M. M., Farrington, D. P., & Lösel, F. (2012). School bullying as a predictor of violence later in life: a systematic review and meta-analysis of prospective longitudinal studies. *Aggression and Violent Behavior*, *17*: 405–418.

Van Noorden, T. H., Haselager, G. J., Cillessen, A. H., & Bukowski, W. M. (2014). Dehumanization in children: the link with moral disengagement in bullying and victimization. *Aggressive Behavior*, *40*: 320–328.

Weiner, B. (2000). Intrapersonal and interpersonal theories of motivation from an attributional perspective. *Educational Psychology Review*, *12*: 1–14.

PART V

TRAINING AND RESEARCH IN SOCIAL TRAUMA

Introduction to Part V

The concluding section of the book closes the circle. We started from our research network's approaches to social trauma in the countries marked by a traumatic history. Now we have a look at academic teaching on social trauma in our countries, and at the network collaboration itself.

The section start with a preliminary report of an ongoing study we are especially proud of. During the summer schools, students decided on their own account to compare their universities, to see whether and how the topic of social trauma is addressed in the psychology master's courses. They performed a qualitative study, which turned out to be all but easy-going (a common phenomenon in qualitative studies), and here they present as a first result, that in most universities the topic was not covered. In fact, we had expected such a result (which, however, will be studied in more detail by the authors), and at the level of network staff and administrations, we had prepared a remedy: all participating departments in the Trauma, Trust, and Memory network decided to design and implement an international master's course called Social Trauma, which can be regarded as one of the great successes of the network collaboration (Hancheva, Scher, & Hamburger, Sofia & Berlin). The section and the volume concludes with a summary by the chair and the coordinator (Hamburger & Scher, Berlin) of the network's aims, measures, and achievements.

CHAPTER TWENTY-THREE

What do psychology students learn about social trauma in study programmes at trauma, trust, and memory network universities?

Maša Božović, Chrysanthi Papadopoulou, Margarita Papazova, Duška Šain, Jusuf Hafizović, Aleksandra Stojilković, Gloria Velinova, Jonas Diekhans, Siniša Lakić, Tomi Tzolov, and Sonja Protić

The main goal of this research was to understand what type of education, about social trauma and about trauma in general, psychology students receive in universities that are part of the Trauma, Trust, and Memory (TTM) project: the universities of Sarajevo, Banja Luka, Belgrade, Niš, and Berlin, and two universities from Sofia. A sample of the literature on trauma provided for compulsory courses of bachelor and master's study programmes for each university during the academic year 2013–2014 was subjected to content analysis. The coding system was developed following the syllabus of specialised international trauma study programmes. In the present chapter, initial results of the ongoing study are presented.

Introduction

Nowadays, mental health professionals are asked to work with large groups of trauma survivors. This is a consequence of the current, rather unstable, global political situation, and includes dealing with terrorist attacks, wars, and refugee crises; the victims of such events require particular readiness from the mental health care system and its professionals (Sitterle & Gurwitch, 1999; Kos, 1997; Summerfield, 2000). Dealing with trauma also demands confronting unresolved issues from the past such as the Bosnian war, the Holocaust, and genocide (Danieli, 1996; Fogelman, 1991). Humanistic sciences must focus on diminishing the influence that these types of traumatic events have on the development of individuals, and on society in general. This draws attention to the education process and to the institutions responsible for it.

In August 2014, after the large floods in the Balkans, and based on the need to implement organised and efficient psychological help, we reflected during one of the Network fellow trainings, on the extent to which we were trained for such situations. What knowledge and skills acquired during our studies could we rely on to respond adequately and help people suffering from social trauma? Participation in the TTM project gave us close insight into other important aspects of this topic, so we discussed whether we were systematically taught to conduct relevant studies in the field of trauma and to be sensitive to specific methodological issues. Could we maintain the necessary high professional and ethical standards when dealing with people who have been in physical or psychological pain? Finally yet importantly, are we trained to take care of ourselves as professionals with our own vulnerabilities?

These have become the main research questions of the present study, with the following three main aims: 1) assess the current quality of trauma education in each psychology department; 2) compare those findings and establish if there are similar trends or significant differences; and 3) suggest how to improve the quality of trauma education in psychology departments. Our research is in progress and only preliminary results are given here.

Methods

Sample

The study sample for each university consisted of the literature on trauma provided for compulsory courses of bachelor and master's study programmes during the academic year 2013–2014. Sample selection went through three round processes in order to be matched between universities and to enable comparison and replication of the results. The outcome of the first round was the list of all the courses in which the syllabus of objectives or teaching units contained one of the terms "trauma", "stress", or "crisis". In the second round only the literature in which these terms are mentioned in the context of traumatic experiences (violence or abuse, neglect, somatic or psychological illness, loss, natural disaster, war and refugee life, suicide attempts) were left. The final sample consisted of literature that has at least one chapter or the whole paper that deals with trauma.

Variables and their operationalisation

Specialist trauma programmes in the USA and Western Europe (such as the MSc in Trauma Studies at the University of Nottingham, UK) were studied in order to provide enough representative and reliable criteria of good educational practice, which could be operationalised through variables. Six main variables containing twenty-seven subcategories resulted from the analysis:

1. *Knowledge of trauma phenomena:* Definitions, Historical overview, Types of trauma, Stages of trauma, Individual reactions to and consequences of trauma, Societal consequences of individual trauma, Risk factors, Protective factors and resilience, Development and trauma, Cultural perspective and trauma.
2. *Practice—assessment of and help for trauma survivors:* Diagnostic, Case report, Development, General interventions, Specific interventions, Stages of treatment, Cultural context, Concentric circles of trauma, Multidisciplinary teams.

3. *Research in the field of trauma:* Design, Instruments.
4. *Scientific thinking in the field of trauma:* Analysing and comparing of arguments, Critical thinking.
5. *Ethics in the field of trauma:* Ethics related to research, Ethics related to practice.
6. *Development of professionals working with trauma survivors:* Long-term learning, Personal development of professionals (coping strategies and self-reflection).

Each variable, with its subcategories, was described in a coding book and coding sheet that can be provided upon request.

Content analysis

Content analysis, as a qualitative method for multimedia material used to describe, classify, understand, and explain with reference to the meanings, contexts, and intentions of the material (Hsieh & Shannon, 2005) was performed in this study. Whole papers or chapters were defined as units of analysis. During two pilot analyses on two papers in English, we worked on obtaining a satisfactory inter-rater reliability between the members of each team and for the whole group.

Initial results

The results come from the content analysis of mandatory literature. This exclusion criterion may limit the actual extent of the provided knowledge at the universities about social trauma and trauma in general, as it is derived from the results of the current study, since some universities do not issue comprehensive lists of compulsory literature but allow students to select the coursework through lists of recommended literature. Thus, these results should be read with caution.

University of Banja Luka

The bachelor psychology programme at the University of Banja Luka lasts for three years, and during this time, students are introduced to fundamental areas of psychology as a science along with clinical psychology and other applied fields. The master's programme lasts for two years. Emphasis is placed on acquiring practical skills together with the advanced methodology courses that introduce various research methods, both quantitative and qualitative. In the third semester, students are asked to choose between two sets of courses in the clinical or the educational field.

Preliminary results suggest that there are no courses dealing either with general trauma or with social trauma. That said, some readings in clinical and social psychology courses did mention certain types of trauma and suggested interventions (for PTSD, for example) or consequences of trauma, but these were extremely short sections, thus they have not met the sample selection criteria.

Based on this we can conclude that psychology students at the University of Banja Luka were not sufficiently trained to recognise and deal with any kinds of trauma, especially social trauma.

New Bulgarian University

The psychology studies at the Department of Cognitive Science and Psychology, at the New Bulgarian University, consist of a four-year bachelor programme and four types of master's programmes, with one of them being a two-year master's in clinical psychology.

Initial results suggest that only the psychopathology course deals with trauma in a way that fulfils the criteria needed for the analysis. Students learn how to identify symptoms and provide a diagnosis of post-traumatic stress disorder (variable Practice, subtype Diagnosis). Trauma is mentioned on several other courses: Introduction to clinical psychology, Psychotherapeutic approaches, and Psychology of personality, but in these cases literature doesn't include a chapter of a book or an article dedicated to the topic. Furthermore, the preliminary review showed that social trauma is not represented in any of the courses.

University of Niš

The psychology studies at the University of Niš consist of a four-year bachelor programme and a one-year master's programme. Since last year there have been modules in the master's degree, including Clinical psychology, but before 2015 it was an encompassing programme. Students learn how to identify symptoms and provide a diagnosis of post-traumatic stress disorder (variable Practice, subtype Diagnosis).

The preliminary literature review revealed no article or book specifically dealing with social trauma, in either the bachelor or master's programmes. The Psychology of mental health BA course is the only one that deals with trauma, and there is one specific book, by a Serbian author, from 2001, on this topic. Students who attend this course may learn about the phenomena of stress, crisis, and trauma, and the distinction between them. The provided knowledge refers to the Knowledge about phenomena variable.

International Psychoanalytic University (IPU) Berlin

The literature for the three-year psychology bachelor programme and the two-year master's programme in clinical psychology was the object of the analysis. The modules that contain literature related to trauma are part of the curriculum of the master's programme. The majority of books and articles are updated (after 2000) and even though most of the authors are German, there are some writings by foreign authors as well.

The courses Scientific theory and epistemology of the subject, General and specific mental disorders, Intervention, and Developmental psychology, refer to trauma as the main topic. Aspects of trauma that are analysed in the literature are focusing on Knowledge about phenomena and more particularly on Definitions, the Historical overview, Individual reactions to and consequences of trauma, Risk and Protective factors, and Development, but also on Practice and more particularly on Case report, General, and Specific interventions. Due to the clear focus of the IPU on the psychoanalytic principles and perspective, basic psychoanalytic developmental theories are a part of many courses as obligatory background literature. Trauma is a core concept in most of these theories and they are thus considered to be trauma relevant.

Social trauma is the main topic in four articles and one book. The aspects of social trauma that are analysed are the interventions and developmental aspects of trauma, mostly from the attachment theory perspective. The transgenerational transmission of trauma is also discussed and thus the Individual reactions to and consequences of trauma.

Students at the IPU can gain knowledge on individual trauma, whereas social trauma although present in literature is not sufficiently covered.

University of Sarajevo

Taught in the psychology department, the bachelor programme lasts three years and the master's programme two years. The majority of the courses both at bachelor and the master's levels are in the clinical psychology field, and many deal with the topic of trauma, including: Mental health, Psychology of pain, Introduction to clinical psychology, Introduction to psychopathology, Psychopathology, Basics of trauma psychology, Psychotherapeutic approaches, Assessment and treatment of psychological disorders, and Developmental psychopathology. The main course dealing with trauma is Basics of trauma psychology. Literature used for all courses is updated and is mostly by foreign authors.

Most of the important definitions of trauma are explained along with historical overviews, types, stages, people involved, consequences, development, risk, and protective factors. There are many case reports about personal experience of trauma, but Interventions are not explained in detail. Instructions for the research about trauma are very well described, except for the information about recommended Instruments. Ethics in research and practice are very well described. Personal development of professionals and coping are mentioned.

University of Sofia, St. Climent Ohridski

There are two psychology departments—Social, work, and educational psychology; and General, experimental, and genetic psychology. Study programmes include a four-year BA course, which focuses on social, clinical, experimental, and cognitive psychology. Master's programmes take 18 months; the majority were not found to deal with the subject of trauma, but with social and organisational psychology instead.

Literature relevant to trauma is included in the BA curriculum and in the two master's programmes: Child and adolescent and school psychology (assessment and counselling); and Clinical and counselling psychology. The course Child and adolescent developmental psychology contains literature referring to individual trauma from the developmental perspective—suicidal risks, attachment trauma, loss, and bullying; the Clinical psychology and Psychopathology courses teach about PTSD and sexual abuse; Counselling psychology teaches about crisis interventions. Material covered fits within the categories Knowledge about the phenomena, Practice, and Research. Literature on psychoanalysis in the curricula is also considered to be relevant to the topic of individual trauma.

Master's programmes go deeper into the topics relevant to individual trauma. The course Bullying and victimisation at school develops students' Knowledge about the phenomena of school victimisation, covers aspects of research and practice (diagnostics, general interventions, risk and protective factors, cultural and developmental aspects, and concentric circles of trauma). Other courses like Psychopathology of development, and Children and adolescent psychiatry, deal with Developmental trauma and sexual abuse. The master's programme in clinical psychology covers material on attachment trauma, PTSD, sexual abuse, suicidal risks, and crisis—students gather Knowledge, Practical, and Research skills, and support in their Development as professionals.

Authors are both domestic and foreign. Literature varies widely with regard to year of publication—some professors give more recent sources, while others tend to prefer the classical ones.

Social trauma was not mentioned in any literature or curricula.

University of Belgrade

The psychology department offers a four-year BA in psychology and a one-year MA comprising four modules. At the beginning of the fourth year, students can choose modules, including Clinical psychology.

By reviewing curricula for the preliminary study, three courses were found dealing with trauma phenomena. Specifically, social trauma was introduced through literature dealing with war trauma and the refugee crisis in the former Yugoslavia, and this concept was studied in the same manner as the other types of trauma.

Regarding trauma in general, during the course Psychology and mental health, students learn the Definitions, Theoretical considerations, Stages of trauma, and Individual reactions to it, as well as the Risk and Protective factors. Later in the Clinical module Psychology and mental health—special course, an understanding of different Types of trauma, such as trauma among children, social trauma, physical, and sexual violence, is offered. The course Crisis intervention deals with the theory about crisis interventions (categories, such as Multidisciplinary teams, Concentric circles of trauma, Treatment stages), but also offers techniques used at individual, family, group, and community level. Some examples of Ethics and Professional conduct were also mentioned (e.g., burnout syndrome prevention).

The impression is that the literature could be more up to date and that foreign authors could be more represented, but it should be mentioned that domestic authors whose books and articles were used as compulsory literature, were actually leading professionals in the field of social trauma. Taking into account the categories and criteria of the codebook, Belgrade students could acquire good Theoretical knowledge about the concept of trauma, its aetiology, Types, and Stages, Prevention and Treatment, and some insights about Ethical standards and Personal development of professionals.

Discussion

The aim of this research was to reveal what kind of knowledge psychology students of the TTM network universities obtain about trauma with a specific focus on the topic of social trauma. Initial results and reports suggest that, regardless of the differences in theoretical backgrounds and curriculum structures of the universities that are enrolled, all study programmes have at least one thing in common: they do not provide comprehensive knowledge about social trauma.

Only two of the seven universities reported the existence of literature in their curricula regarding social trauma (IPU, University of Belgrade).

Nevertheless, the topic is not sufficiently analysed, and these are focusing more on interventions, either specific interventions designed for a certain type of trauma (Specific interventions), or the ones required in crisis intervention (Multidisciplinary teams), interventions applied to people in different positions who are affected by the same traumatic event (Concentric circles of trauma), or certain interventions that are applied in different phases of treatment (Stages of treatment).

Topics that are categorised in the Knowledge about phenomena and are covered are the specificities of trauma in infants, children, and adolescents (Development and trauma) and the intrapsychic processes related to trauma, such as defence mechanisms and transgenerational transmission of trauma in the particular literature; these are only two among others (Individual reactions to and consequences of trauma).

As far as trauma in general is concerned, the latter is present in almost all university curricula. Knowledge about trauma is more sufficiently represented in the literature. The books and articles define trauma (Definitions), describe how trauma theory has changed (Historical overview), provide a taxonomy (Types of trauma), analyse the factors that increase the likelihood of having a pathological response (Risk factors), and the factors that are protecting people from experiencing trauma or helping them overcome it (Protective factors and resilience). Development and trauma, as well as Individual responses to and the consequences of trauma, are also present here.

Literature that deals with topics concerning Practice is found in the universities that provide clinical psychology master's programmes. As in the social trauma literature the Specific intervention, Concentric circles of trauma, Multidisciplinary teams, and Stages of treatment are present along with examples of specific personal experiences (Case reports), certain interventions applied to infants, children, or adolescents (Development and interventions) and trauma interventions designed to be specifically culturally sensitive (Cultural context).

Students from two universities can become familiar with research on trauma (University of Sarajevo, University of Sofia). Students may acquire knowledge about the procedures that are especially relevant in trauma research (Design) and about guidelines of the ethics code, standards of professional conduct, issues, challenges, dilemmas, and/or solutions with respect to doing trauma-related research (Ethics related to research). They may also get an insight into instruments that are used in the assessment of traumatised people (Instruments).

Guidelines concerning the code of ethics, standards of professional conduct, issues, challenges, dilemmas, and/or solutions in the context of professional practice, counselling, supervision or treatment of trauma (Ethics in practice) and the aspects concerning the professional's mental health coping strategies, prevention and/or handling secondary traumatisation (Development of the professionals) are a part of only one university's curriculum.

One of the aspects of trauma learning that has been shown not to be sufficiently represented in the curricula is Diagnostic. Trauma and its consequences seem to be perceived and understood mostly from its post-traumatic (PTSD) symptomatology as presented in the prominent, rather descriptive diagnostic manuals (ICD-10, DSM-5) (Hamburger, 2015). The integration of diagnostic manuals in the curricula that do not focus merely on the symptomatology of

PTSD, but take into consideration the background of the individual along with reactions to stressful events in general (i.e., Operationalized Psychodynamic Manual), would enable students to develop a more complete picture before intervening.

Integration of literature dealing with Research and Ethics on research would encourage more students to conduct research. The techniques and intervention methods can only be adequately evaluated and improved if rigorous research takes place. Finally yet importantly, it is required that students are able to follow codes of ethics when conducting research in such a sensitive population.

Development of professionals is a topic that could be more emphasised, having in mind that specific theories and preventive suggestions have been developed that are dealing with this particular issue, such as vicarious traumatisation under the frame of the constructivist self-development theory (Pearlman & Saakvitne, 1995; Saakvitne & Pearlman, 1996; McCann & Pearlman, 1990).

Moreover, Scientific thinking can be encouraged through proper education that would constantly ask questions, look for diversity in reasoning, and demand careful examination of given literature and answers that are offered. This process requires more thorough and complete literature about social trauma and trauma in general to be integrated in the curricula that would enable students to develop their critical thinking after mastering the theoretical basics of trauma.

In general, the topic of trauma, although it is a core concept for the suffering of the psyche, seems to capture little attention.

Various aspects of the current study process brought us great benefit. The process of preparing the coding book and coding sheet with descriptions of the variables required an extended review of the trauma literature and gave us the chance to enrich our knowledge. We have developed the mentality of evaluating and being interested in the content of our studies. The chance to become familiar with other universities' programmes and teaching practices made us more precise by formulating specific proposals that will enhance the teaching of the trauma topic at our universities.

Besides the positive experiences that we collected during the research process, there were various delays and obstacles. Due to levels of motivation and technical issues that we were dealing with—such as long Skype meetings with many participants, coordination of more than ten or even fifteen people, detailed literature searches, organisation of teams—we faced the problem of some participants dropping out. Elaborating and doing research on the topic of trauma could be seen as a possible explanation of the difficulties, due to specific internal processes, that this topic may evoke in researchers. Moreover, for the teams whose universities do not provide specific lists of mandatory literature, the process of collecting the data proved to be particularly time and energy consuming.

Typical limitations of this particular methodology can be traced. Decisions about which categories should be included in the table of contents fulfilling the criterion of relevance to the topic and which definitions from the available literature should be chosen, were made subjectively. To overcome this issue and to ensure reliability, replicability, and validity we proceeded with a pilot analysis of articles to improve inter-rater reliability. Nevertheless, it should be noted that we both formulated the research question and proceeded in the analysis of the data.

Furthermore, the subject of the analysis was limited in the compulsory literature of the university curricula. Complete results on what we learn about social trauma and trauma in general would have to analyse also internships, guest lectures, presentations, and conferences. As mentioned above, the process of collecting literature differed among teams. In some cases it had to be requested from the professors, whereas in others it existed as standard lists announced on the webpages of the universities. Lastly, the current research was the first independent study we, as a team, conducted under the principles of the qualitative approach.

Taking into consideration the findings of this research and after attending the multidisciplinary joint elective study course of the TTM project, which made us realise how broad and important the intervention and research fields of social trauma are, we cannot but suggest that more attention is drawn to social trauma. This multidisciplinary joint elective study course, which has existed since 2015 as one of the main activities of the TTM network, could be included in the psychology curricula, as it provides a complete picture and insight into trauma phenomena. Further research should be conducted, analogous to our study, in order to decide the precise content of such courses.

Acknowledgments

This research was supported by and is part of the Trauma, Trust, and Memory project. We would like to express our gratitude to Professor Andreas Hamburger of the International Psychoanalytic University of Berlin, chair of the TTM network, who gave us the opportunity, as young researchers, to write this chapter, and supported this study with his knowledge and enthusiasm.

We would also like to thank Biljana Stanković from the University of Belgrade, for her support and suggestions during this research process.

Finally yet importantly, we want to thank our colleagues Petra E. Sailer, Julian Tennstedt, Sonja Mermazadeh, Sabina Hoth, Natalia Goncharova, Ana Perović, and Milena Aranđelović who made essential contributions with their comments, elaboration in methodology, and collection of data.

References

Danieli, Y. (1996). Who takes care of the caretakers? The emotional consequences of working with children traumatized by war and communal violence. In: R. J. Apfel & B. Simon (Eds.), *Minefields in Their Hearts: the Mental Health of Children in War and Communal Violence* (pp. 189–205). New Haven, CT: Yale University Press.

Fogelman, E. (1991). Survivor-victims of war and holocaust. In: D. Leviton (Ed.), *Horrendous Death and Health: Toward Action* (pp. 37–45). New York: Hemisphere.

Hsieh, H., & Shannon, S. E. (2005). Three approaches to qualitative content analysis. *Qualitative Health Research, 15*: 1277–1288.

Kos, A. M. (1997). Mental health workers and refugees. In: C. Segula & S. Thakral (Eds.), *They Talk, We Listen* (pp. 9–24). Ljubljana: Center for Psychosocial Help to Refugees.

McCann, L., & Pearlman, L. (1990). Vicarious traumatization: a framework for understanding the psychological effects of working with victims. *Journal of Traumatic Stress, 3*: 131–149.

Operationalized Psychodynamic Diagnosis Task Force (2008). *Operationalized Psychodynamic Diagnosis OPD-2: Manual of diagnosis and treatment planning*. OPD Task Force.

Pearlman, L. A., & Saakvitne, K. (1995). *Trauma and the Therapist: Countertransference and Vicarious Traumatization in Psychotherapy with Incest Survivors*. New York: Norton.

Saakvitne, K. W., & Pearlman, L. A. (1996). *Transforming the Pain*. New York: Norton.

Sitterle, K. A., & Gurwitch, R. H. (1999). The terrorist bombing in Oklahoma City. In: E. S. Zinner & M. B. Williams (Eds.), *When a Community Weeps: Case Studies in Group Survivorship* (pp. 160–189). Philadelphia: Brunner/Mazel.

Summerfield, D. A. (2000). Childhood, war, refugeedom and "trauma": three core questions for mental health professionals. *Transcultural Psychiatry, 37*: 417–433.

CHAPTER TWENTY-FOUR

International master's study course in social trauma

Camellia Hancheva, Carmen Scher, and Andreas Hamburger

Social trauma is among the most important subjects in clinical, social, and general psychology, as well as in cultural theory (Hamburger, 2017; see also Chapter Two). The elaborated concept of social trauma carries the classical definition and implicit ideas of violent shock, (psychic) wound, and long-lasting consequences affecting psychic organisation but with an important reframing regarding interpersonal dynamics. It is of high interest and practical relevance for researchers and societies that have experienced war, armed or ideological conflicts, and totalitarian regimes. Students in humanities and especially psychology need to be informed about the causes, consequences, and therapeutic options regarding social trauma.

In the syllabus of most psychology study programmes, social trauma is only addressed incidentally (see Chapter Twenty-Three). In clinical psychology, psycho-traumatic pathology and trauma therapy are regularly taught subjects, but the specific conditions of *social* trauma require an interdisciplinary and specific approach. Therefore, the Course in Social Trauma (CST) logically unites in well-developed coordination the overlapping fields of clinical, developmental, social psychological, cultural, theoretical, ethical, and research methodology. The course is jointly offered by psychologists as well as by professors and practitioners working in non-psychological departments.

Crediting and embedding in the syllabus

The course is designed as a supplement to the local master's study programmes in psychology and other subjects or to the respective general education programmes. According to the rules and regulations of the participating departments it can either be acknowledged as one of the obligatory subjects scheduled in the syllabus, or offered as an additional elective subject to one or more study programmes or as part of the continuing education programme.

Introduction and examination are the responsibility of the home department, as well as a part of the teaching, depending on the department's specialisation. Other parts will be taught in the frame of block weekends by other participating departments (see below). The lecturer responsible for the course is each TTM participating professor in regard to his or her own faculty.

The course is taught over one year and comprises fifteen double sessions per semester. With a total workload of sixty hours of presence it is credited with six credit points according to the European Credit Transfer System (ECTS). Since some of the participating universities credit their elective courses with three credit points, according to a workload of thirty contact hours, these credits might be awarded by their home faculties after having completed only one half of the course. Students who have completed the full CST (six credit points) will get a certificate issued by TTM. Universities or departments that wish to offer the course in one semester may accomplish it by partly acknowledging sessions from other semesters.

Each participating department offers an introductory and a concluding session and examination of its own students. In addition, the departments offer block sessions, held in one weekend block (Friday and Saturday, eight hours per subject in total) and/or at the annual TTM summer school. These sessions are open to all CST students. Universities may decide to offer the whole course to their own students; in this case their CST students would nevertheless have to attend at least one block session abroad.

Students attend the introductory and the concluding sessions as well as at least two teaching blocks at their home universities. They travel to one or two teaching blocks offered by partner universities, and they have the option to book several teaching blocks at the summer school. They have to plan their individual study programme in advance.

Funding and sustainability

In the first two years funding for travel and accommodation costs was available. The programme start was supported by the German Academic Exchange Service (DAAD). Places were limited; each participating department is entitled to admit four funded students to CST (IPU Berlin: only one funded student). However, a huge number of students choose to participate in the course and they travel voluntarily, bearing the costs themselves, for participation in the modules offered abroad. This continuous interest indicates that the course will be continued independently from future funding schemes.

Admission

The admission procedure and decision is the responsibility of each department. Optionally, a motivation letter in English and a personal interview are suggested. Students who are admitted are obliged to fulfil the above-mentioned travelling requirements.

With applying for admission, students should carefully outline their study plan, which is subject to specifications by TTM due to the limited funding options for travel and accommodation.

Structure and teaching subjects

In this section, the curriculum of the course is outlined and illustrated by students' reports from their portfolios. The description of the modules should be understood as a set of suggestions. Not everything listed here has to be taught in the course.

The concept of social trauma: starting session at the home university

The introductory session is offered at every participating department for their own students. Participants reflect on their personal interest in the topic. Each student gets a template for his course diary (portfolio), where the study experiences of every session and homework are to be documented. The design of the course is explained and the initial, basic literature is handed out.

In addition, a first working definition of social trauma is given in the form of an interactive lecture. The concept of social trauma needs a precise and scientifically based definition. Examples throughout history (the Holocaust, ethnic cleansing, genocide, war rape) are discussed, and initial questions about the forthcoming course sessions are identified. Students are assigned homework to read individual reports of survivors and perpetrators, highlighting relevant issues for the definition of social trauma. Critical revision of historical, socio-cultural, and political studies and/or texts is required for the construction of understanding of social trauma as a disaster caused by people, targeted at whole groups, aiming at physical and cultural annihilation, and not defined by the external event alone, but by its intra-psychic and socio-psychic processing.

Specific methodology and practice in social trauma research

The specificity of social trauma requires a combination of qualitative and quantitative methodologies to be considered in research plans. The methodology module includes a focus on trauma and extended teaching of research methodologies (lecture and seminar), attachment measurement, and qualitative methods in trauma research. Practical work is in small groups, where students formulate a research question and design a specific research project in the field of social trauma (two workshops). A research plan and design for a hypothetical study is presented in writing after the module completion in students' portfolios.

Ethics

Informed by the concept of secondary traumatisation, the ethics module gives special attention to the possible risks of ill-timed research interventions. A space is created for discussion of contradictory concepts such as "survivors" versus "victims", or post-traumatic disorders.

The module comprises ethical aspects of working with survivors of social trauma, in terms of re-traumatisation by research, reduced capacity to consent, and working with perpetrators (legal aspects of self-incrimination). Students are asked to peer-review research projects under ethical aspects and discuss their reviews in the group. This training enables students to perform the online exam of the Protecting human research participants course of the NIH Office of Extramural Research.

Clinical psychology of social trauma

Introduction of the PTSD diagnosis in the 1970s marked a stage in the development of practice-informed diagnoses. The multi-layered construct of traumatic reaction needs further exploration of the full spectrum of related psychopathology. The content of the clinical module research and therapeutic aspects of social trauma comprises clinical consequences of social trauma as compared to general psychic trauma, complex trauma, neurobiology, sequential traumatisation attachment, and mentalization. Specific diagnostic and therapeutic approaches are discussed using a case example.

Developmental psychology of social trauma

Social trauma as a relational phenomenon requires a focus on development. Trauma as a single event, but also and more often as a cumulative experience in interpersonal relations, leads to diverse outcomes in the lifespan periods from childhood and adolescence to adulthood. Risk factors from neurobiology, physical health of individuals, family history, and socio-economic and socio-political aspects are discussed to map out the field between psychopathology, resilience, and adjustment. Cumulative developmental trauma is discussed, defined as a prolonged interpersonal experience early in the life cycle leading to serious impairment in achievement of secure attachment, mentalization and meaning construction, affect regulation, self-perception, and interpersonal relations. Specific traumatic events as well as specific concepts including transgenerational transmission and vicious circles of violence are discussed.

A small group discussion and case formulation is performed, based on fictional (film or novel) characters. A portfolio presenting a case analysis relating to the concept of developmental trauma is required.

Report on developmental psychology from a Bulgarian student's portfolio

> I was surprised by my reaction watching the still-face experiment. An overwhelming, almost unbearable, sadness took me by surprise. Following the discussion and the explanation of the cycle of ruptures and repairs in mother–baby interactions I felt relief, but still I was puzzled by the echo of my somatic reaction. Thinking it over and searching in my own childhood history made me realise how the impact of loss of a close person that my mother had experienced during my second year had affected both her and me. Ideas about the role of attachment as a protective factor give me insight on my personal experience.

Memory studies

Psychoanalytic conceptualisation of inner reality, fantasy, and the unconscious had been at the centre of the "false memory" debate for more than a century. A meeting point of cognitive neuroscience and psychoanalysis, memory research provides insights of organisation of psychological processes around concepts of personal and collective identity and meaning. The module comprises general psychological theory of traumatic memory (dissociation, implicit memory symbolisation), group traumatic memories and meanings ascribed to certain past episodes, the false memory syndrome, and results in discussion of social implementation of memory versus social extinction of memory.

From a German student's reports on memory studies in her portfolio:

> I found myself in the very awkward position of looking at a room of people who were experiencing war during their early childhood and listening to people talking about what I regarded as "minor, random accidents" that were not caused by any human intention. And again I had to ask myself—what actually is trauma, what classifies as trauma?
>
> As for the actual content of the course, we talked about the memory in context of traumatic events: while experiencing a trauma the frame of references changes, and generalisations after a traumatic event are often anticipated. It is then crucial whether or not the event can be integrated in one's own frame or world view, or can be put in a narration.

Social psychology and cultural theory of trauma

Social trauma is defined at an intersection of sociology, where trauma narratives are regarded as a strong part of social identity, and social psychology, studying the individual's adaption to social constraints and ideologies. The module combines the theory of cultural trauma with specific aspects of social psychology relevant to the study of social trauma. Often, the module is taught by two lecturers specialised in either cultural theory or social psychology.

The social psychology part of the module comprises topics such as the interaction between victims and perpetrators, Stockholm syndrome in large groups, dehumanisation, conspiracy of silence and social psychological aspects of transgenerational traumatisation, and totalitarianism. Here, emphasis can be given to migration and borderland identity.

In the cultural theory part, concepts of cultural and chosen trauma, collective memory and the culture of remembrance, the media, and political and historical aspects of trauma and testimony are addressed.

Theoretical approaches are discussed using the example of a feature or documentary film.

Concluding session and course assessment

The concluding session is offered at every participating department for their own students. Participants deliver their learning portfolios, presenting them to the group of local CST participants. They report and compare their individual education experiences in different universities.

Examination system

The examination procedure is designed according to the rules and regulations of the home department. We suggest the examination requirement should be the written portfolio, including a small research project design from the methodology session, plus its oral presentation and discussion in the group as examination requirement. The portfolio is evaluated by the home university professor.

Students who do not wish to complete an examination can receive a certificate of attendance if they have participated in all the classes.

Concluding remarks

The elective master's course in social trauma is an innovative teaching platform, where the complex topic of social trauma is taught to a group of international students by a group of international lecturers. Besides the quality of the specialised, multidisciplinary teaching, this format enables students to become familiar with international collaboration and exchange. Many of the portfolios finish with sentences like: "The CST was the most important and moving learning experience during my study time. I especially enjoyed the openness of the exchange with my co-students from three countries."

Acknowledgements

This project has been funded by DAAD, grant numbers 57068644, 57173352 and 57246729, and developed with the help of all professors participating in the TTM network. It has been discussed and modified by the TTM network's Deans and Decision Makers Conference, Berlin, December 2013. A complete module handbook for the course including the suggested literature is available at www.ipu-berlin.de/en/study-courses/international/students/network-elective-course-social-trauma.html.

Reference

Hamburger, A. (2017). Genocidal trauma. Individual and social consequences of the assault on the mental and physical life of a group. In: A. Hamburger & D. Laub (Eds.), *Psychoanalysis and Holocaust Testimony. Unwanted Memories of social trauma* (pp. 66–91). London: Routledge.

CHAPTER TWENTY-FIVE

An academic network on social trauma in southeast Europe

Andreas Hamburger and Carmen Scher

Since 2012, and with the active support of the German Academic Exchange Service (DAAD), a network of research groups from Germany and southeast Europe has been working together under the name Trauma, Trust, and Memory—social trauma and reconciliation in psychoanalysis, psychotherapy, and cultural memory. The present book is the first comprehensive summary of its achievements. The network aims at building bridges and enhancing interdisciplinary dialogues between psychoanalysis and empirical research, as well as therapy and cultural theory. In addition, we started this dialogue in a region where there had been much more serious conflicts than the aforementioned academic battles, in several former Yugoslavian countries and Bulgaria.

The topic, task, and region were not arbitrary choices. Building on our own experiences as a social trauma researcher (Hamburger) and a founding director of the Goethe Institute in Sarajevo in 1999 (Scher), we took the initiative to establish a collaboration with colleagues from countries where dictatorship, war, and genocide were still fresh in the collective memory. Together with researchers from the Balkan region we submitted a proposal under the European Programme of Academic Reconstruction in Southeast Europe, which was eventually granted in 2012.

The network came into being with seven participating universities from five countries. Bulgaria, Bosnia and Herzegovina, Macedonia, Serbia, and Germany were the initial five. Over time, some participants changed: Tuzla and Skopje universities left the network, but Niš (Serbia) joined. Altogether, the network has connected eleven universities from six countries. Over time, more than sixty research studies from different research paradigms related to social trauma (war, persecution, genocide) were conducted and more than 700 students and research fellows participated in the network.

The history of the network, its achievements, crises, and impasses reflect the vicissitudes of such an enterprise.

Trauma research and the European perspective

It was no coincidence that social trauma became the topic for a research network under the *Academic Reconstruction in Middle and South Europe* programme. In fact, social trauma is one connecting thread throughout the vicissitudes of South European history.

Since the fall of communism, the end of the Cold War, and the outbreak of war and civil war in the Balkans, and since the realignment of the middle and southeast European countries and the expansion of the EU, Europe has transformed into a completely new entity, unlike anything seen before. It is as marked by deep wounds as it is by the desire for healing and peace. However, it is an entity that has not become anything like a motherland for Europeans. It is a business contract, not a home.

In this historical situation, trauma research is a central concern of European scientific collaboration. Many middle and eastern European psychological, medical, and cultural research initiatives broach the issue of traumata in conjunction with dictatorship experience, war, civil war, mass murder, and despotism, and their traumatic consequences. Attachment disorders, addictions, post-traumatic stress and adaptation disorder, depression and personality disorders, as well as cultural consequences in conjunction with the build-up of civil society and its commemorative culture, are studied. But most researchers refer to Western European and international contexts, and rarely relate to one another: this is because traumatic historical experiences keep regional research groups apart. This Western-oriented interest can only partly be blamed on current, prevalent economic disparities. The western orientation of many elites of middle and southeastern European countries has a long and ambivalent tradition. Historically, it is legitimate to speak of a traumatic identity in the Balkans (see Lovrenovic, Chapter).

Aims

The network tries to connect research groups who want to open up to the regional and international dialogue. Substantial collaboration requires transdisciplinary and trans-regional discussion of all running research processes, from which new research questions and applications can emerge.

The paramount project goals are:

1. Quality assurance through mutual project audits as well as regional and trans-regional training sessions and trans-regional presentations.
2. Project-related scientific collaboration through development of cross-project research questions, replication studies, and validation.
3. Development of cross-project structures and processes, like the creation of a virtual research platform, development of ethical standards, regional research funding, publications, and peer reviews.

Measures

The network has organised two conferences (Berlin, 2013, 2014), five summer schools (Belgrade, 2013; Sozopol, 2013; Banja Luka, 2014; Sarajevo, 2015; Niš, 2016), four workshops, seven fellow trainings, and five research meetings. Research and teaching collaboration were performed through joint study designs and joint supervisions. An online e-learning platform, hosted at IPU Berlin, is frequently used for scientific, informative, and administrative exchange. Publications and presentations in international conferences have made the network visible in the scientific community.

One example is the summer school held in Sarajevo in June 2015, "Traumatic past—posttraumatic present: mental and social long-term effects of war". It was organised by Larisa Kasumagić and her associates from the Faculty of Philosophy of Sarajevo University and had to be prepared years in advance. Eventually, different disciplines, nations, and generations worked together in studying the consequences of social traumatic experiences of different kinds, and discussing ways of mourning and coping. International lecturers from the fields of psychoanalysis, psychology, history, linguistics, literature, arts, education, and teaching pedagogy provided their scholarly input. In a group of seventy international students and close to thirty lecturers, professors, and visiting members, the invited speakers presented their ongoing studies and discussed them with the guest and staff lecturers. Among the keynote lectures, Vamik Volkan stood out with his presentation "From natural disasters to ethnic cleansing: massive trauma and societal responses".

Achievements

From the beginning, the central topic was social traumatisation, requiring precise research approaches in the area of epidemiology of trauma effects. In particular, post-traumatic stress disorders, and attachment and mentalization disorders, as well as approaches for the cultural analysis of social traumata coping mechanisms were relevant. The network yielded increasingly intensive exchange among the participating research centres. To illustrate this with just one example, the aforementioned topic of acknowledgement of social trauma can be highlighted. While in the beginning the differences in knowledge and meaning of the persecution between the participants were treated in a rather "subcutaneous" way, in the course the process they were subject to discursive opening.

The importance of acknowledgement

After the joint visit to the Jewish Museum, Berlin, in December 2013, a group meeting showed how painful the willingness for acknowledgement of historic wounds (see Chapter Four) concerning participants personally is. The positive atmosphere of the new collaboration turned into a lasting silence at the end of the meeting. Professors and students suddenly found themselves sitting in a quiet circle. It became apparent that under the surface of the successful collaboration pre- and unconscious traumatic traces in the experience of the individuals and the represented groups do exist after all. The silence was broken when one of the students, a young man from Serbia, said one wishes for "an army of angels" to prevent such crimes against humanity. This image of an army of angels held all the helplessness and anger that remains inextricably linked with the social trauma of the Holocaust, but also of the genocides in war and civil war.

This process of painful acknowledgement continued during a workshop in Tuzla in May 2013, where colleagues discussed topics such as chosen trauma with its conscious and unconscious mythologisation; the adulteration of historical viewpoints; unconscious fantasies of revenge; victimisation; the dissemination of traumata; and the conspiracy of silence. The next day the TTM group visited the Potočari/Srebrenica memorial, and learned it was only the third group of Serbian participants ever to visit the memorial of Srebrenica in its ten-year existence. This experience initiated intense, personal discussion, far beyond the usual discourse within a research context. The workshop attracted much professional and media attention. The chief editor of the internationally renowned journal *World Psychiatry* requested a report (Delić et al., 2014).

At the summer school in Banja Luka in 2014, the topic of acknowledgement was brought up again. At this summer school, Amra Delić (Sarajevo) presented her work concerning the effects of mass rape in Bosnia. This is not self-evident: Banja Luka, capital of the Serbian-dominated canton Republica Srpska, was the scene of extensive ethnic cleansing in the Yugoslav War. More than 100,000 Muslim Bosnians were exiled from there; exact numbers remain uncertain to this day (Funke & Rhotert, 1999, p. 313). One dedicated presentation on the suffering of this population group at this place was outstanding. Delić's work clearly made an impression on the members of the network. Confrontational debates unfolded between participants. The young Serbians felt wrongly indicted and accused; they could not handle the feeling of being pushed into the role of the offender, with many emphasising that the Serbian population suffered, too.

After the depicted tensions and rejections had been openly addressed, the presentation by Andreas Hamburger, "After Babel. Co-constructing a research network in a former battlefield" (Hamburger, 2017, in press), connected to the group experience in the Jewish Museum, Berlin, but also mentioned the persisting rise, divisions, and repressions in regional discourse—albeit from the viewpoint of a foreigner. The lecture found a receptive audience. It resulted in a programme change: the closing conference in plenum was replaced with two parallel discussion forums for delegates, both students and professors. Topics included fear of taboo, breaking taboos, and assignment of guilt. Both forums agreed to keep the contents of the discussions confidential. However, it can be said that an increased need for discussion and appropriate willingness to open up was recognised and agreed upon.

Joint research and teaching projects

Many research projects were connected or jointly started, such as the studies on attachment in all countries of former Yugoslavia (see Chapters Thirteen and Fourteen). Closely linked to the network's topics and methodology, a series of doctoral and master's theses have been completed. Some are included in this volume, while others have not yet been completed or published (Ilić, 2014; Karadzova, 2014; Papazova, 2015; Perović, 2015; Petković, 2015; Petrova, 2014; Ristein, in preparation; Rumenova, 2015; Stancheva, 2015; Stojiljković, 2015; Zivković, 2015; and others).

Much effort was dedicated to teaching methodologies and supervising research processes. Supervision took place mainly in small research supervision groups during the summer schools but there were also regular supervision sessions via Skype.

In our network trainings and workshops, distinguished international trainers taught the adoption and evaluation of important instruments, such as the Adult Attachment Projective (AAP), Reflective Functioning (RF), the *Grille de l'Elaboration Verbale de l'Affect* (GEVA), the Psychological Mindedness Scale (PMS), Facially Expressed Emotion Labelling (FEEL), Movie for the Assessment of Social Cognition (MASC), and conducting the Adult Attachment Interview (AAI).

Academic collaboration

A key aim of the TTM network is to provide an educational approach. The network has inaugurated an international lecture series, a decentralised international master's study course, and joint thesis supervisions.

International lecture series

Since 2014, six guest lectures on faculty or university level have been held in five universities. As a principle, the visiting professor comes from abroad, and if possible is accompanied by one or two academics from a third country, who give a training session in accordance with the lecture topic chosen by the professor. Thus, students of the host university have the opportunity to learn about social trauma and to get an impression of the network's activities. One outstanding example was Bosnian researcher Amra Delić's deeply moving lecture at Belgrade University on recovery-oriented treatment of the survivors of sexual violence in war. Listeners were informed about war rape, its consequences, and possible therapy approaches. This was the first lecture on this topic ever given at the Faculty of Philosophy, possibly in Belgrade generally. The audience was not large but the important thing to understand is that the door is now open.

Further lectures in the international lecture series addressed, among other topics, post-traumatic nightmares (Lutz Wittmann, IPU Berlin & Siniša Lakić, University of Banja Luka, held in Niš); unmourned loss (Camellia Hancheva, University of Sofia & Slađana Ilić, University of Tuzla); trauma models (Aleksandar Dimitrijević, University of Belgrade); and drug addiction (Nikola Atanassov, University of Sofia), the latter two held in Sarajevo.

Collective learning module at master's level on the topic of social trauma

An exceptional result of the network activity has been the programme for an interdisciplinary course in social trauma, consisting of two contact hours over the course of two semesters (totalling four contact hours, six credit points). The course is allocated to several universities as well as the summer school. The course covers six specialities—methodology, ethics, clinical psychology, developmental psychology, memory research, and social and cultural psychology—offered by experts from the participating universities. Examination accountability remains with the home university. This teaching programme is described in detail in Chapter Twenty-Four.

Outreach

The network has produced a considerable outreach by its presentation on the cooperating universities' websites, presentations at international congresses, and book and journal publications. Congress lectures and panels on the network have been held at a number of important international conferences.

General outreach was achieved by public lectures in connection with the network's activities, and by coverage of the network by regional and international media.

Conclusion

As a network founded and funded to enhance academic reconstruction in southeast Europe, TTM continues to contribute significantly. We now have a lively international collaboration between young researchers, based on an improved methodological basis. As a journey through a former disciplinary, cultural, national, and international battlefield, it is a valuable and sometimes disturbing experience. It teaches us how many steps have to be taken for social growth—which, unlike in nature, is not genetically programmed but has to be achieved by many hands, and many minds, connecting their efforts and addressing, reflecting, and resolving their fears and animosities.

Acknowledgements

This chapter reports on the international research network, currently connecting seven universities from four countries. Responsible division leaders are: Nikola Atanassov, New Bulgarian University Sofia (Bulgaria), Camellia Hancheva, University St Kliment Ohrid, Sofia (Bulgaria), Dzenana Husremović and Maida Koso, University Sarajevo, (Bosnia-Herzegovina), Slavica Tutnjević, University of Banja Luka (Bosnia-Herzegovina), Biljana Stanković, University of Belgrade (Serbia), Vladimir Hedrih, University Niš (Serbia), and Andreas Hamburger, International Psychoanalytic University Berlin (Germany).

References

Delić, A., Hasanović, M., Avdibegović, E., Dimitrijević, A., Hancheva, C., Scher, C., Stefanović-Stanojević, T., Streeck-Fischer, A., & Hamburger, A. (2014). Academic model of trauma healing in postwar societies. *Acta Medica Academica, 43*: 76–80.

Hamburger, A. (2015). Roots in Jewish and Christian soil: a portrait of the Holocaust researcher as an involved person. *Contemporary Psychoanalysis, Special Issue: The Evolution of Witnessing—Emergent Relational Trends in Holocaust Studies, 51*: 289–295.

Hamburger, A. (2017) [in press]. After Babel—teaching psychoanalysis on a former battlefield. *International Forum of Psychoanalysis*.

Ilić, S. (2014). Karakteristike ličnosti i ratna trauma kao determinante pomirenja kod studenata [Personality traits and war trauma as determinants of reconciliation among students]. Master's thesis, University of Tuzla.

Karadzova, B. (2014). *Psychosocial identity development. Case study of women with history of violence.* Postgraduate diploma thesis, University of Sofia.

Papazova, M. (2015). **Емоционални и Социални Особености на Деца от Институции—Силни Страни и Трудности** [Social and emotional specifities in children from protectories: strengths and difficulties]. Master's thesis.

Perović, A. (2015). *Trait emotional intelligence and general intelligence of mothers as intervening variables in the transgenerational transfer of attachment patterns*. Master's thesis, University of Belgrade.

Petković, P. (2015). *Attitudes toward normality, morality and health in the domain of sexual behaviour*. Master's thesis, University of Belgrade.

Petrova, P. (2014). *Child play: implications for the assessment and counselling. Case study of a traumatized child*. Master's thesis, University of Sofia.

Ristein, L. (in preparation). *Translation and Validation of Mentalization Scale (MenteS) from Serbian to German*. Master's thesis, University of Dresden.

Rumenova, J. (2015). *Psychoanalytic interpretation of the film "Fight Club"*. Master's thesis, NBU Sofia.

Stancheva, D. (2015). *Complicated mother's grief and symptoms in grown up child.* Postgraduate diploma thesis, University of Sofia.

Stojiljković, M. (2015). *Ways of portraying psychiatry patients on television: is stigma inevitable?* Master's thesis, University of Belgrade.

Zivković, A. (2015). *Empirical study of the role of psychiatry service users in the process of recovery.* Master's thesis, University of Belgrade.

INDEX